Doing
Research
in the
Real
World

DAVID E. GRAY

SAGE Publications
London • Thousand Oaks • New Delhi

First published 2004

Reprinted 2005, 2006

SAGE Publications Ltd
1 Oliver's Yard
55 City Road
London EC2A 4PU

SAGE Publications Inc
2455 Teller Road
Thousand Oaks, California 91320

SAGE Publications India Pvt Ltd
B-42, Panchsheel Enclave
Post Box 4109
New Delhi 110 017

British Library Cataloguing in Publication data

A catalogue record for this book is available
from the British Library

ISBN-10 0-7619-4878-3   ISBN-13 978-0-7619-4878-0
ISBN-10 0-7619-4879-1 (pbk)   ISBN-13 978-0-7619-4879-7 (pbk)

Library of Congress Control Number 2003109254

Typeset by C&M Digitals (P) Ltd., Chennai, India
Printed in Great Britain by TJ International, Padstow, Cornwall

Contents

List of case studies

List of figures

List of tables

Preface

This book has been written to provide you with an introduction to research strategies and methods, and to help you develop the necessary skills to design and implement a research project. In the 'real world' of commercial businesses, public sector organizations, voluntary services, professional networks and neighbourhoods and communities, pressing issues exist that require answers. Often, we can only arrive at these answers through a systematic process of investigation – that is, research. And, as the real world becomes more competitive, complex and uncertain, many people are recognizing the importance and value of research: surveying employee attitudes or customer responses to a new produce or service; evaluating a professional development programme; discovering how new computer systems can be better implemented; assessing the impact of a drug awareness programme in schools – to name but a few. Hence, research is no longer just the remit of the professional researcher or the university academic. It is increasingly becoming an integral part of the job specification for many occupations.

Why bother reading this book? You may be interested in research because you are undertaking a research project as part of an academic programme such as a doctorate, MBA, MSc or first degree. Or you may be undertaking a programme of professional development that involves you in a research study of some kind, possibly within your own workplace. Alternatively, your job role may require that you undertake a research investigation of some kind. In all cases, this book is for you!

I would like to take this opportunity to express my warm and sincere thanks to a number of people who gave their support and practical help by reviewing and commenting on various chapters of the book, namely: Sally Rumsey, Paul Barber, Josie Gregory and Colin Griffin, at the University of Surrey; Trevor Murrells of Kings College, London; Julia Gaimster, London College of Fashion; and my friend and fellow researcher Ken Marsh at the University of Greenwich. I would also like to thank the students on the doctoral and Work Based Learning degree programmes at the University of Surrey who had the 'pleasure' of reading earlier versions of these chapters and who gave me invaluable feedback. My sincere thanks also to Michael Carmichael, Zoe Elliott and Patrick Brindle at Sage, who were always there with practical assistance, advice and encouragement. Any mistakes, omissions or biases, of course, remain my own.

Finally, good luck in your research – and enjoy it!

David E. Gray,
School of Management, University of Surrey

1 Introduction

Chapter objectives

After reading this chapter you will be able to:

- **Describe why research in the real world is of increasing importance.**
- **Explain the nature of theories.**
- **Outline the stages in the research process.**
- **Distinguish between inductive and deductive methods.**

This book is designed to introduce you to some of the essential methodologies, approaches and tools of research. In doing so, we will explore some of the philosophies and theoretical perspectives behind the many different ways of conducting research, as well as providing practical examples and guidance as to how research should be planned and implemented. Later in this chapter we will look at the structure of the book, but first we need to examine the nature of the research process and why research is being seen as increasingly important in a growing number of organizations and contexts.

The term 'globalization' is often used to describe a world that is becoming increasingly integrated and interdependent and where large, international organizations dominate. Within this globalized world, change in business and working environments has become rapid, pervasive and perpetual. Organizations have adapted to this uncertainty in a number of ways. One approach has been to understand (research) and develop relationships with both markets and supply chains. Most forward-looking organizations have also recognized the need for a multi-skilled and occupationally agile workforce. It has also required that organizations understand what motivates their workforce and how people embrace change. All this has had an enormous impact on the way organizations operate and interact with the 'real world', and how they communicate and work. Small and medium-sized enterprises (SMEs) have also had to modernize their organizational practices and to understand their working environment, as have public sector organizations (including hospitals, schools, colleges and universities) and voluntary organizations.

Faced with a more competitive, dynamic and uncertain world, a knowledge of research methods is important because it helps people in organizations to understand, predict and control their internal and external environments (Sekaran, 1992). It also means that those involved in commissioning or sponsoring organizational research are better placed to understand and manage the work of researchers and to objectively evaluate and interpret the outcomes of research. Hence, it becomes possible to calculate the potential risks and benefits in implementing research projects. But what do we mean by the term 'research'?

ORGANIZATIONAL RESEARCH IN THE REAL WORLD

Research in this context is a 'systematic and organized effort to investigate a specific problem that needs a solution (Sekaran, 1992: 4). Hence, organizational research is often about how (process) to solve real problems (content) (Gill and Johnson, 1997). This may have a very practical focus (applied research), with an emphasis on achieving measurable outputs that are specific to a particular organization. The results of such research may be of significance to that organization, but difficult to generalize elsewhere. On the other hand, organizational research may also be concerned with clarifying, validating or building a theory (basic research). Its importance to individual organizations may be determined by the extent to which this theory is translatable into a specific organizational context. However, most organizations will only see research as valid if it is seen to lead to practical outcomes (Easterby-Smith et al., 1991). Then there are forms of research comprising collaboration between the researcher and professional practitioners (action research). Table 1.1 provides a summary illustrating a continuum between basic and applied research.

TABLE 1.1 BASIC AND APPLIED RESEARCH

Basic research	Applied research
Purpose	*Purpose*
Expand knowledge of organizational processes	Improve understanding of specific organizational problems
Develop universal principles	Create solutions to organizational problems
Produce findings of significance and value to society	Develop findings of practical relevance to organizational stakeholders

Source: Adapted from Saunders et al., 2000

Organizational research is not an easy option. First, there is no single subject called 'organizational research'. It draws upon fields of inquiry such as sociology, anthropology, philosophy, communication, economics and statistics. This often means having to adopt an inter-disciplinary approach, incorporating ideas and approaches from a diverse range of subject backgrounds. Secondly, organizations are complex and the people working within them very busy, making it often difficult for the researcher to gain access to the people that can provide information. Key research sponsors, gatekeepers or stakeholders may also have their own agendas that are not necessarily the same as those of the researcher. Thirdly, research may be influenced by the fact that organizations are working in a world of competition, market influences and financial constraints. Research projects may have to be modified or cancelled. Research sponsors may criticize what they read in research reports, especially when these reveal organizational inefficiencies.

We have looked, briefly, at organizational research, but what do we mean by the 'real world'? To many, it means businesses, companies, hospitals, schools, colleges or other organizations, and certainly these are important sites for, and sponsors of, research. The real world, however, can also include communities where people live, including residential areas, parks, shops, local amenities or areas where young people congregate. It could also mean networks such as community groups, educationalists, professional associations, management associations or trades unions. Increasingly it could also include virtual communities where people communicate with each other through the Internet. In other words, the real world comprises any setting where human beings come together for communication, relationships or discourse.

The real world, of course, contains a myriad of subjects that lend themselves to research. Table 1.2 provides just a general 'feel' for the kinds of areas that this book will explore. You will, of course, be thinking about or developing a research topic of your own.

TABLE 1.2   EXAMPLES OF REAL WORLD RESEARCH TOPICS

Women firefighters – breaking down barriers to recruitment

Disability awareness training – does it change attitudes?

Project management in virtual organizations

Identifying the factors that influence youth club membership and attendance

Why don't people buy recycled paper?

The feasibility of transferring advanced horticultural practices to a poor developing country. A case study of three Romanian villages

Does targeted neighbourhood policing work?

Housing association accommodation and services – an evaluation of tenant attitudes

How can call centre response times and the quality of feedback to customer queries be improved?

The impact of intensive 'exam culture' on pupil sickness and medical referral

An evaluation of government 'special measures' on pupil attainment and teacher retention

Working trajectories – getting disaffected youths from ethnic communities into the jobs market

Measuring and improving customer satisfaction in a library

But how do we go about addressing these kinds of research areas? One way to solve any problem in the real world is to do so *systematically*. While Figure 1.1 presents a very simplified version of such an approach (which will be modified in later chapters), it does at least offer a starting point. Gill and Johnson (1997) rightly caution that the wise researcher is one who gives equal attention to each of these phases. Many naïve researchers are tempted to rush into the 'collect

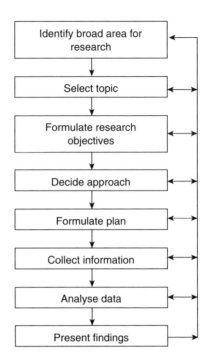

FIGURE 1.1 OVERVIEW OF THE (SIMPLIFIED) RESEARCH PROCESS (ADAPTED
FROM GILL AND JOHNSON, 1997)

information' stage without first very clearly defining the research topic, and its objectives. The results of this fuzziness only become transparent later on, with the effect that the researcher has to cycle back to an earlier stage in the research process, or to start again.

Figure 1.1 shows that it is possible, in principle, to move from the identification of the research focus right through to the presentation of the findings in a neat sequence of steps. This, however, is an idealized model and is not necessarily the norm. The complexities of researching in the real world mean that the researcher may often have to revisit previous stages in the research process. For example, at the analysis stage it might emerge that the collection of important data has been overlooked. New plans will have to be formulated and the data collected before the researcher is able to return to the analysis and presentation of the findings. Indeed, as we shall see in later chapters, it is also valid for the researcher to enter 'the field' to gather data, with only the most general of notion of what she/he is looking for, and for the data to help in the generation of concepts and theories.

Figure 1.1 implies that the research process in a highly practical one. You identify a problem, decide on how to tackle it, collect data (which often involves discussions with other people), analyse and present findings and take action. But research, as was mentioned above, is more than a mere pragmatic activity; behind it lies the foundations of academic theories that have emerged through the process of scientific enquiry and investigation over many decades and even centuries. To theories we now turn.

THE NATURE OF THEORIES

A theory has been defined as:

A set of interrelated constructs (concepts), definitions, and propositions that present a systematic view of phenomena by specifying relations among variables, with the purpose of explaining and predicting phenomena. (Kerlinger, 1986: 9)

One might, for example, have a theory of business failure. The factors that might explain this could be: poor management practices, antagonistic labour relations, insufficient staff training, or a lack of investment. The actual failure of the business has to be explained by examining and understanding the interrelationship between these factors. Such understanding may take the form of a theory that is predictive or explanatory in nature. Indeed, a theory is only worthy of the term if it has some predictive qualities. As we shall see, if a theory is no longer predictive, a crisis ensues and the theory will, over time, be challenged and replaced by a new one.

There is no reason, however, to denigrate organizational research activity that is not theory-orientated. In both educational and organizational research it may be quite valid to undertake an investigation that merely seeks to find the immediate goal of a relationship between two variables (a characteristic that is measurable such as income, attitude, action, policy, etc.) But as Kerlinger (1986) points out, the most satisfying and usable relationships are those that can be *generalized*, that is, applied from the specific instance of the research findings to many phenomena and to many people. This is the nature of theory.

Activity 1.1

Examine each of the following statements and decide whether you agree with them. A theory:

- Is an accumulated body of knowledge, written by acknowledged experts.
- Informs 'state-of-the-art' concepts and innovations.
- Is a body of work where inconsequential or misleading ideas can be filtered out.
- Represents knowledge that should be viewed critically and rejected when incompatible with practice.
- Adds interest and intellectual stimulation to a project.
- Acts as a model against which 'live' business processes can be evaluated.
- Guides the execution of research methodology.

Suggested answers are provided at the end of the chapter.

(*Source*: adapted from Gill and Johnson, 1997)

INDUCTIVE AND DEDUCTIVE REASONING

We have briefly examined the nature and uses of theory – but in research should we begin with theory, or should theory itself result from the research? Dewey (1933) outlines a general paradigm of enquiry that underpins the scientific approach, consisting of inductive discovery (induction) and deductive proof (deduction). Deduction begins with a universal view of a situation and works back to the particulars; in contrast, induction moves from fragmentary details to a connected view of a situation.

The deductive process

The deductive approach moves towards hypothesis testing, after which the principle is confirmed, refuted or modified. These hypotheses present an assertion about two or more concepts that attempts to explain the relationship between them. Concepts themselves are abstract ideas that form the building blocks of hypotheses and theories. The first stage, therefore, is the elaboration of a set of principles or allied ideas that are then tested through empirical observation or experimentation. But before such experimentation can take place, underlying concepts must be operationalized (made measurable) in such a way that they can be observed to confirm that they have occurred. Hence, measures and indicators are created. For example, if research is to be conducted into how organizational communications can be improved, we would first have to establish an operational definition of 'communication' within the context of organizational interactions. Through the creation of operational indicators, there is a tendency to measure and collect data only on what can actually be observed; hence, subjective and intangible evidence is usually ruled out. Table 1.3 provides a summary of this process.

The inductive process

Through the inductive approach, plans are made for data collection, after which the data are analysed to see if any patterns emerge that suggest relationships between variables. From these observations it may be possible to construct generalizations, relationships and even theories. Through induction, the researcher moves towards discovering a binding principle, taking care not to jump to hasty inferences or conclusions on the basis of the data. To ensure a degree of reliability, the researcher often takes multiple cases or instances, through, for example, multiplying observations rather than basing conclusions on one case (see Figure 6.4, Chapter 6).

It would not be true to say that the inductive process takes absolutely no note of pre-existing theories or ideas when approaching a problem. The very fact that an issue has been selected for research implies judgements about what is an important subject for research, and these choices are dependent on values and concepts. This may help to formulate the overall purpose of the research. But the inductive approach does not set out to corroborate or falsify a theory. Instead, through a process of gathering data, it attempts to establish patterns, consistencies and meanings.

TABLE 1.3 SUMMARY OF THE DEDUCTIVE PROCESS WITHIN AN ORGANIZATIONAL CONTEXT

Stages in the deduction process	Actions taken
Organizational mission	Read and take into account
Theory	Select a theory or set of theories most appropriate to the subject under investigation
Hypothesis	Produce a hypothesis (a testable proposition about the relationship between two or more concepts)
Operationalize	Specify what the researcher must do to measure a concept
Testing by corroboration or attempted falsification	Compare observable data with the theory. If corroborated, the theory is assumed to have been established
Examine outcomes	Accept or reject the hypothesis from the outcomes
Modify theory (if necessary)	Modify theory if the hypothesis is rejected

Combining the inductive and deductive methods

Inductive and deductive process, however, are not mutually exclusive. Adapting Dewey's (1933) formulation for a modern problem, let us say a researcher has been asked to investigate the problem of staff absenteeism. Taking a selection of facts (absentee rates over time, in different departments and across staff grades), the researcher is able to formulate a theory (inductive approach) that absenteeism is related to working patterns (see Figure 1.2). It is particularly rife among lower grade workers who are the objects of quite rigorous supervision and control. The researcher then becomes interested in what other impact this form of control may have on working practices (deductive approach). A working hypothesis becomes formulated that over-zealous supervision has produced low morale and therefore low productivity levels amongst sections of the workforce. This hypothesis is tested by the introduction of new working methods in some sections, but not others (an experimental approach using a control group), to compare productivity levels between traditionally supervised and the newly supervised sections. Figure 1.2 provides a summary of this process.

Activity 1.2

For your own research project, consider whether you intend to adopt an inductive approach, a deductive approach, or a combination of the two. List three reasons for your choice.

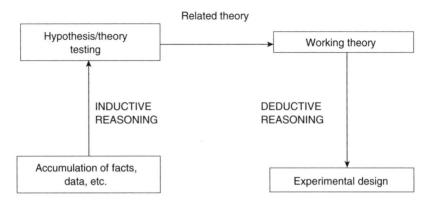

FIGURE 1.2 AN ILLUSTRATION OF HOW THE INDUCTIVE AND DEDUCTIVE METHODS CAN BE COMBINED

THE ORGANIZATION OF THE BOOK

The book is divided into five parts. Part A prepares the way by looking at the underpinning philosophy of research and the selection of suitable research topics. In Chapter 2 the nature and significance of theory is justified and the epistemological (philosophical) basis of theory explored. The chapter also describes how different epistemological perspectives provide the basis for research methodologies like experimental research, surveys, grounded theory and action research, all of which are discussed in detail in later chapters. If you have little or no previous experience of philosophy you may find this chapter rather daunting, but you are encouraged to tackle it, as it will help you to understand the approaches taken in later chapters.

Having provided an overarching view of research philosophy, methodologies and methods, Chapter 3 gets down to the practical issue of selecting and planning a research project. Advice is offered on how to identify research topics that meet your personal needs and experience and how to write a successful research proposal. Some of the ethical issues raised by research are discussed, an important topic that we return to many times in the book.

Part B deals with research methodology, beginning with experimental and quasi-experimental design (Chapter 4). This is an appropriate place to begin our discussion of methodology since this is one of the oldest and, in a sense, the classical approach to research design. The chapter not only describes and justifies alternative experimental designs, but introduces concepts (such as validity and reliability) that are appropriate for, or at least addressed by, many other research methodologies.

In Chapter 5 we take another, and increasingly popular, research methodology, surveys, and describe different types of survey and the process of survey design. A distinction is made between self-administered and interview-administered surveys and the merits of each is discussed. Partly because of their scale, surveys can be prone to sources of error such as sampling error, data collection error and interviewer error. Some practical advice is provided on how to cope with these.

Another widely used research methodology is the case study (Chapter 6). For many years, the case study approach has been wrongfully denigrated by some researchers as lacking in rigour, partly because it is often based upon a small number of cases. However, as this chapter shows, case studies, if carefully planned, can provide a powerful means of exploring situations where there is uncertainty or ambiguity about phenomena or events.

While some research methodologies attempt to uncover new knowledge, evaluation (Chapter 7) involves exploring how existing knowledge is used to inform and guide practical action. Hence, evaluation might be used to gauge whether a teaching or training programme has been successful. But evaluation can also be used to report on much larger units of analysis such as national policies or government-sponsored intervention programmes.

Of course, whichever research methodology (or combination of methodologies) we use, none can be successful without the use of sound and reliable data collection tools (Part C). We start here with a look at, perhaps, one of the most commonly used research instruments, the questionnaire (Chapter 8). This chapter shows how designing valid and reliable questionnaires requires adherence to a large number of design considerations that range from the writing of individual questions to the layout of the questionnaire itself.

Questionnaires are often used as the data gathering instrument for structured or semi-structured interviews. But interviews (Chapter 9) also necessitate that the researcher acquires a wide range of other skills associated with actually conducting the interview. This chapter, then, provides some practical advice on planning and conducting a variety of interview approaches.

But how do we know that interviewees tell the truth? It may be that they do not know the answer to a question or that they want to hide something from us. Another data gathering method, then, is observation (Chapter 10), which could be used either instead of an interview or as a supplement to it (to verify the data). As this chapter shows, observation might be undertaken overtly, where the subjects of the research know that they are being observed or covertly where the role of the researcher is disguised. Observation can also be conducted as either a participant in the research setting or as a non-participant.

One of the problems in using questionnaires, interviews and observations is that they are potentially reactive – that is, the data may become contaminated because of, say, the bias of the research instruments or the way data are interpreted by the researcher. An often neglected but equally powerful data gathering method is what is termed 'unobtrusive measures' (Chapter 11), which offer the benefit of being non-reactive. Unobtrusive measures include physical evidence, documentary evidence and archival analysis, including documents held on the World Wide Web. Unobtrusive measures can offer flexible, creative and imaginative ways of collecting data, often to verify findings from the use of other data collection methods.

Having collected data, they have to be analysed and the results presented (Part D). Of course, plans and designs for analysis should have been completed long before this stage. Chapter 12 looks at techniques for presenting and analysing quantitative data, including ways of categorizing quantitative data and cleaning and coding data. This chapter also examines ways of analysing data using descriptive statistics and the use of some elementary inferential statistical techniques.

In contrast, Chapter 13 looks at the possible sources of qualitative data and approaches to how data can be analysed. It looks particularly at content analysis and grounded theory methods and also includes approaches such as the use of narratives, conversational analysis and discourse analysis. You will probably notice in reading Chapters 12 and 13 how some of the philosophical issues raised in Chapter 2 are given substance in terms of what is researched, and how the research is conducted.

After you have collected your data, you now want to present them in a way that enhances their credibility and impact. Chapter 14 looks at different types of research report including organizational and technical reports, and studies written up as part of an academic dissertation or thesis. Advice is given on key features, such as the use of appropriate language and writing style for the intended audience, and the structure of the report.

In a sense, Chapter 14, covering the final outcome of a research project, the report, might seem a logical place to conclude this book. However, Chapter 15 goes a stage further by exploring the purposes and methods behind action research. In Chapter 1, and, indeed, throughout the book, we look at real world issues and problems. Action research is about addressing and, in some cases, solving these problems. The key focus is not research for the sake of expanding knowledge but on achieving change (often in a company, school, college or community setting). We have, therefore, come full circle from Chapter 1, where we explored the need to address some of the issues in the 'real world', to our final chapter, which demonstrates one methodology that actively engages in the process of change through research.

HOW TO USE THE BOOK

How is the book best used as an aid to research? You could think of it as a research manual that also explains the theoretical underpinnings of research methods and provides guidance on where to find further information. It is recommended that you read through the book, focusing on the objectives listed at the beginning of each chapter. Try to get a feel for which aspects will be of particular interest to you, noting any ideas or topics, approaches and practices that strike you as relevant to your research. During the research process revisit these parts and if you need further guidance, check with the further reading lists at the end of each chapter, which include brief details of the nature of the sources listed. Note also any associated Case Studies (which are designed to illustrate key research methodologies or approaches) and Activities (designed to promote thinking, reflection and skills development and, in the case of websites, a guide to additional information or resources). It is not expected that you attempt to complete all Activities – tackle those that you think would be most useful. Where it is felt appropriate, suggested answers are given for some Activities at the end of the relevant chapter.

As indicated, some of the Activities in the book ask you to visit specified websites. If you do not have access to the Web, then these Activities can be omitted. But do note the growing importance of the Web for research in terms of providing data, tools, resources and access to both research respondents and fellow researchers.

SUMMARY

- The growing complexity of the world means that research in the real world is of growing importance. An understanding of the world is underpinned by theory.
- A theory consists of a set of interrelated concepts, definitions and propositions that demonstrate relationships between variables.
- Through the inductive approach, data are accumulated and analysed to see if relationships emerge between variables. The deductive approach uses a theory to generate a working hypothesis concerning relationships between variables. The hypothesis is operationalized and tested and is either accepted or rejected on the basis of the evidence.
- The inductive and deductive methods are not mutually exclusive. A researcher may turn a collection of data into a set of concepts, models or even theories (inductive approach) which are then tested through experimentation (deductive).

Suggested answers for Activity 1.1

Actually, it is all of them!

PART A

Principles and Planning for Research

2 Theoretical Perspectives and Research Methodologies

Chapter objectives

After reading this chapter you will be able to:

- **Distinguish between ontology and epistemology in research.**
- **Explain the different perspectives taken by positivism and interpretivism.**
- **Describe the different research methodologies and the conditions for their selection.**
- **Distinguish between exploratory, descriptive and expanatory research studies.**

We saw in Chapter 1 that the research process requires us to engage at some stage with theoretical perspectives. Sometimes this will occur before undertaking the research (the deductive approach) and at other times after it (inductive). But the question remains: which theories? The purpose of this chapter is to examine the range of theoretical perspectives available, and also to provide some guidance as to which ones are most appropriate to the research project or task you are undertaking.

This is far from being a simple process. Particularly if you are relatively new to the study of philosophical perspectives, the nature of theories and their significance to research methodologies may not be instantly obvious. Furthermore, the nature and meaning of some philosophical perspectives is still contested and debated.

At this stage it is suggested that you read this chapter without dwelling too much on individual sections. If some of the discussion seems rather abstract do not worry – keep going. It is suggested that you return to this chapter at a later stage when its relevance will, hopefully, be clearer and more easily absorbed.

EPISTEMOLOGICAL AND ONTOLOGICAL PERSPECTIVES

We looked in Chapter 1 at the nature of theories and their relationship to practice. We now need to explore the range of theories available to us as researchers, and how we can select between them. As Crotty (1998) demonstrates, one of the problems here is not only the bewildering array of theoretical perspectives and methodologies, but the fact that the terminology applied to them is often inconsistent (or even contradictory). Crotty suggests that an interrelationship exists between the theoretical stance adopted by the researcher, the methodology and methods used, and the researcher's view of the epistemology (see Figure 2.1).

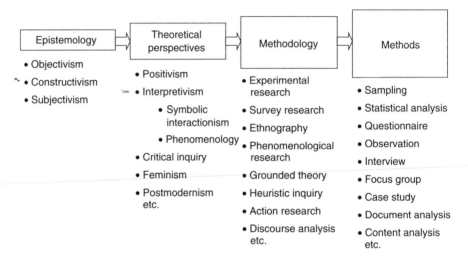

FIGURE 2.1   RELATIONSHIP BETWEEN EPISTEMOLOGY, THEORETICAL PERSPECTIVES, METHODOLOGY AND RESEARCH METHODS (ADAPTED FROM CROTTY, 1998)

Despite the natural tendency for the researcher (and especially the novice researcher!) to select a data gathering method and get on with the job, the choice of methods will be influenced by the research methodology chosen. This methodology, in turn, will be influenced by the theoretical perspectives adopted by the researcher, and, in turn, by the researcher's epistemological stance.

Ontology is the study of being, that is, the nature of existence. While ontology embodies understanding *what is*, epistemology tries to understand *what it means to know*. Epistemology provides a philosophical background for deciding what kinds of knowledge are legitimate and adequate.

Western thought remains divided by two opposing ontological traditions. Heraclitus, (*c*.535–*c*.475BC), who lived in Ephasus in ancient Greece, placed an emphasis on a changing and emergent world. Parmenides (*c*.515–*c*.445BC), who succeeded him, placed quite a different emphasis on a permanent and unchanging reality. Between a Heraclitean ontology of *becoming* and a Parmenidean ontology of *being*, it is the latter that has held sway in Western philosophy. Hence, reality is seen as being composed of clearly formed entities with identifiable properties (in contrast to a Heraclitean emphasis on formlessness, chaos, interpenetration and absence). Once entities are held to be stable they can become represented by symbols, words and concepts. Thus a representationalist epistemology results in which signs and language are taken to be accurate representations of the external world. This representationalist epistemology orientates our thinking towards outcomes and end-states rather than processes of change. According to Chia (2002), only relatively recently has postmodern epistemology challenged traditional *being* ontology with notions of a *becoming* orientation and the limitations of truth-seeking.

It would be a mistake, however, to view *being* ontology as leading to epistemological positions that are unitary and holistic. As Figure 2.1 shows, at least three positions have emerged. Objectivist epistemology, for example, holds that reality exists independently of consciousness – in other words, there is an objective reality 'out there'. So, research is about discovering this objective truth. A theoretical perspective closely linked to objectivism is positivism (see Figure 2.1). In contrast, constructivism rejects this view of human knowledge. Truth and meaning do not exist in some external world, but are created by the subject's interactions with the world. Meaning is *constructed* not discovered, so subjects construct their own meaning in different ways, even in relation to the same phenomenon. A theoretical perspective linked to constructivism is interpretivism. Yet, while interpretivism and objectivism hold different epistemological positions, both are still based upon a *being* ontology (Chia, 2002).

In contrast to constructivism, for subjectivism, meaning does not emerge from the interplay between the subject and the outside world, but is imposed on the object by the subject. Subjects do construct meaning, but do so from within collective unconsciousness, from dreams, from religious beliefs, etc. Despite Crotty's assertion that this is 'the most slippery of terms' (1998: 183), postmodernism can be taken as an example of a theoretical perspective linked to subjectivism (and *becoming* ontology).

As Easterby-Smith et al. (1991) point out, having an epistemological perspective is important for several reasons. First, in can help to clarify issues of research design. This means more than just the design of research tools. It means the overarching structure of the research including the kind of evidence that is being gathered, from where, and how it is going to be interpreted. Secondly, a knowledge of research philosophy will help the researcher to recognize which designs will work (for a given set of objectives) and which will not.

THEORETICAL PERSPECTIVES

Of the different theoretical perspectives available, positivism and various strands of interpretivism are, or have been (arguably) among the most influential. These, and a number of other stances such as critical inquiry, postmodernism and feminism, will be used here to illustrate the value of adopting theoretical perspectives that are congruent with the researcher's epistemology and demonstrate the kinds of research methodologies that emerge from them.

Positivism

Positivism was the dominant epistemological paradigm in social science from the 1930s through to the 1960s, its core argument being that the social world exists externally to the researcher, and that its properties can be measured directly through observation. In essence, positivism argues that:

- Reality consists of what is available to the senses – that is, what can be seen, smelt, touched, etc.
- Inquiry should be based upon scientific observation (as opposed to philo-sophical speculation), and therefore on empirical inquiry.
- The natural and human sciences share common logical and methodological principles, dealing with facts and not with values.

Hence, ideas only deserve their incorporation into knowledge if they can be put to the test of empirical experience. Positivists saw the natural sciences as pro-gressing through the patient accumulation of facts about the world in order to produce generalizations known as scientific laws. To achieve this, the act of scien-tific inquiry was taken to be the accumulation of 'brute data' such as shape, size, motion, etc. For positivists, then, both the natural and social worlds operated within a strict set of laws, which science had to discover through empirical inquiry. This is a brief summary of positivism, but, as Bryman (1988) notes, there have been many different versions of positivism which overlap, and which rarely agreed precisely on its essential components.

The case against positivism

Positivism has been described as 'one of the heroic failures of modern philosophy' (Williams and May, 1996: 27). As Hughes and Sharrock (1997) show, one of the fundamental mistakes of positivism is some of the assumptions it made about scientific inquiry. Science is, certainly, interested in producing theoretical explana-tions but not just on the basis of what can be observed. Indeed, some branches of science consist almost entirely of mathematical formulations. Black holes and sub-atomic particles, for example, have been reasoned from only the most indirect of evidence. Typically, science does not begin from observation, but from theory, to make observations intelligible. Thus, even observations are 'theory laden' (Williams and May, 1996).

Adopting a positivistic stance is not only about adopting certain approaches to the design of research studies. As Crotty (1998) points out, it implies that the results of research will tend to be presented as objective facts and established truths. Popper (1968), however, suggests that no theory can ever be proved simply by multiple observations, since only one instance that refutes the theory would demonstrate it as false. According to Popper, theories cannot be proved to be true – they can only be proved to be false. Hence, with the deductive approach, theories are tested through observation, leading either to the falsification and discarding of the theory, or to the creation of, as yet, unfalsified laws.

Normal science consists of extending the knowledge of the facts that a paradigm suggests are especially important, by extending the match between those facts and the paradigm's predictions, and by further articulation of the paradigm itself. But normal science is a puzzle-solver and if it persistently fails to solve problems, then the failure of existing rules will lead to a search for new ones. This is part of what Kuhn (1970) has called a paradigm crisis. It is a crisis which may turn into a revolution if anomalies continue and new people enter the field, such as researchers who are not committed to the traditional rules of normal science and who are able to conceive of a new set of rules.

Case Study 2.1 provides an illustration of how stubbornly existing paradigms resist change – even in the face of emerging evidence that strongly contradicts their fundamental underpinning principles.

Case Study 2.1   The conflict of paradigms

On 22 June 1633, Galileo Galilei was put on trial by the Inquisition in Rome. Charged with heresy, this old man of 69 was threatened with torture, imprisonment and even burning at the stake unless he renounced his claim that the Sun and not the Earth was the centre of the universe, and that the Earth moved around the Sun, and not vice versa.

The idea of an Earth-centred universe was first promulgated by Ptolemy of Alexandria in AD 150. The beauty of the Ptolemaic system was that it worked with some accuracy, enabling astronomers to predict, through complex geometry, the movements of the heavenly bodies. Later, these geocentric (Earth-centred) ideas became entrenched into the teachings of the Church, largely because they fitted neatly with the Christian notion of the centrality of mankind (Hellman, 1998). Hence, Ptolemaic theory became a combination of science, philosophy and religious ideas. Note the long-standing relationship between science and philosophy!

In 1543 Nicolaus Copernicus, a canon in the Polish Catholic Church, challenged the accepted Ptolmaic paradigm with a heliocentric (Sun-centred) system, but, as was traditional, his book was written in Latin and thus was not widely read. A century later, Galileo's repetition of these ideas in Dialogue on the Great World Systems, Ptolemaic and Copernican (1632) was written in Italian. As such it was widely accessible and seen by the Pope, Urban VIII, as a direct threat to the teachings of the Church.

Under the Inquisition's threats, Galileo retreated. These threats, after all, were not idle. A friend, Bruno, who had advocated the idea of an infinite universe, was tried by the Inquisition, refused to recant and was burned at the stake in 1600. Of course, the Church could not completely suppress the *Dialogue*. In fact, it was published in England before Galileo's death in 1642. But the trial before the Inquisition is an interesting example of the bitterness that can be generated when far-reaching new ideas come into open conflict with the vested interests of long-accepted paradigms – and the entrenched nature of these paradigms.

Activity 2.1

Take a once accepted theory (say, in management, education, or your own professional subject) that has become less popular or even discredited in the eyes of some (theorists and/or practitioners), and show how alternative theories have emerged. What factors have helped to discredit the once 'accepted' theory? What factors have helped to promote the emerging alternative theory?

We have seen that, at least in the social sciences, many of positivism's avowed certainties about the nature and results of scientific inquiry have been strongly challenged. It should be noted, however, that some of the approaches to research developed under positivism, such as an insistence on empirical inquiry, the use of experimental designs and inductive generalization (to name but three), are still with us (as we shall see in later chapters) in one form or other. In general, however, we now inhabit a post-positivist world in which a number of alternative perspectives (for example, anti-positivist, post-positivist and naturalistic) have emerged.

Interpretivism

A major anti-positivist stance is interpretivism, which looks for 'culturally derived and historically situated interpretations of the social life-world' (Crotty, 1998: 67). There is no, direct, one-to-one relationship between ourselves (subjects) and the world (object). The world is interpreted through the classification schemas of the mind (Williams and May, 1996). In terms of epistemology, interpretivism is closely linked to constructivism. Interpretivism asserts that natural reality (and the laws of science) and social reality are different and therefore require different kinds of method. While the natural sciences are looking for consistencies in the data in order to deduce 'laws' (nomothetic), the social sciences often deal with the actions of the individual (ideographic).

> *Our interest in the social world tends to focus on exactly those aspects that are unique, individual and qualitative, whereas our interest in the natural world focuses on more abstract phenomena, that is, those exhibiting quantifiable, empirical regularities.* (Crotty, 1998: 68)

Let us now look at five examples of the interpretivist approach: symbolic interactionism, phenomenology, realism, hermeneutics and naturalistic inquiry.

Symbolic interactionism

Symbolic interactionism grew in the 1930s out of the work of the American pragmatist philosophers, including the social psychologist George Herbert Mead and John Dewey. These philosophers shared a disenchantment with what they saw as the irrelevance of contemporary philosophy and social science. Instead, they wanted to develop a way of conceptualizing human behaviour that focused on people's practices and lived realities. Central to social behaviour is the notion of meaning. Human interaction with the world is mediated through the process of meaning-making and interpretation. The essential tenets of symbolic interactionism are that:

- People interpret the meaning of objects and actions in the world and then act upon those interpretations.
- Meanings arise from the process of social interaction.
- Meanings are handled in, and are modified by, an interactive process used by people in dealing with the phenomena that are encountered.

Thus, meanings are not fixed or stable but are revised on the basis of experience. This includes the definition of 'self' and of who we are. For example, if someone is promoted from supervisor to manager their perception of themselves and the company may change, which in turn leads to changes in the meaning of objects, and thereby to changes in behaviour.

In order to understand this process, researchers have to study a subject's actions, objects and society from the perspective of the subject themselves. In practice, this can mean entering the field setting and observing at first-hand what is happening. The kinds of research methodologies that are often associated with symbolic interactionism include ethnography and the use of participative observation methods (Chapter 10) and grounded theory (Chapter 13).

Phenomenology

Phenomenology holds that any attempt to understand social reality has to be grounded in people's experiences of that social reality. Hence, phenomenology insists that we must lay aside our prevailing understanding of phenomena and revisit our immediate experience of them in order that new meanings may emerge. Current understandings have to be 'bracketed' to the best of our ability to allow phenomena to 'speak for themselves', unadulterated by our preconceptions. The result will be new meaning, fuller meaning or renewed meaning. Attempts are made to avoid ways in which the prejudices of researchers bias the data. The key is gaining the subjective experience of the subject, sometimes by trying to put oneself in the place of the subject. Hence, phenomenology becomes an exploration, via personal experience, of prevailing cultural understandings. Value is ascribed not only to the interpretations of researchers, but also of the subjects of the research themselves. Far from using a theoretical model that imposes an external logic on a phenomenon, this inductive approach seeks to find the internal logic of the subject. Table 2.1 provides a summary of some of the major distinctions between positivism and phenomenology.

Tesch (1994) distinguishes between phenomenological research and ethnography. While both are based upon description and interpretation, ethnographic research is focused more on culture and phenomenology, on human experience of the 'life-world'. So, while the unit of analysis of phenomenology is often individuals, ethnographers make use of 'sites'. Phenomenology makes use

TABLE 2.1   A SUMMARY OF POSITIVIST AND PHENOMENOLOGICAL
PARADIGMS

	Positivist paradigm	Phenomenological paradigm
Basic beliefs	The world is external and objective	The world is socially constructed and subjective
	The observer is independent	The observer is a party to what is being observed
	Science is value-free	Science is driven by human interests
The researcher should	Focus on facts	Focus on meanings
	Locate causality between variables	Try to understand what is happening
	Formulate and test hypotheses (deductive approach)	Construct theories and models from the data (inductive approach)
Methods include	Operationalizing concepts so that they can be measured	Using multiple methods to establish different views of a phenomenon
	Using large samples from which to generalize to the population	Using small samples researched in depth or over time
	Quantitative methods	Qualitative methods

Source: Adapted from Easterby-Smith et al., 1991

TABLE 2.2   DISTINCTIONS BETWEEN PHENOMENOLOGICAL RESEARCH AND
ETHNOGRAPHY

Ethnography	Phenomenological research
Study of culture	Study of the 'lifeworld' human experience
Discovering the relationship between culture and behaviour	Exploring the personal construction of the individual's world
Studying 'sites'	Studying individuals
As many informants as possible	Between 5 and 15 'participants'
Use of observation, and some interviewing	Use of in-depth, unstructured interviews
Unit of analysis: event	Unit of analysis: meaning unit
Reliability: triangulation	Reliability: confirmation by participants

Source: Adapted from Tesch, 1994

almost exclusively of interviews, while ethnography's prime mode of data collection is observation (as a participant or outside observer), which is sometimes supplemented by interview data for clarification. Ethnographers pay particular attention to language and the ways in which terms are used in certain cultures. A summary of the distinctions between phenomenological research and ethnography is given in Table 2.2.

Realism

Realism begins from the position that the picture that science paints of the world is a true and accurate one (Chia, 2002). So for the realist researcher, objects of research such as 'culture', 'the organization', 'corporate planning' exist and act quite independently of the observer. They are therefore as available for systematic analysis as natural phenomena. Hence, knowledge is advanced through the process of theory-building in which discoveries add to what is already known. But although reality comprises entities, structures and events, realism holds that some observable 'facts' may be merely illusions. Conversely, there may be phenomena that cannot be observed but which exist none the less.

Hermeneutics

The hermeneutic tradition is associated largely with nineteenth century German philosophy, but also has connections with phenomenology and the psychoanalysis of Freud. According to a hermeneutic perspective, social reality is seen as socially constructed, rather than being rooted in objective fact. Hence, hermeneutics argues that interpretation should be given more standing than explanation and description. Social reality is too complex to be understood through the process of observation. The scientist must interpret in order to achieve deeper levels of knowledge and also self-understanding.

Naturalistic inquiry

According to Lincoln and Guba (1985), in the naturalistic paradigm there are multiple constructed realities that can only be studied holistically. Inquiry into these multiple realities raises more questions than it answers, so that prediction and control of outcomes is a largely futile expectation, although some level of understanding can be achieved (Guba, 1985). Inquiry itself cannot be detached but is value-bounded by the perspectives of the researcher. Rather than aiming to generalize, inquiry develops an ideographic body of knowledge that describes individual cases. Within these cases, plausible inferences on events and processes are made, but this falls short of claiming causality. Phenomena can only be understood within their environment or setting; they cannot be isolated or held constant while others are manipulated. The real world is too complex, diverse and interdependent for this (Lincoln, 1985).

Research designs cannot be pre-specified, but 'emerge, unroll, cascade, or unfold during the research process' (Lincoln, 1985: 142). Because naturalists believe in the concept of multiple, constructed realities, it would be incongruent to specify these designs in advance. However, the types of research methods usually selected by naturalistic inquirers involve those most closely associated with a human component: interviewing, participant observation, document and content analysis (and other forms of unobtrusive measures).

Critical inquiry

It is worth having a brief overview of critical inquiry because it offers quite a different perspective to positivism and interpretivism. This critical form of research is a meta-process of investigation, which questions currently held values and assumptions and challenges conventional social structures. It invites both researchers and participants to discard what they term 'false consciousness' in order to develop new ways of understanding as a guide to effective action. In a Marxist sense, the critical inquiry perspective is not content to interpret the world but also to change it. The assumptions that lie beneath critical inquiry are that:

23

- Ideas are mediated by power relations in society.
- Certain groups in society are privileged over others and exhert an oppressive force on subordinate groups.
- What are presented as 'facts' cannot be disentangled from ideology and the self-interest of dominant groups.
- Mainstream research practices are implicated, even if unconsciously, in the reproduction of the systems of class, race and gender oppression.

Those adhering to the critical inquiry perspective accuse interpretivists of adopting an uncritical stance towards the culture they are exploring, whereas the task of researchers is to call the structures and values of society into question.

Feminism

Like Marxism and critical inquiry, feminist epistemologies take the view that what a person knows is largely determined by their social position. But whereas Marxism defines social class in terms of a person's relationship to the means of production, feminism regards women themselves as an oppressed social class. Because men come from a position of dominance, their knowledge of the world is distorted. In contrast, women, being subject to domination, have a less distorted social experience that has the potential to produce less distorted knowledge claims (Williams and May, 1996). But what counts as knowledge is also challenged. Attempts at rational or objective approaches to research are seen as the remit of male researchers, reflecting and prioritizing male values. In contrast, women have access to a deeper reality through their personal experiences (of oppression), and through their feelings and emotions.

Postmodernism

Postmodernism is far from being a unified system of thought and is sometimes used interchangeably with concepts such as deconstructionism and post-structuralism. Emerging from the disillusionment of French intellectuals with Marxism after the events of 1968, postmodernism was not just an attack on positivism, but on the entire historical agenda of modernity – and particularly Marxism (Delanty, 1997). Postmodernism rejects any notion of social 'emancipation', emphasizing instead multiplicity, ambiguity, ambivalence and fragmentation. Whereas philosophers such as Habermas had seen fragmentation in negative terms and as a threat to communication, postmodernism views it quite positively as an opportunity for choice. Hence postmodern analysis often focuses on themes within advertising, lifestyles, fashion, subcultures and gender.

In terms of research, the primary task becomes the deconstruction of texts to expose how values and interests are embedded within them (Williams and May, 1996). The focus becomes not one of how these texts describe the 'reality' of the world, but how the social world becomes represented, and how meanings are produced. Texts are therefore seen as social practices, embedded with multiple values and vested interests, not the reporting of independent, objective judgements. As we have seen, in contrast to other epistemologies, postmodernism stresses a *becoming* ontology.

RESEARCH METHODOLOGIES

We have examined, briefly, the significance of both epistemology and theoretical perspectives in research design. Let us now look at applying these in practice by exploring some of the alternative research methodologies. The choice of research methodology is determined by a combination of several factors – for example, whether the researcher believes that there is some sort of external 'truth' out there that needs discovering, or whether the task of research is to explore and unpick people's multiple perspectives in natural, field settings. It is influenced, then, by whether the research is inclined towards a positivist, interpretivist, or other perspective. It will also be influenced, for example, by the researcher's attitude towards the ways in which she or he thinks theory should be used – whether research should begin with a theoretical model or perspective (deductive approach) or whether such models should emerge from the data itself (inductively).

In examining each of the following research methodologies (selected to illustrate a range of approaches), pause each time to consider whether you think each is inclined towards a more 'being' or 'becoming' ontology. A Case Study is provided for each methodology to help you.

Experimental and quasi-experimental research

In classical, scientific experiments, subjects are randomly assigned to either an experimental or a control group. The experimental group receives the 'treatment' and the results are compared with the control group that does not receive the treatment. In the real world, however, it is often not possible to conduct truly experimental research because it is difficult to find experimental and control groups that are closely matched in terms of key variables (such as age, gender, income, work grade, etc). Instead, a quasi-experimental design is used where the researcher, for example, has to take existing groups rather than drawing on random samples. Instead of trying to manipulate an independent variable, the researcher will often attempt to find groups of people who have experienced it in their own natural setting. An attempt is then made to compare the behaviour of this group with that of a similar group that has not experienced the event or phenomenon. In experimental and quasi-experimental research there is also the tendency to make use of hypotheses which the experiment seeks either to support or to refute. In other words, experimental research is usually deductive.

Experimental and quasi-experimental research then places an emphasis on:

- Reproducing the techniques of the laboratory experiment with highly structured methods.
- The generation of initial hypotheses.

- The control of variables.
- Accurate (quantitative) measurement of outcomes.
- Generalization from samples to similar populations.

Case Study 2.2 Experimental research

A global organization selling Internet hardware, software and services, has an extensive set of internal training programmes, each of which is formally assessed. The company wants to reduce the size of the overall training budget through the use of e-learning, but is concerned as to whether learning through this mechanism is more effective, less effective or makes no difference. It is believed by the research team that e-learning will be marginally more effective – thus they have a working hypothesis.

All 200 members of a representative sample are given a pre-test of their understanding of a selected subject. Then, the subject is taught to 100 participants through traditional, classroom learning (the control group) and to the other 100 participants through a specially designed e-learning program (the experimental group). All employees are given a post-test, and the gain-scores (the differences between the pre-test and post-test score) compared between the two groups.

Action research

Action research involves close collaboration between researcher and practitioners, and places an emphasis on promoting change within an organization. While the emphasis is on seeking information on the attitudes and perspectives of practitioners in the field, the way in which data are collected may involve both quantitative and qualitative methods. The main action research medium, however, is the case study, or multiple case studies. In some research designs, both an experimental and a control case study may be used, so emulating the experimental approach. Action research then:

- Involves both researchers and practitioners (or practitioners as researchers within their own organization).
- Can be highly structured and involve the use of experimental and control groups used to test a hypothesis.
- Can also be quite unstructured and used inductively (and qualitatively).

Case Study 2.3 Action research

A group of 20 teachers provide intensive educational support to children with special educational, emotional and physical needs in four community schools. The educational attainment of the special needs children in these schools has remained depressingly low over time. The special needs teachers decide to undertake an action research study using their four schools as the experimental cohort and

(Continued)

---

four other schools in the district as the control. Working collaboratively with their other teaching colleagues in the school, a series of ten 'mould-breaking' workshops are run in which issues are explored and new solutions formulated. These are prioritized and a number of solutions implemented in the second semester. The educational attainment and other indicators are then calculated for the children from the four schools involved in the action research project, and compared to those of children in the other district schools (the control).

Analytical surveys

These attempt to test a theory in the field through exploring the association between variables. Analytical surveys are highly structured and place an emphasis on the careful random selection of samples, so that the results can be generalized to other situations or contexts. On the other hand, the very tightness of the survey structure may hinder the ability of respondents to provide illuminating information in a way that they would like.

Like the truly experimental approach, analytic surveys emphasize:

- A deductive approach.
- The identification of the research population.
- The drawing of a representative sample from the population.
- Control of variables.
- The generation of both qualitative and quantitative data.
- Generalizability of results.

Case Study 2.4   Analytical surveys

A government department is becoming increasingly concerned that the level of waste recycling by domestic households is not increasing despite a major publicity campaign and the provision of local amenities for recycling. The department commissions a nationally based survey to explore for each household contacted:

- the level of recycling
- attitudes to the environment
- attitudes to recycling specific waste products
- the size and location of the household
- the convenience of recycling facilities available
- the household income level
- the number of people and children per house

The survey is constructed so that correlation levels (strength of relationships) between levels of recycling and the other variables can be calculated and analysed. The hypothesis being tested is that levels of recycling are strongly positively correlated

(Continued)

---

with attitudes to the environment (determined through the collection of qualitative data) and moderately positively correlated with access to local recycling amenities. Hence, if the hypothesis is confirmed, government policy will focus on changing attitudes towards recycling rather than on the provision of more amenities.

Phenomenological research

Phenomenology is a theoretical perspective that uses relatively unstructured methods of data collection. One of the advantages of phenomenology is that, because of its emphasis on the inductive collection of large amounts of data, it is more likely to pick up factors that were not part of the original research focus. It is also capable of producing 'thick descriptions' of people's experiences or perspectives within their natural settings. But it is often based upon quite small case studies giving rise to concerns about its generalizability to other situations. Also, because it is generally unstructured, phenomenological research may be difficult to replicate. Phenomenological research, then:

- Emphasizes inductive logic.
- Seeks the opinions and subjective accounts and interpretations of participants.
- Relies on qualitative analysis of data.
- Is not so much concerned with generalizations to larger populations, but with contextual description and analysis.

Case Study 2.5   Phenomenological research

A city police authority has spent three years conducting a 'war' on street soliciting in one of the city's poorest areas. Since the legal crackdown has not had the desired result, the police authority decides that the problem needs to be understood before new solutions are tried. A research study is commissioned to find out why these women turn to prostitution, the attitudes of the local community to their activities, and what sort of clients seek the women's services and where they come from.

Three female researchers rent a flat in the area for six months. They do not try to hide who they are or what they are doing, but nevertheless, manage to build up a rapport and trust with ten of the women. Sometimes this is through visiting their 'pitches' where they are working, at other times it is through chance meetings while shopping, in bars or the launderette. The researchers also take time to talk to local people about the issue, including local police officers, through casual conversations, rather than formal interviews. The team gathers data sets consisting of detailed personal biographies of the women, their own attitudes towards their work, and the range of problems and issues raised by members of the local community. Having written these biographies, the researchers revisit the women to have the transcripts checked for accuracy.

Heuristic inquiry

Heuristic inquiry is a process that begins with a question or a problem which the researcher tries to illuminate or find an answer to. The question itself is usually focused on an issue that has posed a *personal* problem and to which answers are required. It seeks, through open-ended inquiry, self-directed search and immersion in active experience, to 'get inside' the question by becoming one with it.

According to Moustakas (1990), one of the primary processes of heuristic research is self-dialogue in which the researcher enters into a conversation with the phenomenon and is questioned by it. It is hoped that the process will lead to self-discoveries, awareness and enhanced understanding. Through this, the researcher is able to develop the skills and ability to understand the problem itself and, in turn, to develop the understanding of others.

Philosophically, heuristic inquiry does not start from the premise that there is an external 'objective' truth to be discovered. In contrast, it starts phenomenologically from the belief that understanding grows out of direct human experience and can only be discovered initially through self-inquiry. Heuristic research, then, is autobiographical, providing for a deep, personal analysis. It is richly descriptive, but also strongly subjective, and weak in terms of generalizability.

Heuristic research, then, involves the researcher in:

- A deep personal questioning of what it is they wish to research.
- Living, sleeping and merging with the research question.
- Allowing inner workings of intuition to extend understanding of the question.
- Reviewing all the data from personal experiences to identify tacit meanings.
- Forming a creative synthesis, including ideas for and against a proposition.

Case Study 2.6   Heuristic research

The Operations Director of a company finds that he is passed over for promotion to Chief Executive for the third time. In an attempt to understand why this has occurred, he approaches the Chairperson, who has been largely responsible for this decision and asks if she will join him in a heuristic research project to uncover the reasons behind the decision. At first, the Chairperson is reluctant because she thinks (rightly) that the process will reveal some of her confidential thoughts. But she eventually agrees because she realizes that the process of working together might articulate for her the personal qualities she is seeking in a Chief Executive.

The Operations Director, who acts as the researcher, begins with a deep personal reflection on what he wants to achieve in the research. Then, through a series of open and frank discussions with the Chairperson, he works through his feelings towards his current role, his successes and failures in numerous projects, his expectations of the Chairperson and her expectations of him. Over a period of five meetings he begins to understand that the blockage is not based upon prejudice, but on a feeling (shared by other members of the Board), that he is an excellent Operations Director, but lacks the *strategic* vision to be the Chief Executive. Through a process of explication (the full examination of awakened consciousness), he begins to realize that this analysis is probably correct.

> **Activity 2.2**
>
> Examine the range of research methodologies outlined above. Select one methodology that you think could be valid for your own research uses and one that is inappropriate. Justify your choices.

SELECTING RESEARCH APPROACHES AND STRATEGIES

In this chapter we have examined some of the philosophies of research, two approaches to research (inductive and deductive) and, within the context of truth and perspective-seeking objectives, some research methodologies (experimental, survey, phenomenological, etc.). We now need to put these together within a coherent framework (or as near to one as we can get) and to add a time horizon and data collection methods. Notice that data collection methods are being discussed last (see Figure 2.2). Novice researchers may be tempted to begin with the design, say, of a questionnaire, so that data can be gathered without delay, but Figure 2.2 shows that other stages must be considered first.

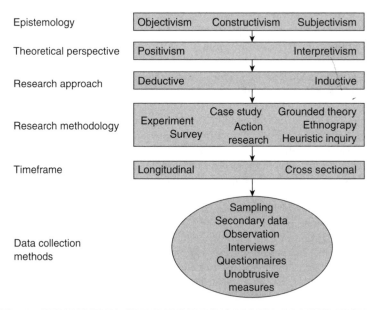

FIGURE 2.2   THE ELEMENTS OF THE RESEARCH PROCESS (ADAPTED FROM SAUNDERS ET AL., 2000)

Connecting the research elements

As we saw earlier, it is wise to start by considering epistemology. At first sight, this might seem rather irrelevant. But your approach to research and the research methods that you use will be influenced by whether you think it is possible (or desirable) to try to measure an objective 'truth', or whether you think that the real world cannot be measured in this way. As we have seen, the theoretical perspective of interpretivism sees the world as too complex to be reduced to a set of observable 'laws'. Generalizability is less important than understanding the real workings behind 'reality'. With your research topic in mind, you will probably have a view as to whether you want to measure and generalize to a larger population or to seek 'thick descriptions', through the collection of qualitative data. Alternatively, your approach might include elements of both. Hence, Figure 2.2 does not illustrate a dividing wall between epistemologies and perspectives, but a gradual shading of one into the other.

We also have access to a range of research methodologies. Figure 2.2 deliberately shows the experimental methodology beneath the deductive/positivism side of the diagram. Conversely, action research has been placed more towards inductive/interpretivism. But it is dangerous to categorize research methodologies against specific approaches and philosophies. Action research, for example, can incorporate a qualitative, inductive approach with an emphasis on seeking the views and perspectives of participants. Equally, it can use, say, a series of case studies involving an intervention with a number of groups, with others used as a control – in other words, an experimental methodology. Figure 2.2, then, illustrates some broad tendencies that should not be interpreted as concrete relationships. What is important, is that whatever philosophy, approach and methodology you adopt for your research, you should be able to justify your mix in relation to your research philosophy and research question(s).

Note that we come to the choice of data collection methods last of all. This is not because the choice is unimportant, but because it is impossible to make one until we have a clear perspective on philosophy, approach and methodology. While claims have sometimes been made that one data collection method or another is more applicable to a particular methodology or research philosophy, in fact, they should be regarded as independent.

Timeframes for research

In planning your research you will usually have some sort of idea as to the timescales you have available to you. If these are short-term, then you will probably have to adopt a *cross-sectional study* using a 'snapshot' approach where the data are collected at one point in time. Cross-sectional studies often use a survey methodology. For example, they might seek to measure staff attitudes towards the introduction of new working practices, or to compare crime rates for particular types of crime between different cities. Most research studies are cross-sectional, mainly because of the pressure of time and resources.

If your timescales are more generous, it may be possible to undertake a *longitudinal study*, to study change and development over time. Taking our example above, a longitudinal study of working practices might examine changes in staff attitudes over time, looking at attitudes before the introduction of new working practices, and then at various periods afterwards. Similarly, crime rates can be studied to identify where rates are falling and rising. This might allow researchers to begin to identify explanatory factors such as demographic changes, social conditions and policing methods.

Exploratory, descriptive and explanatory studies

While we have so far classified studies by their research methodology, they can also be classified according to their purpose. As Robson (1993) explains, there are three possible forms of study: exploratory, descriptive and explanatory.

Exploratory studies

As the name suggests, exploratory studies seek to explore what is happening and to ask questions about it. They are particularly useful when not enough is known about a phenomenon. An exploratory study, then, may help to decide whether it is worth researching the issue or not. As Saunders et al. (2000) suggest, exploratory studies can be conducted by:

- A search of the literature.
- Talking to experts in the field.
- Conducting focus group interviews.

Descriptive studies

According to Hedrick et al. (1993), the purpose of a descriptive study is to provide a picture of a phenomenon as it naturally occurs. This may, indeed, by purely descriptive (for example, the level and nature of crime among 16–21-year-olds). But it may also comprise a normative study, comparing the data against some standard (for example, comparing drug use against legal standards of drug classification to gauge the seriousness of crime).

Explanatory studies

Some studies can also be correlative in nature, with the emphasis on discovering causal relationships between variables. So we could determine the relationship between drug use and other variables such as social class, employment, attitudes to drugs etc.

Using multiple methods

Much of the discussion so far has tended to offer a dichotomy of approaches – inductive or deductive, experimental or case study, cross-sectional or longitudinal. In practice, however, it is often the case that multiple methods will be used. One reason is that research projects usually include a number of different research questions, so a research method appropriate for one question may be inappropriate for another. The second reason for using multiple methods is that it enables *triangulation* to be used. Easterby–Smith et al. (1991) refer to data triangulation as the collecting of data over different times or from different sources. This approach is typical of cross-sectional designs. Methodological triangulation is also possible, with the use of a combination of methods such as case studies, interviews and surveys. All methods have their strengths and weaknesses. So not only does the use of multiple methods assist in data triangulation, it helps to balance out any of the potential weaknesses in each data collection method. But whichever methods are used, in the final analysis Oakley's argument is sound: '*all* methods must be open, consistently applied and replicable by others' (1999: 252, original emphasis).

SUMMARY

- The dominant research paradigm for much of the twentieth century was positivism, but, today, at least in the social sciences, this has been largely replaced by anti-positivist or post-positivist stances such as interpretivism.
- Approaches to research include both truth-seeking and perspective-seeking methods. Truth-seeking methods tend to adopt more experimental or quasi-experimental approaches. Perspective-seeking methods tend to be more interpretivist (for example, phenomenological) and to generate qualitative data. These relationships should be treated as tendencies rather than as laws.
- Selecting approaches to research involves adopting a research philosophy, and an appropriate research approach and methodology. In practice, research often necessitates the use of multiple methods to achieve triangulation.

Further reading

Crotty, M. (1998) *The Foundation of Social Research: Meaning and Perspectives in the Research Process.* London: Sage. Provides a very readable description and explanation of the major epistemological stances and how they originated.

(Continued)

Cohen, L. and Manion, L. (1997) *Research Methods in Education*, 4th edn. London: Routledge. See especially Chapter 1 on The Nature of Inquiry.

Reinharz, S. (1992) *Feminist Methods in Social Research*. New York: Oxford University Press. Covers approaches such as ethnography, survey research, experimental research, case studies and action research, all from a feminist perspective.

Scheurich, J.J. (1997) *Research Methods in the Postmodern*. London: Falmer. Provides an introduction to how postmodernism can be applied to critiquing a wide range of approaches to research, and describes the implications of post-modernism for practice.

3

Selecting and Planning Good Research Projects

Chapter objectives

After reading this chapter you will be able to:

- **Generate new ideas for research.**
- **Identify a good research topic using selected criteria.**
- **Write a proposal for the research project.**
- **Plan the research project and data collection.**
- **Gain the access you need to data.**
- **Conduct research in an ethical manner.**

Having read Chapters 1 and 2, you should now have a clearer idea about the methodologies, approaches and tools that are essential for the design and implementation of a good research topic. The question remains, of course, what *is* a good research topic? Generally, research projects can be designed as part of an academic programme of study, or as a result of a business or organizational need. While the former will probably require a stronger element of theoretical underpinning, both will need a sharp, practical focus or application. The outputs from research projects not only have potential benefits for organizations and their management, they can also be a vital element in personal learning and development. Clearly, the best approach is to select a research topic that interests you, and one that is likely to maintain your interest. The research process can be a long and arduous one, so you need to be committed to your subject. Winkler and McCuen (1985) suggest that you also need to select a subject area that has sufficient scope to generate several research projects. So, for example, investigating how a particular commodity is produced at source and shipped to a retail outlet may not prove particularly illuminating. On the other hand, a study of supply logistics in general may offer greater scope for the research process, the range of literature to be consulted and the value of the research outcomes.

If you find you have difficulty finding a research subject, then talk to colleagues at work to see what sort of issues concern them. Discuss the matter with your academic supervisor or line manager. Other useful sources are professional journals and magazines that often contain articles on issues that are currently engaging the minds of business, commerce, public sector and voluntary organizations. You might also browse through the business or management sections of your local bookshop to see what kinds of titles are being published. Some more practical suggestions for generating ideas are given in this chapter. Some advice is also given on how to select a research topic and on how to write a successful proposal for your research. It also suggests how you can plan a schedule for conducting your research and how you should carry out the project, not only efficiently, but ethically.

SELECTING A RESEARCH TOPIC

You may already have a research topic in mind and hence want to use this section as a means of checking its validity. Alternatively, you may have been commissioned by your organization to undertake a specific piece of research. In the latter case, do not feel that you should be a passive recipient of such projects. Make use of the criteria in this section to evaluate and renegotiate the focus of your project if you feel that this is necessary.

When to select a research topic

Obviously, this is going to be a matter of individual choice. Some researchers have a very clear idea and focus at an early stage. Indeed, they may have embarked on a programme of study precisely because they want to tackle a specific end project. For others, and probably the majority, a research topic emerges only towards the end of the study programme, or as a result of an emerging problem in the workplace. For some, the problem may be making a choice between a number of potential topics; for others, there may be only one focus.

Sources of research topics

There are, essentially, two ways of identifying a research topic. One is through the literature – books and academic and professional journals – which may raise interesting themes and topics that can be related to your own organization. The other route is directly from the workplace or community setting. Line managers, supervisors or project teams may all require assistance, and this can often be a fruitful source of research focus. In effect, the researcher then acts as a kind of internal consultant to a project team.

What is a good research topic?

Whatever topic you choose, it is likely that you will begin to develop or enhance a range of personal skills. A good topic, then, is one that gives you free rein to maximize this self-development. Jankowicz (1991) argues that such personal development might include:

- Improving personal time management.
- Gaining access to respondents.
- Interviewing respondents.
- Speaking to an audience.
- Persuading people to cooperate.
- Dealing with uncertainty about data.

But it must also be a subject that interests you. Since research may involve many hours of planning, execution, data analysis and report writing, you will quickly tire of any topic that you thought was only moderately interesting at the outset. It is also a good idea to choose a subject that allows you to demonstrate your skills and abilities. Hence, if, say, you are undertaking a project at the end of an academic programme, you will need to select a subject that gives you scope for showing the integration of various fields of knowledge and analysis. Within the workplace, being able to demonstrate the skills of planning, data analysis and report writing can enhance your prestige and even promotional opportunities.

Academic requirements

You must ensure that the research subject is capable of meeting academic requirements if you are undertaking a programme of study. As Raimond (1993) suggests, be sure that your topic is capable of being linked to the appropriate academic theory. Management theory, for example, tends to evolve and change quite quickly. Textbooks, however, can take years to write and are often out of date by the time they are published. One solution is to look at the academic journals (many of which are now online), which tend to be more topical.

Access

You will need access to relevant information, material and data. If you select an issue where these are lacking, you have little chance of completing the project. Remember that some issues in organizations, communities or networks are sensitive or confidential, for example, some financial data, redundancy plans, attitudes within a community, etc. Indeed, Flick (1998) warns that a research project is an intrusion into the life of an institution and is inherently unsettling for it. Apart from written or Web-based information, one of the essential elements of research is access to people. Who will you need to meet (perhaps to interview) and how busy are they? A classic contradiction is that the more important your project (to the organization), the more likely it is that the people you need to see are senior in the organization, and too busy to spare the time to be interviewed. The challenge is to gain access to these people despite this. In community settings, the researcher may be seen as an intruder or outsider.

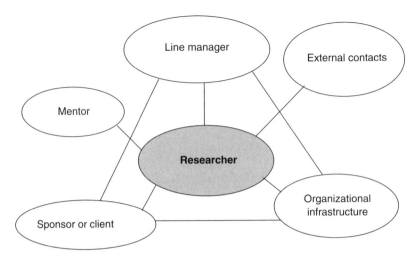

FIGURE 3.1   ORGANIZATIONAL SPONSORSHIP AND SUPPORT NETWORKS

Sponsorship and networking

It helps if you have a sponsor or client who can give you either financial backing, or at least moral or practical support. The latter might involve 'opening doors' in the organization and facilitating your access to people with information. Figure 3.1 shows the kind of networks that may exist, or which you may request are established, to provide you with assistance. Note that not all elements of this network are necessarily connected. They all perform different roles, so you need to understand or negotiate what each can offer you.

Activity 3.1

Make a list of the support networks available to you. Are they readily accessible? Are they sufficient?

Time available

Be sure that the research can be completed within the time available. There is always a tendency to underestimate the time needed for a project. Further difficulties may arise if the topic chosen is dependent upon the implementation of another project within the organization. If this project becomes delayed (which is often the case), or abandoned, then your research project may quickly reach an impasse. The best approach is to draw up a research plan before starting the project, with clear indications of dependencies and potential bottlenecks (see Figure 3.3).

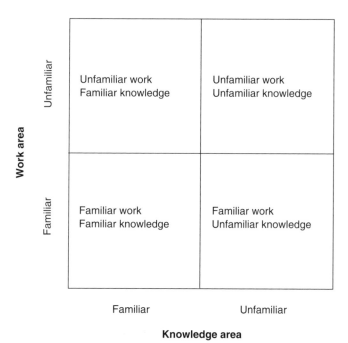

Work area

Unfamiliar

Familiar

Unfamiliar work
Familiar knowledge

Unfamiliar work
Unfamiliar knowledge

Familiar work
Familiar knowledge

Familiar work
Unfamiliar knowledge

Familiar

Unfamiliar

Knowledge area

FIGURE 3.2 JOHARI WINDOW SHOWING CHOICES BETWEEN FAMILIAR AND UNFAMILIAR WORK EXPERIENCE AND PERSONAL KNOWLEDGE

Capabilities and experience

This may seem obvious, but selecting an issue that is within your capabilities is essential. Your skills will, hopefully, develop during the course of the research process; but, say, choosing a topic that requires robust statistical skills when you are comfortable with only basic mathematics may be a recipe for disaster. Experience may be a different matter. As the Johari window in Figure 3.2 shows, you can choose projects that are congruent with both your work area and experience (the safe approach), or, moving towards the top-right side of the diagram, beyond both your work and current knowledge set. This poses greater risks, but also enhances opportunities for personal development. Moving the project into an unfamiliar work area may also provide opportunities for networking amongst new groups of people which can be advantageous for both the project and your own professional future (including your future as a researcher).

Activity 3.2

Take the project that you intend to do, or one or more projects that you are considering. Locate the position of the project(s) within the Johari window. How risky is the project, and are the risks worth taking? How 'stretching' is the project and is such development a personal objective?

Value of the project

Projects that have value to the organization (say, in terms of identifying cost savings, new marketing opportunities, IT strategies, etc.) will have a much greater chance of success than those that merely re-plough old ground. Innovative, provoking and original projects have a better chance of sponsorship and support from within the organization (at the appropriate level), of opening new networks for meeting and interviewing people, and of eventual implementation. A high value project is also more likely to motivate both you and your line manager or sponsor. But ambitious projects may be more difficult to manage and complete. Sometimes, a more modest project may be both more feasible and achievable.

Symmetry of potential outcomes

Gill and Johnson (1997) suggest that one way of reducing the risks involved in a project is to achieve symmetry of potential outcomes. This means that, no matter what the results are, they will be useful. For example, a project to examine whether the company's e-commerce website produced any increase in overall sales would be significant whatever the outcome. Conversely, a project that examined the relationship between levels of stress and output levels amongst line workers would be interesting if strong correlations were found, but would be of little value if they were not.

Career goals

You may consider whether the research topic may be of value to you in the future in terms of your personal career development. The research may make you an 'expert' in a particular subject or area, and enhance your value as an internal consultant.

Generating research ideas

If you are devoid of ideas for a topic, how can you create some imaginative ones? Table 3.1 suggests that new ideas can be generated either through rational or creative processes. Let us look at each of these in turn.

Examining your own strengths and weaknesses

You will benefit from choosing a topic that you enjoy and for which you have probably received good marks for previous assignments and other course assessments, or positive feedback from a work-based project. Why not make a list of your strengths and weaknesses. Get a friend or colleague to critique the list (prepare yourself for a shock!), then amend it as necessary.

Looking at past projects

This is often a useful way of generating new ideas. A glance towards the end of some projects may reveal a section entitled 'Suggestions for future research' that

TABLE 3.1   TECHNIQUES FOR GENERATING AND REFINING RESEARCH IDEAS

Rational thinking	Creative thinking
Examining your own strengths and weaknesses	Brainstorming
Looking at past projects	Exploring personal preferences using past projects
Searching the literature	Relevance trees
Discussion	Keeping a notebook
	SWOT analysis

Source: Adapted from Saunders et al., 2000

may be helpful. There may also be a bibliography which could prove a useful starting point for your own research – although take care that the references are not too dated. Also note that some universities and colleges place *all* theses and dissertations in the library. Their presence there, then, is not a necessary guide to their quality.

Searching the literature

The literature includes articles in the academic journals, reports, books and websites (although be wary of the authenticity and quality of the latter). Becoming aware through the literature of the significance of some issues, or new angles on old ones, can be a stimulus to undertake research in how these ideas can affect your own organization. More detail on reviewing the literature is provided later in this chapter.

Exploring personal preferences using past projects

Here, you simply take a look at the subjects you have chosen for previous modules, programmes or work projects, and identify the kinds of topic areas you have selected. This may be a guide to what you are generally interested in.

Discussion

Ideas might be generated by talking to fellow students, work colleagues, line managers, university tutors, practitioners and professional networks (the latter, possibly, through online discussion groups).

Brainstorming

This is a well-known problem-solving technique for generating and refining ideas. Jarvis (1995) suggests that the quantity of ideas produced by the brainstorming group is more important than the quality. All points made by participants are recorded (for example, on a flipchart) over a mutually agreed period of time. No member of the group may criticize the ideas of another, irrespective of how ridiculous some ideas may sound, since this would inhibit discussion. At the end of the agreed time period, the group discusses and selects from the points raised.

Relevance trees

This is similar to mind mapping, where you start with a broad concept from which you generate more specific topics. From each of these branches, new sub-branches can be generated. Do this quickly with an emphasis on generating ideas rather than evaluating them for quality. Once the process is finished, look over your material and evaluate the results.

Keeping a notebook of ideas

This simply involves noting down any new ideas as and when they occur. It is best to keep the notebook with you at all times. This could be a section in a research log book (see Managing information, p. 46).

SWOT analysis

SWOT stands for Strengths, Weaknesses, Opportunities and Threats. Using this well-known method, you could make a list of ideas under each of these categories. SWOT analysis usually works best, however, when undertaken by a group since good ideas tend to generate others.

Activity 3.3

Begin the process of generating ideas for your project. Note down fresh ideas as they occur. This may be when reading the literature, talking to people at work, or talking to people undertaking a similar programme of study. At some point, you may chose to carry out a SWOT analysis on each subject to see which of them has the most potential.

TOPICS TO AVOID

It is often only possible in retrospect to recognize the topic you should not even have attempted! However, here are a few hints that may help you to avoid the research disaster. The topics to avoid are those that are:

- *Too big*. For example, 'Human resource management – innovative international perspectives'. Some very large projects can be worthy and valuable to an organization, but you need to ask yourself whether you have the time, experience and resources to complete them. Winkler and McCuen (1985) also warn that the big topic is also the most difficult to write about: it is difficult knowing where to begin, and omissions and oversights are more crudely exposed.

- *Traced to a single source.* This may not be a particular problem in pure business research when a single solution is needed to a problem. However, if the research is linked to an academic programme of study, or important for your own professional development, there will usually be a requirement that issues are explored from a variety of different angles.

- *Too trivial.* This may seem rather subjective, but you should use your common sense to evaluate the kinds of projects that are worth doing and those that are not. As a general rule of thumb try using the 'So what?' test. Ask yourself, after completing the research, whether the results have any meaning or significance (to others not just to yourself). For example, a research project that surveyed how to reduce the use of paper in a marketing department of ten people would yield very little of value. On the other hand, a project that took the issue of recycling (paper, printer cartridges, furniture, computers, etc.) across an organization could have considerable scope and link into the broader environmental debate.

- *Lacking in resource materials.* Look out for warning signs – very few references to the topic in the main textbooks, practitioner journals or other refereed journals or websites. If the project is going to rely on access to in-house knowledge experts, make sure (in advance) that they are both available and willing to cooperate with you.

- *Lacking in sponsorship.* This does not necessarily mean financial sponsorship, but it is often important to obtain the support and commitment of key people in the organization or fieldwork setting where the research is taking place. These are likely to be directors, senior managers, or the leaders of networks or groups.

- *Too technical.* Some projects are more concerned with solving highly technical problems rather than organizational research. Leave these to the technical gurus.

- *Intractable.* You may be offered a problem that nobody else has been able to solve. Be highly suspicious of this kind of gift! Ask yourself: 'Why me?' It may be an offer you need to refuse.

- *Dependent on the completion of another project.* Even if you are 'guaranteed' that projects you hope to use as data sources will be completed in time for your use, you are strongly advised not to make your own project dependent on them. If slippage occurs, your own research will be held up or even scrapped.

- *Unethical.* Avoid taking on projects that can damage other people physically, emotionally or intellectually. Refuse to take on a project that forces you to breach confidentiality or trust. When using interviews, observation or surveys, you will need to pay particular attention to politically sensitive issues such as power relationships, race, gender and the disclosure of personal information. Ethics are discussed in more detail at the end of this chapter and elsewhere in this book.

Activity 3.4

Consider each of the following 'big' topics and formulate a more focused, narrower research project from each of them:

- Communication in the workplace
- Mergers and acquisitions
- Health and safety
- Teenage pregnancies
- Equal employment legislation

PLANNING THE PROJECT

It may seem obvious that all research projects should be carefully planned, but it is surprising how many researchers rush forward into data collection without a plan of campaign. Disaster is the inevitable result. Planning also helps with time management, one of the greatest problems when work and research commitments compete. There are many ways of planning a project and presenting the plan. One technique is to make use of a table, which sets out the tasks and the planned dates for their completion. A better approach is through the use of a Gantt chart (see Figure 3.3) through which you not only specify tasks but whether they are going to be completed in sequence or in parallel. Project management software such as *Microsoft Project* not only generates various graphics such as Gantt charts, but also allows you to specify timescales for the completion of each task.

LOCATING THE LITERATURE

This is not simply a sequential process of first finding the literature that you need and then reviewing it. As we shall see, it is more usual for this to be an iterative process, with locating, reviewing and then more searching. There are, essentially, two main areas to be searched:

- The literature dealing with the subject of your research.
- The literature on research methodology and data collection methods.

The challenge is that there is so much information available. Table 3.2 offers a brief overview of some of the sources.

According to Hart (2001), the keys to conducting a successful search of the literature are: planning, understanding the ways in which information is organized and made available, maintaining records, and extracting information from useful sources, including the main arguments, theories, concepts and definitions. We will look at some of these issues in more detail. In doing so, various sources, primarily websites, will be mentioned.

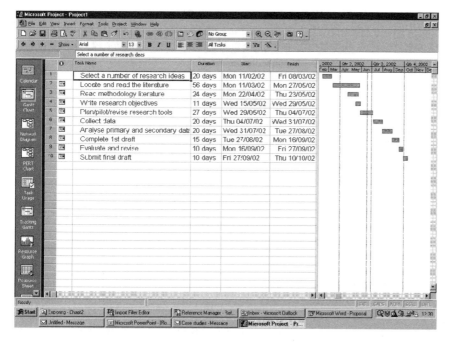

FIGURE 3.3 PLANNING SCHEDULE FOR A RESEARCH PROJECT USING MICROSOFT PROJECT

Search planning

At the outset you may have only a general notion of your research theme (for example, performance management in your company, the effectiveness of mixed ability teaching, public attitudes to the integration of schizophrenic patients into society). This is obviously where you will start. It may happen, however, that your reading takes you down a completely different path. This is acceptable, as long as it results in a coherent topic for your research. Alternatively, your initial theme may appear too wide (for example, brands in marketing), and through reading the relevant literature you may be able to focus on a specific area of the topic which is actually feasible to implement (for example, getting a new brand image accepted and promoted by an organization).

Planning the literature search is not like getting on a train and travelling from A to B. You may have a general intention of getting to B, but your route may involve several modes of transport (sources) and you may find yourself travelling sideways or sometimes backwards! Indeed, you may even decide when on your journey that you intend to travel to C instead! Planning, then, means aiming for a destination (even though this goal may change) and knowing where the modes of transport and timetables are. To modify Hart's (2001) analogy of trawling and mining, the research process is about touring (looking around) and camping (stopping to explore in more depth), as Figure 3.4 shows. Notice that the travelling

45

TABLE 3.2 AN OVERVIEW OF LITERATURE SOURCES

Sources where research and information is published	Sources and organizations providing publications	Tools for searching published works and data
Textbooks	Academic libraries	Library catalogues
Articles	Public libraries	Subject indexes
Theses	National libraries	Subject abstracts
Government publications	Specialist libraries	Bibliographies
Legal and professional publications	Museums	Encyclopaedias
	Archives	Guides to the literature
Trade literature	Special collections	Internet directories
Conference papers	Political parties	Internet search engines
Monographs	Commercial organizations	
Statistics	Trusts	
	Internet	

Source: Adapted from Hart, 2001

process involves an enticing journey around the literature. But camping involves a more discriminating approach, selecting, synthesizing and analysing in more detail. By the end of the literature search journey, you will be familiar with the history of the subject, the key sources and authors, and methodological approaches, theories and findings. Above all, you will be familiar with the problems, debates, arguments and uncertainties within the territory, and these should begin to clarify your own concerns, objectives and research focus.

Managing information

It is all too easy to be enthusiastic and motivated in searching the literature, but sloppy in storing your findings. Without an accurate, consistent and searchable means of storing your literature search data, your efforts will lack the reward that they deserve. The key is the maintenance of a research log. This can be paper-based or a computer file, depending on which you are most comfortable with. The research log could contain sections on:

- Search parameters – details of your main subject focus and the keywords that describe it.
- Search logs – information on what you have searched, when, how and with what results.
- Contact details of people, organizations, Internet newsgroups, online discussion groups, etc.
- Inter-library loans, including what you ordered and when.
- CD ROM and Internet sources.
- Bibliography.

Maintaining an accurate and searchable bibliography is important for a number of reasons. First, it means that you have a printable bibliographical record at the end of your research project. Secondly, keeping a searchable record allows

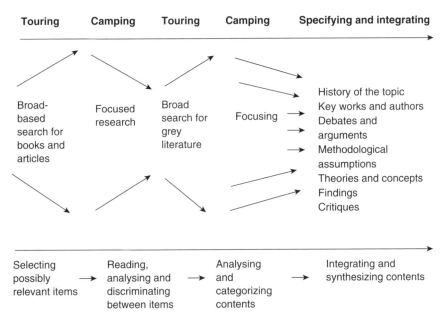

FIGURE 3.4   TOURING AND CAMPING TO ACQUIRE, ANALYSE AND SYNTHE-
SIZE INFORMATION (ADAPTED FROM HART, 2001)

you to locate all your references on specific issues (topics, authors, dates of publication etc.) when you are writing up your research. This is much easier to carry
out if you maintain computerized records. There are a number of bibliographic
software products on the market that allow you to store records in a database, create bibliographies and even conduct Internet searches of online and Web databases.

Activity 3.5

You can download trial versions of two bibliographic software products from
the Adeptscience website at:
   http://www.adeptscience.co.uk

Look for Reference Manager and EndNote.

For the specifications of the two applications see:
   http://www.lib.ucdavis.edu/healthsci/win-bibmanagers.html

For a tutorial on using Reference Manager see:
   http://www.ion.ucl.ac.uk/library/rm.htm

For a tutorial on using EndNote see:
   http://www.endnote.com/support/en4tutorial.asp

Locating reference materials

There is no strict order in which you have to locate source materials. Creswell (1994), however, suggests that the following order is helpful:

- *Journal articles*. But ensure that you concentrate on peer-reviewed journals. This is not to say that you should always avoid, say, professional magazines or periodicals. Articles in credible journals, however, are scrutinized for their relevance, originality and validity by other academic researchers. Hence, the quality and reliability of such articles, while not guaranteed, is more assured.
- *Books*. Begin with research monographs that are summaries of the academic literature on a particular subject. Then look at complete books on a single topic or ones that contain chapters written by different authors. Note, however, that textbooks quickly become dated, so it is best to use them in conjunction with other sources.
- *Conference papers*. These often contain the most up-to-date information and developments in research.

In contrast, Hart (2001) advises that the best start is delving into a library's quick reference section, where you can find sources such as guides to the literature, dictionaries, directories and encyclopaedias. After this, the focus becomes one of using books and bibliographies in more detail. Clearly, there are alternative approaches! Try dipping into the reference sources and see what you find the most rewarding.

Books

The main source for locating relevant books is the Online Public Access Catalogue (OPAC) of a library. These can usually be searched by subject, author, title and key words. They also often offer access to other online catalogues, and gateways. Using the Internet, you can access libraries across the world, as the next Activity shows.

Activity 3.6

Access the BUBL Link public access catalogues and locate the online public catalogues in your own country at:
   http://link.bubl.ac.uk/libraryopacs/

Another source of useful information is Amazon, which not only sells books but also often provides descriptions of their contents. See: http://www.amazon.co.uk

---

When browsing in a library or bookshop, a useful evaluation procedure for deciding on whether a book is worth borrowing or purchasing is to look at a number of features, including the:

- Title and subtitle – are they relevant?
- Preface – does it cover your subject area or at least an element of it, and is it at the right level?
- Contents list – does it offer material on your topic?
- Publisher – is the organization respected for publishing quality texts in your field?
- Bibliography – is there one, and do the references look familiar, at the appropriate level and 'on topic'?

Bibliographic services

Bibliographies are gigantic databases of what is in print and what has been printed, and can be used for locating sources on topics or by specific authors. Take a look at two major national bibliographies in the next Activity.

Activity 3.7

Explore and evaluate the bibliographic services of the British Library at:
http://www.bl.uk/services/bibliographic.html

Also take a look at the National Union Catalogue of Manuscript Collections at:
http://leweb.loc.gov/coll/nucmc/nucmc.html

Journal articles

There are, essentially, two types of journal article: academic articles written in peer-reviewed journals, and articles published in professional journals (that are not usually peer-reviewed). The articles you need can be accessed through using either an indexing or abstracting tool. A keyword search of an index will give you a list of articles, authors, title of article, date of publication and journal title. Examining the article title or knowing the reputation of the author may allow you to evaluate whether the article is worth reading. Abstracting services, however, also give you a brief synthesis and summary of what the article is about, which is much more helpful. Since many (but unfortunately not all) journal articles are now published online, it may even be possible to access the article immediately and print it off (sometimes, however, this will depend on whether your institution subscribes to the journal title). Hart (2001) advises that it is best to search the multi-subject indexes and abstracts first, and subject-specific abstracts (if there are any) last. See the next Activity for an example of a multi-subject index and a subject-specific index.

Activity 3.8

For examples of *multi-subject indexes* see:

The Cambridge Scientific Abstracts and look for Electronic Products at: http://www.bhinet.co.uk/
Catchword at http://www.catchword.com/
Ebsco online at http://www-uk.ebsco.com/home/

For a *subject-specific index* see:
ScienceDirect at: http://www.sciencedirect.com/

Many journals are now either being published in both paper-based and electronic format, or just as e-journals (the latter being increasingly the case). There are also a growing number of gateways to these e-journals that provide access to the full-text articles (either free of charge or for a subscription). Explore some of these very useful gateways in the next Activity.

Activity 3.9

Take a look at the BUBL Journal collections at:
http://bubl.ac.uk/journals/

And then at Ingenta journals at:
http://www.ingenta.com

For a directory of electronic journals see:
http://arl.cni.org/scomm/edir/index.html

Grey literature

This is the sort of published and unpublished material that cannot be identified through the usual bibliographic methods. A growing and significant example here are websites, but grey literature also includes academic theses and dissertations, newspaper and magazine articles, editorials, materials produced by business and trade journals, reports, and publications by clubs and societies.

Activity 3.10

For a search engine providing access to technical grey literature see the Magic Project at:
http://www.magic.ac.uk/

Links to Internet sources on grey literature are at:
http://www.library.drexel.edu/netresources/subject/greylit.html

---

Official publications, statistics and archives

These can be of enormous value to the researcher, but it will depend, of course, on the extent to which a government collects these kinds of data, and the level of access provided to the public. Of the kind of material that is available, an increasing amount is finding its way onto the Web. The next Activity provides links to some multi-subject gateways, sources for statistics and links to data archives.

Activity 3.11

UK statistical sources can be found at:
http://www.statistics.gov.uk/

European Commission statistics can be viewed at:
http://www.europa.eu.int/comm/eurostat/

A source of data archives can be found at:
http://ssda.anu.edu.au/
http://www.psr.keele.ac.uk/data.htm

Using citations and reviews

A citation index records the references made in other works to an author or source. By examining the scale to which an author has been cited, you can quickly see who the acknowledged authorities are in a particular field. Citation indexes also provide reviews of books. Book reviews can also be found in abstracting services, in professional magazines and journals as well as in the academic journals.

Activity 3.12

Point your Web browser to the Institute for Scientific Information (ISI) site at:
http://www.isinet.com/

Find the Journal Citation Report on the Web, which provides access to statistical data to determine the relative importance of journals within their subject categories.

Using authors

Consider making use of networks to access literature sources. It you have been impressed with a particular author's work, why not try contacting her or him? These days, many people are quite easy to locate through their organization's website. You can ask them if they have published anything else in your field of interest, or if they are writing something new at the moment. You may be lucky enough to receive copies of articles, drafts of work in progress, or at least new references. On the other hand, they may be too busy to reply to you, so do not be disappointed!

Joining professional associations

You can join relevant professional associations, many of which publish their own professional journal, and hold conferences or seminars. Some even have their own libraries that can provide a rich source of material in the field.

Using your organization

Do not forget that you can also make use of your own organization as an important source of data. This will include internal documents. But note that the academic literature should underpin the theoretical elements of the project. Using institutional or company documents is valid for providing background information and supporting detail, but they should not carry the main burden of the theoretical argument or analysis.

REVIEWING THE LITERATURE

The critical review of the literature provides the foundations of your research. Not only does it inform and refine your research objectives (for example, are they topical, worthy of research, original?), it provides a benchmark against which you can compare and contrast your results. One of the features of any project is that it should enable you to demonstrate a critical awareness of the relevant knowledge in the field. A comprehensive review of the literature is essential because it:

- Provides an up-to-date understanding of the subject and its significance and structure.
- Identifies the kinds of research methods that have been used.
- Is informed by the views and research of experts in the field.
- Assists in the formulation of research topics, questions and direction.
- Provides a basis on which the subsequent research findings can be compared.

The literature review is not something you complete early in the project and then drop. It is likely to continue almost to the writing up stage, especially since your own research may generate new issues and ideas that you will want to relate to the literature. As we saw in Chapter 2, if you are adopting a deductive approach to your research, your literature review will help to provide a source for the focus of your research, including aims, objectives and hypotheses. Conversely, if you favour a more inductive approach, you may begin with the collection and analysis of data, a process that leads to questions that are then addressed through engagement with the literature.

The critical review

A review can involve a narrative or description of an article or other piece of work. A *critical* review, however, is much more than this and it is important to

TABLE 3.3   SKILLS FOR CRITICAL ENGAGEMENT WITH THE LITERATURE

Skill	Actions	Description
Analysis	Select, differentiate, break up	Dissecting data into their constituent parts in order to determine the relationship between them
Synthesis	Integrate, combine, formulate, reorganize	Rearranging the elements derived from analysis to identify relationships
Comprehension	Understand, distinguish, explain	Interpreting and distinguishing between different types of data, theory and argument to describe the substance of an idea
Knowledge	Define, classify, describe, name	Describing the principles, uses and function of rules, methods and events

Source: Adapted from Hart, 1998

understand the difference. Hart (1998) argues that a reading of the literature should pose questions such as:

- What is the purpose of the study?
- What is the focus of the study?
- What types of data were collected?
- How were the data managed?
- What analytical approach is used?
- How is validity addressed?
- How are ethical issues handled?

Operationalizing the issues listed above means using sets of tools to analyse and evaluate the literature. This means developing a complex set of skills, acquired through practice. Table 3.3 provides a brief overview of the types of skill involved.

In terms of structure, Creswell (1994) suggests that a literature review should comprise five components:

- An Introduction, informing the reader about how the review is to be organized and structured.
- Review of Topic 1, addressing the literature on the independent variable or variables (the influences on the dependent variable or subject, upon which the research is focused). Note: we will explore descriptions of dependent and independent variables in more detail in Chapter 4.
- Review of Topic 2, the literature on the dependent variable. If there are multiple dependent variables, devote a sub-section to each one, or focus on a single important dependent variable.
- Review of Topic 3, the literature that relates the independent variable to the dependent variable. Creswell warns that this section should be relatively short and should focus on studies that are extremely close in topic to the proposed study. If nothing specific has been written on the topic, then review studies that address it at a general level.

- Provide a summary of the review, highlighting the most significant studies and the key themes that have emerged.

This last point is vitally important. It is not enough to simply read around a subject or theme. You must produce a synthesis of subjects or related subjects in the form of an increasingly *focused argument* or set of concerns (recall Figure 3.4). It is the difference between describing a menu – 'first we tried the appetizers, then we ate the main course, after which we sampled the desserts' – and producing the sort of *critical* evaluation of a restaurant's fare that you would read in a gastronomic magazine. Within the five-step structure suggested above, any critical review should also incorporate:

- An assessment of the strengths and weaknesses of some of these theories.
- A clear understanding of the topic.
- A citing of all key studies in the subject territory.
- A clear indication of how the review links to your research questions.
- A definition of the boundaries of your research.
- A selection and synthesis of existing arguments to form a new perspective.
- Through gradual refinement, a clear demarcation of the research problem.

The key word here is 'refinement'. Recalling Figure 3.4, touring the literature, but also pausing to focus on areas that have emerged as important, means that the discussion is gradually refined down to a set of core issues and arguments. These, then, provide the basis for the formulation of research questions and the focus of the research.

Hart (1998) warns that, in evaluating a piece of research, the researcher must be aware of the methodological tradition from which it emanates – even if the researcher is not sympathetic to that tradition. For example, it is not enough to criticize a quasi-experimental research study for taking a quantitative approach to data collection, since this is what one would expect. A more valid argument would be that the research design was not matched to the research objectives, or that assertions made for the study were insufficiently supported by the data or analysis.

Positioning the literature review

Should your review of the literature come at the beginning of your report or dissertation, in the middle or at the end? Creswell (1994) offers three possible locations: in the *Introduction*, as a *separate section* and as a *final section* in the study. Table 3.4 provides a brief summary. For some qualitative studies, for example, the literature can be discussed in the *Introduction* to 'frame' the subject being studied. Using a separate literature review section towards the beginning of a study is typical of a quantitative approach. The purpose of this section becomes to provide a basis on which questions and hypotheses can be based, and can influence the design and direction of the research. In contrast, in some types of

TABLE 3.4 RESEARCH METHOD AND USES OF THE LITERATURE

Research method	Use of the literature	Comments
Qualitative studies: all types	Used in Introduction to 'frame' the problem	Some literature must be available
Quantitative	Located as separate 'review of the literature' section at beginning of study	Helps to generate research questions and hypotheses; also used at end of study against which results compared
Qualitative: grounded theory	To compare and contrast theories generated from the data with theories in the literature	The literature does not guide or direct the study, but becomes an aid once patterns emerge from the data

Source: Adapted from Creswell, 1994

qualitative research, such as the use of grounded theory, theoretical perspectives are developed inductively from the data itself. Any literature review is created towards the end of the research, providing a benchmark against which the results can be compared.

WRITING THE PROJECT PROPOSAL

There are, essentially, two types of proposal:

- An **organizational** proposal, written to gain funding for a project or at least to elicit support and commitment from a project sponsor.
- An **academic** proposal, a plan for conducting research as part of an academic programme of study.

Organizational proposals

There are two main types of organizational proposal, comprising those that are written:

- In response to a request for proposals or 'invitations to bid' from, say, government agencies or companies.
- For submission to an internal organization or department, often in response to a request for help with a problem or a need to improve a product or service.

Whichever kind is written, White suggests that a proposal is a 'sophisticated advertisement of approaches and abilities' (1997: 218) and not just a description of how a project could be tackled.

To bid or not to bid?

Many proposals are written within tight timescales and in the knowledge that other individuals, teams or organizations are competing for the project. In deciding whether to respond to any request for proposals (RFPs), you will need to take a view of:

- Whether you possess the necessary expertise to respond.
- The number of bids you are competing against and the likely strength of opposing bids.
- The number of bids that will be funded.
- Whether all bids are to be fairly evaluated, or whether the process is possibly biased.

These criteria will help you to undertake a risk assessment, weighing up the probability of success and the potential size of the funding if successful, against the time it will take to write the bid.

Preparing to write the proposal

Figure 3.5 illustrates a series of steps that should be observed in writing any project proposal. We will look in detail at each stage.

Review the RFP specifications Take another, careful, look at the request for proposals and make sure that they are complete, consistent and clear. Some RFPs may also contain information on how responses to each of the specifications will be scored – for example, some requirements may be more important to the project than others and receive a higher weighting. If anything in the RFP is unclear, then it is legitimate to contact the creators of the RFP (preferably in writing) and ask for clarification.

Develop a plan of action This should include a rationale for the project, the key research objectives and a plan of how these are to be met, that is to say, the research methodology. Take care to show that the project has value. To do this apply the invaluable 'so what?' test. This means looking at your proposed project outcomes and asking yourself to evaluate honestly whether they have any real worth in terms of practical application or contribution to knowledge.

Determine the human resource requirements of the project Those who commissioned the proposal will be keen to evaluate not only the number of people committed to the project, but also their experience and qualifications. If any element of the project is going to be outsourced to a third party, then again, evidence should be provided of their 'fitness for purpose'.

Develop the project graphics This will be particularly important for more technical projects, but should always be considered for research projects of any kind. Graphics, particularly flow diagrams showing how different elements of a project relate to one another, can be easy to read and understand. Ensure that if

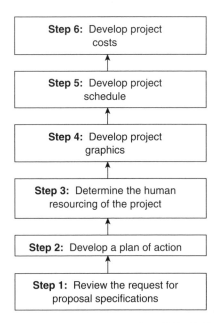

FIGURE 3. 5   PROPOSAL DEVELOPMENT FLOWCHART (ADAPTED FROM
WHITE, 1997)

graphics are used, there is a clear description provided in the text (such as the way
in which this text is describing Figure 3.5).

Develop a project schedule   A project schedule such as a Gantt chart (recall
Figure 3.3) provides a list of the main project tasks and the dates for their completion. These tasks could include arrangements for seeking permissions from an ethics
committee, preliminary arrangements for getting research subjects, a timetable for
constructing research tools, analysing data and writing the research report.

Develop project costs   White (1997) warns that this is more an art than a science because there are so many variables to take into account. Particular care
needs to be taken when estimating labour costs since these often eat up the bulk
of a research project's budget. Since the research process is rarely linear and
smooth, it is prudent to add in some contingency costs in case unexpected results
emerge that require further research. The less experienced the research team, or
riskier the project, the higher the contingency costs should be. Given that commissioning organizations are highly unlikely to pay for contingency costs, these
will have to be built into (i.e. hidden!) in general costs. Of course, the higher your
overall costs, the less competitive your bid.

Preparing the final document

In writing the final project proposal, try to ensure that the document is internally
consistent, and that there are no gaps or contradictions between objectives and

research processes. Remember that once the proposal is submitted you are committed to it, so you need to ensure that all errors have been eliminated. It helps, then, to elicit the assistance of some experienced reviewers who should be asked to answer the following questions:

- Is the proposal clear and understandable?
- Is the proposal realistic?
- Is the proposal consistent with the bid specifications?

Also, get an appropriate person to review the costings. White (1997) makes the useful suggestion that you should do a hand calculation of all columns and rows of financial data, even if they were calculated by computer (in case a decimal point has slipped!). When you have finished the proposal, print it off and read it one more time.

Success or failure?

It is worth having a strategy in place for whether the bid is approved or rejected. If the latter, Williams (1996) offers the advice that you should try to get feedback on the proposal from those who have evaluated it. This may allow you to improve the bid if there are later opportunities for resubmitting it. If the bid is successful, you may be offered less funding than you asked for. At this point you need to decide whether to accept this funding, or, if possible, renegotiate the outputs of the project at a lower level.

Academic proposals

The structure of these proposals is normally specified by the academic institution. An example is given in Table 3.5, where you will note the weight given to academic theory and underpinning.

THE ETHICS OF RESEARCH

We will deal with a wide range of ethical issues that are particular to specific research methods in later chapters. Here, we will examine some of the ethical considerations of more general significance. Ethics is a philosophical term derived from the Greek word *ethos*, which means character or custom. The ethics of research concern the appropriateness of the researcher's behaviour in relation to the subjects of the research or those who are affected by it. Since research in the real world inevitably deals with people and the things that affect them, ethical issues can arise at the planning, implementation and reporting stages of research. Some ethical issues are obvious and a matter of courtesy and common sense but others are less clear. As Korac-Kakabadse et al. (2002) suggest, one of the challenges of ethical behaviour is that it lies in a 'grey zone' where clear-cut dichotomies between what is right and wrong may not exist.

TABLE 3.5 TYPICAL STRUCTURE FOR AN ACADEMIC PROPOSAL

Section	Contents
Working title	Describes the breadth and depth of the topic and gives an indication of the methodology to be used (e.g. case study, evaluation, etc.)
Introduction (abstract)	A summary of the research topic, describing the core problems or issues, the gaps in the research and how the research will address them
Aims	General statements on intent and direction of the research
Objectives	Clear and measurable statements of intended outcomes
Justification	Rationale for the research with reference to gaps in current knowledge, and potential application of results
Review of the literature	Describes the history of the topic and key literature sources; illustrates major issues and refines focus to indicate research questions (qualitative research) or hypothesis (quantitative research)
Methodology	Justifies methodological approach, including data collection and analytical techniques; use of quantitative or qualitative methods; choice of research approach and paradigm; anticipation of ethical issues; how the data will be analysed
Work schedule	A timetable for completing the research, indicating tasks and timescales
References	Bibliography of works cited in the proposal
Related material	For example, letters of support for the research, agreement to collaborate from interested institutions

Source: Adapted from Hart, 1998

Ethical issues arise even at the initial access stage, where the ambitious researcher can unwittingly or otherwise put pressure on people to become participants. If you are a practitioner researcher conducting a project within your own professional context it may be especially tempting to cajole colleagues who may feel obliged to cooperate. The key to ethical involvement is not just obtaining consent but *informed* consent. This includes explaining to gatekeepers such as project sponsors and the participants:

- The aims of the research.
- Who will be undertaking it.
- Who is being asked to participate.
- What kind of information is being sought.
- How much of the participant's time is required.
- That participation is voluntary.
- That responding to all questions is voluntary.
- Who will have access to the data once it is collected.
- How anonymity of respondents will be preserved.

Informed consent may be given through a verbal agreement, but a written statement is probably best. It is also important to keep participants informed if the aims of the research change during the project.

Professional researchers in the fields of sociology and psychology often have a set of ethical guidelines to adhere to, as do members of some professional associations or those working in professional contexts. In the UK health service, for example, many research ethics committees have been established, their work coordinated by the Central Office for Research Ethics Committees. Activity 3.13 provides some useful websites that illustrate different sets of ethical guidelines.

Activity 3.13

Compare and contrast the ethical principles stated at the following sites, noting any difference between codes of conduct for researchers and consultants.

American Psychological Association at:
http://www.apa.org/ethics/code.html

British Educational Research Association at:
http://www.bera.ac.uk/guidelines.html

Central Office for Research Ethics Committees at:
http://www.corec.org.uk/

Institute of Management Consultants (see Ethics and Discipline, under 'Our Standards') at:
http://www.imc.co.uk/index3.html

Table 3.6 summarizes some of the ethical issues the researcher must be aware of and plan for. The following Case Study provides you with an opportunity to apply some of these principles, and illustrates some of the complexities of trying to adopt an ethical stance in 'real world' situations.

Case Study 3.1   Ethical dilemmas in research

A financial services company implements a new information technology system that gives e-mail capability to all employees, irrespective of grade. After 12 months, company directors are anxious to know if the investment is providing a financial payback. One indicator is whether the e-mail facility is improving inter-employee communication and general productivity. Hence, they want an analysis of e-mail traffic. An external researcher is commissioned to conduct the study.

She decides to use a blend of quantitative and qualitative methods. On the quantitative side, negotiating access to the information poses no problems, since all she has to do is contact the head of information services. Given that this is a legitimate

(Continued)

TABLE 3.6 A CHECKLIST OF ETHICAL ISSUES

Ethical issue	Description
Privacy	The right not to participate. The right to be contacted at reasonable times and to withdraw at any time
Promises and reciprocity	What do participants gain from cooperating with the research? If promises are made (such as a copy of the final report) keep them
Risk assessment	In what ways will the research put people under psychological stress, legal liabilities, ostracism by peers or others. Will there be political repercussions? How will you plan to deal with these risks?
Confidentiality	What constitutes the kinds of reasonable promises of confidentiality that can be honoured in practice? Do not make promises that cannot be kept
Informed consent	What kind of formal consent is necessary and how will it be obtained?
Data access and ownership	Who will have access to the data and who owns it? Make sure that this is specified in any research contract
Researcher mental health	How will the researcher be affected by conducting the research? What will they see or hear that may require debriefing or counselling?
Advice	Who will the researcher use as a confidant(e) or counsellor on issues of ethics during the research?

Source: Adapted from Patton, 1990

company project, commissioned by the executive board, he is obliged to give the researcher free access to whatever information she requests.

For the qualitative side of the research she wants to interview a sample of 40 employees. Believing that imposing herself on these people would be unethical, she writes to all of them individually requesting access, and provides details of the purpose of the research, how the information is being collected, and who will read the final report. She had made a request to the executive board that she should be allowed to provide a summary of the final report to all respondents but this was refused. Despite her reassurances, only 12 of the original sample agree to being interviewed, most excusing themselves on the basis that they are too busy. One option would be to obtain an instruction from the managing director, ordering everyone to cooperate. She decides, however, that, not only would this be counter-productive, it would be unethical on a number of grounds not least because the responses would no longer be voluntary. Eventually, she decides that these 12 in-depth interviews will be sufficient to yield high quality data.

Having set up the interviews, the researcher first turns to the quantitative analysis of the e-mails, which she intends to place into a number of categories. However, as the research progresses, she discovers a significant number of personal e-mails, including jokes, a betting syndicate, plans for illicit liaisons and inflammatory comments about senior managers and the executive board!

The researcher now faces a difficult ethical dilemma. She decides to include general descriptions of the personal e-mails in her report but not to reveal the names of individuals (although it will not be difficult for the company to trace them given that it now has an e-mail audit trail). She also decides that she will ask

(Continued)

some questions about personal e-mails in her interviews to gain an employee perspective. Before doing this, she takes another look at her letter to the interviewees and the description of her research. She decides that the description, 'To investigate the purpose of e-mail traffic' is still valid and an additional letter flagging the new 'personal e-mail' probe is not necessary. Participants will still be given the assurance that they can refuse to answer any question and that their responses will be anonymous.

Activity 3.14

Examine Case Study 3.1 and consider the following questions:

1 Is the research conducted by a researcher or a consultant? Does it make any difference to the ethical issues involved?
2 Have sufficient steps been taken to safeguard ethical principles? Are there any additional steps that you would take?
3 Should the research be abandoned before the qualitative stage?

Suggested answers are provided at the end of the chapter.

SUMMARY

- A good research topic must have the potential for demonstrating theoretical credibility, allow access to the relevant data, provide a symmetry of potential outcomes, and be congruent with your own interests, capabilities and career aspirations.
- To generate ideas for a research topic you could look at examples of projects completed by others, or ideas could emerge from your reading of the literature or by a brainstorming process.
- Before starting the project, produce a plan to show when and how you intend to conduct your research including data collection, analysis and the writing up process.
- An important step in any research project is the literature review. This may assist in the formulation of research questions or topics (deductive approach) or illustrate and illuminate research findings (inductive approach).
- Before starting many projects you may be required to write a project proposal. Make sure that, if there is a request for proposals, your bid matches the specifications accurately. Get your proposal evaluated by others before submission.
- Ensure that ethical principles are catered for in the research, including the privacy of respondents and their anonymity (if this has been guaranteed).

(Continued)

Summary of web links

http://www.adeptscience.co.uk
http://www.apa.org/ethics/code.html
http://arl.cni.org/scomm/edir/index.html
http://www.bera.ac.uk/guidelines.html
http://www.bhinet.co.uk/
http://www.bl.uk/services/bibliographic.html
http://bubl.ac.uk/journals/
http://link.bubl.ac.uk/libraryopacs/
http://www.catchword.com/
http://www.corec.org.uk/
http://www.endnote.com/support/en4tutorial.asp
http://www.europa.eu.int/comm/eurostat/
http://www.imc.co.uk/index3.html
http://www.ingenta.com
http://www.ion.ucl.ac.uk/library/rm.htm
http://www.isinet.com/
http://lcweb.loc.gov/coll/nucmc/nucmc.html
http://www.library.drexel.edu/netresources/subject/greylit.html
http://www.lib.ucdavis.edu/healthsci/win-bibmanagers.html
http://www.magic.ac.uk/
http://www.psr.keele.ac.uk/data.htm
http://www.sciencedirect.com/
http://ssda.anu.edu.au/
http://www.statistics.gov.uk/
http://www-uk.ebsco.com/home/

Further reading

Jankowicz, A.D. (1991) *Business Research Projects for Students*. London: Chapman & Hall. Very readable and contains a practical guide to selecting and planning research projects.

Hart, C. (2001) *Doing a Literature Search*. London: Sage. An essential guide that includes plenty of practical advice and also a host of useful online resources.

Hart, C. (1998) *Doing a Literature Review*. London: Sage. Another essential source that justifies the importance of the literature review and demonstrates the review process.

Suggested answers for Activity 3.14

1   Since the researcher is hired from outside the organization, it is probably fair to call her a consultant. Does this make a difference to the ethical stance adopted? Well, possibly, yes. Researchers, for example, may be measured against the code of conduct of their relevant professional association. Consultants may also have a professional association, but also have to answer to the research sponsor or manager who will tend to be more concerned with 'results'.

2   The consultant has adopted a number of ethical safeguards, including asking for participation and providing information about the purposes of the research.

3   If this project was being conducted in a purely research context it would probably have to be abandoned. But for the consultant, while needing to give due weight to stakeholders' interests, the interests of the client come first.

PART B

Research
Methodology

Experimental and Quasi-experimental Research Design

Chapter objectives

After reading this chapter you will be able to:

- **Describe the experimental and quasi-experimental research approaches.**
- **Formulate appropriate questions and hypotheses.**
- **Identify populations and samples.**
- **Describe the principles of research tool design.**

We saw in Chapter 2 that experimental research methodology usually involves truth-seeking (as opposed to perspective- or opinion-seeking) and may often involve the use of quantitative methods for analysis. It tends, therefore, to utilize a deductive approach to research design, that is, the use of a priori questions or hypotheses that the research will test. These often flow from sets of issues and questions arising from the researcher's engagement with a relevant body of literature. The intention of experimental research is the production of results that are objective, valid and replicable (by the original researcher, or by others). In terms of epistemology, then, experimental research falls firmly into the objectivist camp, and is influenced by positivistic theoretical pespectives. It takes, for example, some of the principles of research design (such as the use of experimental and control groups) from the natural sciences. However, given the discredited status of positivism, advocates of the experimental approach are now likely to make more cautious and modest claims for the veracity and status of their research results.

In an organizational context, research might stem not from issues prompted by a body of literature, but from a real, live problem the researcher is asked to solve. The initial focus, then, is the problem itself, but the researcher will probably soon have to access both the academic literature (including technical and institutional sources) and also grey literature such as internal organizational documents and reports. Chapter 3 showed how the researcher journeys through a process of refinement, whereby the territory covered by the research literature becomes

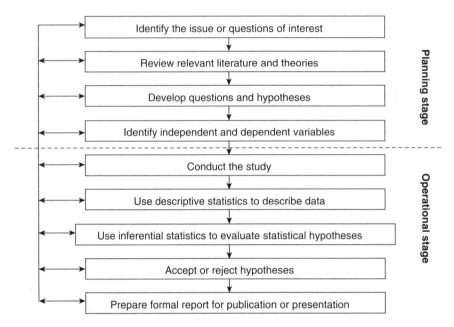

FIGURE 4.1   STAGES IN THE PLANNING AND OPERATION OF AN
EXPERIMENTAL AND QUASI-EXPERIMENTAL RESEARCH PROJECT
(ADAPTED FROM KEPPEL ET AL., 1992)

increasingly focused. But this is not just a question of narrowing the research. The core issues that emerge from the literature gradually build into significant sets of themes, or concerns that link to, and help to specify, the research questions and the research design for solving them.

Note that many of the issues discussed in this chapter (for example, the generation of research questions, the identification of samples from populations and issues of validity and reliability) are also discussed in many of the chapters that follow – even those associated with more qualitative designs.

THE STRUCTURE OF EXPERIMENTAL RESEARCH

The experimental research design process, put simply, comprises two steps: the planning stage and the operational stage (see Figure 4.1). At the planning stage, the main issue or research question may be posed and the relevant literature and theories investigated. From these it should be possible (if the issue is capable of being researched), to formulate research hypotheses. The dependent variables (the subject of the research) and independent variables (variables that effect the dependent variable) are identified and made explicit after which we move into the operational stage. After the experiment has been conducted, the analysis stage may involve the use of both descriptive and inferential statistics (described in Chapter 12).

From the analysis it then becomes possible to either accept or reject the hypothesis. A formal document or presentation is then prepared to report the results. Let us look at each of these stages in more detail.

Identifying the issue or questions of interest

We saw in Chapter 3 that some of the criteria that make up a 'good' research topic include the availability of resources and access to sponsors and other people who may be able to help in the research. Sometimes a research issue may arise from your reading of a body of literature. In a workplace setting, issues or questions spring up as a result of real problems that require a solution, or as a result of a pilot study prior to the implementation of a research project.

Reviewing relevant literature and theories

As we saw in Chapter 2, the experimental approach to research is often deductive, so once an area or issue has been chosen for research, the next stage is to identify and delve into a relevant body of literature. Chapter 3 illustrated some of the sources where you might find the literature you need. Early on in your research, you should try to identify the theories that are relevant to addressing your topic, and also what kind of research methods have been used to address the subject. The literature search will also identify who are the dominant and influential writers in the field. Having looked at the literature, you may decide that the scale of the subject is too large, or that the investigation you were considering has already been done. However, you may also see that previous investigations have been flawed, or that there are gaps in the research that are worth filling.

Developing questions and hypotheses

Research questions and hypotheses are merely the configuration of issues into a transparent and measurable formulation. The way in which research questions are stated, their focus and the kinds of data they seek, are strongly connected to the philosophy and research paradigm of the researcher (recall Chapter 2). As Wield (2002) also cautions, writing questions and hypotheses is not necessarily a linear process. Even after they have been formulated, either further reading of the literature, or surprises at the piloting or data gathering stages, can force the researcher to amend or even rewrite them. Let us look at research questions and hypotheses in more detail.

Research questions

As Alford (1998) points out, research questions are not the same as problems. Problems, themes and concerns may be allocated to you by a sponsor, or may emerge from your engagement with a relevant body of literature. Alford, however, asserts that, in contrast to a problem, a research question comprises two elements: first, a connection to a theoretical framework; secondly, a sentence in which every word counts and which ends (not surprisingly) with a question mark. Questions also describe potential relationships between and among variables that are to be tested.

Kerlinger (1986) argues that a good research question:

- Expresses a relationship between variables (for example, company image and sales levels).
- Is stated in unambiguous terms in a question format

But, as Black (1993) states, a question could meet both of Kerlinger's criteria and still be invalid, because it may be virtually impossible to operationally define some of its variables. What, for example, do we mean by 'image' (in the above example), and how would we define it in ways that could be measured? As Hedrick et al. (1993) argue, researchers may have to receive sets of questions from research sponsors, and these may be posed by non-technical people in non-technical language. The researcher's first step, then, is to re-phrase the questions into a form that is both researchable and acceptable to the client. Research questions can be classified into four major categories:

- Descriptive ('What is happening', 'Which methods are being used?').
- Normative ('What is happening compared to what should happen?')[1]. The standards against which the outcomes are evaluated could include legal requirements, professional standards or programme objectives.
- Correlative ('What is the relationship, and the strength of this relationship, between variable X and Y?'). Note that this establishes a relationship, but it does not imply a cause.
- Impact ('What impact does a change in X have on Y?'). In contrast to correlation studies, impact questions do try to establish a causal relationship between variables.

Table 4.1 provides some examples of research questions for each of these categories.

It is often useful to take a research question and to break it down into subordinate questions. These are highly specific and assist in answering the question to which they are attached. Taking the first question in Table 4.1, we might devise a set of subordinate questions such as:

- How common is drug use amongst male and female students?
- How does drug use compare across different universities?
- How has drug use increased or decreased over the past five years?

This is also a useful exercise because subordinate questions can provide a stage between the original objective and the kinds of detailed questions needed for research tools such as questionnaires and interview or observation schedules. Case

Study 4.1 provides an illustration of how research questions often have to be revised and refined before they become sufficiently focused and usable.

TABLE 4.1   TYPES OF APPLIED RESEARCH QUESTIONS WITH EXAMPLES

Type of research question	Example
Descriptive	How common is drug use among university students? What is the frequency of e-learning to classroom learning in large companies? What proportion of medium-sized organizations have human resource directors?
Normative	How serious is drug abuse among university students? How well run is the local transport system? To what extent are engineering companies complying with health and safety legislation?
Correlation	What is the relationship between gender, academic performance and university drug use? Is there an association between personality type and seniority in companies? What is the relationship between obesity and heart disease?
Impact	Has a drug awareness programme had any effect on the level of drug use among university students? Do increased computer literacy skills have any impact on the probability of future employment? Have new forms of supervision reduced errors in production?

Source: Adapted from Hedrick et al., 1993

Case Study 4.1   Getting those research questions right

A researcher, working for a voluntary association giving advice to the public, is concerned that most of those seeking the bureau's help are white, with very few clients coming from the ethnic minority population. She receives a small grant from the bureau's trustees to carry out a research project. She formulates her research questions as follows:

Research questions

1   To produce a report detailing the research. To check if the bureau is conforming to its organizational aims and objectives and if not how it can improve the delivery of services.
2   To increase awareness of the needs of ethnic minority clients and potential clients of the bureau among staff and to inform the organization of staff training needs.
3   To use this as a starting point for further work to be carried out by volunteers at the bureau.

(Continued)

Take a look at these research questions. What is wrong with them? Well, to be honest, quite a lot. Question 1 is not really a question but an output. This is what will be produced *through* the research. What are listed as research questions do not deserve the description. They may result from the research but are not objectives, since there is nothing here that can be *measured*.

After some thought, the researcher arrives at the following list of questions, namely, that the research will set out to:

1   Identify the needs of ethnic minority groups in the district by:

     • Establishing whether they have access to information about the bureau.
     • Evaluating whether those that access the information, understand its contents.
     • Evaluating whether they trust the information provided by the bureau.

2   Evaluate the degree of awareness of bureau staff (against organizational service levels) about the needs of ethnic minority groups.

Activity 4.1

Examine the final set of questions in Case Study 4.1. Which of these research questions belongs to the descriptive, normative, correlative or impact categories?

Suggested answers are provided at the end of the chapter.

Research questions are formulated as part of many research studies, whether perspective-seeking or truth-seeking, although not necessarily at the same stage of the research. In perspective-seeking studies, for example, questions may emerge as part of the data gathering exercise. For truth-seeking research, including experimental and quasi-experimental research, they are usually formulated at the beginning of the research process. But while perspective-seeking research usually relies just on research questions, truth-seeking approaches usually go further and require the formulation of a hypothesis.

Hypotheses

Research questions are usually broad in nature, and may lend themselves to a number of answers, but a hypothesis is capable of being tested and is predictive. For example, the statement 'Why is street crime more common in inner-city areas' is a research question and not a hypothesis. To convert the question into a hypothesis we might conjecture that: 'High street crime in inner-city areas is a product of liberal policing policies'. Kerlinger suggests that a hypothesis is a 'conjectural statement of the relation between two or more variables' (1986: 17). Good hypotheses, then, should contain a statement containing two or more variables that are capable of measurement. Measurement, however, can only occur if the variables contained in the hypothesis can be operationally defined (see next section). Certainly, in the above hypothesis, the two variables 'street crime' and 'liberal policing policies', can each be operationally defined, compared through a research study, and the statement either accepted or rejected.

In formulating a hypothesis, care should be taken to avoid what Kerlinger (1986) describes as value questions such as those that contain words such as 'should', 'ought' or 'better than'. Similarly, the statement 'The implementation of the new information technology system has led to poor results' is also a value statement because of the use of the word 'poor' – what, exactly, is meant by this? A better approach would be to state the results in measurable terms such as 'reduced output', 'lower staff satisfaction', or 'computer error'. It is useful to reflect that negative findings are sometimes just as important as positive ones since they can highlight new lines of investigation.

Activity 4.2

Examine each of the following statements and decide which (if any) make valid hypotheses.

1   Mixed ability teaching leads to disappointing levels of student attainment.
2   What are the major causes of car theft in inner-city areas?
3   The 'Total Quality Care' system will increase levels of patient satisfaction.

Suggested answers are provided at the end of the chapter.

Operationally defining variables

One of the problems in formulating research questions and hypotheses is that they tend to be somewhat generalized and vague. Before research tools can be drawn up, it is important to operationally define key variables so it is quite clear *what* is being measured. Kerlinger defines an operational definition as something that:

> ... *assigns meaning to a construct or a variable by specifying the activities or 'operations' necessary to measure it.* (1986: 28)

Classifying operational definitions can sometimes be quite challenging. For example, our research question might be: What factors provide the key drivers for ensuring business success in the medium term? As it stands, the question is far too vague to provide a basis for measurement. Returning to the question, we need to operationally define what we mean by 'business success': is it output, profitability, cost control or perhaps a combination of all of these? Similarly, what is meant by 'medium term'? Is it one year, two years, ten years? Going through the process of producing operational definitions allows us the opportunity to rethink some of our assumptions and may even encourage us to rewrite our original research question or questions. Note the loops back to previous stages in Figure 4.1.

Identifying independent and dependent variables

Scientific research aims to identify why conditions or events occur. These causes are called *independent variables* and the resulting effects, *dependent variables*. A variable is a property that can take different values. Thus, the focus of research might be the introduction of a new performance-related pay system (independent variable) which is designed to lead to greater output (dependent variable). But as Black (1993) warns, relationships between variables may be ones of association, but this does not necessarily imply causality, that is, that changes in one variable lead to changes in another. For example, after the introduction of performance-related pay, output may rise, but this increase may have been caused by completely different factors (for example, better weather or victory by the local football team, each of which might boost morale and hence output).

Indeed, independent variables may act upon dependent variables only indirectly via *intervening* variables. Thus, someone may undertake high calibre professional training hoping that this will eventually lead to a higher income level. But in practice, the professional training (independent variable) acts upon income level (dependent variable) via its effects on the person's job prospects (intervening variable, as illustrated in Figure 4.2). The Figure also shows other relationships. For example, it is conceivable that, having achieved a higher level of income, some people may then want to (and be able to afford) more professional training.

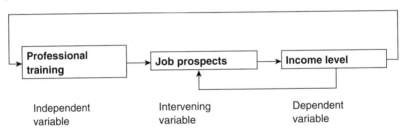

FIGURE 4.2 ILLUSTRATION OF THE RELATIONSHIP BETWEEN DEPENDENT, INDEPENDENT AND INTERVENING VARIABLES

In experiments, it is the independent variable that is manipulated to see the effect. So, using the above example of performance-related pay, we might introduce such a scheme into a company and observe the effect on output. But, as has already been suggested, there may be other factors at work that might influence such changes in output. These are termed *extraneous variables* and must be 'controlled for', that is, the study designed in such a way that the impact of extraneous variables does not enter the calculations.

There are various ways of controlling for extraneous variables. One is through *elimination*. So, using our example of performance-related pay, if the study was concerned about the possible influence of current status or grade, we would only choose people from a certain grade for the study. Another way of controlling extraneous variables is through *randomization*. If randomization is achieved, then it is probable that the experimental groups are equal in terms of all variables. It should be noted, of course, that complete randomization is difficult to achieve in practice. Say, for example, that we know that male and female workers are exactly equally represented in the workforce. If we were to take a random sample of 100 workers, we might expect to finish with 50 men and 50 women. In practice, we often end up with slight variations such as 48 men and 52 women. If gender constitutes the independent variable of interest to the study, we might want to ensure that the groups are equally represented, and randomly select male workers until the numbers reached 50 and likewise for female workers (see Stratified random sampling, p. 87).

Conducting the study

Here begins the operational stage of the research, the success of which depends, not only on how the data are gathered, but on how well the study has been planned. While the research strategy (experimental) has been selected, there are still a variety of research designs at the researcher's disposal (see Design structure, next) and these have to be selected with care.

Using descriptive and inferential statistics

The data are analysed using a variety of statistical methods, all of which should have been selected at the planning stage. Descriptive statistics are used to describe or summarize a set of data, while inferential statistics are used to make inferences from the sample chosen to a larger population (see Chapter 12).

Accepting or rejecting hypotheses

As we saw in Chapter 2, it is impossible to 'prove' that any theory is right. All theories are provisional and tentative (until disproved). However, the weight of evidence must be sufficient that a hypothesis can be accepted as proved. As we will see in Chapter 12, experimental design makes use of inferential statistics and probability to calculate the risk involved in accepting the hypothesis as true (when it is in fact false) and rejecting the hypothesis as false (when it is in fact true).

Preparing the formal report

Particularly when a study has been sponsored or commissioned, the researcher will need to prepare and deliver some kind of formal presentation of the findings. At this stage the focus will be on:

- Why the study was conducted.
- What research questions and hypotheses were evaluated.

- How these were turned into a research design (with sufficient detail that the experiment could be replicated).
- What differences were observed between the hypotheses and the results.
- What conclusions can be drawn and whether they support or contradict the hypothesis and existing theories.

In a more organizational and less academic setting, the formal report will tend to focus on the rationale for the study, the kinds of questions being posed, the results, and what findings, if any, can be implemented. Writing the research report is covered in detail in Chapter 14. For projects that have received research funding, sponsors usually want to go beyond the report and to be provided with information on how the results of the project will be disseminated.

DESIGN STRUCTURE

The basis of true experimental design is that the researcher has control over the experiment, that is, who, what, when, where and how the experiment is to be conducted. This particularly includes control over the 'who' of the experiment – that is, subjects are assigned to conditions randomly. Where any of these elements of control is either weak or lacking, the study is said to be a quasi-experiment. Often, in organizational settings, for example, for practical purposes it is only possible to use pre-existing groups. Hence, it is only possible to select subjects from these groups rather than randomly assign them (as in a true experimental study). Another important difference is that while in experiments we can *manipulate* variables, in quasi-experimental studies we can only *observe* categories of subjects. So, taking the latter case, we could consider the differences between two groups to be the independent variable but we would not be manipulating this variable.

One of the strengths of experimental design is that randomization improves the control over threats to internal validity. In other words, if the experimental intervention (treatment) does lead to a change in the dependent variable, there is some justification for believing that this has been caused by the treatment itself, and not just by the effect of some extraneous variable. Yet it should not be assumed that random assignment is the goal of all experimental studies. As Hedrick et al. (1993) point out, using an experimental group also means using a control group who do not receive the intervention. Even if the treatment does not prove to be effective, it usually comes with more resources. The control group will be denied these, and for a long period if it is a longitudinal study.

One of the strengths of quasi-experimental designs is that it is about as near as one can get to an experimental design, so it can support causal inferences. In the words of Hedrick et al. (1993), it provides 'a mechanism for chipping away at the uncertainty surrounding the existence of a specific causal relationship' (1993: 62). Quasi-experimental designs are best used when:

- Randomization is too expensive, unfeasible to attempt or impossible to monitor closely.

TABLE 4.2 DIFFERENCES BETWEEN EXPERIMENTAL, QUASI-EXPERIMENTAL AND NON-EXPERIMENTAL RESEARCH

Research type	Selection of research sample	Manipulation of variables
Experimental	Random	Yes
Quasi-experimental	Intact	Yes
Non-experimental	Intact	No

- There are difficulties, including ethical considerations, in withholding the treatment.
- The study is retrospective and the programme being studied is already under way.

According to McBurney (1998), generally, experimental designs are usually considered superior to quasi-experimental (and quasi-experimental to non-experimental). However, it may not always be possible to replicate social, organizational or behavioural conditions in a laboratory setting. Therefore, observation in a field setting, say, might be preferable to an experiment because the advantage of realism outweighs the loss of control. The broad differences between experimental, quasi-experimental and non-experimental studies are summarized in Table 4.2, and an example of a quasi-experimental design provided in Case Study 4.2.

Case Study 4.2   A quasi-experimental design

Research has suggested that teenage pregnancy has significant effects on girls in terms of their later income level, educational attainment and general welfare – putting them on a lower part of the economic ladder. But it is also acknowledged that teenage pregnancy is more common among lower income families, a potentially confounding factor.

It is not possible to randomly assign teenage girls to become or not to become pregnant! In the research quoted by Hedrick et al. (1993) this problem was overcome by using as a non-equivalent group the sisters of girls who became pregnant in their teens, but who themselves did not become pregnant until at least the age of 20. This allowed the researchers to control for the family economic disadvantage variable. When the data were analysed, it was found that the previously negative effects associated with teenage pregnancy were not as pronounced as expected.

Activity 4.3

Taking Case Study 4.2, explain:

1   Why this is a quasi-experimental rather than an experimental study.
2   Why the greater incidence of teenage pregnancy among lower income groups is a confounding factor for this particular study.

Suggested answers are provided at the end of the chapter.

TABLE 4.3 NON-EXPERIMENTAL DESIGN WITH INTACT GROUP

Group	Allocation of subjects	Treatment	Test
Single	No – intact	No	No

Let us take a look at a number of research designs, starting with frequently used (but faulty designs) and then some sound designs.

Faulty designs

Design 1: Non-experimental with intact group

In this design, an intact group is taken, and attempts made to discover why changes in an independent variable occurred. There is no attempt made here to manipulate any independent variables – hence the design is non-experimental (see Table 4.3). Say that a voluntary organization analyses its charitable donation patterns over the past three years by geographic region. The dependent variable is the level of charitable donations for each region. The independent variable is not manipulated but is imagined. In other words, researchers would conduct a study that would try to find explanations for any regional differences, perhaps using documentary evidence. Clearly, the problem here is providing convincing evidence of causation – that a particular independent variable caused the changes in the dependent variable.

In their influential work, Campbell and Stanley (1963) describe designs that are devoid of a control group as being of almost no scientific value. This is not to say that they are completely worthless. Each design might reveal some interesting evidence of value to an organization, but they are worthless in the sense that it would be a mistake to draw firm conclusions from them.

Design 2: Post-test only with non-equivalent control groups

In this type of design, a treatment is given to one group (the experimental group), but not to another (the control). Both groups are then given a post-test to see if the treatment has been effective (see Table 4.4). Unfortunately, subjects have not been randomly allocated between the experimental and control groups, so that it is impossible to say that the two groups are equivalent. If, say, the experimental group performs better in the test, it is not possible to rule out the possibility that this was because the subjects in this group were more able or better motivated.

Design 3: One group, pre-test/post-test

In Design 3, a group is measured on the dependent variable by a pre-test, an independent variable is introduced, and the dependent variable measured by a post-test. So, an organization could measure staff attitudes towards racial tolerance,

TABLE 4.4 POST-TEST ONLY WITH NON-EQUIVALENT CONTROL GROUPS

Group	Allocation of subjects	Treatment	Test
1	No	Yes	Yes
2	No	No	Yes

TABLE 4.5 ONE GROUP PRE-TEST/POST-TEST DESIGN

Group	Allocation of subjects	Treatment	Test
Single	No – intact	Yes	Yes

introduce a race-awareness programme, and measure staff attitudes once the programme was completed. Any change in attitudes would be measured by changes in scores between the two tests.

This design is an improvement on Design 1 as it appears that any changes in attitude could be attributed to the impact of the treatment – the attitude training. Unfortunately, as Campbell and Stanley (1963) point out, there are other factors that could have affected the post-test score. These can impact on the experiment's internal validity, that is, the extent to which we can be sure that experimental treatments did make a difference to the independent variable(s). Such factors include:

- *Maturation* effects: people learn over time, which might affect scores on both mental ability and attitude, or they may grow more fatigued over time, which may also affect their post-test scores.
- *Measurement procedures*: the pre-test itself might have made the subjects more sensitive to race issues and influenced their responses on the post-test. Both controversial and memory issues are prone to be influenced in this way.
- *Instrumentation,* in which changes, say, in the observers or scorers used to assess the test results may affect the scores obtained.
- *Experimental mortality,* or the differential loss of respondents from one group compared to the other, for example, through absence, sickness or resignations.
- *Extraneous variables* might influence the results, particularly if there is a large time gap between the pre-test and post-test.

Sound designs

McBurney (1998) states that there is no such thing as a perfect experiment. Nevertheless, there are two elements of design that provide some control over threats to validity and which form the basis of all sound experimental designs: (a) the existence of a control group or a control condition; (b) the random allocation of subjects to groups.

TABLE 4.6   EXPERIMENTAL GROUP WITH CONTROL

Group	Allocation of subjects	Treatment	Pre-test	Post-test
1	Random	Yes	Yes	Yes
2	Random	No	Yes	Yes

TABLE 4.7   QUASI-EXPERIMENTAL DESIGN WITH NON-EQUIVALENT CONTROL

Group	Allocation of subjects	Treatment	Pre-test	Post-test
1	No – intact	Yes	Yes	Yes
2	No – intact	No	Yes	Yes

Design 4: Experimental group with control

In this design, subjects are randomly assigned to each of the experimental and control groups, which means that, at least theoretically, all independent variables are controlled. Hence, again using our racial tolerance example, the study would randomly assign groups of people to both the experimental and control groups. The experimental group would receive the treatment (the race-awareness training) while the control group would not receive the training. Notice that any extraneous variables, such as the effects of the pre-test on attitudes, would be controlled for since the impact should be the same on both the experimental and control groups. If the training has been genuinely successful, then the improvements in test scores for the experimental group should exceed those for the control.

Design 5: Quasi-experimental design with non-equivalent control

Recall that one of the features of quasi-experimental designs is that it is not possible for the researcher to control the assignment of subjects to conditions, and will often have to take groups that are intact. For example, studies in education will often have to use classes that already exist. A typical feature of quasi-experiments is where we have an experimental and a control group, but subjects have not been randomly allocated to either of the two groups.

The use of a control group makes this design superior to Designs 1, 2 and 3, since at least the impact of extraneous variables is controlled for, but not as reliable as Design 4. If steps can be taken to improve the equivalence between the two groups then this will improve the validity of the study. Matching, for example, will help in this direction. Here, steps are taken to match subjects between groups against significant variables such as age, sex, income, etc. If matching is not possible, then at least both groups should be chosen from the same population.

One of the challenges of using a non-equivalent control group design is in the analysis of the results. McBurney (1998) distinguishes between desired result patterns and those that it is impossible to interpet. In pattern A (Figure 4.3), for example, both the experimental and control groups exhibit the same performance in a pre-test, but only the experimental group improves its performance in the

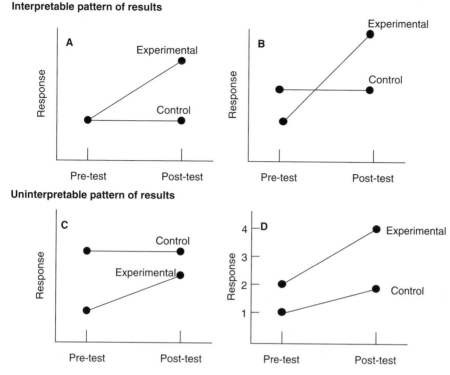

Interpretable pattern of results

Uninterpretable pattern of results

FIGURE 4.3 INTERPRETABLE AND UNINTERPRETABLE PATTERNS OF RESULTS IN A NON-EQUIVALENT CONTROL GROUP DESIGN WITH PRE-TEST AND POST-TEST (ADAPTED FROM McBURNEY, 1998)

post–test. Although the experimental and control groups are not equivalent, their performances can be compared because their behaviour was the same at the beginning. A similar situation pertains for pattern B – the experimental group performed worse than the control group in the pre-test but improved in the post-test, with the control showing no improvement. It would be difficult to find a reason as to why this process had occurred by chance alone.

Pattern C, however, is much harder to interpret. Although it is true that the performance of the experimental group has improved, the lack of improvement by the control group may be due to the ceiling effect – they began by being better than the experimental group and it may not be possible to improve on this level of performance. Hence, it cannot be deduced that the improvement in the experimental group was due to the treatment. In pattern D the performance of both the experimental and control groups has improved, with the experimental group improving to a higher level. At first sight this might appear to be a significant result but a claim for this would be mistaken since both groups have improved their performanance by the same proportion.

Design 6: Developmental designs

Like interrupted time-series designs, developmental designs involve measurement across time and, again, do not involve the use of control groups. One kind of developmental design is the use of a *cross-sectional study*, which looks at a phenomenon at a particular period of time. For example, a cross-sectional design might study the determinants of accidents in an organization. A survey might be used to calculate an average number of days lost in accidents per employee. The next stage of the survey might examine accident rates by age group, gender, occupational role and seniority. One of the advantages of cross-sectional design is that it can reveal associations among variables (age, gender, etc.). But what it cannot do is reveal causation. To achieve this, we would have to turn to a *longitudinal study*, taking a series of samples over time. The problem here, however, is that it may be difficult to gain access to the same set of people over a long period. Indeed, even different sets of researchers may have to be employed.

Design 7: Factorial designs

The designs we have considered so far have involved manipulation or change in one independent variable. Sometimes, however, it becomes necessary to investigate the impact of changes in two or more variables. One reason for this could be that there is more than one alternative hypothesis to confirm or reject. Another reason might be to explore relationships and interactions between variables. Here we use a factorial design which allows us to look at all possible combinations of selected values.

The simplest form is where we have two variables, each of which has two values or levels. Hence, it is known as a two-by-two (2×2) factorial design. In Figure 4.4, for example, the two variables are light and heat, each of which has two levels (cold/hot and dull/bright). Hence, we have four possible combinations, as illustrated. We could conduct an experiment to see which combination of factors gives rise to the most attentiveness (measured, say, by production levels, or on a self-assessment questionnaire) in a workplace. We might find, for example, that dull light combined with both heat and cold leads to low levels of attentiveness, as do bright/hot conditions; but the interaction of brightness with cold temperatures keeps all workers 'on their toes'!

GENERALIZING FROM SAMPLES TO POPULATIONS

A typical human trait is to make generalizations from limited experience or information. For example, we may ask a member of staff what they think of the new company intranet system. We may infer that this could be the opinion throughout the organization, the entire workforce constituting what in research terms is known as the *population*. A population can be defined as the total number of possible units or elements that are included in the study. If it is not possible to evaluate the entire population (because of its large size or a lack of research resources),

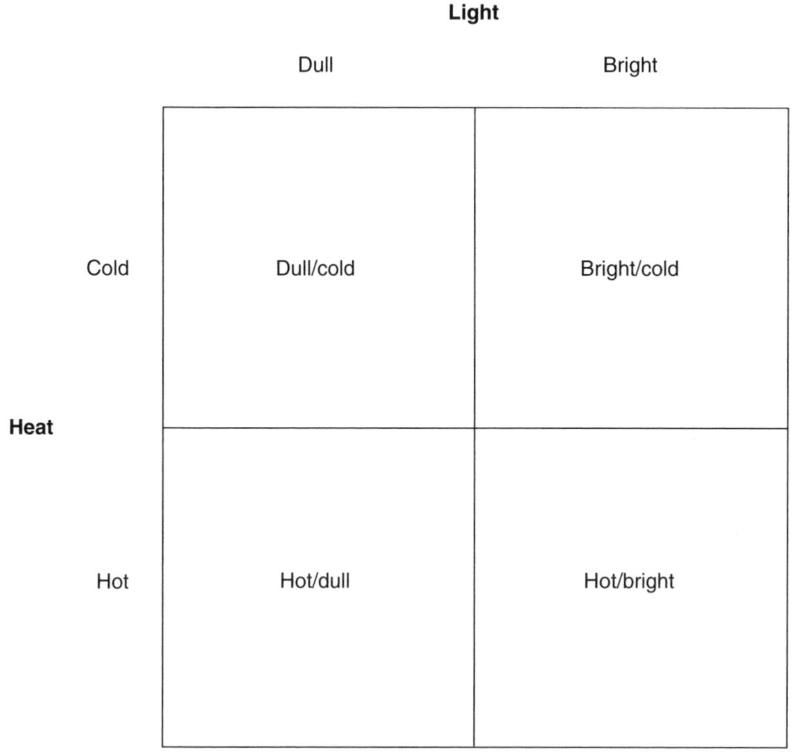

Light

	Dull	Bright
Cold	Dull/cold	Bright/cold
Hot	Hot/dull	Hot/bright

Heat

FIGURE 4.4   A 2 × 2 FACTORIAL DESIGN SHOWING ALL POSSIBLE
COMBINATIONS OF FACTORS

then we might select a *sample* of employees for evaluation. According to Fink, 'A good sample is a miniature of the population – just like it, only smaller' (1995a: 1).

The process of selecting samples

A sample will be chosen by a researcher on the basis that it is *representative* of the population as a whole, that is, the sample's main characteristics are similar or identical to those of the population. Samples are selected from a sampling frame, that is, a list of the population elements (see Figure 4.5). Notice that, while every attempt will be made to select a sampling frame that provides details of the entire population, practical circumstances may make the sampling frame incomplete. For example, the population may comprise all people working in a company, but the personnel records may have missed out some staff by mistake, whilst new starters have not even been entered onto the database yet. The research sample itself might be less than the sampling frame just because using all sampling frame records is too expensive. But having established the sampling frame and how many people we are going to use, how do we choose them?

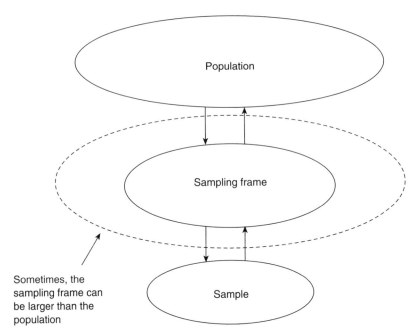

Sometimes, the
sampling frame can
be larger than the
population

FIGURE 4.5 RELATIONSHIP BETWEEN THE POPULATION, SAMPLING FRAME
AND SAMPLE

Most methods utilized to achieve representative samples depend, in some way, on the process of random assignment. Random sampling is the selecting of a random sample such that each member of the population has an equal chance of being selected. Clearly, this can present practical problems. Can we, for example, acquire a full list of company employees from which to draw the sample (the sampling frame)? But as Black (1993) warns, even after taking a random sample, there remains a finite possibility that it may not be representative of the population after all. The chances of this happening are reduced if the study can be replicated, that is, other random samples are used and studied. Nevertheless, the chances of a sample being representative are higher through *random* selection than if the sample is purposive (specifically selected by the researcher).

Of course, we may not always want to attain completely random samples. Again using the simple example of gender, a factory workforce of 100 people might comprise 90 women and 10 men. A random sample of 25 people might give us 23 women and 2 men. Clearly, if gender is the independent variable, a sample of 2 men would probably be of little value to the study. In this case, we might use stratified random sampling by deciding to random sample female workers until 15 are picked and follow the same strategy but oversample for men until we have a sample of 10. Let us look at some of the approaches to achieving representativeness in samples.

What size sample?

The first stage is to determine the actual size of the sample needed. Before doing this, we need to decide on the size of the confidence interval. This is the range of figures between which the population parameter is expected to lie. Say we set the *confidence interval* at 4 per cent, and 45 per cent of the population pick a particular answer. This means that we are saying that we are confident that between 41 per cent (45–4) and 49 per cent (45+4) of the entire population would have picked that answer. We also decide on a *confidence level*, usually of either 95 per cent or 99 per cent. This states the probability of including the population mean within the confidence interval. This is chosen before working out the confidence interval. In many studies, a confidence level of 95 per cent is often deemed sufficient. In medical research, a level of 99 per cent is usually taken because of the need to be highly confident of estimates. Experimenting with the next Activity should make this clearer.

Activity 4.4

To calculate the size of sample you need from a given size of population, point your Web browser to:
http://www.surveysystem.com/sscalc.htm

Randomization

Having estimated the size of sample you need, you can now go about randomly selecting it. As we have seen, randomization is the process of assigning subjects to experimental and control groups such that the subjects have an equal chance of being assigned to either group. The process of random selection can be accomplished either by using the appropriate statistical table (see Table 4.8) or using a special computer program (see Activity 4.5).

Say you have acquired a list of 1000 of the company's staff from which you want to randomly select 50 as your research sample. First, ascribe a number to each staff member on the list. Then, using a pencil, close your eyes and point to part of the table. If you happen to select, say, 707, the top number of the third column, take the first two numbers, 70, and work down your list of random numbers in the table to the 70th. Hence, your first number is 799. Then, using the last digit from 707 and the first digit of the next three digit figure, 872, you get 78. Select the 78th position down the list which gives you 343. Go back to the number 872 and choose the last two digits of that number, 72, and take the 72nd number from the table, etc. Repeat this process until 50 names have been selected. Now take a look at the Web randomiser (Activity 4.5) – you may find it easier!

TABLE 4.8   A THREE DIGIT RANDOM NUMBERS TABLE OF NUMBERS BETWEEN
0 AND 999 (FROM BLACK, 1993)

777	841	707	655	297	947	945	734	697	633
297	522	872	029	710	687	64	660	555	489
672	573	065	306	207	112	703	768	377	178
465	436	070	187	267	566	640	669	291	071
914	487	548	262	860	675	846	300	171	191
820	042	451	108	905	340	437	347	999	997
731	819	473	811	795	591	393	769	678	858
937	434	506	749	268	237	997	343	587	922
248	627	730	055	348	711	204	425	046	655
762	805	801	329	005	671	799	372	427	699

Activity 4.5

Your sample comprises 100 people from whom you want to randomly select 10 as your sample. All people are allocated a number from 1 to 100. You now want to produce a set of 10 random numbers ranging from 1 to 100. In your Web browser, go the following address:

http://www.randomizer.org/

Click on [Randomiser] then respond as follows to the questions presented:

- How many sets of numbers do you want to generate? = 1
- How many numbers per set? = 10
- Number range = 1 to 100
- Do you wish each number in a set to remain unique? = Yes
- Do you wish to sort your outputted numbers (from least to greatest?) = Yes
- Click on [Randomise Now!]

You should see a set of 10 random numbers arranged in a row.

Types of random sample

In an ideal world, you would have sufficient time and resources to choose completely random samples. In the real world, due to practical constraints, you may have to choose other types of sampling techniques. Random samples are preferable to non-random.

Simple random sampling

This relies on taking a completely random sample of the population (as in Activity 4.5) and is used when it is believed that the population is relatively homogenous with respect to the research questions of interest. It relies, however, on having access to a complete list of the population (the sampling frame is equal to the population) so this may not always be practicable.

Stratified random sampling

This consists of taking a sample from various strata. Let us take the example of a large fashion retailer that wants to examine the reliability of its supply chain. Hence, it would take a random sample of its women's clothes suppliers, a random sample of its shoe suppliers, a random sample of its clothes accessory suppliers, etc. Stratified random samples are used because the researcher believes that the identified sub-groups are likely to markedly differ in their responses. In effect, the stratified random sample treats the population as separate sub-populations. If there are 50 women's clothes suppliers, 20 shoe suppliers and 200 accessory suppliers, the samples selected should reflect these proportions.

Cluster sampling

This acknowledges the difficulty in sampling a population as a whole, especially when convenient sampling frames are not available. For example, in an educational study, you might not be granted access to a college's enrolment list. Instead, you could obtain a list of all the classes in the college and randomly select 10 per cent of them. You would use the students from these classes as your sample.

Stage sampling

This is an extension of cluster sampling that involves successive random selections. So, using the education example, the researcher randomly selects 10 per cent of the college's classes and then randomly selects 20 per cent of the students from each of these classes.

Types of non-random sample

As we have seen, random samples are preferable to non-random samples. Sometimes, however, for practical or other reasons, we have to make do with non-random samples.

Purposive sampling

Here, the researcher deliberately selects the subjects against one or more trait to give what is believed to be a representative sample. This approach may, indeed, succeed in achieving a true cross-section of the population. For example, market research may seek a sample that includes a balance between males and females in the sample and across all age ranges. The disadvantage of purposive sampling is that the researcher may inadvertently omit a vital characteristic or may be sub-consciously biased in selecting the sample.

Quota sampling

In this approach, the researcher non-randomly selects subjects from identified strata until the planned number of subjects is reached. So, the researcher may chose to stratify the study according to social class, and go on selecting subjects until each of the strata is filled to a chosen level. An advantage of this approach is that each group is of equal size which can be important for certain inferential statistical tests (see Chapter 12). The disadvantage is that the size of certain strata may not accurately reflect their proportion in the overall population. For example, production workers outnumber managers in most industrial organizations.

Convenience or volunteer sampling

Here, the sample is selected purely on the basis that they are conveniently available. So, a staff 'suggestion box' will contain the views of those who volunteer their views, but there is no way of telling how representative these are of the workforce in general. Convenience samples such as this may be useful indications of trends but need to be treated with extreme caution.

Snowball sampling

With this approach, the researcher identifies a small number of subjects, who, in turn, identify others in the population. Davenport and Prusak (2000) describe how, in a study of knowledge management in an organization, researchers interview someone who is a 'knowledge source', who then suggests other likely persons, etc.

Activity 4.6

A large multinational computer manufacturing company has two factories in the UK, one in Eire, five in Japan and three in the USA. In total it employs 25,000 people world-wide. The Board of Directors wishes to sponsor a survey of staff attitudes towards a proposed branding change in the company's name, logo and marketing profile. It does not wish to poll the entire workforce since this would resemble a plebiscite that the company might, then, find itself

(Continued)

morally obliged to implement. To aid decision-making flexibility, it decides to use a sample of 2,500 employees. Examine each of the following scenarios and decide which constitutes (a) stratified random sampling; (b) random sampling; (c) stage sampling; (d) purposive sampling; (e) volunteer sampling.

1 Five of the company's eleven factories are randomly selected. A random selection is then made that selects five departments in each factory and 100 people are interviewed in these departments in each of the factories chosen.
2 Ten per cent of staff are chosen from each individual grade of staff in each factory in the organization.
3 A sample is chosen to ensure an even distribution between males and females in the sample, and a balance in terms of grade, age, seniority and years of service in the organization.
4 A central computer holds details of all employees in the organization across the globe. A computer program is written that randomly selects 2,500 names.
5 A Web-based questionnaire is designed for the company intranet, and an e-mail sent to each employee inviting them to complete it. Once 2,500 responses have been received, the website is shut down.

Suggested answers are provided at the end of the chapter.

Generalizing

One of the objectives of experimental research is to achieve a situation where the results of a study using a sample can be generalized. According to Kerlinger (1986), generalizing means that the results of a study can be applied to other subjects, groups or conditions. Generalizing means that the fruits of research can have a broader application than merely being limited to a small group. On the other hand, just because a study does not find results that are capable of generalization does not mean they have no relevance. A small case study, for example, may produce findings that are interesting and possibly indicative of trends worthy of replication by further research. And from a perspective-seeking view they may be seen as valid in their own right. The important point is that you should not make firm or exaggerated claims on the basis of small, unrepresentative samples.

DESIGNING RESEARCH INSTRUMENTS

We have looked, so far, at some of the general principles of research design, including the uses of experimental and control groups and the selection of representative samples so that results can be generalized to a larger population. However, for defensible inferences to be made on the basis of the data, any research tools used (such as questionnaires, interview schedules and observation

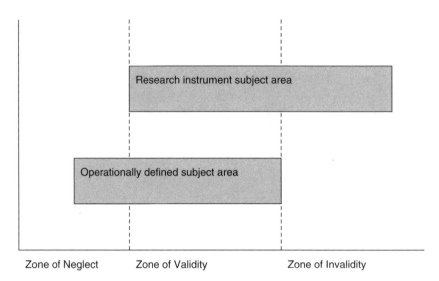

FIGURE 4.6 RELATIONSHIP BETWEEN RESEARCH INSTRUMENT AND OPERATIONALLY DEFINED SUBJECT AREAS AND THE ISSUE OF VALIDITY

schedules) must be internally valid and reliable. To achieve external validity, such instruments must be designed in such a way that generalizations can be made from the analysis of the sample data to the population as a whole.

This section deals with some of the general principles of validity and reliability, but these important issues are taken up in more detail when describing the design of specific data collection tools in later chapters.

Validity

To ensure validity, a research instrument must measure what it was intended to measure. This may sound like an obvious statement, but many novice researchers make the mistake of asking spurious questions in a misguided attempt to collect as much data as possible – just in case some of it may be needed at the analysis stage! McBurney (1998) poses the interesting analogy of using a measurement of hat size to determine intelligence. You could measure someone's hat size, say, every hour and always come up with the same result. The test, then, is reliable. However, it is not valid, because hat size has nothing to do with what is being measured.

In Figure 4.6 we can see that only part of the research instrument covers the subject areas that have been operationally defined. Some operationally defined subjects have not been addressed by the instrument (Zone of Neglect), while other parts of the instrument cover issues of no direct relevance to the research study at all (Zone of Invalidity). To achieve validity, the research instrument subject area and operationally defined subject areas must exactly match (Zone of Validity).

The issue of validity, however, is much more complex than this. At a basic level, it can be defined as seven types: internal, external, criterion, construct, content, predictive and statistical validity.

Internal validity

Internal validity refers to correlation questions (cause and effect) and to the extent to which causal conclusions can be drawn. If we take, for example, an evaluation of the impact of a health education campaign, one group receives the educational material (the experimental group) while one does not (the control group). Possible confounding variables are controlled for, by trying to make sure that participants in each group are of similar ages and educational attainment. Internal validity (the impact of the campaign) may be helped by testing only those who are willing to participate in the experiment. But this reduces the completely random nature of the experimental group and hence the external validity of the study (see next).

External validity

This is the extent to which it is possible to generalize from the data to a larger population or setting. Clearly, this is important in experimental and quasi-experimental studies where sampling is required and where the potential for generalizing findings is often an issue. As Robson (1993) points out, the argument for generalization can be made by either direct *demonstration* or by *making a case*. The problem of generalizing from a study, is that cynics can argue that its results are of relevance only to its particular setting. Direct demonstration, then, involves carrying out further studies involving different participants and in different settings. If the findings can be replicated (often through a series of demonstrations), then the argument for generalizing becomes stronger. Making a case simply involves the construction of a reasoned argument that the findings can be generalized. So, this would set out to show that the group(s) being studied, or the setting or period, share certain essential characteristics with other groups, settings or periods.

Criterion validity

This is where we compare how people have answered a new measure of a concept, with existing, widely accepted measures of a concept. If answers on the new and established measures are highly correlated, then it is usually assumed that the new measure possesses criterion validity. However, as de Vaus (2002) suggests, a low correlation may simply mean that the old measure was invalid. Furthermore, many concepts have no well-established measures against which to check the new measure.

Construct validity

Construct validity is concerned with the measurement of abstract concepts and traits, such as ability, anxiety, attitude, knowledge, etc. As we saw above, each of these traits has to be operationally defined before it can be measured. Taking each trait, the researcher proceeds to elaborate on all of the characteristics that make up that trait. For example, if we use the construct 'confidence' within a particular research context this might be defined as:

- The ability to make quick decisions.
- Sticking with personal decisions once these are made.
- Strong interpersonal skills.

You might reflect here that, in fleshing out traits to this level of detail, it is only a relatively short step to the creation of a research instrument like a questionnaire.

Content validity

Content validity is associated with validating the content of a test or examination. Since it is important to create a match between what is taught and what is tested, this might include comparing the content and cognitive level of an achievement test with the original specifications in a syllabus. Let us take the case of a computer company that provides a training programme in fault finding and rectification for those retail companies that sell its products. After a two-day training programme, participants are given a 50-question multiple-choice test. The computer company will want to ensure that the content of the test is matched with the content of the training programme so that all the syllabus is covered, and only issues that have been taught are assessed. Equally, it will want to assure itself that it has delivered the training programme at a level so that attendees learn the skills of problem solving. The assessment, then, will also have to be at this problem solving level (rather than, say, merely applying rules, or recalling facts) for the test to be valid.

Predictive validity

This shows how well a test can forecast a future trait such as job performance or attainment. It is no use if a test has both construct and content validity if it fails to identify, say, those who are likely to be 'high performers' in a key work role.

Statistical validity

This is the extent to which a study has made use of the appropriate design and statistical methods that will allow it to detect the effects that are present.

Reliability

According to Black (1999) reliability is an indication of consistency between two measures of the same thing. These measures could be:

- Two separate instruments.
- Two like halves of an instrument (for example, two halves of a questionnaire).
- The same instrument applied on two occasions.
- The same instrument administered by two different people.

If we were to take another sort of measuring device, a ruler, how sure can we be that it is always a reliable measure? If it is made of metal, does it expand in extreme heat and therefore give different readings on hot and cold days? Alternatively, we might use it on two different days with similar temperatures, but do we mark off the measurement of a line on a piece of paper with the same degree of care and accuracy? For a research tool to be reliable we would expect it to give us the same results when something was measured yesterday and today (providing the underlying trait(s) being measured have not changed). Similarly, any differences found in traits between two different people we would expect to be based on real differences between the individuals and not be due to inconsistencies in the measuring instrument. Reliability is never perfect and so is measured as a correlation coefficient. In the social and business sciences it is rarely above 0.90. If a research instrument is unreliable, it cannot be valid. Like validity, there are several ways of measuring reliability. Black (1993) describes five of them.

Stability

This measures the scores achieved on the same test on two different occasions. Any difference is called *subject error*. For example, a survey of employee attitudes towards their workplace may yield different results if taken on a Monday than on a Friday. To avoid this, the survey should be taken at a more neutral time of the week.

Equivalence

Another way of testing the reliability of an instrument is by comparing the responses of a set of subjects with responses made by the same set of subjects on another instrument (preferably on the same day). This procedure is useful for evaluating the equivalence of a new test compared to an existing one.

Internal consistency

This measures the extent to which a test or questionnaire is homogenous, and allows a reliability coefficient to be calculated. In the words of Sekaran, the items in the measuring instrument should 'hang together as a set' (1992: 174).

Inter-judge reliability

This compares the consistency of observations when more than one person is judging. An example would be where two people judge the performance of a member of an organization's marketing staff in selling a product over the telephone to the public. The reliability of the observation is provided by the degree to which the views (scores) of each judge correlate. *Observer error* can be reduced by using a high degree of structure to the research through the use of a structured observation schedule or questionnaire.

Intra-judge reliability

Where a large amount of data have been collected by a researcher over time the consistency of observations or scores can be checked by taking a sample set of observations or scores and repeating them. A further problem, and often a significant one, is *bias* on the part of respondents. It is quite common, for example, for respondents to provide a response they think the researcher is seeking. Particularly if the researcher is seen to be representing 'management', respondents may be reluctant to provide honest answers if these are critical of the organization. Even assurances of confidentiality may not be enough to encourage complete honesty.

Activity 4.7

A district police force plans to conduct a survey to discover the attitudes of recent victims of crime to the way police officers have handled their cases. The aims of the survey are to: (a) measure public perceptions of the speed of police responses to reports of the crime; (b) reveal whether victims believe police are collecting appropriate information on the case; (c) evaluate whether victims feel they are receiving appropriate and sufficient help/support from the police; (d) establish whether, as a result of the case, victims feel more or less confident in the police.

There are insufficient financial resources to send the questionnaire to *all* the district's victims of crime so you must select a sample that comprises no more than 10 per cent of all crime victims in the district over the past 12 months.

1 What is the population for this research?
2 What is the sampling frame?
3 What kind of sample will you select? Justify your choice.
4 Identify dependent and independent variables.
5 Produce an appropriate research design.
6 Using the aims outlined above, construct a valid and reliable research instrument.

Suggested answers are provided at the end of the Chapter.

SUMMARY

- The structure of experimental research generally comprises two stages: the planning stage and the operational stage.
- Experimental research begins from a priori questions or hypotheses that the research is designed to test. Research questions should express a relationship between variables. A hypothesis is predictive and capable of being tested.
- Dependent variables are what experimental research designs are meant to affect through the manipulation of one or more independent variables.
- In a true experimental design the researcher has control over the experiment: who, what, when, where and how the experiment is to be conducted. This includes control over the who of the experiment – that is, subjects are assigned to conditions randomly.
- Where any of these elements of control is either weak or lacking, the study is said to be a quasi-experiment.
- In true experiments, it is possible to assign subjects to conditions, whereas in quasi-experiments subjects are selected from previously existing groups.
- Research instruments need to be both valid and reliable. Validity means that an instrument measures what it is intended to measure. Reliability means that an instrument is consistent in this measurement.

SUMMARY OF WEB LINKS

http://www.randomizer.org/

http://www.surveysystem.com/sscalc.htm

Further reading

Kerlinger, F.N. (1986) *Foundations of Behavioural Research,* 3rd edn. Orlando, FL: Holt, Rinehart and Winston. Excellent on the pros and cons of various experimental designs and on quantitative research design in general.

McBurney, D.H. (1998) *Research Methods*, 4th edn. Pacific Grove, CA: Brookes/Cole. Although written for a psychology perspective, a useful quantitative approach to research design.

Suggested answers for Activity 4.1

1 Descriptive.
2 Normative.

Suggested answers for Activity 4.2

1 Not a good hypothesis, since it contains the subjective word 'disappoint-ing'. The statement should contain a parameter capable of measurement.
2 This is a research question (to which there could be a variety of answers) not a hypothesis, capable of being tested.
3 A good hypothesis since it is testable. Levels of patient satisfaction can be measured and we can see whether levels increase, decrease or stay the same.

Suggested answers for Activity 4.3

1 This is a quasi-experimental study because there was no opportunity to randomly assign subjects to the condition (pregnancy!).
2 The objective of the research is to examine the impact of teenage preg-nancy on later income levels, educational attainment and general welfare. If teenage pregnancy was evenly spread across all income groups the independent variable of income level would be controlled for. Unfortunately, as we are told, this is not the case. Lower income families tend to have higher incidences of teenage pregnancy – which could confound the results.

Suggested answers for Activity 4.6

1 Stage sampling. But note that if the factories vary in size, taking 100 people might constitute a different proportion of each factory. The employees in very large plants, for example, might hold different views to those in the smaller ones. Hence, you might want to weight the results.
2 Stratified random sampling.
3 Purposive sampling.
4 Random sampling.
5 Volunteer sampling.

Suggested answers for Activity 4.7

1   The population comprises all the victims of crime within the police district.

2   The sampling frame consists of 10 per cent of the district's population who were victims of crime during the past 12 months.

3   One approach would be to take a completely random sample by allotting a number to each crime victim and selecting a series of numbers randomly. However, it might be hypothesized that certain groups, for example, the elderly, are highly anxious about crime. Hence, an alternative approach would be to take a purposive sample which focuses more heavily on the older age groups. The results might highlight the perceptions of these groups, but could not be claimed to be representative of crime victims as a whole.

4   The dependent variable is the attitude of crime victims to police handling of their cases. There are many potential independent variables but some might include those identified for study by the research – the speed of police responses to the crime, whether police are seen to be collecting appropriate evidence, the extent of police help and support, etc.

5

Designing Descriptive and Analytical Surveys

Chapter objectives

After reading this chapter you will be able to:

- **Distinguish between descriptive and analytical surveys.**
- **Describe and apply different approaches to both analytical and descriptive surveys.**
- **Select alternative survey data collection methods.**
- **Implement special approaches to maximize response rates to organizational surveys.**
- **Take steps to counteract some of the limitations of survey design.**

In the previous chapter, we looked at experimental and quasi-experimental design, in many senses one of the classic and long-standing methodologies. In this chapter, we examine surveys, today one of the most popular methodologies and widely used in the business and commercial worlds. Surveys are described by Fink (1995b) as a system for collecting information to describe, compare, or explain knowledge, attitudes and behaviour. They are a common methodology in research because they allow for the collection of significant amounts of data from a sizeable population. But many surveys go further than this, looking for associations between social, economic and psychological variables and behaviour. Market researchers, for example, may be interested in how changes in income level and status affect people's spending patterns. The results of surveys, whether commissioned by organizations, companies or the government, are frequently quoted in the media. Most surveys are conducted using a questionnaire, but structured observation and structured interviews may also be used. Unlike many other research methodologies, surveys are often a team effort, involving a division of labour between survey designers, interviewers and those who capture the data into computer files prior to analysis.

Surveys fall into two categories: *analytical* and *descriptive*. Analytical surveys take many of the features of experimental, deductive research and so place an emphasis on reliability of data and statistical control of variables, sample size, etc. It is hoped that the rigour of these controls will allow for the generalization of the results. In contrast, descriptive surveys tend to use an inductive approach, often using open-ended questions to explore perspectives. Descriptive surveys may be quite ethnographic in character. If a theory does emerge, it may be tested, subsequently, using more structured research instruments. This chapter, then, looks at how surveys are planned, the types of designs available, some of the special features of organizational surveys, as well as some limitations of survey methodology.

WHAT IS A SURVEY?

According to Sapsford (1999), a survey is a detailed and quantified description of a population – a precise map or a precise measurement of potential. Surveys involve the *systematic* collecting of data, whether this be by interview, questionnaire or observation methods, so at the very heart of surveys lies the importance of standardization. Precise samples are selected for surveying, and attempts are made to standardize and eliminate errors from survey data gathering tools. The very first survey, the Doomsday Book of 1085, was largely an exercise in counting (people, ownership of land and livestock, etc.) but modern surveys are usually exercises in measurement (often of attitudes). They attempt to identify something about a population, that is, a set of objects about which we wish to make generalizations. A population is frequently a set of people, but organizations, institutions or even countries can comprise the unit of analysis. Since populations often tend to be fairly large, and therefore time-consuming and expensive to survey, we tend to collect data from samples, as we saw in Chapter 4, a portion or subset of the population.

Conducting surveys is now a thriving business, and being on the receiving end of surveys is often a component of modern life. Companies make use of surveys to measure customer attitudes towards their products and services. Educational establishments survey (evaluate) student opinions about courses and programmes as part of their quality assurance processes. Governments and politicians pay close attention to surveys of public opinion to gauge the mood of the populace on issues such as transport, education, health, the environment, and, of course, voting intentions. For example, in 1982 the Policy Study Institute obtained UK government funding for a national survey of ethnic minorities, using a sample of 5,000 adults (Hakim, 2000). The survey considered the extent and causes of 'racial disadvantage' in relation to residential segregation, housing, education, employment and health care.

A particular form of survey, a census, is a study of every member of a given population and *the* Census is an official survey of a country's entire population – in the case of the UK, one that is carried out every ten years. A census provides essential data for government policy makers and planners, but is also useful, for example, to businesses that want to know about trends in consumer behaviour – such as ownership of durable goods, and demand for services.

An increasingly common focus of surveys is employees' attitudes. Hartley (2001) reports research showing that in the USA employee surveys are becoming an integral part of human resources strategy. In the UK, in large firms employing over 5,000 people, nearly half have reported using employee surveys. Surveys, then, have moved from being used as barometers of attitudes and opinions, to constituting essential links to business strategy and organizational change.

TYPES OF SURVEY

As we have seen, surveys fall into two broad categories: descriptive and analytical.

Descriptive surveys

Descriptive surveys are designed to measure the characteristics of a particular population, either at a fixed point in time, or comparatively over time. They are designed to measure *what* occurred, rather than *why*. Descriptive surveys are used in a wide range of areas such as market research, public opinion polling, voting intention surveys and media research (ratings surveys). Surveys of this kind have often been used to identify the scale and nature of social problems, including poverty, crime and health-related issues. Hence, descriptive surveys can be the source and stimulus for policy changes and social action.

Characteristics of descriptive surveys

While, generally, inductive in approach, it would be entirely wrong to assume that descriptive surveys are devoid of theory. Indeed, reference to relevant theories may be necessary before the research can be formulated. De Vaus (2002) goes further, arguing that good description is the basis of sound theory. Unless something is described accurately and thoroughly, it cannot be explained. Illuminating descriptions can highlight puzzles that need to be solved, and thus provide the inspiration for the construction of theories. Furthermore, the identification of problems can provide the cornerstone for action.

Descriptive surveys are often undertaken to ascertain attitudes, values and opinions. For example, a survey might examine staff views about whether the organization's customers seem content with the service they are receiving. Indeed, the working practices of organizations would be a typical subject for descriptive surveys. But as Black (1993) notes, there may be differences between the opinions found through a survey, which is a description of people's *perceptions*, and the actual reality of practice. In other words, people may articulate a particular view, but in practice behave differently. Hence, caution needs to be exercised in drawing conclusions from such surveys.

Mass descriptive surveys: the opinion poll

In modern, democratic societies, one particular type of descriptive survey, the opinion poll, has become an essential arm of the government policy making process. Sometimes large corporations also commission their own surveys to check on shifting public priorities and attitudes that could influence government initiatives (Ferguson, 2000). The following Case Study, however, shows how difficult it is for opinion polls to make accurate predictions.

Case Study 5.1   Survey lessons from US opinion polls

Should we trust opinion polls? The track record is patchy because signs that the methods used are failing can be ignored until disaster strikes – like calling the wrong winner in an election! This happened to the *Literary Digest* in 1936. The magazine had been polling since 1916 and getting its predictions acceptably close. In 1932, for example, it predicted Roosevelt's victory within a fraction of a percentage point. But in 1936 it predicted a victory for Alfred Landon when Roosevelt won again. So what went wrong?

The problem was that the *Literary Digest* accessed its sample by using telephone directories and car registrations. But Roosevelt's New Deal coalition had brought minority groups, such as Southern farmers and organized labour, towards his Democratic Party. But these were precisely the kinds of groups under-represented in terms of telephone and car ownership.

The next major polling crisis came in 1948 when they failed to predict the victory of Harry Truman. Statisticians later found that the polls had stopped asking questions too soon. Many people switched their votes at the last minute, largely due to Truman's effective campaigning. After this, the polls stayed in the field longer. They also replaced quota sampling with probability sampling, meaning that respondents were chosen purely on chance. Polling accuracy improved dramatically, and was further improved in the 1970s with the introduction of telephone polling. This was cheaper and therefore allowed for much greater sample sizes (and therefore purer samples).

But in the 1990s the average error (the difference between the final pre-election poll and the winner's vote) rose to over 3 per cent. Why the rise? Well, a major factor must be the problem of public resistance to telephone interviewing, probably as a result of being burdened with too many junk phone calls. People are wary of strangers calling at inconvenient times.

One result of this has been a growing interest in Net polling. The problem here, of course, is that not everyone is linked to the Internet. The polls try to get around this by giving more weight in the survey to those Internet users who are most like (in key variables such as social groups) non-Internet users. In the 2000 US presidential election some of these Net polls were predicting a win for Gore. Back to the drawing board!

(*Source:* Adapted from Meyer, 2000)

Activity 5.1

Go to Social Surveys Online at:
  http://qb.soc.surreyOnline.uk

Click on Surveys to view a wide range of surveys including:

- British Election Surveys
- Family Expenditure Surveys
- Labour Force Surveys

Also, take a look at Resources.

Now take a look at
  http://www.yougov.com

Pay particular attention to the sampling methods. To what extent do you think they could be justified as representative?

From descriptive to analytical surveys

Often, descriptive surveys might only be the precursor to more detailed analytical studies. For instance, a descriptive survey of UK management attitudes towards sterling currency integration with Europe might reveal the strength of feelings one way or another. But we might quickly come face-to-face with the 'so what?' question. If a trend or attitude has been described, what caused it? As Saunders et al. (2000) make clear, descriptive studies in business and management research have their place, but they are generally a means to an end rather than an end in themselves.

In practice, what determines whether a survey is analytical or descriptive is often the size of the sample. If the sample is relatively small, and the research deals with relationships between multiple variables, it is unlikely that any associations found will be statistically significant. In these circumstances, an analytical survey would be of little value so the survey will be largely descriptive.

Analytical surveys

As has been pointed out, analytical surveys attempt to test a theory in the field, their main purpose being to explore and test associations between variables. As Oppenheim (1992) shows, analytical surveys take on typical characteristics of experimental research when it comes to dealing with these variables. As was shown in Chapter 4, the survey will have to distinguish between:

- *Dependent* variables – the subject of the research, the gains or losses produced by the impact of the research study.
- *Independent* variables – the 'causes' of the changes in the dependent variables that will be manipulated or observed, then measured by the analytical survey.

- *Uncontrolled* variables – including error variables that may confound the results of the study. It is hoped that such variables are randomly distributed so any confounding effects are limited.

Controlling extraneous variables can be achieved in a number of ways through careful planning of the survey. They can be controlled, for example, through *exclusion* (such as only using females in the study so as to eliminate the possible confounding effects of gender). Variables can also be controlled by *holding them constant* (for example, by interviewing respondents on the same day so as to eliminate the effects of time). Randomizing can also assist in controlling extraneous variables, since, if the sample is truly random, any extraneous variables should, in all probability, be represented in the sample in the same proportions as in the population being studied.

Activity 5.2

Take a look at the website for the NOP Research Group at http://www.nop.org.uk and examine some of the surveys conducted. Pay special attention to the size of some of the samples used. Can you pick out any particular designs such as longitudinal or cross-sectional?

STAGES IN THE SURVEY PROCESS

Before conducting a survey it is essential to understand the phases and steps involved. Conducting a survey is much more than just a process of designing a questionnaire and collecting data. Czaja and Blair (1996) suggest a five-stage process (see Figure 5.1).

Stage 1: Survey design and preliminary planning

As with most research strategies, the first step involves the specification of the central research questions that the survey needs to address. These might be articulated in a number of different ways, for example:

- A *hypothesis*: Industrial workers are more likely to favour 'blood sports' than service-sector workers.
- A *causal hypothesis*: People who like classical music are more likely to visit art galleries.
- A *description*: What proportion of people believe that all first-time offenders should be jailed?

Some research questions may focus on the views or actions of individuals, others on groups, organizations, networks or businesses. In formulating research questions

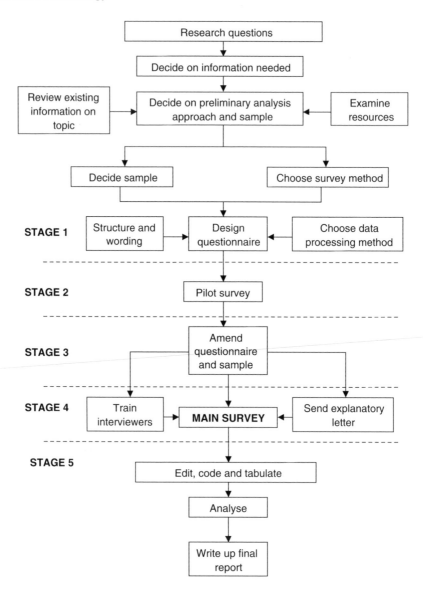

FIGURE 5.1 STAGES IN THE SURVEY PLANNING PROCESS (ADAPTED FROM CZAJA AND BLAIR, 1996)

it is important that they achieve a sense of specificity and focus. De Vaus (2002) suggests that this can be achieved by asking the following questions:

- What is the *time frame* for the survey? Do we need to know about the issue now, in the past, or do we need to project trends into the future?
- What is the geographical *location* of the research? Is it local, regional, national or international?

- Is the focus of the research broad and general, or does it need to *compare* and *specify* patterns among sub-groups? For example, in looking at absentee levels in a country, are we also interested in a breakdown of data by region, sector, industry or gender?
- What *aspect* of the topic is of interest? If, for example, the research issue is e-commerce, are we interested in trends in its growth, companies who do (and who do not) use e-commerce and why, or what kinds of software platforms firms are building their e-commerce Web system on?
- How *abstract* is the research interest? Is the main focus of the research on the gathering of raw data, say, the sale of expensive consumer durables, or what this might reveal about general consumer confidence and standards of living?

In writing research questions for surveys, it is important to establish the research's frame of reference. Hence, if we find that in a customer satisfaction survey, 56 per cent of customers expressed themselves as 'broadly satisfied' with the service they were receiving, what are we to make of this figure? It would be helpful to know before we start the survey the benchmark criteria for 'good', 'bad' and 'indifferent' performance. One way of achieving this is by benchmarking against other companies in the field. If we found, for example, that no industry competitor had achieved a satisfaction rate above 40 per cent, then any figure above 50 per cent would look relatively good.

Collecting benchmark data, of course, is not always a simple exercise. If we need data on competitors they are unlikely to give it to someone working in a rival organization. There are a number of possible solutions, including the use of:

- Overseas organizations. Concentrate on overseas organizations who are in the same business or service but not in direct competition (due to geographical distance). Sometimes organizations might have websites that offer data on their mission, structure, products and services, etc. There may be articles about the organization in trade or professional magazines or journals.
- Organizations in different industries that share similar problems or have business activities in common. A researcher, for example, working for an airport might research customer satisfaction data for bus or train companies. The challenge here is to show how the lessons from a related but different industry can be transferred to the target area for the research.

Whatever the focus of the study, one of the key issues is the selection of the *sample*. For example, in surveying attitudes of residents towards a city transport system, do we contact those who live in the city centre, in the suburbs, or also include people who commute into the city from outlying towns? What age groups do we use? Do we only count people who are 18 years old and above? What about young adolescents, say, above the age of 14 who also use the transport system? There needs to be an age cut-off point somewhere, so it is sensible to limit the sample to those people who are capable of providing accurate information.

Another important issue is the selection of the *sampling frame*, that is, the source or sources that include the population members from which the sample is to be selected. For general population surveys, the most common source for the sampling frame is telephone directories. If we were to conduct a survey of teaching staff in a university, the sampling frame would be the names held on personnel records. As we saw in Chapter 4, of central importance is the question of how much the sampling frame is representative of the eligible population. If we take the example of telephone directories, obviously not everyone has a telephone. Telephone ownership tends to be lower for poorer social groups and in certain localities, and these people may hold different views from those of telephone-owning households. How much bias does this generate in a survey? Czaja and Blair (1996) suggest that most researchers are not too concerned by this threat because non-telephone households are proportionately so small (at least in most industrialized countries).

At this preliminary design stage other factors that need to be considered are the budget for the study and the time available. In general, the cheapest form of survey is through using mail, then telephone surveys. Face-to-face surveys are the most expensive, particularly for large-scale studies, when interviewers will have to be recruited and trained. This is also the stage at which careful thought needs to be given to how the data are to be collected, captured and analysed.

Stage 2: Pre-testing

This stage involves the testing or piloting of elements such as the sampling frame (is it representative of the target population?), survey questions and data collection tools. It is likely that several drafts of the research tool will have to be tested before a satisfactory version is reached. If resources permit, focus groups can be used to discuss the validity of individual questions, or to evaluate the overall design of the survey. If interviewers are going to be used, they will require training and debriefing to ascertain whether the training has been successful. Only when it is felt that the research instrument is ready will it be pre-tested on a group of, say, 20–40 interviewees.

Stage 3: Final survey design and planning

The pre-testing will inform planners as to what changes need to be made to the various elements, such as the choice and size of sampling frame, the questionnaire itself, interviewer training, data coding and plans for data analysis. A common occurrence at this stage is to find problems with the representativeness of the sampling frame. For example, it might be found that the responses of a particular subgroup (say, male nurses) were quite different to the main group (female nurses). A decision would have to be made (within the constraint of time and budgets) on whether to increase the size of this sub-group sample. Of course, if the budget is fixed, this implies that the size of the other sub-group (female nurses) will have to be reduced. Researchers, then, need to consider what impact this may have on the reliability of the results.

Stage 4: Data collection

Apart from the data collection and coding process itself, at this stage one of the most important activities is to monitor the rate of completed interviews and the rate of non-response. The latter should be measured by specific category, each of which has different implications for the research, namely:

- Non-contacts (try to re-contact).
- Refusals (try to ascertain reasons for refusal).
- Ineligibles (replace by eligible respondents).

If interviews are being conducted, the performance of individual interviewers needs to be checked for their success rate at achieving interviewee cooperation and the quality of the interview data. For example, are there some interviewers who consistently fail to get all questions in the questionnaire completed? Is this accidental or does it point to a problem? The importance of reducing sources of error will be explored in more depth later in the chapter.

Stage 5: Data coding, analysis and reporting

At the coding stage, a number is assigned to the responses to each survey question, and these are then entered into a data record that includes all the responses from one respondent. Each respondent is then given a unique identity number. Before data analysis can begin the data have to be 'cleaned', that is, checked for obvious errors. If, for example, a question has only two possible responses, 'Yes' (= 1), or 'No' (= 2), but the data file contains the number 3, then clearly an error has been made and must be corrected.

Activity 5.3

Take a survey that you have conducted or intend to carry out. Are there any steps in Figure 5.1 that you would omit? If so, justify your decision.

Survey methods

Saunders et al. (2000) comment that the design of a survey questionnaire will depend on how it is to be administered, that is, whether it is to be self-administered, or interviewer-administered. Within these categories, they distinguish between six different types of questionnaire (see Figure 5.2). Of these, the most commonly used are postal questionnaires, structured (face-to-face) interviews and telephone questionnaires, although the use of the on-line questionnaire is becoming increasingly popular. The starting point for selecting between them is the purpose of the survey and the kinds of questions that the research intends

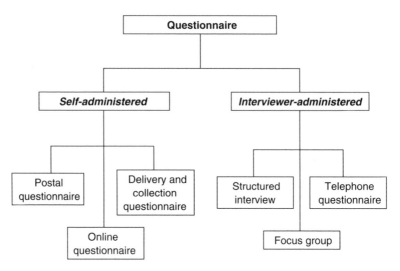

FIGURE 5.2   TYPES OF QUESTIONNAIRE (ADAPTED FROM SAUNDERS
ET AL., 2000)

to ask. Resources such as time and budgets are also part of the decision making equation.

Self-administered questionnaires

Postal questionnaires

Mangione (1995) suggests that postal surveys are best considered when:

- The research sample is widely distributed geographically.
- Research subjects need to be given time to reflect on their answers.
- The research subjects have a moderate to high interest in the subject.
- The questions are mostly written in a close-ended style.

Certainly, postal questionnaires are most suited to situations where the questions are not over-elaborate and require relatively straight-forward answers. They also allow respondents time to consult documents and to complete the questionnaire in their own time. Respondents may also be more amenable to answering personal and delicate questions through this more anonymous medium. It is possible that answers may be more honest than when faced by an interviewer, whom they may be tempted to impress by exaggerated responses or a socially desirable response (SDR). Postal questionnaires are normally one of the cheapest methods to use and can achieve relatively high response rates when the topic is relevant to the audience.

Kerlinger (1986), however, warns that the postal questionnaire has serious drawbacks unless it is used with other techniques. Problems include a low return rate and an inability to check the responses that have been given. He warns that response rates as low as 40 or 50 per cent are common, which means that the researcher has to be careful about making strong generalizations on the basis of the data. Czaja and Blair (1996) also caution that postal surveys are prone to response bias because of lower returns from people with low levels of literacy and education. This group are more compliant with, say, interviews, because no demands are made on their reading abilities. If response rates are low, those responding may be doing so on the basis of some interest or commitment to the subject, making them a volunteer rather than a genuinely random sample. Kerlinger (1986) argues that with postal questionnaires only a response rate of 80 or 90 per cent is acceptable, and every effort should be made to achieve this. Ways of improving response rates are explored later.

Delivery and collection questionnaires

Delivery and collection questionnaires are simply delivered by hand to each respondent and collected later. This has the advantage over postal questionnaires in that there is some direct contact with potential respondents, that might in turn induce a greater proportion of people to complete the questionnaire. But like all questionnaires, this will largely be determined by how interesting the audience finds the survey. One of the considerable disadvantages of this approach, obviously, is the time and effort of delivering and collecting the questionnaires.

Online questionnaires

Online questionnaires are a relatively new, but an increasingly popular way of conducting surveys. Essentially, there are two ways in which an online question-naire can be delivered – as a word processed document attached to an e-mail, or via a website. With e-mails, the researcher will have to know the e-mail addresses of respondents so that the sample can be targeted. With Web-based surveys, if the site is not password-protected, there is no control over who completes the survey form. This means that respondents will comprise a volunteer rather than a ran-dom sample, with corresponding threats to the validity of the data. Conversely, if the site is password-protected, this presents a further barrier to respondents and could tend to push the response rate down. The problem of security is partially solved if the research is focused on just one organization that possesses an intranet, with firewalls to block access from external visitors. But again, the researcher may find it difficult to control who responds.

Being more impersonal, it might be assumed that on-line surveys are less prone to elicit socially desirable responses (SDRs) that might bias the results. Hancock and Flowers (2001), however, report that while some studies have sug-gested that computer responses are more candid and less influenced by social desirability than responses provided on paper (such as postal questionnaires and structured interviews), their own research did not support these findings. At best, online responses were no worse. Online surveys, then, should probably be chosen more on the basis of lower costs, than for the reduction in response bias.

Activity 5.4

For an example of software tools that you can use to build an online survey, see each of the following:

http://www.infopoll.com/
http://www.surveywriter.com/HomePage.html

In addition to constructing online questionnaires, Web-based surveys can also be carried out via a Web discussion group. Here a question, or set of questions, can be posted to the group in the form of a simple e-mail. Since discussion groups (such as listservs) are set up around specific discussions, you need to be sure that the research subject is of relevance and interest to the group. The next Case Study provides an example of how a discussion group was used to conduct a research study.

Case Study 5.2   Conducting a survey through an e-mail discussion group

Two researchers were interested in the views of fellow researchers on the safety procedures necessary in being a lone researcher. To gather data, they chose six e-mail discussion groups. Initially they sent an e-mail requesting only basic information, but after an encouraging response, they sent a more structured set of questions in a second e-mail. This requested details on respondents': gender; age; occupation; area of work; country of fieldwork; whether they had been given safety guidelines; whether they had experienced incidents while conducting research; and recommendations for 'best practice' when researching alone.

A total of 46 responses were received, of which 13 were from males and 33 from females, with ages ranging from the late 20s to the early 60s. Thirty-one were from the UK (possibly resulting from the UK bias of four of the discussion lists). Four were from Australia, six from the USA, and one from each of Finland, Norway, Sweden, Italy and Canada. Some of the replies were quite detailed.

While the sample could not be regarded as representative, this survey method proved to be cheap, speedy at gathering data, and illuminative in terms of the quality of data it elicited. Also note its international character.

Source: Adapted from Kenyon and Hawker, 1999

Activity 5.5

Take a look at some of the e-mail discussion groups available at:
http://www.mailbase.ac.uk/

Interviewer-administered questionnaires

Structured interviews

Structured, face-to-face interviews are probably the most expensive survey method because they require large amounts of interviewer time, a significant proportion of which is often spent travelling to and from interviews. The questionnaires on which the interviews are based can be difficult, time-consuming and costly to produce. However, response rates are usually slightly higher than for methods such as telephone interviews, particularly if a letter can be sent in advance, explaining the purposes of the structured interview. Response bias is also fairly low because refusals are usually equally spread across all types of respondent. Structured interviews are the most effective method for asking open questions and for eliciting more detailed responses. Like telephone interviews but unlike postal questionnaires, structured interviews allow for the use of probing questions in response to unclear or incomplete answers.

Interview schedules may begin with factual information: the respondent's sex, marital status, education, income, etc. This is often referred to as the 'face sheet' and is vital for two reasons; first, it allows for the later studying of relationships between variables – for example, an attitude towards an organization's product or service and respondents' educational background, or income level. Secondly, it allows for some rapport to be built with the interviewee at the start of the interview. The personal interview helps in ascertaining a respondent's reasons for doing something or holding a personal belief. Of course, there may be differences between what people believe and what they do, and between what they think they do and their real actions in practice. There is also the problem that respondents are more likely to over-report socially desirable behaviour than when answering through postal interviews.

Focus group interviews

The use of focus groups allows for a sample of respondents to be interviewed and then re-interviewed so that attitudes and behaviours can be studied over a period of time (a longitudinal survey). An advantage of focus groups is that they allow for a variety of views to emerge, while group dynamics can often allow for the stimulation of new perspectives. Indeed, sometimes these new perspectives may provide the basis for a survey.

Focus groups are increasingly used in the political arena and are also a common tool in market research. Within a business or organization, they can be useful in engaging the commitment of people, especially in circumstances where there is cynicism or hostility towards the research theme.

Telephone surveys

The telephone survey is the most widely used of all the survey methods. One factor in its favour is the growth of household telephone ownership, reaching over 90 per cent in some countries. Indeed, with the spread of cellphones, many households are now multiple telephone owners. Most surveys are currently conducted through home telephones, but it is likely that cellphone surveys will spread, especially when they want access to younger age groups, for whom the cellphone is now a social accessory.

Response rates for telephone surveys are relatively high (60–90 per cent when repeated callbacks are made) because most people are willing to be interviewed by telephone (although recall the resistance to junk calls noted in Case Study 5.1). In contrast to postal surveys, it becomes possible for interviewers to convince people of the significance of the research or to reschedule the interview for a more convenient time. If people prove difficult to contact, Czaja and Blair (1996) recommend five to nine callbacks on different days of the week and at different times of day. With some groups, for example, older adults, making contact through either an interview or postal questionnaire prior to a telephone follow-up can boost the response rate (Wilson and Roe, 1998).

One of the limitations of telephone interviews is the type of questions that can be asked. Questions need to be short and fairly simple, and the kinds of response choices few and short. Sentences should be limited to 20 words or less and language kept as simple as possible. If calling groups who are not conversant with a country's first language, then it is prudent to use interviewers who can speak the respondent's language.

Activity 5.6

In deciding between the various survey methods, make a list of the advantages and disadvantages of each. Which, on balance, is the best for your own survey? Justify your choice.

CONDUCTING A STAFF OPINION SURVEY

Perhaps the most common survey in business is the staff opinion survey, which can provide valuable insights into many elements of an organization's operations, including working practices, communications, management structures, leadership, general organization, and customer relations. For example, a staff survey might be invoked to assess attitudes towards proposed changes, or to predict problems before they occur, or to ascertain what actions need to be taken to improve staff morale, confidence and loyalty. Their value can be greater if a survey can be compared with a similar one conducted in the past (a longitudinal design), or with surveys conducted in similar organizations, or with other sources of benchmarking data. Whatever the subject of the staff opinion survey, it is essential that the results are fed back to all staff, particularly those who provided information, otherwise the response rates to future surveys is likely to be low.

As Figure 5.1 showed, all surveys must be conducted according to a carefully devised plan, and staff opinion surveys are no exception. Indeed, because they involve contacting many people within an organization, it is essential that, if 'political fallout' is to be avoided, they must be seen to be professionally designed and conducted. This is also essential in assisting a high return rate – vital if the organization's policy is to be influenced by the results. We will look in turn at the typical stages involved in a staff opinion survey, many of which should, by now, be familiar.

Aims and objectives

An organization must have a sound reason for wanting to conduct the survey in the first place, since money and resources are going to be used in its planning and implementation. The anticipated results need to outweigh the costs of the survey. Once the organization is satisfied that this is the case, a concise set of aims and objectives should be drawn up. If, for example, a company has just taken over a rival firm, it might want to conduct a survey among the new set of employees on how they have reacted to the take-over and their perceptions of their new employers (including their fears and anxieties). A well-defined set of aims and objectives provide a basis for also determining the scope and structure of the survey and for evaluating its effectiveness.

Planning the survey

Scope
Assessing the scope of the survey is important. It is relatively easy to construct long surveys that attack a range of themes, none of which fits comfortably together. The reports that result from surveys of this kind will have difficulty in providing coherent, focused recommendations for implementation. One approach is to start with a broad but shallow survey that addresses a range of topics, but not in significant depth, to highlight key themes. This could be followed with a detailed survey on prime concerns. If one of these problems was, say, the emergence of a key competitor, the survey could focus on corporate direction, customer focus and innovation. If, on the other hand, the problem was the emergence of a high staff turnover rate, the scope of the survey could be confined to employee appraisal systems, motivation, pay and benefits, and training and development.

Audience
We saw in Chapter 4 that, often for practical reasons, representative samples must be chosen from the population. With staff surveys, however, it is often possible (and desirable) to contact the entire population. In designing a survey for a specific audience, it is necessary to consider their traits and attributes. For example, their educational and literacy levels (including first language), qualifications, experience in the sector or business, technical knowledge and national culture. A survey, say, that asked respondents to provide information on their 'Christian' name, would be offensive to people of non-Christian religions, or of no religious

persuasion. No matter what the social or ethnic composition of an organization, survey designers need to be aware of multicultural sensitivities.

Timing

Even short-term changes in an organization can have an effect on staff morale and hence the chances of people being willing to complete a survey. This can also include rumours, whether substantiated or not, of changes about to occur. It is important to conduct staff opinion surveys during periods when the organization is not affected by these one-off developments. This is particularly important when the results are going to be compared with those from a previous survey. It will almost certainly help to pilot the survey first to make sure that there are no embarrassing misunderstandings. Staff opinion surveys are high profile!

Publicity

Taking Dillman's (2000) advice, advance notice of the survey is important for assisting the return rate. Employees need to know why the survey is being carried out and what will be done with the results. A guarantee of confidentiality is, of course, essential. Publicity for the survey and its credibility will be most effective if this comes from the highest level of the organization, particularly if this is the organization's chief executive or managing director. For many organizations, this publicity will be delivered via its intranet, or staff newsletter.

Selecting research tools

As we have seen earlier, there are a number of alternative survey methods, and any staff opinion survey will benefit from the use of a variety of approaches. Hence, a typical survey may use not only paper-based questionnaires, but questionnaires delivered via e-mail and the intranet. Interviewer-administered questionnaires are less likely to be used for staff opinion surveys due to the time and costs involved as well as the lack of confidentiality.

Analysing the results

The impact of a survey is enhanced if comparisons can be drawn between different categories of respondent in the organization. Hence, for the analysis to have much significance, the survey should be aimed at capturing the opinions of staff in different departments or business units, functions, locations, age groups, levels of seniority, length of service, etc.

Care should be taken, however, to ensure that the use of these categories is accurate. In the modern world, organizations change quickly. Departments get renamed, moved or closed down. New departments or sections open up but news of this may not be generally shared throughout the organization, especially large ones. People get promoted or leave the organization. You need to ensure that you are working from the latest records (sampling frame) of organizational information.

Using the results

Reporting results to management

Many staff opinion surveys may require two different kinds of report. If the organization is a large company, a Corporate Report might be needed at top management level. The Corporate Report should include:

- An overview of the results for the whole organization.
- A comparison, if possible, between the current survey and previous surveys to illustrate trends over time.
- An executive summary that features key points, conclusions and recommendations.

Corporate Reports may also sometimes include the results of similar surveys conducted in other companies to establish benchmarks. An essential feature of a Corporate Report is that it should be easy to read, and so presenting data in tabular and graphical form is very important.

Another kind of document, a Management Report, is needed by the managers of individual business units, divisions, departments or locations. The Management Report might include a comparison between:

- Different business units, departments or locations within the organization.
- The views of people of different grades or levels.
- Different age ranges or length of service.

For very large surveys in complex organizations there can be quite a significant time gap between the collection of the data and the publication of the report. In this case the publication of a short one- or two-page Flash Report, summarizing the findings, could be useful, particularly if these could be broken down, by department or section. In some cases this could comprise a small set of Web pages that are linked from the 'What's New?' section of an organization's main Web home page.

Reporting the results to employees

Staff opinion surveys create expectations amongst employees, hence, it is essential that results are disseminated as soon as possible. This should include those cases where the results of the survey are not in line with management hopes or expectations. Not to publish a report will only fuel resentment and make any future staff opinion survey difficult to implement. The best approach is for management to show that they are willing to acknowledge the results and to take action. Reporting results to staff could be through staff newsletters, bulletin boards, e-mails or team meetings – or all of these.

Implementing the results

For the results of a staff opinion survey to have any lasting impact it is necessary that a planned and coherent series of actions be conducted. These could include:

- The appointment of a director or senior manager responsible for coordinating follow-up actions across the organization.
- The appointment of a senior manager responsible for coordinating follow-up actions in each division or department.
- Agreement on a timetable and process for implementation.
- Agreement on a system for monitoring the implementation of recommendations stemming from the survey and for communicating the effectiveness of the implementation.

REDUCING SOURCES OF ERROR

In an ideal world, the selected sample exactly mirrors all facets of the target population. Each question in the survey is clear and precise and captures the sphere of interest exactly. Every person selected for the sample agrees to cooperate; they understand every question and know all the requested information and answer truthfully and completely. Their responses are accurately recorded and entered without error into a computer file. If only real world surveys were like this! In the real world, gaps and distortions in the data become sources of error.

The two main sources of error are *variance* and *bias*. Variance results from different measures occurring in repeated trials of a procedure. One of the most common sources of this is sampling error (see next section). Variance can also refer to the variability of the dependent variables in a study that cannot be associated with changes in the independent variable. McBurney (1998) suggests that changes in the dependent variable associated with changes in independent variables is fine, but variance is an example of 'bad' variability' because it distorts the data and should be controlled. Other sources of variance are the percentage of respondents who can be contacted for an interview, or the number of refusals to answer a particular question.

Bias occurs when a measurement tends to be consistently higher or lower than the true population value. If, say, we conducted a survey of income levels in a community, there might be a tendency for those on lower incomes to report that they earn more due to social embarrassment. Conversely there might also be a tendency for wealthier social groups to report lower income levels than they earn, perhaps because they subconsciously fear the listening ear of the tax authorities!

Sampling error

Sampling error, as we have seen, is one of the sources of variance. If the population for the study is split between males and females, even a random sample can finish up with, say, 52 per cent females and 48 per cent males. A common source of sampling error, however, lies with sampling frames. We would like the frame to list all members of the population that have been identified, and to exclude all others. Unfortunately, this is often not the case. One problem is that of *undercoverage*, where people are missing from the sampling frame. For example, if telephone directories are used as sources of the sampling frame some groups of people may have their numbers excluded from the directory. This is not a problem if the under-coverage is random, but poses problems if the exclusion is more prone amongst some groups than others. Furthermore, the sampling frame may not include people who have just moved house. This is not problematic if such people are typical of the population as a whole, but, again, becomes an issue if they are different in terms of key characteristics.

A reverse problem is that of *over-coverage* where the sampling frame contains people who are not members of the target population. This occurs, for example, when quite generalised sampling frames are available (such as telephone directories, or membership lists of clubs or associations) but specific groups are required for the sample. This difficulty can be overcome in several ways. One is to contact members of the sampling frame and ascertain whether they belong to the required sample. Another is to design the questionnaire or interview schedule in such a way that ineligible respondents are identified early and screened out.

Activity 5.7

To calculate sampling error for a given size of sample, population and confidence interval, explore the following website calculator:
http://www.dssresearch.com/SampleSize/sampling_error.asp

Data collection error

One of the simple solutions to reducing error at the data collection stage is maintaining a robust record-keeping system so that the amount of missing data can be minimized. At the unit level (person or household), records will include details of all those who have responded, non-respondents and follow up mailing or interview details, and the number and timings of re-attempted telephone calls. Apart from well-organized follow-up processes, non-response can also be reduced by making questionnaires easy to answer. In the case of interviews, non-respondents can be re-contacted by more experienced and persuasive interviewers.

In addition to non-response, missing data is also a problem. In postal surveys there are several ways of coping with missing data:

- Ignoring the items and code as 'missing' in the data set.
- Trying to determine what the answer should be.
- Re-contacting the respondent.

The choice of steps taken partly depends on the value of the missing data. If it is of central importance to the study, then rather than ignoring it, or guessing what it might have been, the best step is to try to contact the respondent. Copas and Farewell (1998) discuss some of the statistical methods for dealing with non-response when these gaps in the data cannot be ignored. If the level of data loss is small, however, and of relatively low importance, then it may be safe to ignore the problem.

Improving response rates

To improve low response rates it is often necessary to locate their causes. Dillman (2000) suggests that low response rates may result from:

- Difficulties in defining the organizational entity. Does the survey deal with individual 'units' of the organization or the organization as a whole?
- Problems in getting to the targeted correspondent. In large organizations, for example, senior managers may have their post opened by administrative staff and personal assistants who may make the decision on whether the survey is passed on for completion.
- Organizations having a policy of not responding to surveys.
- Data sources needing to be consulted, taking up time, even if records are available and not confidential.

In general, response rates will be higher if the respondent has the authority to respond, the capacity to respond (access to the information) and the motivation to respond (it is in his or her interests to do so). Dillman suggests that a number of factors are critical to achieving a high return rate from organizational surveys.

- Identifying the most appropriate respondents and developing multiple ways of contacting them. This is particularly helped if names and job titles are known in advance. Prior telephone calls can help here, and can also assist in identifying where in the organization the survey should be sent.
- Planning for a mixed-mode design, using not only a questionnaire but other forms of contact such as e-mails or the telephone. While surveys targeted at individuals may require about five contacts, organizational surveys may require more.
- Developing an easy-to-complete questionnaire with embedded instructions on how to complete the questions (see Chapter 8).
- Conducting on-site interviews to help tailor the questionnaire to the knowledge and cognitive capabilities of the audience. This may also help identify questions that are too sensitive.
- Targeting organizational surveys on gatekeepers if possible.
- Being cautious about the use of financial incentives (unlike individual surveys), as this may not be ethically acceptable in some organizations.

Jobber and O'Reilly (1996), however, do suggest the use of direct incentives for responding. Table 5.1 illustrates data on monetary incentives taken from the authors' analysis of 12 studies. Even though the sums are relatively modest, the act of 'giving' helps to build an obligation to respond on the part of the recipient. Non-monetary incentives include the use of gifts such as pens or pocket-knives,

TABLE 5.1   METHODS FOR INCREASING RESPONSE RATES WITH POSTAL
            QUESTIONNAIRES

Treatment	Response increase over control (percentage points)
Prior telephone calls	19
Monetary incentives	
10 cents (US)	17
25 cents (US)	19
$1 (US)	26
20p (UK)	15
Non-monetary incentives	
Pen	12
Pocket knife	15
Stamp business reply	7
Anonymity (in-company)	20
Anonymity (external)	10
Follow ups	12

Source: Adapted from Jobber and O'Reilly, 1996

but the data suggest that these are slightly less effective than direct monetary incentives. When using pre-paid envelopes for the return of questionnaires, evidence suggests that stamped rather than business reply envelopes elicit the larger response. Assurances of anonymity can also have an impact, whether the survey is organized from within the organization or from the outside. Finally, it makes sense to follow up any non-respondents with a letter and questionnaire.

Reducing item non-response

At the item (question) level, missing data may be far from random and pose a threat of bias to the study. For example, people may refuse to answer questions that are seen as intrusive or sensitive, or they simply may not know the answer. In interviews it is essential that interviewers are skilled in handling non-response to individual questions. This is helped by interviewers being able to remind respondents about the confidentiality of their answers (if they believe that the problem is one of sensitivity). Mangione (1995) argues that, for postal surveys, any problem of non-response should have been picked up at the piloting stage where it should have been clear which questions were giving respondents a problem. This is particularly the case with attitude surveys where subjects do not feel that their views have been represented in the questions or they dislike the way in which potential responses are phrased.

Reducing interviewer error

Unskilled, untrained or inexperienced interviewers can also be a source of error due to the way in which they handle the interview. The key is that the respondent should answer against the categories that are presented, and no other. So if these categories are 'Strongly agree', 'Agree', 'Disagree' and 'Strongly disagree', or 'No response', these are what are marked down and coded on the interview schedule. If such responses are not forthcoming, the interviewer responds with a probe, a question designed to elicit an acceptable response. So, say a respondent answered: 'Yeh, you're absolutely right!' the correct probe is: 'Would that be ...' [read the categories again]?' The incorrect probe would be: 'So, would that be "Strongly agree", then?', as this, obviously, would be biasing the response.

ETHICS AND GOOD PRACTICE IN SURVEY DESIGN

As we saw in Chapter 3, two of the essential principles of ethical conduct are informed consent and the protection of confidentiality, and these apply to the use of surveys as to any other research method. This means that respondents must be told about the nature and purposes of the survey, who is sponsoring it and how much of their time will be required in answering it. They should also know about the purposes to which the survey data will be put. Subjects should take part purely voluntarily and not as a result of pressure being imposed on them. In protecting confidentiality, care must be taken to ensure that data sets or the results of the study do not allow individuals to be identified. Sampling frame lists should not be passed on to third parties, including other researchers, without the consent of survey participants. Even if consent is given, care must be taken to remove all identifying features that could link specific data to individuals. When research is being conducted by professional survey researchers, these kinds of principles are usually codified into a set of ethical guidelines or rules. The next Activity provides an opportunity to evaluate some examples.

Activity 5.8

Take a look at the American Association of Public Opinion Research for both the *Best Practice for Survey and Public Opinion Research* and *Code for Professional Ethics and Practices* at:
  http://www.aapor.org/

Then examine the following sites:
1 World Association of Public Opinion Research at:
    http:www.unl.edu/WAPOR/ethics.html

2 The World Association of Research Professionals at:
    http://www.esomar.nl/codes_and_guidelines.html

SUMMARY

- Surveys are a common research tool because they allow for the collection of large amounts of data from large samples.
- Stages in survey design include the definition of research objectives, questionnaire design, piloting, survey distribution, coding and analysis.
- There are, essentially, two kinds of survey: analytical and descriptive. Descriptive surveys can provide illuminating data which may provide the basis for more detailed analytical investigations. Analytical surveys are capable of finding associations between dependent and independent variables and between the independent variables themselves.
- Survey methods include self-administered questionnaires (postal, delivery and collection and online) and interviewer-administered questionnaires (structured, focus groups and telephone). Postal and online questionnaires are usually the cheapest to use, but interviewer-administered questionnaires allow interviewers to explore issues of non-response and to follow-up with probes.
- Sources of error include variance and bias. To reduce sources of error, steps must be taken to minimize under-coverage and over-coverage in sampling frames, and to minimize the amount of missing data, including non-response to the survey and to individual items.
- In encouraging high response rates, care must be taken to abide by research ethics in not pressurizing people to participate or to answer questions that they find intrusive.

Summary of web links

http://www.aapor.org/

http://www.dssresearch.com/SampleSize/sampling_error.asp

http://www.esomar.nl/codes_and_guidelines.html

http://www.infopoll.com/

http://www.mailbase.ac.uk/

http://www.nop.org.uk

http://qb.soc.surrey.ac.uk

http://www.surveywriter.com/HomePage.html

http://www.unl.edu/WAPOR/ethics.html

http://www.yougov.com

Further reading

Czaja, R. and Blair, J. (1996) *Designing Surveys: A Guide to Decisions and Procedures*. Thousand Oaks, CA: Sage. An excellent introduction to the various survey methods, plus practical advice on survey design and writing questionnaires.

De Vaus, D.A. (2002) *Surveys in Social Research*, 5th edn. London: George Allen & Unwin. One of the most comprehensive texts available, it includes useful advice on constructing and administering questionnaires for surveys and details of statistical tests used in survey analysis. An added bonus is the presentation of many useful websites.

6

Designing Case Studies

Chapter objectives

After reading this chapter you will be able to:

- **Describe the purpose of case studies.**
- **Plan a systematic approach to case study design.**
- **Recognize the strengths and limitations of case studies as a research method.**
- **Compose a case study report that is appropriately structured and presented.**

We saw in Chapter 5 that surveys are used where large amounts of data have to be collected, often from a large, diverse and widely distributed population. In contrast, case studies tend to be much more specific in focus. While surveys tend to collect data on a limited range of topics but from many people, case studies can explore many themes and subjects, but from a much more focused range of people, organizations or contexts. The case study method can be used for a wide variety of issues, including the evaluation of training programmes (a common subject), organizational performance, project design and implementation, policy analysis and relationships between different sectors of an organization or between organizations. According to Stake (2000), case studies can prove invaluable in adding to understanding, extending experience and increasing conviction about a subject. Yin (1993) is insistent that the case study approach can be used as both a qualitative *and* quantitative method. However, just a brief look at case studies shows why they are more often used qualitatively. Yin (1994) defines the case study as

... an empirical inquiry that

- *Investigates a contemporary phenomenon within its real-life context, especially when*
- *The boundaries between phenomenon and context are not clearly evident.* (Yin, 1994: 13)

Case studies, then, explore subjects and issues where relationships may be ambiguous or uncertain. But, in contrast to methods such as descriptive surveys, case studies are also trying to attribute *causal* relationships and are not just describing a situation. The approach is particularly useful when the researcher is trying to uncover a relationship between a phenomenon and the context in which it is occurring. For example, a business might want to evaluate the factors that have made a recent merger a success (to prepare the ground for future mergers). The problem here, as with all case studies, is that the contextual variables (timing, global economic circumstances, cultures of the merging organizations, etc.) are so numerous that a purely experimental approach revealing causal associations would simply be unfeasible.

The case study approach requires the collection of multiple sources of data but, if the researcher is not to be overwhelmed, these need to become focused in some way. Therefore case studies benefit from the prior development of a theoretical position to help direct the data collection and analysis process. Note, then, that the case study method tends to be deductive rather than inductive in character (although, as we shall see, this is not always the case). It is also, contrary to popular opinion, often a demanding and difficult approach, because there are no particular standardized techniques as one would find, say, with experimental design. Yin (1994), one of the authorities on case study research, who we will refer to extensively in this chapter, also stresses the wide range of skills and flexibility required by case study investigators.

WHEN SHOULD WE USE CASE STUDIES?

The case study method is ideal when a 'how' or 'why' question is being asked about a contemporary set of events over which the researcher has no control. As Table 6.1 shows, 'what', 'who' and 'where' questions are likely to favour a survey approach, or the use of archival records (unobtrusive measures – see Chapter 10), where it is important to show the incidence of a factor. So, a business that needs to identify how many of its workforce are aged 55 or more, will either turn to its human resource records or, if these are so fragmented as not to contain this kind of information, conduct a survey amongst its employees. This would reveal *who* and *where* these older workers were located. If, however, the organization wanted to know *how* an ageing workforce affected its business, a case study would be able to deal with this more explanatory issue and to illuminate key features.

Activity 6.1

Examine the following social policy problem and, using Table 6.1, suggest which research strategy or strategies could be used to address it:

Government statistics reveal a disturbing rise in inner-city drug addition and substance abuse over the past five years. Increased policing and greater legal penalties have had no effect. Drug rehabilitation experts have recommended the provision of 'safe housing' for persistent offenders where their drug intake can be monitored, regulated and reduced over time. Apart from the threat of political 'backlash', the government wants to understand more about the effectiveness of such a programme before deciding whether to support it.

TABLE 6.1   SELECTION CRITERIA FOR DIFFERENT RESEARCH STRATEGIES

Strategy	Form of research question	Requires control over behavioural events?	Focuses on contemporary events?
Experiment	How, why	Yes	Yes
Survey	Who, what, where, how many, how much	No	Yes
Unobtrusive measures	Who, what, where, how many, how much	No	Yes/No
Case study	How, why	No	Yes

Source: Adapted from COSMOS Corporation, in Yin, 1994

You probably decided that the safe houses approach could be used as a case study to explore *how* the drug intake methods affected addiction. The case study approach is not dissimilar to the use of unobtrusive measures such as documents, archives and the use of historical evidence – in each case no attempt is made to manipulate behaviours. But while unobtrusive measures can only rely on the use of existing documentation (historical or contemporary), case studies tend to focus on collecting up-to-date information. For this reason, data collection may involve the use of not only contemporary documentation, but also direct observation and systematic interviewing.

Nevertheless, as Yin (1994) makes clear, the case study approach has not been universally accepted by researchers as reliable, objective and legitimate. One problem is that it is often difficult (indeed, dangerous) to generalize from a specific case. But, in defence of case studies, Yin points out that most scientific inquiries have to be replicated by multiple examples of the experiment, and case studies too can be based upon multiple cases of the same issue or phenomenon. Gummesson (2000) supports this view, asserting that, even in medicine, doctors' skills are often built up from a knowledge of many individual cases.

Another criticism of case studies is the amount of time they take and the volume of documentation they generate. But Yin argues that this is to confuse case studies with one particular type, the use of ethnographic or participant-observation studies where the amount of data collected can be vast. The one argument that Yin (1994) does concede is that conducting case studies successfully is an uncommon skill.

THE CASE STUDY DESIGN PROCESS

Before embarking on the design process itself, Yin (1994) recommends that the investigator is thoroughly prepared for the case study process. This includes being able to formulate and ask good research questions and to interpret the answers. This means 'switching off' his or her own interpretative 'filters' and actually noting what is being said, or done (recall the discussion of phenomenology in Chapter 1). The investigator must be able to respond quickly to the flow of answers and to pose new questions or issues. Having a firm grasp of the theoretical principles involved will obviously help because issues will be thrown into

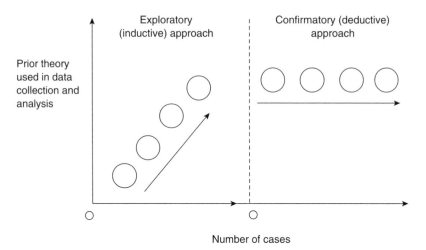

FIGURE 6.1   A COMPARISON OF TWO CASE STUDY POSITIONS: INDUCTIVE
AND DEDUCTIVE (ADAPTED FROM PERRY, 1998)

sharp relief if the data contradict what was expected. This, again, reinforces the importance of the deductive approach. But the case study approach can also generate data that help towards the development of theory – and is, hence, inductive. So which is most important?

Inductive or deductive?

A possible relationship between induction and deduction in case study research is illustrated by Perry (1998). In the left side of Figure 6.1, the first (extreme left hand) case study is purely inductive or exploratory, starting from no theoretical position (pure grounded theory – see Chapter 10). Data collection and analysis in the next case study are informed by some of the concepts found in the first study. But it is difficult to draw inferences through this approach because, as new findings are generated with each study, the focus of subsequent studies (and the kinds of questions that are asked) begins to shift. Hence, data from each study cannot be compared, because we would not be comparing like with like.

This problem is overcome by the more deductive, or at least confirmatory, approach on the right side of Figure 6.1. Here, the first case study could constitute a pilot case, which establishes the theoretical boundaries and then the data gathering protocol and tools for all the remaining studies. The initial theory is then confirmed or rejected by cross-case data analysis across all the main case studies.

This approach is confirmed by Yin (1994), who also argues that, after adopting a particularly theoretical position, the research proceeds through a series of

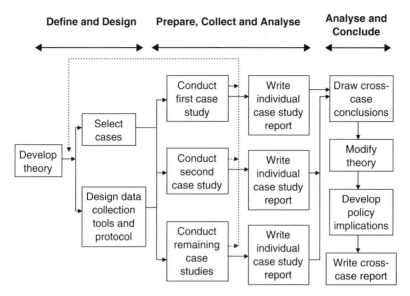

FIGURE 6.2   MULTIPLE CASE STUDY METHOD (ADAPTED FROM YIN, 1994)

case studies, allowing for cross-case comparisons to be taken. In essence, Yin suggests that the research should progress through a series of stages (see Figure 6.2), each of which is described in more detail in the next section.

A case study process

Develop a theoretical stance

A provisional hypothesis or set of questions is developed – provisional in the sense that they are open to further improvement or modification during the process of the study. Hypotheses or questions should be linked, where possible, with previous research. This is also an opportunity to identify rival hypotheses and theories, both of which will help in the analysis of the results.

Let us take the example of a case study that seeks to evaluate the software development process for the building of an organization's intranet Web portal. The hypothesis is that: for Web portal design, the traditional principles of the software development 'life cycle' are inappropriate. Then, using what Yin (1993) calls *analytical generalization*, we are able to compare and contrast the results of the case study with an accepted set of principles or theory. If two or more cases are shown to support the theory, then it becomes possible to make a claim that the theory has been replicated. Yin warns, however, that while analytical generalization is appropriate, statistical generalization is certainly not. It should not be assumed, for example, that the results of a case study can be generalized to a larger population as one would do in an experimental or quasi-experimental design.

Select cases

Cases are selected and the main and subordinate units of analysis provisionally defined. For example, the organization itself might be the main unit of analysis, with departments or geographically dispersed sites the subordinate units. Note that the main and subordinate units of analysis may require different research tools.

Design and pilot research tools, protocols and field procedures

In the design process, care should be taken to ensure that all tools match the original hypothesis and research objectives. Protocols involve the design of a structured set of processes or procedures, often linked to how the research tool is to be administered. For example, a protocol might be used to specify to an interviewer exactly how the interview is to be conducted, and how the interview schedule is to be used.

One of the key design issues in the case study method is the definition of the *unit of analysis,* and then ensuring that this unit of analysis fits with the research objectives of the study. Taking our Web portal development example, it is this *process* that is the unit of analysis and not the look or functionality of the portal itself (although this could be the subject of a different case study). The conceptual framework here is the software development process, including design, prototyping, development, testing and implementation. The study could also explore the group dynamics (another process) between the Web development team involved in building the portal, to understand how their efforts can be improved in future Web projects.

Conduct case study (or studies)

The data are collected, analysed and synthesized into individual case study reports. This is unlikely to occur in a sequential process. So there may be circumstances when analysis raises new questions for which new units of analysis may have to be formulated and additional data collected. Each of the case studies is regarded as a study in its own right, and the findings of each needs to produce *converging evidence,* so that the data from one case replicate the data from another. Think in terms of the police detective at the scene of a crime looking for multiple pieces of evidence that, together, add up to a clear 'picture' or solution.

However, while much of the data may serve to 'prove' or illustrate an issue or phenomenon, negative instances may also make a vital contribution to the analysis. Kidder (1981), for example, shows how an initial hypothesis can be continually revised (on the basis of negative or contradictory data) until it can be validated by the data. Case studies can also sometimes be illuminated by key events. The routine of office or factory life, for example, may serve to obscure phenomena or trends whereas a key event such as a staff 'away day' or a new computer system going 'live' may throw up revealing tensions and social dynamics.

In terms of data collection, the case study method requires the use of *multiple sources of evidence*. This might include the use of structured, semi-structured or open interviews, field observations or document analysis. As we saw in Chapter 3, multiple sources of data also help address the issue of construct validity because the multiple sources of evidence should provide multiple measures of the same construct. The next Case Study provides an example of how rich data can be collected from multiple sources in order to develop a case study.

Case Study 6.1   The taxi-dance hall

In 1932, a group of researchers from Chicago carried out an ethnographic study of an institution called the taxi-dance hall. These halls had developed in the nineteenth century during a period of mass immigration to the USA and were clubs where men could pay for dances with young women. The city social services department were concerned that these dance halls were dens of vice and prostitution.

Four research assistants were employed to collect data by attending dances as participant observers and later to interview taxi-dancers, their clients and the businessmen who ran the halls. The study is vague on precise methodological details, such as the length of the project or ethical or practical issues. But the study is rich in description, as the following passage shows:

Before long the patrons and taxi-dancers began to arrive. Some patrons come in automobiles, though many more alight from street cars. Still others seem to come from the immediate neighbourhood. For the most part they are alone, though occasionally groups of two or three appear. The patrons are a motley crowd. Some are uncouth, noisy youths, busied chiefly with their cigarettes. Others are sleekly groomed and suave young men, who come alone and remain aloof. Others are middle-aged men whose stooped shoulders and shambling gait speak eloquently of a life of manual toil. Sometimes they speak English fluently. More often their broken English reveals them as European immigrants, on the way towards being Americanized. Still others are dapperly little Filipinos who come together, sometimes even in squads of six or eight, and slip quietly into the entrance. Altogether the patrons make up a polyglot aggregation from many corners of the world. (Cressey, 1932: 4–5)

Analysis of the data reveals that many of the girls see dancing as a glamorous and well-paid alternative to an early marriage, or to factory or office work. The backgrounds and motivation of the clients are revealed, and show them as isolated and lonely people. There is discussion of the language used by the dancers and their descriptions of clients as 'suckers', 'fruit' and 'fish'. As Travers points out, the result of the study is 'a revealing and intimate portrait of this social world, built up through a careful study of different group and individual perspectives' (2001: 28).

Source: Cressey, 1932, in Travers, 2001

Activity 6.2

Look back at Case Study 6.1.

1 Identify the implicit working hypothesis of the study.
2 What are the multiple sources of evidence?
3 On the basis of the evidence presented in the study, should the original hypothesis be accepted or rejected?

Suggested answers are provided at the end of the chapter.

Create a case study database (optional)

This process is to ensure that information is collected systematically and that it is logically ordered in the database as well as being easily accessible. One factor that distinguishes the case study approach from other research methods is that the case study data and the case study report are often one and the same. But all case studies should contain a presentable database so that other researchers and interested parties can review the data as well as final written reports. Allowing other researchers to evaluate the data or to replicate it increases the *reliability* of the case study. Case study databases can take a variety of formats, including the use of:

- *Case study notes* resulting from observations, interviews or document analysis, and may take the form of computer files (word processed or an actual database), diary entries or index cards. Whatever form they take, it is essential that they are put into categories and that these can be accessed quickly and easily. Obviously, computer-based files are more efficient in terms of both storage space and search facilities.
- *Case study documents*, which need to be carefully stored and an annotated bibliography produced for ease of later analysis and retrieval.
- *Tabular materials* of quantitative data.

Draw cross-case conclusions

This can include a broad range of analytical techniques involving both quantitative and qualitative approaches. A result of data analysis may also require that further data need to be collected. If the results are unexpected (in the light of current theory) the researcher may have to return to the theory and suggest modifications. The analysis may also have implications for policy making and organizational practice.

Write the case study report

One of the problems with case studies is that they tend to produce large volumes of data, held in a case study database. The report writing stage, then, can sometimes

TABLE 6.2 THE PROCESS OF CASE STUDY CONSTRUCTION

Stage	Process	
Step 1	*Assemble raw case data.* Consists of all the information collected about an organization, person(s) or event	▲ Chain of evidence
Step 2 (optional)	*Construct case record.* Organize, classify and edit raw data to condense it	
Step 3	*Write case study narrative.*	▼

Source: Adapted from Patton, 1990

appear quite daunting. Patton (1990) suggests that a useful intermediary step between this database and the writing of the case study report (which he terms a narrative) is the construction of a case record (see Table 6.2). Each record contains an edited and more condensed version of each case.

The case study report is conceptually linked back to the case study records and raw case data through a 'chain of evidence', including tables, reproduced documents, vignettes etc. These allow the reader (such as another researcher, or the case study's sponsor) to question and even re-interpret the data if necessary. The evidence in the database should also be consistent with the questions and procedures cited in the case study protocol. Allowing a researcher to successfully check the chain of evidence increases the *reliability* of the case study if more than one researcher uses the data to come to similar conclusions (inter-judge reliability).

The task of report writing is much easier, and the results are likely to be more coherent, if the previous stages have been observed carefully. For example, if a case study protocol has been drawn up and implemented, and if individual case study reports have been written up and conclusions drawn (See Composing case study reports, p. 143, for details of report types and structures.)

TYPES OF CASE STUDY DESIGN

Whatever the precise case study design chosen, it is essential that the case study takes the reader into the case situation. This means that descriptions should be holistic and comprehensive and should include 'myriad dimensions, factors, variables, and categories woven together into an idiographic framework' (Patton, 1990: 387). The design process for case studies involves deciding whether the unit of analysis for the study will be an individual case (for example, a person or organization) or multiple cases. Yin (1994) proposes four main types of case study design, as represented in Figure 6.3, each of which need to be selected on the basis of particular sets of conditions. This shows that case studies can be based upon single or multiple case designs and on single or multiple units of analysis.

Type 1: single case study, holistic

In this type of study, only a single case is examined, and at a holistic level, for example, an entire programme, not individual elements within it. The single case

	Single case designs	Multiple case designs
Holistic (single unit of analysis)	**Type 1** Single/holistic	**Type 3** Multiple/holistic
Embedded (multiple units of analysis)	**Type 2** Single/embedded	**Type 4** Multiple/embedded

FIGURE 6.3   MAIN TYPES OF CASE STUDY DESIGN

study should be chosen when it can play a significant role in testing a hypothesis or theory. Another reason is when the case study represents a unique or extreme case, or a revelatory case, where, for example, a researcher is allowed into a previously sensitive or secretive organization to carry out research. There may be other times when a single case study is merely the precursor to further studies and may perhaps be a pilot for a later multiple study.

Type 2: Single case, embedded

Within a single case study, there may be a number of different units of analysis. For example, let us take a case study looking at the implementation of a mentoring system. This is a single case (the mentoring system) but the multiple units of analysis here might comprise:

- The official mentoring processes as laid down by the company's mentoring handbook.
- The perspectives of mentors.
- The perspectives of mentees.
- Tangible evidence that the mentoring system improves company collaboration, networking and morale.

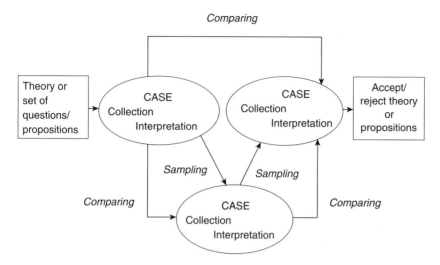

FIGURE 6.4 REPLICATION THROUGH USE OF MULTIPLE CASES (ADAPTED FROM FLICK, 1998)

Type 3: Multiple case, holistic

Where the multiple case study approach is needed (say, to improve the reliability or generalizability of the study) but it is not possible to identify multiple units of analysis, then a more holistic approach can be taken. Let us use the example of a region comprising several hospitals that is attempting to improve its communication processes through the implementation of a specially designed training programme. A researcher might use this communications training programme as a single, holistic unit of analysis, but look at the operation of the programme in all of the hospitals (multiple cases) and over a number of months. The aim here is not to increase the size of the hospital 'sample', but to *replicate* the findings of one case across a number of cases. In this sense, the approach is not very dissimilar to that of experimentation, where an attempt is made to replicate the findings of one experiment over a number of instances, to lend compelling support for an initial set of propositions. Figure 6.4 illustrates this.

     Yin (1994), however, warns that a very serious danger of holistic designs is that the nature of the study may begin to shift under the very nose of the researcher. Hence, the researcher may have begun the investigation on the basis of one set of questions, but the evidence from the case study may begin to address a very different set of questions (recall the left-hand side of Figure 6.1). This is such a threat to the validity of the study that Yin (1994) argues that the only recourse is to begin the study again with a new research design.

Type 4: Multiple case, embedded

The problems faced by holistic case studies can be reduced if multiple units of analysis are used which allow for more sensitivity and for any slippage between research questions and the direction of the study to be identified at a much earlier stage. But one of the dangers of embedded designs is that the sub-units of analysis may become the focus of the study itself, diverting attention away from the larger elements of analysis. For example, with our communications case study, the researcher may examine how the training programme has improved communications between certain groups of nurses and doctors. But if the study remains at this level, it may fail to use this data to explore the wider issue of organizational communication (say, the role of senior management directives) where more significant problems may lurk.

Nevertheless, one of the advantages of multiple case studies is replication (see Figure 6.4, above). But how many case studies is sufficient for multiple case design? The answer, as you would probably expect, is not simple. If external validity (the generalizability of the results – see Chapter 3) is important, or if it is feared that each study may produce quite divergent results, then it is safest to maximize the number of studies. The key here will not to be to aim for measures of statistical significance but for at least some semblance of reliability and credibility.

DATA COLLECTION SOURCES

Yin (1994) suggests that there are broadly six main sources of case study data, each of which have their own strengths and weaknesses, which are summarized in Table 6.3. It should be noted that these sources are not mutually exclusive, with a good case study tending to use multiple sources of evidence. Note that each of these data collection sources is discussed in detail in later chapters.

Activity 6.3

A new Managing Director takes over at Zenco, a manufacturer of engine parts for the automobile industry. His first decision, in a major cost-cutting exercise, is to scrap the headquarters' Reception desk and make the staff who work in it redundant. In its place, visitors have to complete their own security passes and use the internal company telephone directory to inform their client that they have arrived. After six months, you are asked by the MD to carry out a small case study on how the new system is working.

1   What kind of research questions would you seek to address?
2   Which of the following data gathering methods would you use: survey, observation, interview, archival records? Would you favour just one of these methods or use a combination?

Suggested answers are provided at the end of the chapter.

TABLE 6.3   SIX SOURCES OF EVIDENCE AND THEIR STRENGTHS AND
WEAKNESSES

Source of evidence	Strengths	Weaknesses
Documentation (see Chapter 10)	Stable – can be reviewed repeatedly Unobtrusive – not created as a result of the case study Exact – contains precise details of names, positions, events Broad coverage – long span of time, events and settings	Access – problems of confidentiality in many organizations Reporting bias – reflects (unknown) bias of document author
Archival records (see Chapter 10)	(Same as above for documentation) Precise and quantitative	(Same as above for documentation)
Interviews (see Chapter 8)	Targeted – focus directly on case study topic Insightful – provide original and illuminating data	Danger of bias due to poorly constructed questions Response bias Inaccuracies due to poor recall Reflexivity – interviewee gives what interviewer wants to hear
Direct observation (see Chapter 9)	Reality – covers events in real time Contextual – covers context of events	Time-consuming and costly Narrow focus – unless broad coverage Reflexivity – event may proceed differently because it is being observed
Participant observation (see Chapter 9)	(Same as for direct observation) Insightful into interpersonal behaviour and motives	(Same as for direct observation) Bias because investigator unwittingly manipulates events
Physical artefacts (see Chapter 10)	Insightful into cultural features Insightful into technical operations	Selectivity – may be based upon idiosyncratic choices Availability

Source: Adapted from Yin, 1994

QUALITY IN CASE STUDIES: VALIDITY AND RELIABILITY

As we have seen in other research methods, and already in this chapter, the issues of validity and reliability are never far from the surface. They are probably of particular importance for the case study method because of the reliance on data that is generated from either limited or particular samples or situations.

Construct validity

Yin (1994) points out that construct validity is particularly problematic for case studies, because of the difficulty of defining the constructs being investigated. For example, let us say that a researcher is asked to investigate the extent to which team work between different members of a project group has improved over a 12-month period. The problem here is how the concept of team work is defined, leaving the danger that the researcher will base this on his or her personal impressions. This can only be avoided if the researcher:

- Operationally defines the concept 'team work' at the outset.
- Selects appropriate measurement instruments and/or data sources for the defined concept.
- Uses multiple sources of data in a way that encourages divergent lines of inquiry.
- Establishes of a chain of evidence during the data collection process.
- Evaluates the draft case study report through feedback from key informants.

Internal validity

This issue only arises with causal (as opposed to descriptive) case studies where the researcher is attempting to show whether event *x* led to outcome *y*. As we saw in Chapter 3, in research designs that attempt to demonstrate causality, the dangerous impact of extraneous variables always threatens. Taking our previous example of team work within the project group, we may be trying to 'prove' that improvements have occurred as a result of an intensive training programme in team building initiated by senior management. The challenge will be to find significant associations between the training programme and better team work and that the recent introduction of 'flat' management structures (in this case, an extraneous variable) was not the main source of improvement.

Another threat to internal validity comes from the problem of making inferences from the data, when it is simply not possible to actually observe the event. Hence, the researcher will 'infer' that something has occurred based upon case study interview data or documentary evidence. But is it logical and safe to make this inference? Yin (1994) suggests a number of ways of increasing the confidence of making the inference, namely: *pattern matching, explanation building* and *time-series analysis* (see pp. 139–42).

External validity

This addresses one of the most problematic issues faced by the case study approach – whether its findings can be generalized beyond the study itself. Of course, not all would agree that generalizability should be a goal of research. Lincoln and Guba (2000) assert that generalizations inevitably alter over time, so that they become of only historical interest. There are no absolutes and all 'truth' is relative. But Schofield (2000) argues that generalizing is also becoming important in qualitative research. This is partly because the approach is becoming used in high profile studies often linked to evaluation. Funding agencies for large-scale projects also want to see that findings have a wider applicability than to just the project itself.

Taking our example of team work in the project group, to what extent are we able to say that if the training programme did, in fact, help towards better team work, the programme would have a similar impact in other project groups within the organization, or, indeed, in quite different organizations? Gomm et al. (2000) point out that a significant amount of case study research does, indeed, try to make claims for studies that go beyond the original case. They also claim that case study research should be directed towards drawing general conclusions. But how, in practice, should this be done?

The problem faced is that the data collected in the case study may not be representative of the population as a whole (or at least representative of those features that are the focus of the research). Nevertheless, Gomm et al. (2000) advise that researchers can improve the empirical generalizability of a case study by:

- Providing evidence about the 'fit' of key characteristics between the sample and the population; if information about the population is not available, a warning should be issued about the risks of generalizing from the particular case study.
- Using a systematic selection of cases for study, that is, making efforts to ensure, if possible, that cases are typical of the population. Too often cases are chosen on a convenience basis only.

Yin (1994) also defends case studies by pointing out that safer grounds for making generalizations can be established if a study is replicated three or four times in different circumstances.

Before accepting this, however, it is worth noting Lieberson's (2000) note of caution. Referring to what he calls 'small-Ns' (a small number of cases), he warns that it is a bad basis from which to generalize. This is because causal propositions are either *deterministic* or *probabilistic*. In the case of determinism, it is argued that 'If x, then y', that is, the presence of a given factor will lead to a specified outcome. Probabilistic perspectives are more modest, claiming that 'the presence of x increases the likelihood of y occurring or its frequency'. The problem with small-N studies is that probabilistic measurement is ruled out because of the small size of the sample – which leaves us with deterministic measurement.

Lieberson uses the example of drink–driving and accidents. Cases can be shown where drunken drivers are involved in accidents, generating a deterministic relationship between the dependent variable (accidents) and the independent variable (alcohol consumption). But there are also cases where sober drivers have accidents and drunk drivers do not. Small-N studies cannot deal with interaction effects between variables (for example, the interaction between alcohol consumption and driving speed, or running through a red light), because they arbitrarily assume that such interactions do not operate. According to Lieberson, exceptionally rigorous practices are required to avoid these methodological pitfalls. If a small number of cases is selected, then it makes a great deal of difference whether the outcomes are the same in each case, or not. A defensible solution for generalization occurs where:

- One variable is constant across all cases – so, the same independent variable, x, leads to the same dependent variable, y, over a range of cases.
- The dependent variable is different across the cases, and all but one independent variable is constant – so pointing to that independent variable as the cause of the changes.

Reliability

Conditions for reliability are met if the findings and conclusions of one researcher can be replicated by another researcher doing the same case study. Bryman (1988) supports this approach, arguing that case study generalization is made more feasible by team research where a group of researchers investigate a number of cases. As we have seen, this can only be achieved if researchers conscientiously document procedures through what Yin (1994) calls *case study protocols* and *case study databases*. As discussed earlier, a protocol is a plan of data collection instruments and also the procedures for using these instruments (which subsequent researchers can follow). The production of a protocol forces the investigator to think not only about how the final case study report might be completed, but also its intended audience. Yin (1994) recommends that a protocol should contain the following sections:

- An overview of the case study project, including objectives and theoretical issues.
- Field procedures, including access to the case study 'sites' and people; general sources of information; back up procedures including eliciting help, if needed, from colleagues; timescales; contingency plans – for example, if interviewees decide not to cooperate.
- Case study questions, table templates for collecting data and the potential sources of information for answering each question.
- A structure and guide to the final report.

ANALYSING THE EVIDENCE

The case study approach can be one of the most productive in terms of collecting data, but here the problems can often begin. In contrast to other methods, such as experimental design, there is less experience and fewer developed strategies for analysing case study data. Nevertheless, there are some general approaches that can be used with effect. We will look, first of all, at some general strategies, and then at some specific analytical methods.

General strategies

There are, essentially, two ways in which the case study evidence can by analysed. The first is to analyse the data on the basis of the original theoretical propositions and the research objectives that flowed from them. The other is to develop a descriptive framework once the case study has been completed. Yin (1994) recommends that the former is preferable.

Theoretical propositions

One of the purposes of theory is to assist the researcher in making choices between what is worth investigating and what should wisely be ignored. Hence, the objectives and questions of the study are very likely to have been guided by its theoretical underpinning. At the analysis stage itself, data can be compared and contrasted with what the theoretical models have predicted, and suppositions made about the extent to which the original propositions can be supported or rejected.

Descriptive framework

The approach, as its name implies, is more descriptive than analytical, and can be used when perhaps a case study is chosen for a subject or issue for which an underlying theoretical proposition is not obvious. The descriptive framework can operate perhaps to identify the types of cases for which further, more quantitative analysis, should be applied.

Analytical methods

Since one of the objectives of data analysis is to find relationships and contrasts between variables, some techniques are presented here that facilitate this process.

Pattern matching

The logic behind pattern matching is that the patterns to emerge from the data, match (or perhaps fail to match) those that were expected. Figure 6.5 illustrates two possible scenarios. With *non-equivalent dependent variables as a pattern*, a research study may have a number of dependent variables or outcomes that emerge from it. If, before the research is carried out, a number of predictions about the expected dependent variables are made, and are subsequently found, then this supports the internal validity of the study. Hence, in Figure 6.5 dependent variables A, B and C are predicted, resulting from changes in one or more independent variable.

Another type of pattern matching approach is the use of *rival explanations as patterns*. Here, several cases may be known to have a certain outcome, but there may be uncertainty as to the cause, that is, which independent variable is the determining one. Each of the different theoretical positions must be mutually

Non-equivalent dependent variables as a pattern

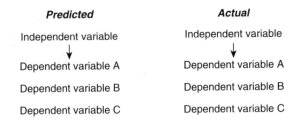

Predicted	*Actual*
Independent variable	Independent variable
↓	↓
Dependent variable A	Dependent variable A
Dependent variable B	Dependent variable B
Dependent variable C	Dependent variable C

Rival explanations as patterns

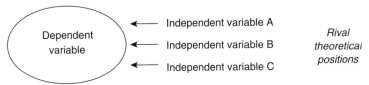

FIGURE 6.5   PATTERN MATCHING OF CASE STUDY DATA

exclusive, so finding the presence of one position excludes the presence of any other.

Take the example of a charitable organization that wants to understand the factors that increase its donation receipts (dependent variable). Case study research is initiated that explores several cases of positive fluctuations in its income stream. It finds two cases when extensive media coverage of a national overseas disaster leads to a 40 per cent short-term rise in donations. A rival theoretical position, that media advertising produces a higher income stream, is found to be inconclusive – on some occasions income rises modestly, on other occasions hardly at all. Hence, the theoretical position, that donations are a product of media coverage of disasters, is accepted. Case Study 6.2 provides an illustration of how pattern matching can be used.

Case Study 6.2   A case study of team working

A year ago, the CopyMatch printing company faced mounting financial losses and decided that it needed to restructure its organization. Its sales representatives earned most of their income through incentive bonuses and, therefore, tried to maximize both their number of clients and sales per client. But often this meant that they took very specialist and small-scale orders that were time consuming to set up, and therefore unproductive and costly to execute. This, of course, was of little concern to the sales 'reps' since they were maximizing their own income.

(Continued)

As part of the restructuring, the workforce was divided into five teams, each of which contained different combinations of sales representatives, production managers, production supervisors and print workers. Through these cooperative teams it was intended that sales representatives would be influenced and informed by those more knowledgeable of the production cycle. The company wanted to monitor the impact of the reorganization and set up a research project, based upon this single case study. The dependent variables (outcomes) of the reorganization were predicted as:

- More orders will be fulfilled to specified times.
- Estimates of customer satisfaction will rise and there will be fewer customer complaints.
- Larger-scale print runs will be undertaken.
- Levels of employee satisfaction will rise.

The research study measured the impact of each type of team (non-equivalent independent variables) to find whether the new structure was more effective than the old one, and which combination of workers had the greatest effect on outcomes.

Activity 6.4

For Case Study 6.2:

1 Suggest an appropriate case study design. For example, what would you choose as the source of measurement?
2 What are the independent variables? Would you treat the project as one case, or each of the teams as sub-cases?

Suggested answers are provided at the end of the chapter.

We saw in Case Study 6.2 that all the predicted independent variables were present, lending considerable weight to the validity of the assertion that the use of production teams increases efficiency, productivity and customer and employee satisfaction. If, however, even just one of these outcomes was not found, the initial proposition could not be supported. Conversely, if another company also used this type of team organization and came up with equivalent results, then this replication of the findings would lend further weight to the proposition.

Explanation building

This strategy is a special kind of pattern matching, but is less structured. Let us say that we want to find an explanation for a problem – to reveal its underlying causes. If these are not to be either subjective or anecdotal, it helps if these causes are located within some sort of theoretical proposition. We would first of all make an initial statement or proposition based upon this theoretical position. Next, we would compare the findings of an initial case study against this proposition, and amend the proposition if necessary. Another case study is taken and the proposition amended, etc. The process is repeated as many times as is considered necessary. At all times it is essential that rival explanations are also considered and solid grounds sought for accepting or rejecting them.

Time-series analysis

In time-series analysis, data on dependent or independent variables are traced over time so that predicted patterns can be compared with the actual patterns that emerge and inferences drawn. What is important here, is that valid indicators are selected that match the objectives of the study. Case Study 6.3 provides an illustration.

Case Study 6.3   Time-series analysis

A large-scale retail park is built on a green-field site on the periphery of a medium-size city. The impact of such a development is measured over time, so a time-series analysis is appropriate here. As usual, we start with a theoretical position or proposition, in this case, that the retail park will impact on the nearby town and locality in a number of ways. First, it will increase the pace of mid-town urban degeneration, in the first place by the closure of various shops and stores, followed, in time, by changing patterns of urban residence – higher income families moving out towards the suburbs. Secondly, increased urban degeneration will increase crime patterns in this locality. Thirdly, traffic flows will change with new congestion 'blackspots' emerging in feeder roads to the retail park. Data are collected on an annual basis over five years through observation, local government records and crime statistics.

Activity 6.5

In Case Study 6.3 identify the independent and dependent variables. To what extent can you be sure that changes in the dependent variable result from the impact of the independent variable and not from other factors?

Suggested answers are provided at the end of the chapter.

Case Study 6.3 is an example of an *interrupted time-series* because the data on, say, patterns of retail spending in the inner city are known before the retail park is built and can be compared with those after its completion. Using a *complex time-series*, we could postulate that a negative trend in a set of data points will be followed by a rise. Using our retail example, we could predict that after a period of several years, the cheap rents and land prices in the inner city (plus state grants and programmes) will attract new entrepreneurs, small businesses and service industries, resulting in urban regeneration.

Another form of time-series analysis is the use of *chronologies*, tracing events over time. The aim here is to compare the chronology of predicted events with what actually occurs. A theoretical proposition may predict that one set of events should be followed by another and that the reverse sequence is impossible; similarly, it may predict that one event should be followed by another after a prescribed period of time. Thus, chronologies not only allow for a description of events, but also for the analysis of causes.

Programme logic models

This combines both pattern matching and time-series approaches. Here, it is postulated that an initial event (independent variable) will produce an intermediate result which, in turn, will produce a final outcome (dependent variable). So, for example, improvements in health and safety procedures in a factory might, indeed, produce better safety standards and lower accident rates. The final result of this might be less disruption to production (through sickness and absence) and higher levels of worker satisfaction, both leading to higher productivity levels. Pattern matching would predict a number of dependent variables (worker satisfaction and higher productivity) as outcomes whilst the time-series approach would measure these outputs over time.

COMPOSING CASE STUDY REPORTS

We will deal with the skills in writing business research reports in general in Chapter 13, but here we will focus on some of the skills and issues that are specific to the case study approach. Given that, as we have seen, the planning and execution of case studies is one of the least systemized of all the research approaches, this, in principle, leaves the case study report also less precisely structured. Nevertheless, following some of the ideas below will help.

Know your audience

Typical recipients of case study reports may be business managers, health professionals, government planners and policy makers, community leaders and special interest groups. As with any report, it is essential that you know whom you are writing for and what it is that they are interested in and what they want to know.

Sometimes case studies can be particularly effective when read by non-specialist or non-technical readers because their descriptive basis and findings can be both illuminating and memorable. For example, consider the relative impact of two reports on the effect of government aid programmes to developing nations. One report is based on a thorough statistical analysis and plentiful quantitative data presented in tabular form. The other report is a case study of an African village showing both the dramatic fall in the mortality rate following the installation of clean water supply but also the continuing grinding levels of under-employment and poverty.

Activity 6.6

Which of the reports just described do you think will have the greatest impact on (a) public opinion; (b) government opinion?

Clearly, government opinion is more likely to be influenced by facts, statistics and rational analysis, while the public tend to favour more of the 'human element' that would emerge through the case study of the African village. Imagine the potential impact if the African village report was taken up and illustrated through a television programme.

One type of audience we have not mentioned so far are the readers and examiners of dissertations and theses. If you are conducting a case study as part of an academic programme then this type of audience will be interested, amongst other issues, with the theoretical propositions on which the study is based, and the extent to which your analysis supports claims that are consistent with the evidence.

Above all, you must ensure that you are actually writing for an audience and not for yourself. This is a particular danger if you are conducting a case study within your own particular work environment, or in a situation within which you have a strong emotional connection. Take, for example, a voluntary worker with an Aids charity conducting a case study into how a particular group of HIV-infected men and women support each other. The danger is that the final report deals with a catalogue of issues that have worried the voluntary worker for some time. But if the report is aimed at changing public perceptions and attitudes towards HIV-infected people, then it must objectively address these wider social values and interests if it is to have any chance of changing ideas.

Types of case study report

Case study reports are usually written, but, in principle, they can also be presented orally, or through photographs, film or video. If a case study is not subject to confidentiality, then it can also be placed on the Web for wider public dissemination. Indeed, if the intended audience is a public one, it would be difficult to find a better delivery medium than the Web. In general, whether presented as a traditional document, or via the Web, written communication is likely to be the most familiar medium to both writer and reader.

Type of case study	Report structure		
Single case study	Case study description and analysis		
Multiple case study	Cross-case analysis and results	Appendix: Narrative Case Study 1 Narrative Case Study n	
Multiple case study: without narrative	Case study 1	Question 1 Question 2	Answer Answer
	Case study 2	Question 1 Question 2	Answer Answer
Multiple case study: integrated	Cross-case issue 1 – data and analysis from all cases Cross-case issue 2 – data and analysis from all cases		

FIGURE 6.6   FOUR WRITTEN FORMS OF CASE STUDY

Figure 6.6 gives examples of four structures that can be used for the generation of written reports, broadly following typical case study design formats. For the classic single case study, the report simply consists of the description and analysis of the data. In the multiple case study, the main body of the report could begin with narrative descriptions of each of the case studies, but these can be bulky and could be confined to the appendices. In this case, the main body of the report would consist of the analysis and supporting data of the cross-cases. A more focused approach would be to present the findings in the form of a question and answer format for each of the case studies. Here, the reader is then in a position to go to those questions of particular interest for each of the cases. This can be both efficient in terms of the reader's time and allow the reader to draw comparisons across each of the studies. The fourth example takes this a stage further using an integrated approach that takes issue by issue (using each case study to supply the underlying data and analysis).

Yin (1994) warns that the selection of one of these approaches for the final report needs to be made during the design of the case study and not as an afterthought, and should be contained in the case study protocol.

Written report structures

A number of alternative report structures are possible, depending on the audience and what the researcher is trying to achieve (see Figure 6.7). If, for example, the final case study report is being written for a largely academic audience, then the linear-analytic structure would probably be acceptable, since its format would be readily recognized by academics. These structures could be used with any of the single or multiple case studies just discussed.

The *comparative* structure takes the same case study and repeats it two or more times, comparing and contrasting the results. This could be done through

LINEAR-ANALYTIC	THEORY BUILDING
Statement of problem Literature review Methodology Findings/analysis Conclusions	Theory/model

COMPARITIVE	SUSPENSE
Case study 1: description A Case study 1: description B	Answer Background Alternative explanations

CHRONOLOGICAL	UNSEQUENCED (example)
Event A Event B Event C	Product development Health and safety improvement Business planning Human resource development

FIGURE 6.7   ALTERNATIVE WRITTEN REPORT STRUCTURES

beginning each time with different underpinning theoretical models, allowing the case to be viewed from an alternative perspective. These repetitions are typical of pattern matching approaches.

The *chronological* structure simply takes a series of events over time and sets them out in sequence. It should not be supposed, however, that this approach is purely descriptive – it can also be used both from explanatory and exploratory studies. For example, setting out a logical sequence of events may not only describe them, but provide insights into linkages and causes.

With the *theory building* structure the purpose is to build a series of chapters or sections that develop a theoretical perspective behind the case study. The theory may serve an explanatory purpose, seeking connections between cause and effect, or an exploratory one, suggesting new research questions and propositions.

The *suspense* structure is probably one of the most valuable in a business environment because it begins with the 'answer' or key findings of the case study. This is what managers, planners and the sponsors of research want to know. Subsequent chapters provide the background to the study and may even look at alternative perspectives on the findings.

Finally, in the *unsequenced* structure, the actual sequence of sections or chapters has no particular significance for the report. Findings can be presented in any order, provided that they are compatible. So, in Figure 6.7, the unsequenced example illustrates a case study of a company where each section can be presented independently in its own right, with no requirement for sequencing the sections in a particular order.

The final Case Study in this chapter brings together many of the principles of case study design that we have discussed. These include the role of theoretical propositions, the design of clear research methodologies and data gathering tools and the use of multiple sources of evidence.

Case Study 6.4   Japanese transplant companies in the UK

A major theoretical theme of management–worker relations in Japanese (transplant) firms based in the UK, is that of strong management control (hegemony) based upon sophisticated recruitment policies, surveillance and performance monitoring. This is facilitated by a compliant local environment with national and local state bureaucracies, development corporations and trades unions eager to offer cooperative working arrangements in exchange for inward foreign (Japanese) investment.

A case study was carried out (Elger and Smith, 1998) working on the hypotheses (based upon previous research) that:

- Despite the use of 'greenfield' sites and inexperienced labour, recruitment and retention of labour still poses problems for Japanese transplant companies.
- In response to these circumstances, management policies are not neatly predetermined but involve debate, conflict and often piecemeal innovation.
- Management policies among Japanese transplants are influenced not only by local and national environments, but by patterns of ownership and company traditions.
- These sources of differentiation help to explain the variations in the ways in which managers respond to common problems within a shared labour market.

A research methodology for the case study was established with the selection of four Japanese greenfield transplant companies, all based in Telford, a 'new town' in the West Midlands of the UK. Ten per cent of managers in these companies were interviewed, plus a number of other 'key informants' in the locality. Documentary evidence and observational data were gathered on both corporate policies and the local labour market. The impact of 'location' as an independent variable was controlled for by holding it constant – that is, by using a set of case study companies from the same location. So, by focusing on four companies operating in the same labour market, it became feasible to identify key features of this environment that impact on their labour relations. It also became possible to explore the impact of individual company policies and strategies on the management of labour relations.

Data on the production and personnel policies in each of the four case study workplaces were gathered using a template (see Table 6.4).

The authors acknowledge that the data need to be treated with some caution:

Of necessity, this table captures only a snapshot of what are evolving patterns of employment practices, and the uniform terminology glosses over important differences in the implementation and meaning of the various features in the different workplaces. (Elger and Smith, 1998: 193)

(Continued)

TABLE 6.4   PERSONNEL AND PRODUCTION PRACTICES IN THE CASE STUDY
PLANTS

| | Company name | | | |
Practice	Copy Co.	PCB Co.	Assembly Co.	Car-part Co.
Team briefing	+	+	P	+
Performance appraisal	+	P	X	+
Formal consultation	X	+	X	+
Use of temporary workers	+	+	X	+
Performance-related pay	+	+	X	+
Systematic hiring policy	X	X	X	P
Operator responsible for quality	+	+	+	+

Key: + = practice exists; P = partial application; X = practice does not exist.

But the evidence (from the table and from the interviews) shows that in all four transplant companies, managers are implementing procedures for quality management. But the form taken by quality and just-in-time measures varies significantly between the factories. Thus, the case study highlights the danger of treating specific transplant workplaces as merely exemplars of generalized Japanese ways of working. There seemed to be no uniform or systematic set of personnel policies designed to shape and induct new recruits. Rather, employee policies seemed to emerge in a much more ad hoc way, in response to emerging problems and pressures, often based around the problems of recruitment and retention of young labour. The case study data reveal that transplant operations are embedded within the influences of the local as well as the national economy and are influenced by the distinctive nature of local labour markets, patterns of trades unionism and employer organization and the politics of local state and development agencies.

Source: Adapted from Elger and Smith, 1998

The Case Study reveals a number of typical issues in case study design. The following Activity asks you to identify what they are.

Activity 6.7

In Case Study 6.4, identify the following:

1   The theoretical underpinning of the case study.
2   The number and type of data collection sources.
3   Protocols used for data collection.
4   The analytical method: pattern matching, explanation building or time-series.
5   The extent to which the original hypotheses are supported or refuted.

Suggested answers are provided at the end of the chapter.

SUMMARY

- Case studies are used for a variety of subjects, including organizational performance, evaluating relationships between individuals, teams or departments and project implementation.
- Case studies are often deductive in character, beginning from a theoretical premise or stance.
- They should be used when there is no opportunity to control or manipulate variables, but when there is an interest in explanations and analysis of situations or events.
- While procedures are not as well defined as those for experimental research, case study research should involve the development of an initial hypothesis or set of questions, and the design of research tools, protocols and field procedures.
- Case studies can involve single or multiple units of analysis (individuals, departments, objects, systems, etc.) in combination with single or multiple case designs.
- In case studies, researchers should aim to collect multiple sources of evidence that should evolve into a chain of evidence, linking research questions, data, analysis and case study reports.
- Data for case studies are typically collected from multiple sources including documentation, archives, interviews and direct or participant observation.
- Internal validity in case studies is strengthened by pattern matching, explanation building and time-series analysis. Reliability is strengthened by multiple replication of the same or similar cases.

Further reading

Yin, R.K. (1994) *Case Study Research: Design and Methods*, 2nd edn. Thousand Oaks, CA: Sage. Yin is widely recognized as one of the leading authorities on case study design. There is no better starting point.

Gomm, R., Hammersley, M. and Foster, P. (eds) (2000) *Case Study Method: Key Issues, Key Texts*. London: Sage. Not for the novice researcher, this book explores some of the complex issues associated with case study research, including external validity and the generation of theory.

Suggested answers for Activity 6.2

1 The implicit working hypothesis is that taxi-dance halls are dens of vice and corruption.

(Continued)

2 The multiple sources of evidence used include observation (of people arriving, their means of transport, the look and demenour of both clients and taxi-dancers, etc.), and interviews with clients, taxi-dancers and the owners of the halls.

3 This is a matter of interpretation! Clearly, however, the hypothesis that the halls are merely vice dens is too simplistic. Both the taxi-dance girls and their clients reveal a wide mixture of hopes, aspirations and incentives.

Suggested answers for Activity 6.3

1 Research questions might include: (a) What is the attitude of customers towards the new system? (b) What is the attitude of staff to the system? Does the system work – are customers able to understand and use it?

2 Data collection methods could include covert observation of the customers as they arrive to see how easily they manage to use the new system. Later, a selected sample of customers could be interviewed as they left the building to ascertain their views on the system. The views of staff could be tapped through a small-scale survey using a structured questionnaire (perhaps distributed in the next issue of the company newsletter).

Suggested answers for Activity 6.4

1 The source of measurement would include the number of orders filled to specific timescales, levels of customer satisfaction, the scale of print runs and the levels of employee satisfaction.

2. Independent variables include the new team structures, but you would need to look out for other extraneous variables that might confound the results (for example, do some teams contain more experienced workers?). Since the project is looking at the impact of different combinations of workers (compared to the old one) then sub-cases would be used, comprising each of the new team structures. One sub-group could comprise the old structure which could then act as a control to see if the more collaborative team approach was, indeed, more effective.

Suggested answers for Activity 6.5

The new retail park is acting as an independent variable on its environment, within which dependent variables include urban degeneration, traffic congestion and crime. One of the challenges here is to measure the impact of the retail park itself, since there are likely to be many other independent variables at work. Taking just traffic as an example, car ownership tends to rise over time, so will add to traffic congestion.

Suggested answers for Activity 6.7

1 The theoretical underpinning of the study revolves around the literature on management–worker relationships in Japanese transplant companies.
2 Data collection sources include secondary sources (previous studies), interviews with 10 per cent of company managers, some key informants in the locality, documentary evidence on company policies, plus observational data.
3 The protocols used for data collection are illustrated in the template at Table 6.4.
4 The analytical method comprises a form of explanation building.
5 The original hypothesis could be accepted on the basis of the results.

7

Designing Evaluations

Chapter objectives

After reading this chapter you will be able to:

- **Describe the purposes of evaluations.**
- **Distinguish between the different schools of evaluation.**
- **Identify suitable data collection sources.**
- **Design valid and reliable evaluation tools.**
- **Produce readable and informative evaluation reports.**
- **Adhere to ethical principles in conducting evaluations.**

Often surveys (Chapter 5) can be used to evaluate public perceptions of a product or service. Equally, a case study approach (Chapter 6) can be adopted, which consists of the evaluation of, say, a new factory system or process. Evaluation involves the systematic collection of data about the characteristics of a programme, product, policy or service. As part of this process, evaluation will often explore what needs to be changed, the procedures that are most likely to bring about this change, and whether there is evidence that change has occurred (Warr et al., 1970). Indeed, as Clarke (1999) points out, while the purpose of basic research is to discover new knowledge, evaluation research studies show how existing knowledge is used to inform and guide practical action. A significant amount of evaluation research revolves around training or professional development programmes, and some of the chapter will focus on this area.

Interest in the process of evaluation can be traced back to the 1970s and was strongly influenced by the work of Donald Kirkpatrick, who focused on the evaluation of programmes. The emphasis was often on the accuracy, or otherwise, of evaluation measuring techniques, and was strongly positivist in orientation (Lincoln, 1985). In recent years, with the expansion of action learning, work-related learning and self-development programmes, learning is now seen as arising *within* and *through* the work situation rather than just through formal programmes. Hence, for evaluation, the focus has shifted to a certain extent away from measurement and towards issues of *what* is evaluated, *why* and *for whom*. This includes issues around subjectivity and the ethics of evaluation.

It has been suggested by Campbell (1997) that the process of evaluation suffers from a lack of accurate and complete information, bad information or untimely information, that is, a lack of information when it is really needed. In this chapter, then, we will look at different sources for collecting data for evaluation, and the design of valid and reliable tools for use in the field. We will also look at ways of enhancing the quality and accuracy of evaluation studies and therefore the chances of them being accepted by their sponsors – so that the effort of planning and implementing an evaluation study produces positive outcomes.

THE FOCUS OF EVALUATION

In his original, seminal work, Kirkpatrick (1959) made recommendations for evaluation that have laid the basis for thinking about the subject ever since. He argues that, in essence, the evaluation of training programmes should concentrate on four levels:

- *Level 1, Reaction:* evaluating the reactions of trainees to the programme (usually by the use of a questionnaire).
- *Level 2, Learning:* measuring the knowledge, skills and attitudes that result from the programme and which were specified as training objectives.
- *Level 3, Behaviour:* measuring aspects of improved job performance that are related to the training objectives.
- *Level, 4 Results:* relating the results of the training to organizational objectives and other criteria of effectiveness.

Unfortunately, as Bramley and Kitson (1994) suggest, in the UK and USA over 80 per cent of training is only evaluated at Level 1, with participants commenting on how much they enjoyed or thought they benefited from the programme. This information is gathered through the issue of evaluation forms or, in modern jargon, 'happiness sheets'.

At Level 2, Rowe (1995) distinguishes between three levels of work-related outputs:

- Knowledge (understanding of a subject or skill).
- Skill (the practice of the skill itself).
- Competence (showing one's ability in applying a skill).

As Rowe points out, competence often means 'the minimal standard required', whereas in many work situations what is needed is *excellence* in performance. Also, many highly competent teams will include incompetent individuals. Perhaps, then, it is the competence of teams that we should be evaluating.

Bramley and Kitson (1994) caution that the problems of evaluating at Levels 3 and 4 are not well understood. Measuring changes in job performance,

Behaviours expected of, and benefits to, trainees
Improved and new skills, leading to:
• Improved job prospects
• Higher earnings
• Access to more interesting jobs
• Improved job satisfaction
Behaviours expected of, and benefits to, supervisors and line managers
Improved and new skills, leading to:
• Increased output
• Higher value of output
• Greater flexibility and innovativeness
• Likelihood of staying longer
• Less likelihood of sickness/stress
• Less likelihood of absence
• Less need to supervise
• Increased safety
Benefits to customers
• Better quality work
• Less need to return work
• More 'on time' deliveries

FIGURE 7.1 COST–BENEFIT ANALYSIS OF A PROPOSED TRAINING EVENT
(ADAPTED FROM BRAMLEY AND KITSON, 1994)

for example, is problematic, partly because of the amount of work involved in designing measurement criteria. They proceed, however, to offer some solutions. As Figure 7.1 shows, cost–benefit analysis is one way of measuring the benefits emerging from a programme, described as a list of performance indicators.

Activity 7.1

Taking Figure 7.1, think of ways of measuring some of the performance indicators listed. What sort of data should be collected? Are some indicators easier to measure than others?

Suggested answers are provided at the end of the chapter.

Another way of evaluating the effectiveness of a programme is through impact analysis. Here, all stakeholders get together before the start of the programme and discuss its objectives and the behaviours that are likely to change as a result. Through a snowballing process, each participant is asked to write down the three results they see as most important. These are pinned to a noticeboard, then reorganized into clusters or themes. Each cluster is then given a title, and stakeholders asked to award ten points across the clusters so that a ranking of clusters is achieved. Having done this, enabling and inhibiting factors are discussed to create a force-field analysis. Finally, stakeholders discuss how the purposes of the programme can be evaluated. The following Case Study provides yet another approach to programme evaluation, and one that is widely used in business and organizational contexts.

Case Study 7.1   Programme evaluation through force-field analysis

A hospital senior management team has planned a programme of workshops spread over 12 months, the purpose of which will be to instigate major organizational change. Before this can happen, the programme itself must be evaluated. If this proves successful, then the change programme will be cascaded down through the entire organization.

To prepare for the evaluation, the participants carry out a snowballing process which crystallizes sets of enabling and inhibiting factors that may influence the programme's likely impact on the rest of the organization. The participant evaluators (and programme planners) convene an *impact workshop* during which they come up with four factors that are likely to restrain the spread and success of the programme and four factors that are driving for its full implementation. As Figure 7.2 shows, leadership is seen as both a restraining *and* a driving force, that is, there are groups of managers in favour of change and those who oppose it.

Use of the force-field analysis process and diagram allow the participants to debate and analyse the various strengths of the restraining and driving forces. As a result, the budget for the change management programme is re-examined (evaluated) to see if it is sufficiently large. The impact workshop is reconvened after three months and the on-going programme evaluated against the driving and restraining forces that have been anticipated to see what remedial action needs taking.

(Continued)

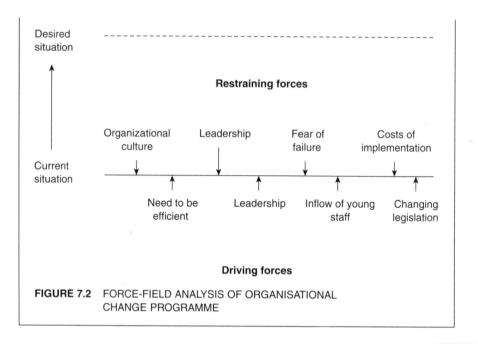

FIGURE 7.2 FORCE-FIELD ANALYSIS OF ORGANISATIONAL
CHANGE PROGRAMME

Activity 7.2

Take a programme or change process with which you are familiar and conduct a force-field analysis on it. This works better if you are able to conduct the evaluation with colleagues who are also familiar with the programme/process. How useful is force-field analysis as an evaluation method?

An increasingly popular focus of evaluation is through the Total Quality Management (TQM) process, the European model of which is set out in Figure 7.3. As Bramley and Kitson explain, each of these nine elements can be analysed in terms of an organization's progress towards TQM. Hence, leadership is defined as 'How the executive team and all other managers inspire and drive total quality as the organization's fundamental process for continuous improvement' (Bramley and Kitson, 1994: 14). Since the focus of evaluation is results, this is at Level 4 of Kirkpatrick's (1959) model.

Focusing on outputs, however, may cause us to miss other important features that deserve evaluation. Easterby-Smith (1994), for example, argues that it is virtually impossible to understand a programme without evaluating the *context* in which it takes place. This might include why the programme was sponsored or devised in the first place (and any differences between overt and hidden agendas), and the different aims and objectives of the various stakeholders. Another focus of evaluation could include *administration*. This includes the processes that occur before the training (for example, nomination for the training, selection of participants)

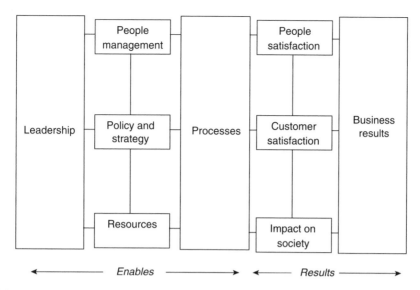

FIGURE 7.3 THE EUROPEAN TQM MODEL (BRAMLEY AND KITSON, 1994)

and what happens once the training is complete (such as follow-up activities). The selection of candidates is often an illuminating place to start. They may find themselves on a programme because they have been identified as a 'high flier', but alternatively it may be because they have been underperforming on the job, and need help.

Evaluation schemes that concentrate narrowly on inputs and outputs of programmes are in danger of missing vital, often illuminating information on *processes*. Process evaluation may involve merely observing what is occurring and keeping a narrative record of events. But it may go further than this, trying to understand the programme or event from the perspective of participants. Another element of process evaluation might be to focus on interactions between facilitators and participants or between participants themselves. Process evaluation may not only describe events, but seek to *interpret* what is happening. Table 7.1 provides an overview of all the many different types of evaluation, some of which we have mentioned above.

Two of the evaluation types in Table 7.1, formative and summative, have a long pedigree. Scriven (1967) uses these terms to describe educational curricula, and the terms have been widely used in an educational context ever since. Formative evaluation is undertaken to provide feedback to people who are trying to improve something. It is often relatively informal, with the evaluator working alongside practitioners to identify the strengths and weaknesses of a programme or intervention. In contrast, summative evaluation aims to determine the overall effectiveness of a programme or project, and to provide a judgement on whether it should continue to run. Summative evaluation is usually more formal in character, with the evaluator operating in a more independent role. In formative evaluation,

TABLE 7.1   TYPES OF EVALUATION AND THEIR DEFINING QUESTION OR
APPROACH

Focus or type of evaluation	Key questions or approach
Accreditation (validation) focus	Does the programme meet minimum standards for accreditation (validation)?
Comparative focus	How do two or more programmes rank or compare on specific indicators, outcomes or criteria?
Compliance focus	Are rules and regulations followed?
Context focus	What is the social, economic, political and cultural environment within which the programme operates?
Cost–benefit analysis	What is the relationship between programme costs and programme benefits (outcomes) expressed in monetary terms?
Criterion-focused evaluation	By what criteria (quality, costs, client satisfaction) should the programme be evaluated?
Decision focus	What information is needed to inform specific future decisions?
Descriptive focus	What happens in the programme? What can be observed?
Effectiveness focus	To what extent is the programme effective in attaining its goals? How can the programme be more effective?
Efficiency focus	Can inputs be reduced and the same level of output be maintained? Can outputs be increased with no increase in inputs?
Formative evaluation	How can the programme be improved (during its planning and delivery phases)?
Goal-based focus	To what extent have the programme goals been attained?
Impact focus	What are the direct and indirect impacts on participants, the organization, the community?
Input focus	What resources (money, staff, facilities, technology, etc.) are available and/or necessary?
Knowledge focus	What can be learned from this programme's experiences and results to inform future efforts?
Longitudinal focus	What happens to the programme and to participants over time?
Needs assessment	What do clients need and how can these needs be met?
Norm referenced approach	How does this programme population compare to some specific norm or reference groups on selected variables?
Outcomes evaluation	To what extent are desired clients/participant outcomes being attained? What are the effects of the programme on clients or participants?

(Continued)

TABLE 7.1 *(Continued)*

Focus or type of evaluation	Key questions or approach
Process focus	What do participants experience on the programme? How can these processes be improved?
Quality assurance	Are minimum standards (of teaching/training/health care, etc.) being provided? How can quality be monitored and demonstrated?
Summative evaluation	What is the overall merit or worth of the programme? Should it be modified? Should it be continued?

Source: Adapted from Patton, 1984

feedback to practitioners may be written or provided through discussions, but in summative evaluation feedback is usually in the form of a formal, written report to the commissioning body.

Activity 7.3

Take a look at the various types of evaluation in Table 7.1. Which of these would you consider selecting for your own evaluation projects? Can several approaches be combined at the same time?

Clearly, these different approaches to evaluation stem from differences of opinion as to what evaluation is for. Such differences can be classified into schools of evaluation, to which we now turn.

SCHOOLS OF EVALUATION

Easterby-Smith (1994) categorizes the various approaches to evaluation into four schools of thought: experimental, systems, illuminative and goal-free. To these we can add: decision making, goal-based, professional review and interventionist (see Figure 7.4). It is worth noting the views of Ballantine et al. (2000) that the philosophy underlying an evaluation has a great influence on how it is conducted, the tools used and also its goals. So, evaluations that focus on technical issues (such as computer information systems) are likely to be summative and formal in approach, regarding people as automata, or mere cogs in a process (see experimental and systems evaluation). In contrast, the more moral approach to evaluation is likely to be more formative and human-centred (see illuminative and goal-free evaluation). Clearly, implicit in some of these approaches are some of the ontological and epistemological assumptions discussed in Chapter 2.

The role of the evaluator is likely to be quite different according to which type of evaluation process is being followed. For example, in more formal, 'scientific' approaches, the evaluator may often be an independent and detached 'outsider' providing feedback to a commissioning body. In contructivist or more

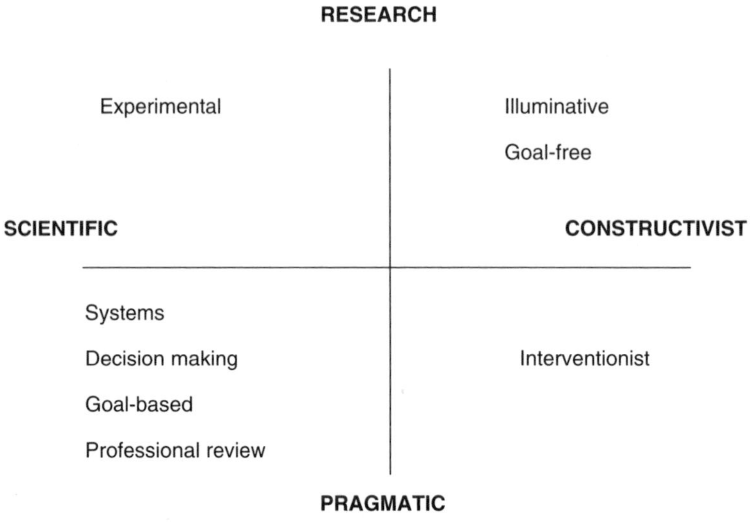

RESEARCH

Experimental	Illuminative
	Goal-free

SCIENTIFIC   **CONSTRUCTIVIST**

Systems	
Decision making	Interventionist
Goal-based	
Professional review	

PRAGMATIC

FIGURE 7.4   MODEL OF SCHOOLS OF THOUGHT IN EVALUATION
(ADAPTED FROM EASTERBY-SMITH, 1994)

naturalistic approaches, the evaluator may work quite closely with practitioners in a more collaborative, participatory style, acting not only as an evaluator but as a facilitator of change. The evaluator is expected to enter the evaluation setting free of predetermined views, and hence is unlikely to start with a particular research design or set of research questions. These emerge as part of the process of inquiry. Evaluators approach the research context with an open mind.

Experimental evaluation

Experimental evaluation seeks to demonstrate that any observed change in behaviour or outcomes can be attributed to the intervention (for example, the training or development provided). There is an emphasis on research design, and quantitative measurement, and sometimes the use of control groups and treatment groups – just as we would expect to see in any, typical, experimental approach. Clarke (1999) posits the example of a training programme for the unemployed. An evaluator may attempt to measure the causal effect of the programme by comparing the future employment records of those who participated in the programme with unemployed adults living either in the area where no training is provided, or residing in the same area but receiving no training.

Easterby–Smith (1994), however, cautions that there are a number of reasons why experimental evaluation may have limited applications. For example, if statistical techniques are going to be applied, sample sizes must be sufficiently large. If control groups are used, they must be properly matched to the experimental group; even when associations between variables can be identified, there is still the problem of showing causality, that is, that changes in one variable led

TABLE 7.2 AN EVALUATION SCHEMA BASED ON THE SYSTEMS APPROACH

Part 1 Plan the evaluation
1.1 Determine evaluation requirements
1.2 Specify evaluation purposes and objectives
1.3 Identify sources of information
1.4 Prepare an evaluation schedule with stakeholder involvement

Part 2 Collect and interpret information/data
2.1 Prepare and pilot test instrument(s)
2.2 Administer instrument(s)
2.3 Collect and tally data

Part 3 Prepare recommendations and an action plan
3.1 Formulate recommendations
3.2 Draw up a plan for corrective action
3.3 Write a report

Source: Campbell, 1997, adapted from L'Angella

to changes in the other. Clarke (1999) also argues that experimental evaluation faces all the kinds of problems that typify experimental research in general. For example, there may be differential attrition rates between the experimental and control groups, meaning that the two groups are no longer equivalent. Furthermore, the research may actually serve to create inequalities between the two groups, since one group receives the treatment and the other does not. This can work in unexpected ways. For example, if the control group learns that it *is* a control, members may be tempted to perform better than the experimental group; conversely, they may feel deprived and resentful and their performance may deteriorate.

Systems evaluation

In the *systems* approach, there is emphasis on specifying the objectives of the evaluation, with identifying outcomes, and on providing feedback on these outcomes to those providing the training. An example of the systems approach process is provided by Campbell (1997), who describes a schema for conducting an evaluation (see Table 7.2).

A typical example of systems evaluation would be where evaluators are brought in to investigate the effectiveness of a new financial accounting system. Objectives might be discussed with stakeholders and defined as:

- How robust is the system – does it 'crash'?
- Does its functionality match the original specifications?
- How 'user-friendly' is the system, and what are its implications for staff development and training?

A structured evaluation schedule is then drawn up containing questions matched against design specifications. An interview schedule is also designed so that issues can be explored with those who work on the system. Once the data have been collected, they are analysed and a formal report prepared containing recommendations for change.

One of the criticisms of the systems approach is that it represents rather a mechanistic view of the world that fails to recognize that objectives, for example, can never be neutral. Critics of the approach would point out that objectives tend to be selected by one particular social group (for example, often senior managers) and reflect the vested interests of such groups. A systems approach to evaluation may also fail to pick up the subtleties and complexities of both the products and processes of training or systems because it does not recognize that such complexities exist.

Goal-based evaluation

Like systems evaluation, goal-based evaluation is focused on the achievement of pragmatic outcomes. Here, however, the emphasis is not so much on designing systems to measure outcomes, but on identifying any discrepancies between planned and actual goals. This evaluation approach has been extensively used by educationalists from the behavioural school, who believe that the outcomes of programmes should be expressed in behavioural terms (for example, 'the learner should be able to *demonstrate* the ability to plan a project'). This does, however, raise questions about the extent to which what is observed in terms of human behaviours infers what people are actually thinking. It also assumes that the stated goals of a programme against which outcomes are to be evaluated can be accepted at face value. Yet people may hold tacit goals that they choose not to articulate or are not consciously aware of. Furthermore, there are issues of democracy and power relationships: who selects the goals that are to be evaluated? Whose interests do they represent?

Decision making evaluation

The decision making approach suggests that evaluation should be structured by the decisions that need to be made – often by top decision makers or managers. This resolves one of the evaluator's dilemmas of not always knowing at whom the evaluation should be directed (House, 1980). A drawback is that it can often ignore other potentially interested parties and stakeholders, although this can be overcome to some extent by gathering evaluative data from groups outside the original sponsors of the evaluation. As an evaluation approach it makes extensive use of survey methodology, often using tools such as questionnaires and interviews.

Professional review: validation and accreditation

Many professional associations for people such as lawyers, accountants, doctors, social workers, consultants and human resource managers set professional standards and then assess and accredit individual members of the profession against these standards. Indeed, possession of the prerequisite accreditation is often the passport required for entry into the profession. If professional training and assessment are delivered by organizations (such as institutions of higher education) external to the professional association itself, then the association is likely to set in motion evaluation (validation) processes to assure the quality of the training and professional development programmes.

In many countries, validation is seen as an essential quality assurance process to ensure appropriate standards for courses delivered by colleges and universities. In the UK, for example, the Quality Assurance Agency for Higher Education sets out a code of practice for the approval, monitoring and review of programmes (QAA, 2000). Hence, higher education institutions are charged with the task of ensuring that programmes are compatible with the goals and mission of the institution and with its academic planning and resources. In the course of the approval (validation) process, institutions are asked to give consideration to:

- The design principles underpinning the programme.
- The definition and appropriateness of standards in accordance with the level and title of the award.
- The resources needed and available to support the programme.
- Anticipated demand for the programme.
- Monitoring and review arrangements.
- The length of time for which approval is granted (which will normally be between one and five years).
- The contents of the programme specifications.

On-going monitoring will normally be undertaken by the department delivering the programme and will include the use of student feedback (often through evaluation forms), student progress information, reports from accrediting or other external bodies and examiners' reports (an important form of external evaluation of assessment standards).

Illuminative evaluation

Illuminative evaluation takes a much more flexible and open-ended approach. Rather than focus on measurement, it seeks the views of participants, recognizing that there are 'multiple perspectives' on any matter under scrutiny. So illuminative evaluation will seek to promote communal awareness about a programme, rather than aiming to achieve pre-specified outcomes, results and recommendations. In terms of methodology, it is often associated with the case study approach we discussed in Chapter 6 and will tend to use qualitative methods such as in-depth interviews and direct observations of programme activities.

A danger of using illuminative evaluation, apart from the time and costs involved, is that clients and sponsors may want more than just 'illumination', but rather results that can lead to action. These do not always emerge from approaches of this kind. Furthermore, as with the case study approach in general, the results may be heavily influenced by the subjective views of the evaluator. As House (1980) warns, illuminative evaluation faces the difficulty of proving its authenticity and confidence in its outcomes.

Goal-free evaluation

Goal-free evaluation suggests that evaluations should totally ignore the formal objectives of a programme, since these may fail to reflect what is actually happening. Indeed, according to Scriven (1973), knowing the goals of a programme will bias the evaluator. The evaluation, then, should aim to look for unanticipated outcomes and, above all, processes. So this may mean observing pre-course planning meetings, mixing with participants socially and discussing the training event with them afterwards. In terms of research paradigms, goal-free evaluation may typify a constructivist approach, exploring how participants make sense of their experiences. Ballantine et al. (2000) support this approach, arguing that evaluation should look less at financial measures, and more at subjective views where personal judgements are made explicit. The results of this approach to evaluation may reveal illuminating insights but may not always produce results that can easily be implemented. There are also the dangers of the objectivity of evaluations being compromised by evaluators becoming too involved in events.

Interventionist evaluation and action research

This encompasses a number of different approaches, but here we will focus on two of the most widely used. In contrast to experimental evaluation that uses predefined objectives and measuring instruments, *responsive* evaluation concentrates on a programme's activities rather than its planned intentions, and explores the different stakeholder perspectives involved. Responsive evaluation, as the name implies, is more likely to be adaptive as the needs and circumstances around a programme change. Rather than act in a detached capacity, responsive evaluation favours the evaluator in a more involved, interventionist mode, often working in close collaboration with programme staff and participants.

Another approach to interventionist evaluation is *utilization focused* evaluation. Here, the stress is on the importance of identifying the motives of key decision makers before deciding on what types of information need to be collected. So evaluators must discuss with stakeholders both before, during and after the programme what it is that they need to know and the ends to which the emerging data may be put. This has much in common with action research (see Chapter 15), in which practitioners set out to solve problems through planning, implementing and evaluating change processes and strategies.

Both approaches have in common a commitment to achieve a direct impact on a programme and those involved in it. One problem with interventionist evaluation is that it might become too adaptive to changing situations, with evaluators becoming too involved with clients to maintain detachment and objectivity.

DATA COLLECTION SOURCES

There are many channels available for collecting data, and the type of medium used will often depend on the objectives of the evaluation. Easterby-Smith (1994) suggests that there are three kinds of medium available, all of which are discussed in detail in other parts of this book. The media comprise: the use of *informants,* where data are collected through, for example, questionnaires (Chapter 8); direct *observations* by the evaluator of what is taking place (Chapter 10); and accumulated *records* of what has taken place in the past (Chapter 11). In this section, then, we will only look at some ideas that are specific to the evaluation process.

Informants

Easterby-Smith (1994) classifies informants into four categories: direct participants, observers, controls and stakeholders.

* *Direct informants* are the programme delegates and the tutors or facilitators. Depending on the extent of their involvement, it might also include programme sponsors or the colleagues of programme participants.
* *Observers* may include course participants, if they are able to become sufficiently emotionally detached to be able to comment on the outcomes and processes objectively. The views of managers and sponsors can be useful in commenting on the effectiveness of a programme in terms of its impact on the subsequent work performance of learners.
* *Controls* are identical to the people in the experimental group, except that they do not receive the intervention. Using this approach, it is possible, in principle, to measure the effectiveness of a training or development programme. As we saw in Chapter 4, however, it is often difficult to find two groups that can be matched in this way and also difficult to control for the effects of extraneous variables.
* *Stakeholders* are those who do not have direct contact with a programme but have a legitimate interest in it none the less. Top managers, for example, may be very interested in the success of a sponsored MBA programme because it is hoped that some 'high fliers' will emerge that are vital for medium-term succession-planning at executive level.

Observations

Evaluating a training session or project by observing it may appear not only a perfectly sensible but also a fairly unproblematic approach. As we will see in Chapter 10, however, there are different ways of observing, including overt and covert observation and evaluating a programme or project by joining it as a participant or from the outside as a non-participant. Covert observation whether as a participant or looking in from the outside may reveal information that would not emerge if participants knew they were under scrutiny. Of course, the fact that they are being observed secretly raises ethical issues that require addressing.

Whichever approach is adopted, it is simply not possible to observe everything that occurs. Those that advocate using a video recorder to solve this problem forget that even this medium is selective in what it can 'see'. Of course, observing, taking notes and using video and audio media all help to build data sets that can provide a more comprehensive (reliable) picture for subsequent analysis. For practical purposes, it may be necessary to be selective in collecting data, which may involve a number of approaches including:

- *Time sampling*. Here 'snapshot' observations are made over a period of time. For example, as part of a job evaluation study a shop floor packer could be observed every 20 minutes against the categories: walking, packing, discussing, requesting, taking instructions, absent.
- *Incident sampling*, involves looking for critical incidents that might have an important impact on what is being evaluated. For example, a training programme may involve arguments and hostility between participants that could be documented.
- *People sampling,* involves observing a sample of people in the belief that the sample selected is representative of the population from which it is drawn. So, in evaluating the impact of a new bonus scheme, a number of people who had recently received bonuses would be observed to evaluate whether this had had any impact on their behaviour or performance.
- *Analytical categories sampling* involves looking for, and recording, instances of specific behaviours or verbal interchanges. A classic example of this is the work of Bales (1950), who observed interactions amongst groups to determine broad categories of group behaviour comprising: asking questions, attempted answers to these questions, followed by either positive or negative reactions.

Methods of recording the data collected using these techniques are examined in detail in Chapter 10.

Accumulated records

While the use of informants and observations requires the collection of data in the field, it is possible to evaluate programmes on the basis of data that were collected in the past. Examples of typical sources include:

- Programme or project plans and specifications.
- Communications between those responsible for the commissioning, planning or delivery processes.
- Comments written on flipcharts.
- E-mails between participants.

Records, for example, might also show that it is taking participants longer than in the past to achieve a particular programme objective – based on this fact, personnel records might be checked to see if recruitment standards were being observed (Campbell, 1997). Sometimes, it is the lack of recorded information that might be significant – for example, the fact that few participants completed the pre-course activities that were vital to the programme's success. Accumulated records are an example of unobtrusive measures that are discussed in more detail on Chapter 11. Having identified appropriate sources, the next step is actually to collect the data.

DATA COLLECTION TOOLS

There are a wide variety of tools available for collecting evaluation data, some of the commonest techniques including questionnaires and interview schedules. Since these are discussed in considerable depth in Chapters 8 and 9 respectively, they will be discussed only briefly here. As in any type of questionnaire, the content must be designed to be both valid and reliable. In Figure 7.5, for example, 18 questions are asked about a training programme – probably a sufficient number to produce a reliable estimate of people's opinions. Note that Campbell (1997) calls this not a questionnaire but an opinnionnaire, since it is eliciting participants' opinions about a training programme.

It is worth, however, noting the concern of Campbell (1997), who warns against too much reliance being placed on the use of numerical ratings and statistical calculations in evaluation questionnaires. He cautions that the data on the feelings and opinions collected remain subjective.

Assessment tests

It is important to differentiate between assessment and evaluation. Put simply, we evaluate products, policies, programmes, etc., but we assess people. So what is the connection between evaluation and assessment? The answer is that we can evaluate the success of a programme by assessing what people have learned from it in terms of knowledge, skills or comprehension – and above all, performance. Hence, controlling for other variables, if post-course assessments reveal that new skills and knowledge have been acquired, we can attribute this (through evaluation) to the training programme itself. Thus, the outcomes of assessment can comprise an important element of the evaluation process.

Repertory grid

The repertory grid technique is based upon the original work of Kelly (1955), who argued that people's behaviour is influenced by the way in which they classify what is going on around them. People construe and interpret events, noting features of a series of events that characterize some and are particularly uncharacteristic of others. In doing this, they erect constructs involving similarity and contrast. So, if someone is construed as having leadership qualities, this would imply

Directions: Please read the following 13 statements and indicate your level of disagreement or agreement by making a check mark in the column that corresponds to your opinion. Add a written comment to support your opinion on the line provided below each statement.

Statements	Strongly disagree	Disagree	Agree	Strongly agree
1 Learning objectives were adequately discussed at the beginning of sessions	❑	❑	❑	❑
Comment				
2 Including learning objectives on instructional materials enhanced learning	❑	❑	❑	❑
Comment				
3 The instruction included all that was necessary to perform	❑	❑	❑	❑
Comment				
4 Sufficient opportunities were provided to practise the skills taught	❑	❑	❑	❑
Comment				
5 The instructor encouraged trainee involvement	❑	❑	❑	❑
Comment				
6 The instructor was available for help when needed	❑	❑	❑	❑
Comment				
7 The instructional methods used (lecture-discussion, demonstration, etc.) helped me learn	❑	❑	❑	❑
Comment				
8 The audio-visual media used (transparencies, video tapes, etc.) and training aids used helped me understand	❑	❑	❑	❑
Comment				

(Continued)

9 The instructional materials used (books, modules, job performance aids, instruction sheets, etc.) helped me learn	❑	❑	❑	❑

Comment

---

10 The criterion-referenced performance tests helped me become proficient	❑	❑	❑	❑

Comment

---

11 The training environment enhanced my motivation and helped me learn	❑	❑	❑	❑

Comment

---

12 All the necessary tools and equipment were available	❑	❑	❑	❑

Comment

---

13 The facilities in which training took place supported my learning	❑	❑	❑	❑

Comment

Directions: Please write your answer to items 14 to 18 on the lines provided

14   What subject/topics should be added?

---

15   What subjects/topics should be deleted?

---

16   What part of the training was most helpful?

---

17   What part of the training was least helpful?

---

18   What changes do you recommend for the future?

Your feedback will remain confidential and your assistance is greatly appreciated.

THANK YOU.

FIGURE 7.5   SAMPLE OPINIONNAIRE (ADAPTED FROM CAMPBELL, 1997)

they shared similar characteristics to other people seen to have this quality *and* contrast with characteristics shown by people with no leadership ability. But this does not imply that the person identified as a leader would be seen in this light by everyone. Constructs are personal, with different individuals giving different interpretations of events or characteristics. They are also hierarchical, with some constructs seen as more important than others. In particular, *core* constructs allow an individual to maintain their sense of identity and continuing existence, while *peripheral* constructs can be altered without any change in core structures. Some (permeable) constructs may change on the basis of new evidence, but other constructs (impermeable) prove more resistant to change. Hence, a technique is used, the repertory grid, to elicit these constructs for analysis and interpretation. Since the result of using this technique is the production of quantitative data, repertory grids have proved popular for evaluating the outputs from training programmes in terms of people's views, behaviours or perceptions.

Using an example (Figure 7.6), let us say we want to evaluate an organization's appraisal system through the perspectives of an employee. Designing a questionnaire or interview schedule might bias the evaluation towards the issues and concerns of the evaluator. Using personal construct theory, however, this should not occur. The employee is asked to identify a set of events connected to her recent appraisal that were of particular significance to her (Elements in Figure 7.6). She is asked to identify what it was about these elements (constructs) that had been of particular significance to her. Hence, for example, she decided that she had found some elements motivating whilst others were demotivating. She then uses the grid to allocate a score between 1 and 4 against each of her constructs for each of the elements.

Just glancing at Figure 7.6 reveals some quite startling results. We can see that the appraisee found nearly all aspects of the appraisal process either fairly or completely demotivating. The reasons for this are not hard to identify. While she found the preparation of the documentation for the appraisal very helpful (perhaps in focusing her thoughts and identifying her achievements) if time-consuming, the actual appraisal itself obviously did not go well. She found the reviewing of progress and the setting of new work objectives not at all helpful – indeed, destructive. Feelings rather than analysis emerged – and probably very negative feelings at that.

This is a relatively simple example of a repertory grid, with some detailed and complex examples benefiting from the use of especially designed computer software programs. Nevertheless, it serves to illustrate the power of allowing someone to identify their own constructs and interpretation of events. From an evaluation perspective, it allows us to identify which aspects of the appraisal programme may need review and overhaul – in this case, not the documentation, but the interaction dynamics between appraiser and appraisee. Perhaps we should continue the evaluation by looking at the appraiser's personnel records – is he sufficiently trained?

Critical incidents

A critical incident is something that produces an emotional response (whether positive or negative) in a person (Gray et al., 2000). As an evaluation tool, this is a qualitative approach that asks participants to comment on such events, often through the use of a log or diary (see next). There may be a pact between evaluators

CONSTRUCTS							Significant ELEMENTS of the appraisal			
							Pre-appraisal planning	Appraisal: reviewing progress	Appraisal: agreeing objectives	Post-appraisal: documenting/signing
							1	2	3	4
	Motivating	1	2	3	4	Demotivating	3	3	4	3
	Helpful	1	2	3	4	Unhelpful	1	3	3	3
	Quick	1	2	3	4	Time-consuming	4	1	3	1
	Encouraged analysis	1	2	3	4	Encouraged feeling	2	4	4	3
	Creative	1	2	3	4	Destructive	1	3	4	3

FIGURE 7.6 REPERTORY GRID SHOWING AN INDIVIDUAL'S CONSTRUCTS OF AN APPRAISAL

and participants before the start of the evaluation process whereby such diaries are acknowledged to be confidential, with participants revealing and commenting on only those critical incidents they are willing to divulge.

The analysis of critical incidents may also be useful in the workplace itself. Here the effectiveness of a training or development programme is evaluated (say, by managers or supervisors) when they see how staff respond to critical incidents following a training programme.

Learning logs

We have already seen how logs or diaries can be used to keep a note of critical incidents. But they can also be used by participants to keep a note of any events, incidents, thoughts, learning outcomes or unanticipated results of a programme. This can often provide a rich source of illuminative data for evaluation – providing that participants are willing to divulge the contents of such logs.

QUALITY ISSUES IN EVALUATION

One of the challenges of evaluations is that there are no precise rules on how to plan and implement them. Judgement is called for. As Patton (1984) warns, an inevitable trade-off will be faced between gathering as much data as possible (and then face the costs of doing so) or reducing costs, time and hence data, but then reducing confidence in the evaluation findings. Looking at a problem in depth may produce detailed results but leave other problems unanswered; conversely, examining a range of problems might provide insufficient depth to be able to arrive at any sensible conclusions. So, especially at the planning stage, an evaluator needs to decide on what aspects of a programme should be evaluated, and whether all the outcomes require scrutiny or only selected elements. The evaluator's role, then, may be to get stakeholders or sponsors to narrow the focus of the evaluation to a more feasible list of questions.

The quality of any evaluation process is also deeply influenced by the familiar issues of validity, reliability and objectivity. Let us look at each of these in turn, within the context of the evaluation process.

Validity

As we saw in Chapter 4, for a research instrument to be valid, it must measure what it was intended to measure. Sometimes face validity may be sufficient, that is, the extent to which an instrument *looks* as though it will measure what it is intended to measure. This, rather unscientific approach is held in low regard by measurement experts. Patton (1984), however, advises more optimistically that it may have some value. It may, for example, help managers and those responsible for implementing evaluation findings to have confidence in the evaluation instrument – and hence in the evaluation results. House (1980) suggests that goal-based evaluations often offer high levels of face validity because their objectives are made explicit to all concerned.

One of the most sought after measurements is that of predictive validity, that is, the extent to which the results of an evaluation can be used to predict events, usually the impact of a programme on participant performance. As we saw earlier, one of the weaknesses of many evaluation studies is that they tend to focus on whether participants liked, or thought they benefited from, the programme rather than measuring whether new skills or attitudes resulted.

As Patton (1990) points out, validity may be threatened when observation methods are being used and participants know that they are being observed. This is because they may behave quite differently in situations where they are not observed. This suggests that covert observation may be more valid and reliable (although ethical considerations then arise). Yet, it needs to be borne in mind that even covert observation only picks up observable behaviours and not what is in people's minds. The data, therefore, are selective. Validity may be improved by long-term observations where observers and participants get to know one another (longitudinal evaluation, see Table 7.1).

House (1980) contends that systems evaluation often tends to produce valid and reliable evidence because data are produced in a way that lends them to replication by other evaluators. Contrast this with other evaluation approaches where data can involve large elements of personal interpretation. Reay (1994) provides a useful example (Case Study 7.2) of what can, at least potentially, go wrong when the evaluation process fails to address validity issues.

Case Study 7.2 Invalid evaluation – getting it wrong on a Friday afternoon

A company training department trained workers in the goods depot to stock-take every Friday afternoon. All aspects of stock-taking were demonstrated and explained and at the end of the course there was an evaluation which gathered data on the costs of the training programme (including down time and the costs incurred in lost production when trainees were not working), the likely savings through increased productivity and an assessment of what people had actually learned. The evaluation 'proved' that the course was successful.

Then, one Friday afternoon, the depot became extremely busy and the stock-taking was not done. Next week chaos resulted as the computer systems failed to cope with out-of-date information. The result was that orders were not met and customers complained.

Why had this happened? The reason was that nobody had explained to the stock-taking employees that stock-taking was *important* on a Friday afternoon. They had simply assumed that it was something they did when they weren't busy. The evaluation had been invalid. It hadn't asked the question: 'Do these people know *why* they are performing this task?' The evaluation had failed to spot a vital missing training objective.

Source: Adapted from Reay, 1994

Activity 7.4

Using the summary of evaluation types in Table 7.1, suggest which evaluation approaches were applied in Case Study 7.2. Are there any additional ones that you think *should* have been applied?

Suggested answers are provided at the end of the chapter.

Reliability

Recalling Oppenheim (1992), for a research instrument to be reliable, it must be consistent. So to prove the reliability of an evaluation tool, we could attempt to confirm its findings by looking at other data sources. For example, say a study found that a once popular course was now receiving quite negative evaluations.

It might be prudent to look at documentation on the kinds of participants coming on the programme – they might be more experienced or senior than previous participants and not find the course of particular value or sufficiently demanding. Reliability can also be measured by giving the data to another trainer or evaluator to see if they reach similar conclusions (inter-judge reliability).

Essentially, as Patton (1990) advises, a trade-off exists between the size and significance of a programme and the amount of evaluation error that can be tolerated. In the case of a summative evaluation of, say, a major national education programme, involving large amounts of expenditure, we would want to see a robust evaluation involving reliable instruments (or at least as reliable as possible) using a large sample. In contrast, a small-scale training programme involving few people might only require a relatively informal, formative evaluation to highlight areas for improvement, reliability not being a major point of concern.

Objectivity

Concern for objectivity may be particularly strong from evaluators who believe in forms of 'scientific' or experimental evaluation and an emphasis on measurement, manipulation of variables, quantifiable outputs and distance (physical and critical) from what is being observed. But, as Patton dryly comments: 'Distance does not guarantee objectivity; it merely guarantees distance' (1990: 480). This issue, according to Patton, is not one of objectivity as such, but is about the credibility of the evaluator and the extent to which fairness and balance are addressed. This may mean abandoning any positivist notion that there is one objective 'truth' out there, and instead focusing on people's multiple perspectives and interpretations of events.

Certainly, there are dangers when those designing and delivering a programme are also those who conduct the evaluations. There may be a sense of ownership that might be difficult to overcome. Either evaluators must be aware of the danger of subjectivity and try to address it, or they could bring in external consultants to conduct the evaluation. Of course, even when all the issues of validity, reliability and objectivity have been addressed, we may end up with the 'so what?' conclusion. If evaluation results tell us that 82 per cent of respondents scored a programme as either 'excellent' or 'good' what does this really tell us? Probably not very much. As Patton (1984) suggests, the outcomes of evaluation have to be compared with something else for them to have any meaning, such as:

- The outcomes of similar programmes.
- The outcomes of the same programme delivered on a previous occasion.
- The outcomes of model programmes in the same field.
- The stated goals of the programme.
- External standards developed by professional bodies.

Hence, evaluation should be seen less as a 'snapshot', than a measurement of indicators over time.

PLANNING THE EVALUATION REPORT

Evaluation reports may have a multiplicity of potential audiences with quite different needs. Funding agencies, steering groups and managers may be interested in technical issues arising from evaluation, not least because some of these may require action. This does not mean that they need all of the report – they may prefer an executive summary – but they will expect that the technical detail is available should they need it. Programme clients may not require so much technical detail but will want to know the evaluation's findings and its impact on themselves personally. Morris et al. (1987) present a summary (Figure 7.7) of the kinds of communication methods that can be used to report evaluation findings to different groups.

Clearly, some of the formats suggested in Figure 7.7 require the production of quite formal and large-scale documents. If effective action is to result from these reports, it is important that they are properly structured, a typical example being a table of contents, an executive summary, the main body of the report and appendices. Campbell (1997) suggests the following outline, described in Figure 7.8.

Remember, you will have to write clearly and concisely for your intended audience (see Chapter 14). Make as much use of figures and tables as is feasible, as these provide accessible summaries of the data and serve to break up the text. Planning the evaluation report may include allowing time for the review (evaluation!) of the report by a colleague or a helpful member of the intended audience, so that errors, inconsistencies and misunderstandings can be eliminated.

ENHANCING THE IMPACT OF EVALUATION

Having completed an evaluation, how can you ensure that its findings lead to change or improvements? As Patton (1984) points out:

> The challenge in evaluation is getting the best possible information to the people who need it – and then *getting those people to use the information in decision-making.* (Patton, 1984: 39–40; emphasis in original)

This may not always be easy. Evaluations may be 'ritualistic', conducted so that an agency can delay having to make a decision on a difficult subject (Weiss, 1984). One, obvious, approach is to ensure that the evaluation report is of high quality and worth reading and acting on. For example, make sure that conclusions and recommendations actually fit the data and are compatible with the objectives of the evaluation study. Campbell (1997) also strongly recommends the production of action plans, providing precise details of remedial measures required and their timing.

A key factor here is making sure that these findings do not come as a shock to the programme or evaluation sponsors. People do not like surprises, particularly when money and resources have been invested in a policy, system or programme. A number of steps can be taken to improve the probability of an evaluation being accepted.

Possible communication form	Technical report	Executive summary	Technical/professional paper	Popular article	News release/press conference	Public meeting	Media appearance	Staff workshop	Brochure/poster	Memo	Personal discussions
Audience/users											
Funding agencies	•	•									•
Programme administrators	•	•	•	•	•			•		•	•
Board members, trustees		•		•							
Advisory committees	•	•	•								
Political bodies		•		•							
Community groups				•		•					
Current clients				•		•	•				
Potential clients											
Programme providers		•		•				•	•	•	•
Media					•	•					

FIGURE 7.7   COMMUNICATION METHODS FOR A VARIETY OF AUDIENCES
(ADAPTED FROM MORRIS ET AL., 1987)

- Involve sponsors in formulating the objectives and the design of the evaluation to gain their interest and commitment.
- Get commitment from senior stakeholders in advance of the evaluation that action will be taken on the basis of results.
- Consider establishing a steering group to monitor and help the evaluation project and get senior stakeholders onto the group if possible to increase its credibility.

Cover page

Typically includes a fully explanatory report title, specifies when the evaluation was conducted, when the report was prepared and who it was submitted to. It may also identify those who prepared it, reviewed and approved the report

Table of contents

Lists all headings in the report, especially the evaluation objectives and attachments/appendices, by page number

Acknowledgements

Identifies colleagues' professional contributions and provides an expression of thanks. When appropriate, the source(s) of financial support is recognized

Part 1 – Summary

Sometimes called an Executive Summary – for those who are too busy to read the full report

1.1 Introduction – background information, etc.
1.2 Purpose of the evaluation
1.3 Objectives of the evaluation
1.4 Summary of the evaluation project

    1.4.1 A brief presentation of evaluation procedures, including a summary statement on the collection as well as the analysis of information and data
    1.4.2 The conclusion(s) drawn from the information and data
    1.4.3 The recommendations made

Part 2 – Report body

2.1 Evaluation objective 1

    2.1.1 Description of evaluation activities – how the evaluation was conducted, development and validation of the instrument(s), collection of information and numerical data, etc.
    2.1.2 Responses, including tables and figures
    2.1.3 Analysis and interpretation of the information and data
    2.1.4 Conclusion(s) formed and recommendation(s) made for the objective

2.2 Evaluation of objective 2

    2.2.1 Etc.
    2.2.2 Etc.
    2.2.3 Etc.

2.3 Plan for corrective action

Part 3 - Appendices

3.1 Instrument(s) used in the evaluation, i.e., reaction form, questionnaires, etc.

3.2 Presentation of raw data (if too bulky for main report)

FIGURE 7.8 FORMAT FOR AN EVALUATION REPORT (ADAPTED FROM CAMPBELL, 1997)

- Keep sponsors informed of outputs (particularly unexpected ones) as they occur.

Consider producing several reports, one for each type of audience. Senior managers, as we have seen, may not have either the time or the inclination to read complete reports and may prefer an executive summary. But take care to ensure that different versions contain similar content and recommendations – the difference should be one of presentation. Ensure that not only managers receive the report but all other relevant stakeholders.

THE ETHICS OF EVALUATION

Ballantine et al. (2000) provide a framework of considerations to be taken into account in any attempt to mount an ethical approach to evaluation. Referring to the work of Habermas (1972), they warn that society is becoming less aware of ethical choices because these are being rationalized as either technical or economic decisions. Science is being absorbed into this discourse and presented as politically neutral and theoretically objective. According to Habermas (1972), however, knowledge always serves the vested interests of one group or another. Ballantine et al. (2000) therefore suggest five constraints (based on the work of Kettner, 1993) that can set the conditions for a 'truly moral dialogue'. These comprise:

- *The generality constraint:* participation in a discourse or discussion must be as wide as possible, and present the views of all affected interest groups.
- *The autonomous evaluation constraint:* participants must be allowed to introduce and challenge any assertions and any interests stated.
- *The role taking constraint:* participants must give equal weight to the interests of others alongside their own interests.
- *The power constraint:* a participant should not appeal to any hierarchical authority to legitimate their argument.
- *The transparency authority:* participants must openly declare their goals and intentions.

To illustrate these, Ballantine et al. (2000) present a real life example from the City of London that is summarized in Case Study 7.3.

Case Study 7.3 Short supply of ethics at the Stock Exchange

In the late 1980s and early 1990s, the London Stock Exchange invested £80 million in Taurus, a major new information systems project. The project failed and the system was never completed. Ballantine et al. (2000) suggest that this was due to a failure to engage in rational moral discourse (discussion) during its evaluation, design and development.

(Continued)

The *generality constraint* was met during the project to the extent that there were a large variety of stakeholders (the Stock Exchange itself, its stockbroking member firms both large and small, company registrars and other financial institutions). One of the problems, however, was that these stakeholders held conflicting requirements. The *autonomous evaluation constraint* played a significant part in the demise of the project because the planning process was quite well developed before participants really began to challenge its rationale and make their own case. The design team were motivated by largely technical considerations and failed to question whether the project was actually worthwhile.

There is little evidence that the *role taking constraint* was adhered to because the more powerful stakeholders (institutional investors) paid little attention to the interests of smaller parties (for example, private investors and small stockbroking firms). Indeed, the inability of different stakeholders to take the views and interests of others seriously was one of the main reasons that led to the Taurus project's collapse. The result was that rather than the creation of one seamless system, about 17 alternative systems were welded together. The *power constraint* was not met because, although the chief executive of the Stock Exchange had wanted to stop the project, it had already gained too much momentum and support from the international banks. Finally, in terms of the *transparency authority*, it is clear that not all participants' objectives were made explicit from the start.

Ballantine et al. caution that if the managers and designers involved in the project had paid more attention to a moral discourse, then the political and ethical issues at stake might have been given more consideration. The result would have been either a project that was more in line with what stakeholders wanted, or the project would have been suspended long before it was, and losses minimized.

Source: Adapted from Ballantine et al., 2000

Activity 7.5

Taking the information provided in Case Study 7.3, and using Ballantine et al.'s five constraints, describe a 'truly moral' and ethical process of collaboration and dialogue that could, in principle, have led to a more positive outcome.

Using some of the principles outlined in the discussion of constraints, above, Ballantine et al. (2000) have constructed a framework for the ethical evaluation of a programme. While they focus this on information systems, it also offers a useful guide for evaluations of any kind (see Figure 7.9). They argue that there are six, general factors that influence the choice of evaluation approach: philosophy, power, culture, management style and the kind of evaluator and resources available (see left column in Figure 7.9). As we saw earlier, different schools of evaluation (and therefore philosophical approaches) have a direct bearing on what is evaluated, the purpose of evaluation and the tools used.

So, in Figure 7.9, the left hand side of each of the ranges represents a more expert and controlling approach to evaluation, while the right hand side emphasizes

Ethical attributes Evaluation influences	Purpose of evaluation		Process of evaluation		People affected by the evaluation	
Philosophy	Summative	Formative	Positivist	Interpretivist	Automata	Human
Culture	Control	Learning	Ritualistic	Purposeful	Organiza-tional	Individual
Management style	Covert	Overt	Implicit	Explicit	Directive	Consensual
Power	Manipulative	Emancipate	Autocratic	Democratic	Dictatorial	Participative
Evaluator	Judgemental	Assist	Investigative	Collaborative	Control	Facilitate
Resources	Minimalist	Comprehen-sive	Limited	Sufficient	Constrain	Enable

FIGURE 7.9   A FRAMEWORK FOR ETHICAL EVALUATION (BALLANTINE ET AL., 2000)

participation and learning. The framework can be used to consider the amount of thought given to ethics by each of the evaluation approaches. According to Ballantine et al. (2000), the more ethical approaches are to be found at the right end of each of the ranges, because more consideration is given to the views of those on the receiving end of the evaluation process. But the authors acknowledge that there may be organizational circumstances when priorities other than ethical factors may be uppermost.

The ethical framework can be used to provide guidance on how ethics can be incorporated into the decision making process. It can also be used as a check on internal consistency, to see whether ethical approaches are consistent across all six influences.

SUMMARY

- Evaluation involves the systematic collection of data about the characteristics of a programme, product, policy or service.
- The focus of evaluation can be on trainees' reactions to a programme, how much new knowledge they have gained, how much this is transferred into better job performance and other organizational criteria.
- Like most approaches to research, evaluation involves different schools or per-spectives, ranging from experimental and quasi-experimental with an emphasis on the measurement of outcomes and quantifiable data, to illuminative perspectives with a focus on processes and the multiple perspectives of participants.
- Data can be collected from various informants and through observations, involving a wider range of stakeholders than just participants.
- Data collection tools include questionnaires, assessment tests (since an important outcome of evaluation is a measurement of what participants have actually learned), learning logs and documentation of critical incidents.
- The principles of validity, reliability and objectivity apply as much to evaluation as they do to many other aspects of research.
- The impact of evaluation is enhanced if stakeholders are kept informed of outcomes as they arise – particularly if they are going to be unwelcome or unexpected. Care should be taken to avoid redundancy of information, providing different stakeholders with different versions of evaluation reports on the basis of what they need to know.
- Evaluation that fails to take into account ethical issues will often be doomed to fail-ure. Ethical approaches include a focus on the individual needs of people rather than the goals of organizations, on making the purpose of the evaluation transparent to those being evaluated, and encouraging participation in the evaluation process.

Further reading

Patton, M.Q. (1990). *Qualitative Evaluation and Research Methods*, 2nd edn. Newbury Park, CA: Sage. Still one of the best books on qualitative methods, with a substantial section on models of evaluation.

(Continued)

Morris, L.L., Fitz-Gibbon, C.T. and Freeman, M.E. (1987) *How to Communicate Evaluation Findings.* Newbury Park, CA: Sage. No evaluation study is worth the effort if the results cannot be effectively communicated to others. This book provides practical advice on how.

Clarke, A. (1999) *Evaluation Research: An Introduction to Principles, Methods and Practice.* London: Sage. Deals with a range of evaluation paradigms, and data collection methods and provides some case studies of evaluation in the education, health care and criminal justice systems.

Suggested answers for Activity 7.1 (selected examples)

Focus or type of evaluation	Type of data collected	Ease or difficulty of measurement
Accreditation (validation)	Market research data (is the programme needed?); course structure and content; module descriptions and objectives; links to other courses; resources supplied (including staff and their qualifications), etc.	Usually a significant quantity of data have to be collected. Evaluators (validation panels) will look for accuracy and coherence of data
Compliance	Case studies of breaches of regulations; performance indicators for compliance – e.g. speed of performance, customer satisfaction rates, etc.	Data may be hidden by those organizations seeking to escape compliance. Costs of data collection may inhibit the setting up of robust systems, but in some cases systems may be required by legislation
Formative evaluation	Participant evaluation forms; tutor observation and self-reflection	How honest are the participants? How self-reflective are tutors? Are a sufficient number of indicators used?
Quality assurance	Minutes of meetings; evaluation of accuracy and completeness of staff and student handbooks; student evaluations; resources etc.	The data may not be particularly complex, but the quality assurance exercise may demand large quantities!

Suggested answers for Activity 7.4

The main evaluation approach seems to have been confined to a cost–benefit analysis. Perhaps a more prudent approach would have been to evaluate the outcomes, goals or the effectiveness of the programme. A descriptive focus might also have illuminated what was actually happening to participants when taking the course.

PART C

Data Collection Methods

8 Collecting Primary Data: Questionnaires

Chapter objectives

After reading this chapter you will be able to:

- **Plan and design valid and reliable questionnaires.**
- **Describe the processes involved in collecting primary data, including piloting.**
- **Demonstrate the skills for writing appropriate individual questions and designing questionnaires.**
- **Write appropriate documentation to accompany questionnaires.**

As an important data gathering tool, questionnaires are used as part of many of the research methodologies described in Part B of this book. Indeed, it is difficult to imagine a large-scale survey (Chapter 5), for example, without the use of a carefully constructed questionnaire. Similarly, case studies (Chapter 6) can use a combination of data gathering tools, with the use of questionnaires, sometimes in the form of an interview schedule (see Chapter 9).

Questionnaires are research tools through which people are asked to respond to the same set of questions in a predetermined order. Since questionnaires are one of the most widely used primary data gathering techniques, considerable space will be devoted here to their design and construction. Many people in the business and educational worlds have had experience in data gathering using questionnaires, but fewer are knowledgeable about how difficult it is to construct questionnaires that are valid, reliable and objective. It is thus relatively easy to produce reports and recommendations based upon the most spurious of data. Hopefully, after reading this chapter you will understand many of the pitfalls of questionnaire design so that you can avoid them.

Questionnaires should be used when they fit the objectives of the research. Hence, in a case study that involves seeking the in-depth opinions and perspectives of a small number of respondents, a highly structured questionnaire might be completely inappropriate. Here you might want to construct an interview schedule containing open-ended questions, adopting a descriptive approach. But where the audience is relatively large, and where standardized questions are needed, the questionnaire is ideal, and will allow, if this is required, an analytical approach exploring relationships between variables. Of course, in many cases questionnaires will be only one tool used in the general research effort. The research design may plan for a wide-scale survey using questionnaires, to be followed up by in-depth structured interviews or observations with a target sample, identified to be of interest by the survey.

In this chapter we will explore some of the essential principles in question-naire design including how to write appropriate questions, whether to use open or closed questions, how to sequence questions and questionnaire layout. We also look at some of the more specific principles behind designing Web or Internet ques-tionnaires, and how questionnaires of any kind should be administered.

WHY QUESTIONNAIRES?

Questionnaires are perhaps one of the most popular data gathering tools, proba-bly because they are thought by many researchers to be easy to design. This belief, as we shall see, is not necessarily supported by the evidence. As Gillham (2000) points out, the popularity of questionnaires is also probably based on some of their inherent advantages. For example:

- They are low cost in terms of both time and money. In contrast to, say, inter-views, questionnaires can be sent to hundreds or even thousands of respon-dents at relatively little cost.
- The inflow of data is quick and from many people.
- Respondents can complete the questionnaire at a time and place that suits them. Contrast this with interviews, when it can be difficult to find conve-nient times to meet the respondent.
- Data analysis of closed questions is relatively simple, and questions can be coded quickly.
- Respondents' anonymity can be assured. But Gillham (2000) rightly notes that in small-scale surveys, this can be largely nominal in character – it may not be difficult for the researcher to recognize the responses of individuals. But real anonymity can also be double-edged. If you do not know who has not responded, to whom do you send reminders?
- These is a lack of interviewer bias. There is evidence that different interviewers get different answers – because of the way in which they place different emphasis on individual words in questions and because of the different probes (additional questions) that they follow up with.

Of course, not surprisingly, using questionnaires also has its drawbacks. Unless we can make completing the questionnaire intrinsically rewarding, the response rate can be depressingly low. This is even more of a danger if questionnaires are too long. Gillham (2000) advises that questionnaires should be limited in length to four to six pages, otherwise the return rate may be adversely affected. Few people greet receiving a questionnaire with unbounded enthusiasm, particularly long ones. Most people find verbal communication easier than using the written word, yet questionnaires demand a certain level of literacy. But there is no opportunity to ask questions or clear up ambiguous or ill-conceived answers. Respondents may give flippant, inaccurate or misleading answers, but the researcher is not in a position to detect this. In contrast, the face-to-face interview might reveal underlying problems through observing body language or the verbal tones of the respondent.

Activity 8.1

Take a questionnaire that you have designed, preferably quite recently. Was it less than six sides in length? Was it well designed and easy for respondents to complete? Were the answers, in your view, honestly given? Overall, how successful was the questionnaire in eliciting the required data and how could you explain its success or failure?

DESIGNING QUESTIONNAIRES

Questionnaires reflect the designer's view of the world, no matter how objective a researcher tries to be. This is true not only for the design of individual questions, but often about the very choice of research subject. Furthermore, what we choose *not* to ask about, may just as easily reflect our world view as what we include in the questionnaire. It is important, then, that, as a researcher, you are aware of this and try, as far as possible, to be objective. Indeed, it is the values, perceptions and interests of the respondent that you should be attempting to capture, and the questionnaire should reflect this as much as possible. In this section, we will look at the design of individual questions, including open and closed questions, the sequencing of questions and questionnaire layout.

Writing individual questions

Piloting a questionnaire usually helps to eliminate or at least reduce questions that are likely to mislead. But it needs to be understood that people may read and interpret questions in quite distinct ways. It is naïve to believe that standardized questions will always receive standardized, rational, responses. Nevertheless, it helps if questions are phrased in ways that are clear, concise and unambiguous (to everyone in the sample), and free from jargon and abbreviations. While the overall content, style and structure of the questionnaire must satisfy the respondent, each individual question must stand on its own merits. Arksey and Knight (1999) provide a useful list of what to avoid when constructing individual questions.

Prejudicial language Try to avoid language that is prejudicial or contains sexist, disablist or racist stereotyping. A question that annoys, irritates or insults a respondent may affect the way they respond to questions that follow – if they decide to complete them at all! For example, the question: 'What is your marital status?' may annoy those who live with partners or who are not living in a heterosexual relationship (assuming that the society allows only heterosexual marriages).

Imprecision Avoid vague phrases such as 'average', 'regularly' and 'a great deal' since they are likely to be interpreted in different ways by different respondents.

Leading questions These suggest a possible answer and hence promote bias. Questions such as 'Why do you think the organization has been successful in the past three years' are leading because they are making an assumption with which the respondent may not necessarily agree.

Double questions These should be avoided because they are impossible to answer. For example, if the question: 'Do you like chocolate and strawberry ice-cream?' receives a reply of 'Yes' you would be unclear as to whether this relates to both of the ice-cream flavours or just one of them.

Assumptive questions Avoid questions that make assumptions about people's beliefs or behaviours. For example, 'How often do you drink alcohol?' makes an assumption about the respondent's drinking habits which may be entirely false (and even hurtful – see prejudicial language, above).

Hypothetical questions Try to avoid hypothetical questions such as: 'Suppose you were asked to ...' since these have been shown to be poor predictors of people's actual subsequent behaviour. A useful check on whether the content and structure of a question is right is to ask whether a respondent would understand why the question was being asked within the overall context of the study. Arksey and Knight (1999) also argue that such questions can generate insightful data when people have some direct knowledge or experience of the subject being discussed.

Knowledge Make sure that the group that has been targeted to answer the questions has the knowledge actually to do so. Sometimes it may be necessary to provide people with some background information if the subject is quite technical.

Memory recall People may have difficulty recalling what has occurred even quite recently. If, say, you are constructing some questions around recent newsworthy events, then it would be appropriate to present respondents with a list of such events before asking them questions about them.

In determining how to ask individual questions consider the following:

- Can the question be misunderstood? Does it contain difficult or unclear phraseology?

- Is the question misleading because of unstated assumptions or unseen implications?
- Is the wording biased? Is it emotionally loaded or slanted towards a particular kind of answer?
- Is the question wording likely to be objectionable to the respondent in any way?
- Can the question be asked in a more direct or a more indirect form?
- Are double questions avoided?
- Are leading questions avoided?
- Is attention paid to detail – e.g. overlapping categories such as 'age 30–35, 35–40'
- Do questions avoid taxing respondents' memories?
- Can the questions be shortened?
- Are categories such as 'Don't Know' and 'Not Applicable' provided?
- Will the words used have the same meaning for all respondents, regardless of nationality, language, culture, etc.?
- Is the frame of reference clear – e.g. if asking how often, is the range of possible responses made obvious?
- Do questions artificially create opinions on subjects where respondents really do not have any?
- Is personal wording preferable (e.g. 'How do *you* feel?), or impersonal (e.g. 'How do you think people feel'). The first is a measure of attitudes, the second a measure of respondents' perceptions of other people's attitudes.

Classification questions

One type of question often required by a survey is the *classification* question, dealing with, for example, the name, sex, age, status, etc. of the respondent. These are important for providing the basis for analysing associations between variables (for example, a respondent's gender and attitude towards sexual harassment issues in the workplace). These questions should be introduced by a gentle 'It will help us in further analysis if you would tell us a little about yourself'. Take care not to run the risk of alienating the respondent by prying for information that is not, subsequently, needed. For example, is it necessary to know the respondent's exact age, or would a response within a range of ages suffice? People may also be reluctant to reveal details of their salary, particularly to a stranger within their own organization. It may be easier to obtain their response to a question on job grade that may provide an indirect indication of salary.

> **Activity 8.2 Anyone can write a questionnaire?**
>
> Evaluate the questions in the short questionnaire shown in Figure 8.1.
>
> *Suggested answers are provided at the end of the chapter.*

1 State your age

Under 20   20–25   25–30   Over 30

2 What are your views on appraisal?

3 Do you consider appraisal to be vital for organizational development or a way of wasting time?

Yes   No

4 Do you consider that appraisal should be:

- Integrated with training plans
  so people are better trained?   1

- Linked to the reward system so   2 Please tick one
  everyone earns more money?

5 Without effective 'best practice' appraisal the organization cannot prosper

Yes

No

6 Give details on the number of appraisals conducted within the organization over the recent time period.

7 How many of your appraisals have you failed?

8 How often do you think that people should be appraised: (a) once a year (as now); (b) twice a year; (c) once every two years; (d) never (the scheme should be abandoned); (e) other (please specify)

Name:

Department:

Salary:

Complete and return

FIGURE 8.1 EXAMPLE QUESTIONNAIRE

Question content

Clearly, in writing questions issues such as validity need to be borne in mind. Hence, the content of the questionnaire needs to cover the research issues that have been specified. But Foddy (1993) points out that this is by no means a simple matter. A series of precise steps must be followed:

- The researcher has to be clear about the information required and encode this accurately into a question.
- The respondent must interpret the question in a way that the researcher intended.
- The respondent must construct an answer that contains information that the researcher has requested.
- The researcher must interpret the answer as the respondent had intended it to be interpreted.

Unfortunately, as Foddy (1993) comments, there is ample opportunity for the process to break down at any stage, with resulting threats to validity. Even if the respondent understands the question, there also needs to be some confidence that he or she will know the answer, and that they will be willing to provide it. In deliberating about question content ask yourself the following questions:

- Is the question necessary? Just how will it be useful?
- Are several questions needed on the subject matter of this question?
- Do respondents have the information necessary to answer the question?
- Does the question need to be more concrete, specific and closely related to the respondent's personal experience?
- Is the question content sufficiently general and free from spurious concreteness and specificity?
- Is the question content biased and loaded in one direction, without accompanying questions to balance the emphasis?
- Will the respondents give the information that is asked for?

Cannell (1985) deals with the issue of how to ask difficult or embarrassing questions. Referring to the work of Barton, he illustrates a number of ways in which the cooperation of respondents can be maintained. The possible approaches are illustrated in Table 8.1, in which, by means of illustration, a set of hypothetical questions are asked about whether a respondent sabotaged the organization's intranet.

Drafting the answer

Decide on how you want people to respond and stick with it. So, if you require respondents to *tick* their responses, get them to do this throughout the questionnaire, rather than to also incorporate *underlining* and *circling*. In general, people seem to be used to box-ticking. The golden rule is that it should be absolutely clear how the respondent is to complete the questionnaire.

Types of question

With the above warnings in mind, we can now move on to look at the types of questions that can be posed in a questionnaire. Oppenheim (1992) suggests that a

TABLE 8.1   APPROACHES TO ASKING THE EMBARRASSING QUESTION: 'DID
YOU SABOTAGE THE INTRANET?'

Approach	Question
Casual approach	Do you happen to have sabotaged the intranet?
Give a numbered card	Would you please read off the number on this card which corresponds to what became of the intranet [*Hand card to respondent*]: (a) It went down of its own accord (as usual) (b) I hacked into it and programmed a bug to make it self-destruct (c) Other (what?)
The Everybody approach	As you know, many people are tempted to sabotage the intranet these days. Do you happen to have done it recently?
The Other People approach	(a) Do you know any people who have sabotaged the intranet? (b) How about yourself?
Sealed Ballot technique	We respect your right to anonymity. Please complete this form, indicating whether, or not, you sabotaged the intranet, seal it in the envelope and place it in the box marked 'Secret Ballot'

Source: Adapted from Cannell, 1985

funnel approach can often be used, whereby the questionnaire starts off with a broad set of questions and then progressively narrows down the questions to target specific areas. This is sometimes achieved by *filter* questions that are designed to exclude some respondents. So, for example, in a survey of employee commuting experiences, a question might be posed: Have you ever had difficulty in getting to work? If the answer is 'Yes', then more market research questions follow; if the answer is 'No' then the respondent is routed to a later part of the questionnaire on different transport issues. The main body of the questionnaire, however, will comprise either open or closed questions. It should be noted that different formats can be used for questions. Cannell (1985) argues that using a variety of such formats adds interest and can even help increase questionnaire response rates. Let us look at some now.

Open questions

Open questions have no definitive response and contain answers that are recorded in full. Hence, the questionnaire must be designed in such a way that respondents are able to provide such a response without the restriction of lack of space. Open questions often begin with words such as 'How', 'Why', 'What', etc.

The advantage of open questions is the potential for richness of responses, some of which may not have been anticipated by the researchers. But the downside of open questions is that while they are easy to answer they are also difficult to analyse. At first sight much of the information gathered may seem varied and difficult to categorize. Generally, the solution to this is the use of *coding* and the adoption of a *coding frame*.

Open questions may lead to interesting or unexpected responses, so as we saw in Chapter 5, follow-up questions called probes or *probing questions* can be used (if the questionnaire is administered by an interviewer). These probes should be general in nature, and should not try to lead the respondent – for example, 'Could you say a little more about that accident report'; 'How do you feel about those new operational procedures'. Probing questions can also be used to add some clarity where the interviewer has not understood a response. Clearly, it is easier to ask probing questions when conducting a structured interview than when using a postal questionnaire.

The simplest form of open question is the specified response, as illustrated in Question 1.

Question 1   Specified response question

What aspects of the government's healthy living campaign do you find the *most* useful? Please write in. _____

What aspects of the government's healthy living campaign do you find the *least* useful? Please write in. _____

(You could follow up each response with a 'Why?' question.)

Closed questions

A closed question is one to which the respondent is offered a set of pre-designed replies such as 'Yes/No', 'True or False', multiple-choice responses, or is given the opportunity to choose from a selection of numbers representing strength of feeling or attitude. In contrast to open questions, closed questions may restrict the richness of alternative responses, but are easier to analyse. They also make it easier to compare the views of one group with another. Closed questions can be useful in providing respondents with some structure to their answers. There are a number of approaches to asking closed questions.

List questions   These provide the respondent with a list of responses, any of which they can select. This approach avoids making the answering of a questionnaire a test of memory. If list questions are being presented as part of a structured interview, then prompt cards can be used, which list responses and which are shown to respondents. So, rather than read out Question 2 and rely on respondents to remember each item accurately, a card is given to them that reproduces the question and the possible responses.

Question 2   List question

What do you think is the most important influence on the success of the organization in the next two years? Please ✓ as many responses as you think accurate.

Changes in government policy affecting the legal regulation of the market	☐
The entry of new competitors to the market	☐
The impact of the company's current reorganization strategy	☐
Foreign exchange rates	☐

While the list will, clearly, influence the direction of people's responses, this does not make the approach invalid. If the questionnaire is concerned with issues that require recall of information, the list might act as a useful memory-jogger. But it must be recognized that influencing respondents in this way may affect their response to any later open questions.

Category questions   These are designed so that only *one* response is possible. For structured interviews there can be any number of categories, provided a prompt card is used. But for self-administered questionnaires and telephone questionnaires Fink (1995c) suggests a maximum of no more than five alternative responses (see Question 3).

Question 3   Category question

How often in an average week do you use our e-banking facilities? Please ✓ one response.

Never	☐
Once	☐
2–3 times	☐
4–5 times	☐
6 times or more	☐

Ranking questions   This requires the respondent to rank responses in order. With this kind of question it is important to make the instructions for completing the question clear and explicit. Be aware that more than seven or eight items in the list may make it too complex for many respondents to complete. For face-to-face interviews use will have to be made of prompt cards and for telephone interviews, items should be limited to no more than three or four. Note that an 'other' category is also provided to catch any features not mentioned in the list (see Question 4).

Question 4   Ranking question

Please indicate in the boxes provided which features you believe are the most important when visiting our superstore (1 indicating the most important, 2 the next most important, etc.) Please leave blank those features that have no importance at all.

Ease of car parking □
Low prices □
Friendly staff □
Store loyalty card □
Variety of goods □
Other (please specify) □

Scale questions   Scale or rating questions are used to measure a variable, and comprise four types of scale: nominal, ordinal, interval and ratio. A common type is the Likert scale on which respondents are asked to indicate how strongly they agree or disagree with a series of statements (see Question 5). This is an example of an ordinal scale. Further details of all these scales are presented in Chapter 12. Most Likert scales use either a four- or five-point scale.

Question 5   Scale question (ordinal)

As a loyal electricity customer we would like to know your views on the service we provide. Please put one ✓ for each of the following statements

	Strongly Agree	Agree	Disagree	Strongly Disagree
I have been pleased with the emergency 24-hour call out service	□	□	□	□
Electricity prices have been competitive with gas prices	□	□	□	□

Other forms of scaling can also be used. The number of response categories, for example, can be changed. Common formats are 'True/False', 'Yes/No'.

Another approach would be to get respondents to mark a point on a continuum. Question 6 seeks responses on the quality of helpline support. Czaja and Blair (1996) warn, however, that this approach can lead to complexities at the data analysis stage. For example, do we calculate the average rating; combine parts of the scale into high, medium and low categories; or use a threshold that indicates a trend in one direction or another?

Question 6 Continuum scale											
Please circle one number that reflects your opinion of our helpline support											
Quick	1	2	3	4	5	6	7	8	9	10	Slow
Friendly	1	2	3	4	5	6	7	8	9	10	Discourteous
Informative	1	2	3	4	5	6	7	8	9	10	Confusing

Oppenheim (1992) provides a useful table comparing the advantages and disadvantages of open and closed questions, reproduced in Table 8.2. Note that often a questionnaire will use a mixture of both open and closed questions. Indeed, it is often useful to follow up a closed question with an invitation to add comments.

TABLE 8.2   THE ADVANTAGES AND DISADVANTAGES OF OPEN AND CLOSED QUESTIONS

Advantages	Disadvantages
Open questions	
Freedom and spontaneity of the answers	Time-consuming
Opportunity to probe	In interviews: costly of interviewer time
Useful for testing hypotheses about ideas or awareness	Demand more effort from respondents
Closed questions	
Require little time	Loss of spontaneous response
No extended writing	Bias in answer categories
Low cost	Sometimes too crude
Easy to process	May irritate respondents
Make group comparison easy	
Useful for testing specific hypotheses	

Source: Adapted from Oppenheim, 1992

Sequencing questions

There should be a logical flow to the sequence of questions, just as you would expect in a formal written text. Such a flow will aid the respondent in understanding

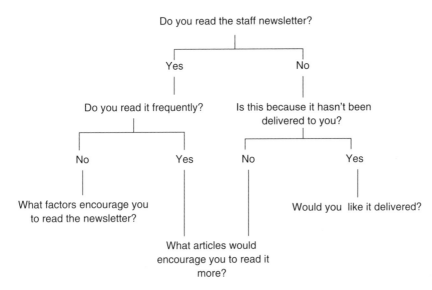

FIGURE 8.2 FLOWCHART FOR PLANNING OF QUESTION SEQUENCES

individual questions and the overall purpose of the questionnaire. One way of designing the flow of questions is to use a flowchart, as shown in Figure 8.2.

Oppenheim (1992) points out that after reading the accompanying documentation that tells them all about the survey, respondents may be quite eager to answer some of the questions. Therefore, the last sort of question they want to see is what is presented in many surveys – a list of personal questions about age, gender, rank, status (work and marital, etc). These types of questions should be kept to nearer the end of the questionnaire, and should be preceded by a short statement explaining that this data is needed for making statistical comparisons, so the respondent's help would be appreciated. De Vaus (2002) argues that questions that should come first include those that are easily answered, factual questions and those that are obviously key to the purposes of the survey. Indeed, as Dillman (2000) points out, if the covering documentation has highlighted the key themes of the questionnaire, it is sensible to start with questions that deal directly with the theme. He also suggests that special attention be given to the first question since this will help determine whether the questionnaire is answered or put in the wastepaper bin.

Other useful advice includes going from easy to more difficult questions and from more concrete to abstract. Any sensitive questions should be left until the end. Where possible, a variety of answering formats should be used to provide interest, some additional advice on the sequencing of questions being:

- Is the answer to the question likely to be influenced by the content of preceding questions?
- Is the question led up to in a natural way? Is it in correct psychological order?
- Does the question come too early or too late from the point of view of arousing interest and receiving sufficient attention, avoiding resistance, etc?

> **Activity 8.3**
>
> Take a questionnaire that has been designed either by yourself or a colleague (it could be the one you used for Activity 8.1). Evaluate individual questions. Are they clear, concise and unambiguous? Would the intended audience be able to answer them? Are instructions on answering the questions clear? Is the sequencing of questions appropriate?

Providing response categories

Asking a question like 'What employment sector did you work in before your present job?' is asking for trouble. It might both confuse the respondent ('What do they mean – sector?') or the respondent might be uncertain as to whether their classification is acceptable. So, for the question cited, it would be appropriate to provide a list of categories such as: Finance, Retailing, Education, Commerce, Agriculture, Other (please specify), etc. Providing these categories also yields a standardized set of responses that will make the data easier to analyse. Note that we have been careful to provide an 'Other' category, just in case. Some common response category statements are provided by Czaja and Blair (1996) and are summarized in Table 8.3.

TABLE 8.3 COMMON RESPONSE CATEGORY QUANTIFIERS

Category	Quantifiers
Opinions	Very satisfied/Somewhat satisfied/Somewhat dissatisfied/Very dissatisfied
	Very important/Somewhat important/Not too important/Not at all important
	Oppose/Support
Knowledge	Very familiar/Somewhat familiar/Not too familiar/Not at all familiar
	True/False
Frequency of events or behaviour	Always/Frequently/Seldom/Never
	Often/Sometimes/Rarely/Never
	Per day/Per week/Per month/Per year/Never
Ratings	Excellent/Good/Fair/Poor
	Got better/Got worse/Stayed the same
	Very fair/Fair/Unfair/Very unfair
	High/Medium/Low

Source: Adapted from Czaja and Blair, 1996

Questionnaire layout

One way of improving the rate of response to a questionnaire is by making it as attractive as possible. Hence, factors such as the general layout, choice of paper, line spacing and answering directions should be considered. So, the way of answering multiple-choice questions should be consistent throughout – for example, ticking boxes or circling numbers. Boxes or lines should be provided for open question responses. It is best to avoid making the questionnaire too cramped as this can be off-putting to respondents.

Dillman (2000) warns against unconventional designs, such as printing on both sides of paper with a staple to bind the pages together, or using landscape (horizontal) orientation. He argues strongly for a booklet format which, he says, is understood automatically by respondents. With this format, people start on page 1 and turn over to page 2 which is to the left of page 3. If the budget is tight, then it is legitimate to print on one side only and to staple sheets together. Carroll (1994) suggests that other typographical issues require careful consideration such as:

- Putting boxes around groups of questions.
- Shading multiple-choice questions.
- Selecting clean, clear typefaces.
- Using lines to take the respondent's eye from question to response.
- Numbering all questions and sections.

Instructions

Most questionnaires will also contain, probably at the start, a set of instructions for completing them. This is important, and it should not be assumed that respondents will all know that they should, say, only tick one choice for each question. Unless instructions are made absolutely specific, it is almost certain that questionnaires will be returned completed incorrectly resulting in a loss of data. Cohen and Manion (1997) even suggest that with postal questionnaires it is advisable to repeat the instructions. Carroll (1994) supports this idea, arguing that providing additional instructions for groups of questions will help the response rate.

One of the problems with instructions is that they are either not read or are misread. Dillman (2000) suggests that respondents can be helped by careful use of typography and design. De Vaus (2002) suggests that, to improve the flow of a questionnaire, the following instructions should be considered:

- General instructions, dealing with the purpose of the questionnaire, assurances of confidentiality, how and when to return the questionnaire.
- Section introductions when the questionnaire is divided into subsections.
- Question instructions (e.g. tick only one response).
- 'Go to' instructions.

Dillman (2000) refers to these 'go to' instructions as 'skip instructions' and argues that they are important because they avoid respondents reading or completing questions that do not apply to them. But in self-administered questionnaires the problem is getting people to *read* the skip instructions correctly. Figure 8.3 illustrates a poorly constructed skip question and an improved version. Note that in the

---

A problem skip question

12 **Do you use public transport to get to work?**

        ❑   Yes (Go to 13)

        ❑   No (Go to 18)

13 **How long does your journey take you (in minutes)**

An improved skip question

12 **Do you use public transport to get to work?**

        ❑   No ☛ (Skip to 18)

        ❑   Yes

13 **How long does your journey take you (in minutes)**

FIGURE 8.3   USES OF TYPOGRAPHY AND EMPHASIS TO AID THE
FUNCTIONALITY OF SKIP INSTRUCTIONS (ADAPTED FROM
DILLMAN, 2000)

improved version, the 'No' response is presented first and respondents re-routed if necessary. Instructions are in bold and a pointed finger used for emphasis.

Similarly, the use of spacing can help to improve the understanding of a question, as illustrated in Figure 8.4. See how a quite densely packed question is laid out so that different elements are separated.

DESIGNING INTERNET AND WEB-BASED QUESTIONNAIRES

As we saw in Chapter 5, the advent of the Internet and World Wide Web has transformed the way in which many surveys are conducted. Given that many organizations, particularly larger ones, have good connections to the Internet, the use of online surveys is especially advantageous in terms of convenience and access to large samples and populations.

E-mail questionnaires

E-mail questionnaires (often used as part of surveys) are relatively easy to compose but offer fewer opportunities to provide visual stimulation or interactivity. It is difficult, for example, to use the kind of skip patterns discussed in the previous section. On the whole, the principles of e-mail questionnaire design are very

---

A problem question

1   When you joined the company, what were your major ambitions (a) promotion; (b) job satisfaction; (c) a rise in salary; (d) learning a new skill; (e) all of these? Mark. one answer.

2   How long have you now worked for the company? _____ Years

An improved question

❶   When you joined the company, what were your major ambitions? Mark one answer

   ❑ Promotion

   ❑ Job satisfaction

   ❑ A rise in salary

   ❑ Learning a new skill

   ❑ All of these

❷   How long have you now worked for the company?

   _____ Years

FIGURE 8.4   THE USE OF SPACING TO HELP IDENTIFY GROUPS OF ELEMENTS

similar to many of those concerned with paper-based design. Dillman (2000) suggests the following strategies:

- Use multiple contacts (e.g. preliminary e-mail, questionnaire e-mail, 'thank-you' e-mail, etc.)
- Personalize all e-mail contacts, do not send them via a listserv. One reason for this is that a response would be sent to all others on the list – so much for confidentiality!
- Keep the covering (introductory) text brief, avoiding the need for the respondent to scroll down the page.
- Suggest alternative ways to respond, such as printing out the questionnaire and completing it by hand. Some respondents may feel insecure about e-mail responses, which can always be checked by an employer.
- Limit column width to 70 characters to decrease the likelihood of text wrapping around to the next line.
- Start with an easy but interesting question.
- Provide instructions on completing questions, such as putting an X inside the brackets.

- In the case of non-response, include a replacement questionnaire with the reminder message.

Web-based questionnaires

Web-based questionnaires offer many facilities for questionnaire design that are not available in traditional, paper-based formats, such as the use of drop-down menus, pop-up instruction boxes and sophisticated skip patterns. However, the very flexibility of the Web makes the opportunities for making design errors all the greater, which may, in turn, affect response rates. It is extremely easy to get 'lost' in a website, at which point many users exit the site quickly. Hence, following some simple design instructions is all the more important. Dillman (2000) makes a number of recommendations:

- Introduce the Web questionnaire with a welcome screen that is motivational, that emphasizes the ease of responding, and shows how to proceed.
- Provide a login to limit access to the site to the selected sample.
- Choose a first question that is easy and stimulating to answer.
- Present questions in a similar format to that used in a conventional questionnaire.
- Use colour appropriately and not just for the sake of it.
- Unless you are sure that all respondents have the same screen configuration, test the Web pages on different screen resolutions and Web browsers to ensure that the appearance is always the same.
- Use drop-down boxes sparingly and identify each with a 'click here' instruction.

All questionnaires, whether paper-based, e-mail or Web-based need careful piloting before dissemination to a wider audience.

Activity 8.4   Evaluating Web-based questionnaires

Take a look at the following website, which contains a wide variety of Web-based questionnaires:
  http://www.accesscable.net/~infopoll/Library.htm

Now find examples of:

- Accompanying documentation, including information letters.
- Different question formats (open/closed; listing questions; category questions; ranking questions; scale questions).
- The use of skip questions.
- Face sheet information.
- The use of response category quantifiers.

Also take a look at Sample Web Questionnaires at:
  http://www.surveysystem.com/websurveys.htm

PILOTING QUESTIONNAIRES

Research instruments such as interview schedules can be modified if certain questions appear to be ineffective, but questionnaires, particularly if used for large surveys, are a 'one-shot' attempt at data gathering. It is therefore essential that they are accurate, unambiguous and simple to complete. As we saw in Chapter 5, that piloting is vital. Judicious piloting will reduce the incidence of non-response to the questionnaire. Gillham (2000) suggests that it is wise to pilot at least 50 per cent more questions than you need so that confusing or unreliable questions can be thrown out at this stage. What else should be piloted? Well, basically, anything and everything! But you could consider the:

- Instructions given to respondents.
- Style and wording of any accompanying letter.
- Content of face-sheet data, that is, respondents' names, addresses, etc.
- Formality or informality of the questionnaire in terms of tone, presentation, etc.
- Length of the questionnaire – if too long, is the response rate likely to be reduced?
- Sequence of questions.
- Quality of individual questions in terms of whether they are understood and answered in a way that was intended.
- Scales and question format used, for example, Likert scales, Yes/No responses, etc.

Oppenheim (1992) even suggests that the tables for the data analysis phase of the final report should be piloted (that is, dummy tables written) before the questionnaire is issued. This might highlight new issues or problems that could require consideration and inclusion in the questionnaire itself.

De Vaus (1986) suggests that evaluation is important in a number of design areas, including checking for:

- The ability of a question to discriminate. If everyone responds with the same answer to a question this is often not very useful, since one purpose of using a questionnaire is to examine the diversity of views on a subject.
- The validity and reliability of questions.
- Redundancy, so if it is found that two questions measure the same thing, one of them can be dropped.
- The response set. With some respondents, a pattern of answering Likert-type questions quickly sets in. So, if they tick 'Strongly agree' for, say, the first three questions, this response becomes habitual and they tick all remaining questions with this response. To avoid this happening, it is wise to alternate responses, for example, by using a negative statement on which the respondent will have to disagree.

Who can help you with piloting? Gillham (2000) advises trying out your initial list of questions with one or two people who are not part of the target group. Explain that you are trying to get the questions right, and that they should indicate where a question is unclear. Even sit with them as they look through the questions, noting their comments and your own observations on a spare questionnaire. Once you have amended the questionnaire, re-trial it with another two or three people who are similar to, but not part of, the target group. The procedure is the same, but this time also ask for improvements, deletions and additions. You are now ready to start designing the layout of the questionnaire.

Of course, if the survey is delivered via the Web, in addition to the issues raised above a whole new set of problems have to be faced. As we saw earlier, the design of Web-based surveys offers both flexibility but also opportunities to get things spectacularly wrong. As in any software development, it is sensible to design and pilot a prototype of the final site, so that user problems can be identified. Issues to look at here include the use of colour, on-screen instructions, navigational routes (especially for skip questions) and how respondents handle inputting their responses to questions (do they know what to do?). Observation at the piloting stage with respondents actually using the website questionnaire may also reveal some entirely unanticipated problems. Case Study 8.1 provides an example of how piloting can help to improve a questionnaire.

Case Study 8.1   Questionnaire piloting to get it right

A research project is set up to study public attitudes towards the decriminalization of certain categories of drugs. The study starts with the question:

Would you say that most people think that certain 'soft' drugs should be decriminalized?

1   Yes
2   No
3   Don't know/not sure

Piloting the questions reveals that:

- Most respondents cannot report in general what 'most people' think, they only know what they, personally, think.
- Some people did not understand the concept 'decriminalize'.
- Some could not differentiate between 'soft' and 'hard' drugs.
- Respondents resisted selecting between just 'Yes' and 'No' and wanted an opportunity to express their feelings between alternatives.

The question then was modified to read:
Do you think that people arrested for the possession of drugs such as cannabis are sentenced fairly (a) almost always; (b) most of the time; (c) some of the time; (d) never?

Piloting shows that this is an improvement because it asks people what they themselves think, and it is more specific about the type of drugs being discussed. It also provides a range of categories. Its disadvantage is that it has become too specific and shifted away from the central theme of the original question, decriminalization.

The third and final version becomes:

Please indicate your view on each of the following statements:
Fining someone for possession of cannabis is: Very fair, Fair, Unfair, Very unfair.
Imprisoning someone for possession of cannabis is: Very fair, Fair, Unfair, Very unfair.
Fining someone for dealing in cannabis is: Very fair, Fair, Unfair, Very unfair.
Imprisoning someone for dealing in cannabis is: Very fair, Fair, Unfair, Very unfair.

Activity 8.5

Take one or a small number of questions from a questionnaire you are designing and pilot them with a sample audience. Amend the questions on the basis of the responses and advice given. Pilot the amended questions. Amend them again. How similar is the third version of the questions to what you started with?

MAINTAINING QUALITY: VALIDITY AND RELIABILITY

Since questionnaires are one of the most popular instruments for data gathering, you will not be surprised that we pause yet again to discuss the issues of validity and reliability.

Validity

We saw earlier in this chapter that the validity of a questionnaire can be affected by the wording of the questions it contains. But even if individual questions are valid, a poor sequencing of questions or confusing structure or design of the questionnaire can all threaten its validity.

The questionnaire must cover the research issues both in terms of content and detail. Recall Figure 4.6 in Chapter 4 which shows the dangers of a questionnaire not covering the research area (Zone of Neglect) and some questions being asked that are irrelevant to the study (Zone of Invalidity). It should be noted that asking spurious, irrelevant questions increases the length of a questionnaire, which in turn, may reduce the number of responses. If the response rate becomes too low, this may limit the generalizability of the findings, and hence external validity.

As we saw in Chapter 5, two threats to the validity of postal questionnaires are the extent to which respondents complete the questionnaires accurately, and the problem of non-response. Accuracy can be checked by interviewing a sample of respondents, and probing for how carefully they have answered the questionnaire. For non-response, again follow-up interviews can be used for those who did not reply, and their responses compared with those who did answer the questionnaire to see if the two sets of responses are similar. If they are, it suggests that the responding and non-responding populations are the same, and there is no threat from this source to the validity of data collected.

Reliability

In terms of questionnaire design, a high reliability means that if you measured something today, you should get the same results at some other time, assuming that what is being measured has not changed (Black, 1993). As we discussed in Chapter 4, reliability is a measure of consistency and can include measures of

- Stability (over time).
- Equivalence (administering two versions of a test instrument to the same people on the same day).
- Inter-judge reliability.

The extent of this consistency is measured by a reliability coefficient using a scale from 0.00 (very unreliable) to 1.00 (perfectly reliable). In practice, a score of 0.9 is generally deemed to be acceptable. There are several ways in which this coefficient can be calculated. One of the most common is Cronback's alpha, which presents the average of all possible split-half correlations, and so measures the consistency of all items, both globally and individually.

QUESTIONNAIRE ADMINISTRATION

Even the best-designed questionnaire will not create an impact if care is not taken with its administration, one of the fundamental objectives of which is to maximize the return rate. We examine next some of the techniques associated with different kinds of survey methods that were discussed in Chapter 5.

Self-administered questionnaires

Postal questionnaires

It is usual for a questionnaire to be accompanied by a letter. Getting the content, style and tone of this letter right is just as important as achieving the quality of these elements in the questionnaire. Indeed, since respondents will probably read the letter first, it could be argued that it is even more important. It is essential that you get the respondent's name, initials and preferred title absolutely right. Documentation sent to women should usually be titled Ms unless you know that they prefer another form.

The letter should cover issues such as the aims of the research, its importance (particularly its importance to the respondent's company or organization, if applicable), how long it will take to complete, and an assurance of confidentiality. The name of the sponsor or researcher should appear on the letterhead, and details of where to return the questionnaire should appear both on the letter as well as the questionnaire itself. Above all, the letter should be as brief and concise as possible, and should contain a note of thanks for the questionnaire's completion. If there are instructions that you particularly need to emphasize, state them as part of a postscript as people often notice these below the main text.

Saunders et al. (2000) list six further techniques that researchers will find useful:

TABLE 8.4   LIKELY TIMING OF RESPONSES FOR POSTAL SURVEY

Distribution	Timing (P-day)*	Responses
First posting	P-day + 10 days	50 per cent of final return
First reminder	P-day + 17 days	80 per cent of final return
Second reminder	P-day + 27 days	A few more

* P-day = Postal-day, i.e. the initial posting.

- Ensure that questionnaires and letters are printed and envelopes properly addressed.
- Make a pre-survey contact with recipients either by e-mail, post or phone to warn them that the questionnaire is on its way.
- Post the questionnaire and covering letter to arrive at a convenient time.
- One week after the initial posting, send out the first follow up reminder letters to all recipients.
- Send the second follow up reminder to those who have not responded after three weeks.
- Post out a third follow up if the response rate is low.

Of course, before reminders can be sent, it is necessary to know who has not responded. A useful technique is to number the questionnaires, but this will not work if anonymity has been promised to respondents. In this situation, a 'scatter-gun' approach may be necessary, reminding all respondents but apologizing in advance to those who have already responded.

When sending reminders, emphasize the importance of the study and do not imply that the initial response has been poor – imply the contrary, if anything (providing this is truthful). When prompting, it is important not to be apologetic. Enclose another copy of the questionnaire and another stamped addressed envelope in case people had not receive or had 'mislaid the original'. In terms of responses and timings, Table 8.4 suggests a typical pattern. It can be seen that after just over two weeks you will have received about 80 per cent of what will prove to be your final total. You will know by this point whether your final return rate is going to be successful, or not.

Postal questionnaires should be sent by first class post and include a stamped addressed envelope. If the questionnaire is going to an individual in their home, Gillham (2000) suggests Thursday as the best day for posting as people have more time at weekends. Letters to organizations should be sent on Mondays or Tuesdays so that they can be completed at work.

Delivery and collection questionnaires

Since questionnaires are to be collected, clearly one of the prime factors is to ensure that respondents know exactly when this will occur. Saunders et al. (2000) advise that, when conducting research in an organization, response rates can be dramatically improved by calling all respondents to a meeting in the organization's time, explaining the purpose of the questionnaire, and getting it completed before people leave the meeting. A box near the exit to the room for collecting questionnaires may help to assure confidentiality.

Online questionnaires

As we saw earlier, online questionnaires can be administered either by e-mail or via the Web. For e-mails, it is relatively easy to obtain people's e-mail addresses, but to contact a sample of respondents 'cold' would risk the accusation of 'spamming', that is, sending unsolicited messages. Another danger is that anonymity will be lost as respondents can be identified by their e-mail addresses.

Nevertheless, e-mails can be used effectively for surveys either by including the questions in the main body of the e-mail or sending the questionnaire as an attached document. Including questions in the body of an e-mail message makes the questionnaire simple to return, but there is little opportunity for using the kind of layout and design that encourages the completion of a questionnaire.

If you are, say, conducting a survey within an organization that uses one software application standard, then you may be able to attach the document in a word processed application version that can be read by all. If the survey is cross-organization there will be risks that not all will be able to read the attachment, so including questions in an e-mail is the safest approach. After this, procedures for sending reminders are the same as for postal questionnaires.

Interviewer-administered questionnaires

Structured interview

Since structured interviews involve face-to-face contact, one of the essential administrative factors is arranging meetings with respondents, and improving the chances of respondents turning up for the interview. This chance will be increased if respondents are contacted in advance of the meeting and advised of dates, times and location, etc. If the structured interview involves some open as well as closed questions, it might be advisable to tape record the interview since transcribing verbal dialogue is difficult unless you are skilled at shorthand. The use of tape recorders involves ethical issues including confidentiality, so you must ask permission before using one. Once interviews are completed, times for any return visits should be arranged.

Telephone questionnaire

For telephone questionnaires it is important that respondents know when they are to be interviewed, so they must be contacted by post and given clear details of dates and times (including the likely length of the interview). When calls are unsuccessful, the reasons should be noted, such as the fact that the respondent has moved or did not pick up the telephone. In the latter case, call three more times at different times of the day.

SUMMARY

- Designing individual questions involves a rigorous process of analysis to avoid ambiguity, leading questions, double questions and simply misleading questions.
- Questions must be clearly linked to the purpose of the research (as specified in the accompanying letter or documentation).
- Questionnaires should start with questions that are easy to answer, interesting and transparently linked to the purpose of the research.
- Questionnaire layout and the use of typography can make a questionnaire easier to complete and more appealing to respondents, enhancing the response rate.
- Clear, well set out instructions on completing the questionnaire can also boost the response rate.
- Web and e-mail questionnaires offer a new and potentially powerful tool, but also require additional design skills.
- All questionnaires, whether paper-based, e-mail or Web-based, require thorough piloting which will include evaluation of accompanying documentation, instructions, individual questions, types of question, question sequencing, the use of scales and skip instructions – basically, everything!

Summary of web links

http://www.accesscable.net/~infopoll/library.htm
http://www.surveysystem.com/websurveys.htm

Further reading

Gillham, B. (2000) *Developing a Questionnaire*. London: Continuum. A small and simply written book that provides an excellent introduction to the subject. Includes chapters on questionnaire design, distribution, data presentation and the analysis of open and closed questions.

De Vaus, D.A. (2002) *Surveys in Social Research*, 5th edn. London: George Allen & Unwin. See specifically Chapter 7 on constructing questionnaires and Chapter 8 on administering questionnaires.

Suggested answers for Activity 8.2

1 An *ambiguous* question since the categories overlap. Also *impertinent* in two ways – the fact that age is asked for (why is this necessary?) and the curt way in which this is demanded.
2 *Vague* and therefore probably unreliable.
3 *Double question* and therefore also ambiguous.
4 *Loaded question.*
5 *Double negative.* It also contains the phrase 'best practice' – what does this mean?
6 Demands either *memory recall* (if the person is in a position to know the answer) or an expectation that they have the *knowledge*, which may not be the case.
7 *Impertinent.*
8 *No instructions.* It is unclear how to complete an answer – ticking or circling? The fact that only one answer can be given is assumed, but should be made explicit.

Finally, the questionnaire contains no introductory paragraph nor explanation of its purpose. It asks for respondents to give their name, which does not appear necessary, and asks for their salary, which is both unnecessary and impertinent. It offers no assurances of confidentiality, does not explain what is going to be done with the information and is unclear as to where it can be returned (and when).

9

Collecting Primary Data: Interviewing

Chapter objectives

After reading this chapter you will be able to:

- **Describe and choose between structured, semi-structured, non-directive, focused and informal interviews on the basis of the objectives of the research.**
- **Select between using interviews and self-completed questionnaires.**
- **Produce valid and reliable interview schedules.**
- **Conduct an interview skilfully, tactfully, safely and ethically.**

An interview is a conversation between people in which one person has the role of researcher. Very often, the interviewer will have on hand a set of written questions which are posed in a structured and methodical fashion (a structured interview). Alternatively, these questions might only be used as an *aide-mémoire*, to remind the researcher of the key areas that need probing. In either case, interviews often make use of questionnaires, so this chapter has much in common with Chapter 8. However, whereas the previous chapter focused on the design of questionnaires, this chapter looks at one way, the interview, in which they can be used. Hence, we are shifting from product (the questionnaire) to process.

Interviewing may pose challenges because of human interaction between the interviewer and respondent. The interviewer has to pose questions (in either a structured, semi-structured or unstructured format), listen to (and data capture) the responses and pose new questions. If the interview format is relatively unstructured, then these questions have to be constructed 'on the fly'. The interviewer may also not only be listening to the verbal responses, but be noting other elements of the interview process such as the body language of the interviewee. However, despite the challenges involved, the well-conducted interview is a powerful tool for eliciting rich data on people's views, attitudes and the meanings that underpin their lives and behaviours.

In this chapter, we will examine some of the different interview approaches, and look at some of the essential interviewing skills you will need to acquire. We will also look, briefly, at telephone interviews, and conclude with some thoughts on safety and ethical issues in interviewing.

WHY INTERIEWS?

There are a number of situations in which the interview is the most logical research technique. If the objective of the research, for example, is largely exploratory, involving, say, the examination of feelings or attitudes, then interviews may be the best approach. The use of semi-structured interviews also allows the researcher to 'probe' for more detailed responses where the respondent is asked to clarify what they have said. This phenomenological approach, then, is concerned with the *meanings* that people ascribe to phenomena. As Arksey and Knight (1999) comment:

> *Interviewing is a powerful way of helping people to make explicit things that have hitherto been implicit – to articulate their tacit perceptions, feelings and understandings.* (Arksey and Knight, 1999: 32)

Interviews are also useful where it is likely that people may enjoy talking about their work rather than filling in questionnaires. An interview allows them an opportunity to reflect on events without having to commit themselves in writing, often because they feel the information may be confidential. They may never have met the researcher and may feel concerned about some of the uses to which the information may be put. Also, with questionnaires the concise meaning of a question may not always be clear, whereas with an interview meanings can be immediately clarified. Potentially, at least, interviews can produce a greater response rate for these reasons.

As Cohen and Manion (1997) point out, the interview can serve a number of distinct purposes. First, it can be used as the means of gathering information about a person's knowledge, values, preferences and attitudes. Secondly, it can be used to test out a hypothesis or to identify variables and their relationships. Thirdly, it can be used in conjunction with other research techniques, such as surveys, to follow up issues. For example, a survey by a clothing company might find a relationship between age and the tendency to purchase certain kinds of clothes. The company might then follow this up with structured interviews among a sample of people from the original survey to explore in more depth the values and motivation behind these buying patterns.

Interviews are also preferable to questionnaires where questions are either open-ended or complex, or where the logical order of questions is difficult to predetermine. But whether an interview is successful in eliciting the range and depth of answers required will depend on large part on the skills of the interviewer.

Essentially, the interview is the favoured approach where:

- There is a need to attain highly personalized data.
- There are opportunities required for probing.

- A good return rate is important.
- Respondents are not fluent in the native language of the country, or where they have difficulties with written language.

In contrast, standardized questionnaires are more powerful where:

- Large numbers of respondents must be reached.
- Better reliability of data is desired.

A summary of some of the pros and cons of interviews and self-administered questionnaires is presented in Table 9.1.

SELECTING INTERVIEW APPROACHES

There are several different types of interview, so the choice of interview technique will depend in large part on the aims and objectives of your research. Indeed, one of the purposes of the interview may be to determine these research objectives themselves. There may also be occasions when more than one interview type is used for a research project.

Interviews may be divided into five categories:

- Structured interviews.
- Semi-structured interviews.
- Non-directive interviews.
- Focused interviews.
- Informal conversational interviews.

We will look at each of the five interview approaches in turn.

Structured interviews

Structured interviews are used to collect data for quantitative analysis, and use pre-prepared questionnaires and standardized questions, that is, the same questions are posed to all respondents. Responses are recorded by the interviewer on a standardized schedule, and, while there is some interaction between interviewer and respondent, this is kept to a minimum. Ideally, questions are read out in the same tone of voice so as not to influence answers. Structured interviews are often used as a precursor for more open-ended discussions such as non-directive interviews.

Semi-structured interviews

Semi-structured interviews are non-standardized, and are often used in qualitative analysis. The interviewer has a list of issues and questions to be covered, but may

TABLE 9.1 COMPARISON OF INTERVIEWS AND SELF-ADMINISTERED QUESTIONNAIRES

Characteristics	Interviews	Self-administered questionnaires
Provide information about	As for questionnaires, but potential for exploring in more depth	Attitudes, motivation, opinions, events
Best at	Exploring stories and perspectives of informants	Testing the validity of a hypothesis
Richness of responses	Dialogue between interviewer and respondent allows for nuances to be captured and for questions to be clarified and adapted or improvised Long interviews common	Questions cannot be modified once printed, and nuances of respondent's voice cannot be heard Long questionnaires rarely acceptable
Ethics	Interviewers know whom they have interviewed, although transcripts can by anonymized	Anonymous questionnaire responses can be assured
Sample size	With the exception of telephone interviews, less suitable for wide coverage	If generalizing to a population, samples often have to be large
Time cost Planning and design	Devising interview guide, piloting, etc., may be less of an issue	Devising questionnaire (checking validity and reliability), piloting,etc. may be very time-consuming
Operation	Arranging interviews, travelling, establishing rapport – all time-consuming	Distributing questionnaire
Data transcription	Typically 7–10 hours for 1 hour interview	Usually swift, especially where optical readers are used
Data analysis	Time needed usually underestimated	Usually swift (unless there are many open-ended questions)
Money costs	High if includes interviewers, travel costs, tapes, batteries, transcription of tapes	Mainly costs of printing, distributing and receiving questionnaires. Looks cheap per questionnaire, but looks more expensive if return rate low

Source: Adapted from Arksey and Knight, 1999

not deal with all of them in each interview. The order of questions may also change depending on what direction the interview takes. Indeed, additional questions may be asked, including some which were not anticipated at the start of the interview, as new issues arise. Responses will be documented by note-taking or possibly by tape-recording the interview.

The semi-structured interview allows for probing of views and opinions where it is desirable for respondents to expand on their answers. This is vital when a phenomenological approach is being taken where the objective is to explore subjective meanings that respondents ascribe to concepts or events. Such probing may also allow for the diversion of the interview into new pathways which, while not originally considered as part of the interview, help towards meeting the research objectives.

Non-directive interviews

Non-directive interviews are used to explore an issue or topic in depth and questions are not, generally, pre-planned. Clearly, though, the researcher must have a notion of the objectives of the research and, therefore, what issues are going to be addressed in the interview. The format of the interview will be such that the respondents are allowed to talk freely around the subject. The input of the interviewer is mainly confined to checking on any doubtful points and rephrasing answers to check for accuracy of understanding. Like semi-structured interviews, non-directive interviews tend to collect data for qualitative analysis.

Focused interviews

The focused interview is based upon the respondent's subjective responses to a known situation in which they have been involved. The interviewer has prior knowledge of this situation and is, thus, able to re-focus respondents if they drift away from the theme. An analogy would be the celebrity television interview in which the interviewer has already analysed the interviewee's autobiography and wishes to probe certain issues in more depth.

Informal conversational interviews

The informal conversational interview relies on the spontaneous generation of questions as the interview progresses. This is the most open-ended form of interview technique. One of the advantages of this approach is the flexibility it offers in terms of what path the interview takes. Indeed, the interviewee may not even know an interview is taking place. This, though, will rule out the taking of notes during the interview. In cases where the fact that an interview is taking place *is* known, it is appropriate to take notes or to use a tape recorder.

One of the drawbacks of the conversational interview is the danger of the 'interviewer effect', that is, the interviewer may begin to influence the course and direction of the interview. Another disadvantage is that it may take some time before the interviewer has posed similar questions to the set of people being interviewed.

TABLE 9.2 CHARACTERISTICS OF STRUCTURED, SEMI-STRUCTURED AND UNSTRUCTURED INTERVIEWS

Structured	Semi-structured	Unstructured (non-directive, focused and informal conversation)
Quick to data capture	Slow and time-consuming to data capture and analyse	As for semi-structured
Use of random sampling	The longer the interview, the more advisable it is to use random sampling	Opportunity and snowball sampling often used. In organizations, targeting of 'key informants'
Interview schedule followed exactly	Interviewer refers to a guide containing mixture of open and closed questions Interviewer improvises using own judgement	Interviewer uses *aide-mémoire* of topics for discussion and improvises
Interviewer-led	Sometimes interviewer-led, sometimes informant-led	Non-directive interviewing
Easy to analyse	Quantitative parts easy to analyse	Usually hard to analyse
Tends to positivist view of knowledge	Mixture of positivist and non-positivist	Non-positivist view of knowledge
Respondents' anonymity easily guaranteed	Harder to ensure anonymity	Researcher tends to know the informant

Source: Adapted from Arksey and Knight, 1999

Finally, the data collected through conversational interviews may be difficult to analyse because different questions have been asked of different people. As a result, the researcher will have to sift through the data to find emerging patterns.

A summary of the characteristics of the different types of interview is provided in Table 9.2.

DESIGNING CREDIBLE INTERVIEWS

One of the prime driving forces behind the design of interviews is the search for credibility by ensuring that the findings can be trusted, which includes issues of validity and reliability. But since interviews often come from a more qualitative perspective, it would be a mistake to apply these concepts rigidly. Instead, we might want to also make use of other indicators of credibility. We also need to ask some familiar questions about the extent to which the findings from the interview study can be generalized to a wider population.

Validity

As we saw in Chapter 4, validity means that an instrument must measure what it was intended to measure. In the case of structured and semi-structured interviews, the issue of validity can be directly addressed by attempting to ensure that the question content directly concentrates on the research objectives. For informal conversational, focused and non-directive interviews, the issue of validity is more problematic because, by their very nature, the direction questions take will depend, in large part, on the responses of the interviewee. In a sense, instead of these approaches commencing with a rigid set of objectives, the subject matter emerges inductively from the interview itself. But the research will need to ensure that, if any research questions require addressing, this is achieved by the end of the interview.

According to Arksey and Knight (1999), validity is strengthened by:

- Using interview techniques that build rapport and trust, thus giving informants the scope to express themselves.
- Prompting informants to illustrate and expand on their initial responses.
- Ensuring that the interview process is sufficiently long for subjects to be explored in depth.
- Constructing interviewing schedules that contain questions drawn from the literature and from pilot work with respondents.

Another important issue of interview design is that of external validity, as we have seen, the extent to which findings from a study can be generalized. As we saw in Table 9.1, interviews are best used when the study is relatively small scale, since interviewing very large samples can be both expensive and time-consuming. Hence, external validity may be restricted. Arksey and Knight (1999), however, offer two practical principles that can be adopted in making a more plausible case for generalizing from interview findings:

- Try to select a sample that allows for a subject to be viewed from all relevant perspectives.
- Keep increasing the sample size, or sub-samples that represent different perspectives, until no new viewpoints are emerging from the data. A sample size of eight is often sufficient, although a survey should then be used to verify the data.

In a practical sense, this means that interview data need to be studied and analysed as they are collected, until it is clear that perspectives are being repeated and data saturation reached.

Reliability and bias

For a research instrument to be reliable it must *consistently* measure what it set out to measure. There is, at least, some potential for such consistency when an interview is standardized, with the same questions being asked of each respondent. However, even with standardized questions the issue of interviewer bias comes into play – does the interviewer ask the questions in the same way and with the same tone of voice with all respondents? In other words, what must be avoided is the 'interviewer effect'.

Interviewer bias can creep into the interview situation in many subtle, and not so subtle, ways. An interviewer, for example, might (unconsciously) give less time to shopfloor workers when conducting an interview than to supervisory and management grade employees. Similarly, prompt cards might be issued to shopfloor workers but not to 'more intelligent-looking' office workers. The only way to avoid this kind of systematic error is to standardize not only the interview schedule, but the behaviour of the interviewer. This is especially important if interviews are being conducted by more than one person. This does not mean that all interviews will be identical, since sometimes an interviewer will have to depart from a script to provide guidance or clarification. The skill of the interviewer is to provide such explanation without influencing the answer of the respondent.

Oppenheim (1992) suggests a number of ways in which bias occurs, namely:

- Departures from the interviewing instructions.
- Poor maintenance of rapport with the respondent.
- Altering factual questions.
- Rephrasing of attitude questions.
- Careless prompting.
- Biased probes.
- Asking questions out of sequence.
- Biased recording of verbatim answers.

One way of avoiding, or at least minimizing, interviewer bias is to require all interviewers to follow the same protocol. Hence, a set of guidelines might be drawn up which ask the interviewer to read the questions *exactly* as they are written, to repeat a question if asked, to accept respondent's refusal to answer a question without any sign of irritation, and to probe in a non-directive manner. The following Case Study gives a practical example of how bias can occur if guidelines such as these are not followed.

Case Study 9.1 Interviewer bias – it can drive you to drink!

In 1929, during the Great Depression, a New York researcher hired several interviewers to ask destitute people about their situation. Several years later the researcher reviewed some of the interviews. He noticed that the responses of one interviewer attributed most of the causes of destitution to economic factors such as unemployment, while the responses of another interviewer focused on problems with alcohol abuse. The researcher located the two interviewers and talked to them. He found that the first one was a socialist and the second, a prohibitionist. There was, thus, a strong suggestion that the causes of bias were located in the behaviour of the interviewers.

Source: Adapted from Beed and Stimson, 1985

Activity 9.1

Video record a 'serious' television interview. From the content of the interview look for evidence of interviewer bias either in the content of the questions, the way in which they are expressed, or the non-verbal behaviour of the interviewer. Political interviews, of course, are not necessarily intended to exemplify the degree of objectivity of a research interview, but they may illustrate the issue of bias more clearly.

Quality indicators

We have looked so far at validity and reliability as factors that enhance the credibility of an interview study. We need, however, to find some alternative, or at least additional, sources of quality. One important indicator is *consistency*, showing how the research has been conducted and the plausibility of the researcher's actions and analysis. The study should also provide evidence of *accuracy*, showing that the data is a fair representation of what informants have actually said. This might mean checking with interviewees that they have not been misinterpreted. Finally, the study must attempt to demonstrate *neutrality*, showing that the researcher is aware of the possible confounding effects of their own actions and perceptions and that these, as far as possible, have been accounted for.

INTERVIEWING SKILLS

Interviewing is a skill that must be learned through experience and practice. Of course, the respondent must first of all agree to be interviewed, and this might depend on a number of factors. Arksey and Knight (1999) suggest that getting an interview might depend upon:

- *Your status.* Are you 'internal' to the organization, or, say, someone completing a research project for an external client? If you are an internal researcher, how senior are you in the organization – and particularly, how senior compared to the interviewee?
- *The project.* Is the project of interest to the potential respondent? Is there a potential pay-off?
- *Yourself.* Do you seem trustworthy, personable and professional?

Once agreement is obtained, there is some preparatory work to be done, after which there is a number of techniques that help in the interviewing process.

Getting started

Preparation

Interviews cannot be rushed. Wengraf (2001) advises that you should arrive at least 30 minutes before the scheduled interview to make the necessary preparations and put aside at least an hour after the interview to make field notes. So, a 45 minute interview, for example, could take up to 2–3 hours to complete. Only by allowing yourself a clear stretch of time will you be assured that the interview will be conducted in a stress-free and unhurried fashion.

Wengraf sets out a schedule that should be followed, even before the day of the interview. About three weeks before, it is sometimes useful to get respondents to complete a pre-interview questionnaire dealing with demographic issues (for example, age, occupation and other details) so that the interview can focus on more substantive matters. Or you may have requested material from the respondent, and you will need time to read and reflect on it. About 7–10 days before the interview, you need to contact the respondent to make sure that they are still available, provide final confirmation about the exact location of the interview, and respond to any last-minute queries or concerns. The day before the interview you need to check that you have all the material you need at your disposal, and especially that you have an up-to-date version of your interview schedule. Obviously, make sure that any equipment such as tape recorders are working and that you have spare batteries, plenty of blank tapes, cables to the electricity supply and extension leads, note paper, pens and perhaps two bottles of mineral water in case you or the interviewee gets thirsty.

Preliminaries

The first task of the interviewer is to explain the purpose of the interview, who the information is for, how the information is going to be handled (including issues of confidentiality), why the information is being collected and how it will be used. This should not require a long speech, but should be done quickly and simply. Above all, the importance of the information should be stressed. If the research has been commissioned by a particular division or department of the organization this should be made clear.

Also ensure that the seating arrangements are acceptable to both parties. Sitting closely and face-to-face can feel confrontational and threatening. It is usually best to face each other but at a slight angle. Having some furniture such as a table between the interviewer and respondent also provides something on which to place note-paper and creates safe 'distance' between the parties. The seating should also be arranged so that the interviewee cannot read forthcoming questions or any notes that are being made.

Building rapport

Rapport means an understanding, one established on a basis of respect and trust between the interviewer and respondent. To establish a rapport it is particularly important to make the respondent relaxed and to get the interview off to a good start. This means you should:

- Describe how the interview will be conducted, how long it should last and the general subjects that are to be covered.
- Ask for permission to audio-tape the interview (and listen attentively for responses and note body language).
- Make guarantees of confidentiality.
- Ask if the respondent has any questions.

Rapport is described by Oppenheim as an 'elusive quality' (1992: 89), and one that often only experienced and skilled interviewers possess. If an interviewer has little rapport, the respondent may be unwilling to answer questions or may cut the interview short. If the interviewer has too much rapport he or she may soon find themselves cast in the role of social worker or counsellor. The secret is to remain objective, professional and detached yet relaxed and friendly (who said that interviewing was easy?!)

Conducting the interview

Impression management

Oppenheim (1992) warns that an interviewer creates an impression on the respondent, even before he or she opens their mouth. Features such as general appearance, mode of dress, accent (see next section), hairstyle, ethnicity and social background may all play a part. Different respondents will be affected in different ways. If an interviewer wears an expensive business suit and interviews top management, this might be acceptable, but would it receive the same reaction in the machine shop? As Oppenheim warns, however, there are no hard and fast rules here. Production line workers might be quite intrigued about being interviewed by someone in a suit and tie.

The key is that the interviewer should be aware of the process of impression management, and should try to avoid giving expression to her or his own distinctive style. The aim is for bland, social neutrality.

Use of language

One problem that needs to be borne in mind is that words can have different meanings to different people. In the UK, especially, there are difficulties stemming from the way different social classes use vocabulary. The word 'dinner', for example, has a meaning that is different in middle and working class language. In a business setting, the word 'management' may have different connotations. Managers themselves, for example, may see it as a way of steering the company (in the interests of *all* employees) towards profit and efficiency. Some employees, however, may view the word more negatively in terms of interference and control from 'above'. The key is making use of language that is accessible to your audience.

Maintaining control

Since time is usually of the essence, it is important that the interviewer keeps control of the interview, minimizing long-winded responses and digressions. Patton (1990) argues that control is maintained by:

- Knowing what the interview is seeking to find out.
- Asking the right questions.
- Giving appropriate verbal and non-verbal feedback.

This means listening carefully to responses and channelling the interview back onto the right tracks if necessary. As Patton (1990) warns, it is not enough to have an excellent list of questions if the respondent is permitted to stray from the point.

Activity 9.2

Consider the following exchange:

Interviewer: Could you tell me something about your feelings when voluntary redundancies were called for.

Respondent: The request for redundancies came in a letter to all of us just before Christmas last year. They were asking for 200 people to go, out of a workforce of just 850. Quite a few people I know were very interested in the package on offer from day one.

Is the response an acceptable reply to the question?

Suggested answers are provided at the end of the chapter.

Verbal and non-verbal communication should be used to provide appropriate feedback. If, for example, the respondent is on-track, head nodding, the active taking of notes and the occasional verbal acknowledgement, should all help. Similarly, the use of a silent probe, remaining quiet when further elaboration of a point is desired, is quite valid. If the respondent is straying off the point, then the usual cues such as head nodding should cease, and a new question interjected as soon as the respondent hesitates. As Patton (1990) warns, it may sometimes become necessary to actively intervene with a statement such as:

> Let me stop you here, for a moment. I want to make sure I fully understand something you said earlier. (Then ask the question aimed at getting the response more targeted.) (Patton, 1990: 332)

Do not be embarrassed about interrupting the interviewee if this means getting the interview back on track. But one of the skills of interviewing is knowing what is relevant and irrelevant as the interview progresses (so think back to your research objectives or general theme!).

Improvising

In semi-structured or unstructured interviews, improvisation may be the key to success. Arksey and Knight (1999) offer the following tips:

- Vary the question order to fit the flow of the interview.
- Vary the phrasing of the questions to help the conversation seem natural.
- Let the interview seem to go off track.
- Build trust and rapport by putting something of the interviewer's self into the interview, possibly by raising similar or different experiences.

Improvising, of course, is a skill that needs to be built through experience.

Activity 9.3

Having used a semi-structured or unstructured approach, go through the transcripts and note where you improvised. What was the result? How else could the question or comment have been phrased to improve the response? Was the eventual outcome a success? Should you continue with this approach, or adopt a more structured one?

Questioning techniques

As with the case of questionnaires, interview questions should be phrased so that their meaning is unambiguous, and they should be delivered in as neutral a tone of voice as possible. As we saw in Chapter 8, there are also certain ways of formulating questions that must be avoided. These include questions that:

- Contain jargon.
- Use prejudicial language.
- Are ambiguous.
- Lead the respondent.
- Include double questions.
- Contain hypothetical statements.
- Probe personal or sensitive issues.
- Require memory recall or knowledge the respondent does not possess.

Cluster groups of questions that deal with similar issues, and then sequence these blocks of questions in a logical order.

Active listening skills

Active listening involves attentive listening, that is, not just listening to the words that are being said, but also to the tone and emphasis. Attentive listening also means that the respondent should be doing most of the talking! If attentive listening is achieved, it should be possible to pick up new or significant themes that can be probed with new questions. Sometimes silences or incomplete statements can reveal more than what is actually said. Attentive listening involves identifying these incomplete replies and following them up.

It should be remembered that an interview is not a normal conversation and therefore the usual norms of human interaction do not necessarily apply. Where in normal conversation it might be acceptable to occasionally glance at one's watch or look away, in interviews a far greater degree of attentiveness is required. This means listening to and interpreting the meaning of what is being said, but also noting the tone and delivery of the dialogue to pick up any traces of irritation, confusion or boredom.

Observing

Like listening, careful observing helps to detect information on how the interview is progressing. Observation of the respondent's body language, for example, is important, to detect important clues on the respondent's concentration level, motivation to continue with the interview and whether she or he is at ease. If negative signs are detected, it may mean changing the sequencing of questions, bringing easier or less controversial ones up the order.

Of course, self-observation (reflection) is just as important. Self-understanding helps us to make our questioning and probing more sensitive. If, for example, the interviewer knows that he tends to dominate most natural conversations, he might make a conscious effort to hold back and leave spaces for the respondent to fill.

Testing and summarizing understanding

A useful approach is occasionally to repeat back to the interviewee what you believe they have just told you. This is particularly important if there are statements or issues that are not fully understood.

Closing the interview

It is at this point that you should check that you have asked all the questions that you intended. It is worthwhile asking the interviewee if they have any questions or final comments that they would like to make.

It is important that both you and the respondent leave the interview with a positive sense of achievement. Even if you feel less than elated by the data you have gathered, thank the interviewee for their help and their valuable observations. Then describe what happens next, particularly in terms of whether the respondents will be needed for checking the accuracy of transcripts, and the reporting process and follow up work. It is worth noting that interviewees often make some of their most interesting and valuable points once they think that the interview is over. Interviewers should not then suddenly scramble for note paper, but should remember and note these remarks once the respondent has left the interview setting.

Recording and transcribing data

There should be no short cuts when it comes to recording data. The analysis stage is made superfluous if the data have not been collected carefully. Patton (1990) puts it bluntly:

> No matter what style of interviewing is used, and no matter how carefully one words interview questions, it all comes to naught if the interviewer fails to capture the actual words of the person being interviewed. (Patton, 1990: 347)

Taking notes may be useful for a number of reasons, since it:

- Can help in the formulation of new questions.
- Provides a means for locating important quotations during later analysis.
- Is a non-verbal behaviour that helps pace the interview, providing the interviewee with a cue that they have said something significant.

Note taking, however, is much harder than it sounds, particularly because making handwritten notes is a slow and often inaccurate process. You will also be observing the respondent and thinking of the next question. It is probably best to jot down key words and occasional verbatim comments. It is usually better to make notes in conjunction with an audio or video recording. Particularly in the case of the former, it should be possible to note the tape recorder counter number where a key statement has been made.

The use of a tape recorder is vital for conducing interviews. Not only does it record the essential data, it permits the interviewer to concentrate on the process of listening, interpreting and re-focusing the interview. Using a tape recorder, though, is not always without its problems. In the workplace, respondents may, initially, feel uneasy about being tape-recorded. They will need reassurance as to confidentiality. In terms of the ethics of research, they should also be given the right to turn off the tape recorder at any time.

Give some careful consideration to the recording equipment you will need. Ensure you have enough tapes for the length of interview. Always make use of an external microphone rather than relying on the tape recorder's internal microphone, as this will give you superior sound reproduction.

Activity 9.4

Test out the quality of reproduction of your tape recorder by making practice recordings at different distances from the microphone. What is the furthest distance that gives you a quality of recording from which you can comfortably transcribe? If you are doing group interviews, will you need two microphones?

Patton (1990) suggests that the ideal objective is to achieve a full transcription of the interview. This process, however, is both expensive and time-consuming, with perhaps each hour of live interview requiring between 7 and 10 hours of transcribing. Nevertheless, there is really no substitute for being able to see all the transcribed data at a glance during the analysis stage of the research. If it is simply impractical to achieve full transcription, an option is to use notes taken at the interview to locate key quotations or passages that can be accessed on the tape for transcription.

Dealing with problem respondents

Interviewing presents a wide variety of potential difficulties. Within the workplace, people may be very reluctant to answer questions connected with their job responsibilities because they may feel vulnerable. Why am I being asked about my job? Why have *I* been picked out? What are they going to do with the information? Similarly, they may be nervous about expressing their views about issues and subjects connected with the company, and may be tempted to provide answers they think are wanted (socially desirable responses) rather than what they actually believe. Also, unless the research is seen to be officially sponsored by the organization in some way, it might be viewed as irrelevant snooping. If the research *is* sponsored, the level of this sponsorship within the organization hierarchy may prove a factor in eliciting cooperation.

Knowledge questions can also prove to be an embarrassment if people do not know the answer. The interviewer must never show surprise at a wrong answer or hint what the correct answer should be. Keep a look out for body language that signals discomfort, anger or irritation, and be prepared to switch questions or even to curtail the interview. Table 9.3 provides a simple summary checklist of do's and dont's of conducting interviews.

Using multicultural interviews

It is worth considering the implications of conducting interviews with people who are of a different ethnic, social or cultural group to that of the interviewer. We have seen the importance of building rapport between the two parties, and the significance of impression management and the use of language. It is extremely easy for any of these elements to go wrong unless the interviewer is aware of, and prepared for, the kinds of problems that can arise. Vazquez-Montilla et al. (2000) talk about the need for *culturally responsive* interviewing that is more sensitive to and aware of multi-ethnic cultural perspectives, and they introduce the notion of 'Triple A' (AAA) practices: authenticity, affinity and accuracy.

Working with Hispanic families in Florida, USA, the researchers found that their own Hispanic backgrounds were vital in establishing authenticity since the researchers were able to 'validate their ethnic match and cultural backgrounds' (Vazquez-Montilla et al., 2000: 4). To accomplish this task they were able to make reference to specific cities, events, characteristics of their native country, foods, etc. Since respondents were made aware of the interviewer's shared cultural perspectives, they became more confident that their message would not be misunderstood. Affinity was established through the interviewer spending time building up a

TABLE 9.3   CHECKLIST OF DO'S AND DON'TS OF INTERVIEWING

Do	Don't
Establish clearly what the interviewee thinks	Do not give an indication to the interviewee of *your* meanings and understandings or appear to judge their responses
Provide a balance between open and closed questions	Do not ask leading questions or questions to which it is easy for interviewees to simply agree with all you say
Listen carefully to all responses and follow up points that are not clear	Do not rush on to the next question before *thinking* about the last response
If necessary, either to gain interviewer thinking time or for the clarity of the audio recording, repeat the response	Do not respond with a modified version of the response, but repeat exactly what was said
Give the interviewee plenty of time to respond	Do not rush, but do not allow embarrassing silences
Where interviewees express doubts or hesitate, probe them to share their thinking	Avoid creating the impression that you would prefer some kinds of answers rather than others
Be sensitive to possible misunderstandings about questions, and if appropriate repeat the question	Do not make any assumptions about the ways in which the interviewee might be thinking
Be aware that the respondent may make self-contradictory statements	Do not forget earlier responses in the interview
Try to establish an informal atmosphere	Do not interrogate the interviewee
Be prepared to abandon the interview if it is not working	Do not continue if the respondent appears agitated, angry or withdrawn

Source: Adapted from Arksey and Knight, 1999

knowledge of the community, often through community agencies and groups. During the interviews, the interviewer attempted to match the respondent's conversational and interaction style, terminology and gestures (although stopping short of mirroring exaggerated mannerisms which would probably appear mocking and offensive). To enhance accuracy, interviewers made themselves aware of basic language terms used by participants by keeping a list of words and idiomatic expressions commonly used by the group. A second researcher always validated the analysis so that cultural stereotyping was avoided.

Keats (2000) suggests that some cultures would find the following actions unacceptable:

• Sending a woman to interview a man.
• Sending a man to interview a woman.
• Sending a person of one religion to interview a person of a different religion when factions from each are in conflict.
• Making direct rather than circuitous replies.
• Looking directly into a person's face when speaking.

Clearly, when conducting interviews with people of a different cultural or ethnic background to yourself, you need to be sensitive to these kinds of issues.

GROUP INTERVIEWS

So far we have assumed a one-to-one situation between an interviewer and single respondent. But, of course, other combinations are possible. Group interviews can comprise a number of different formats, including multiple interviewers, joint interviews and focus groups. An advantage of using group interviews is that costs can be drastically reduced, while the chance of non-response is reduced to about zero. But a drawback is that the social nature of responding may have an influence. Furthermore, as Dillman (2000) reports, group interviews using a questionnaire may invoke test-taking behaviour. He observed respondents checking through questions after completing them and even changing their answers.

Multiple interviewers

It can be very useful to have more than one interviewer present since different roles can be performed. For example, one interviewer can act as chairperson, controlling the pace and direction of the interview, while the other takes notes. At the end of the interview, each researcher can compare thoughts and observations to ensure that nothing has been missed.

Joint interviews

Joint interviews involve one researcher talking with two people simultaneously about one phenomenon. This can facilitate collecting differing or corroborating perspectives of the one event. Having both parties present can also allow for them to fill in details that the other has omitted. Against this must be set the danger of interviewees diverting each other's attention, or one respondent dominating the interview.

Focus groups

Focus groups originated in market research in the 1950s when people were brought together so that their attitudes to new products could be tested. Today, focus groups are still used for this purpose, but their popularity has spread to wider aspects of research. They can be a low cost way of collecting data, but require a considerable amount of cooperation and enthusiasm from participants. Logistical problems can also arise. If the focus group contains only six or seven participants, then tape recording may not pose a major problem. But if the group size is 20 or more, you may need two good quality tape recorders strategically placed to pick up usable recordings.

So far, we have assumed that interviews can be successfully conducted either in an unstructured manner or through the use of various types of questionnaires or interview schedules. However, there may be some special groups for which these techniques will either be inappropriate or entirely ineffective. The next Case Study provides an illustration of some more creative and imaginative approaches.

Case Study 9.2   Secret boxes, soap operas and spiders

Punch (2002) reports on a research study she carried out that explored young people's perceptions of their problems, coping strategies and help-seeking behaviour. The sample was drawn from both young people living at home and in residential care. The interviews were conducted using single sex friendship groups of five people. Clearly, because of the private nature of their problems and often their difficulty or unwillingness to articulate their worries, some innovative approaches were required. These included:

- *A 'secret box'*. The young people were asked to write down any current or recent problem and to post their anonymous response into a box. This was then sealed with sticky tape with the assurance that responses would only be read by the researcher after the completion of the last interview with each sample. It was also shaken up to ensure that the last response would not be on the top. Respondents were also permitted either to write a response or to post a blank piece of paper. This process both assured anonymity but also that questions would not be asked about the responses. Typical concerns to emerge concerned puberty, grief at the death of a close relative and illegal activities (drinking, drug taking and stealing). However, one of the limitations of this technique is that, because of anonymity, it is impossible to probe any of the responses.
- *Stimulus material: video clips from soap operas*. Three short clips from recent soap operas were recorded onto one video tape, each one depicting a typical problem that young people have to cope with. During a group interview, each of the clips was discussed in relation to young people's coping strategies. They were firstly asked how the people in the clip had coped. Secondly, they were asked how they would cope in similar circumstances. Punch describes these video clips as visual vignettes. The clips were highly effective in sparking off memories of personal experiences and provided a stimulus for discussions. One of the drawbacks was the time it took to locate appropriate clips and the time taken up by the clips in the interview sessions.
- *Stimulus material: problem letter pages* were used in a similar way as video clips to discuss issues such as eating disorders, sexual activity and depression.
- *Stimulus material: task-based activities*. A grouping and ranking exercise was used where the young people grouped 20 different problems written on plain index cards and placed them into three piles: big, middle and small worries. Then each pile was ranked from the most to the least worry. This was then used to provoke a group discussion about the nature of different problems. Spider diagrams were also used. Using a large sheet of paper, 'coping with problems' was circled in the middle and each person was asked to add a 'leg' indicating how they dealt with problems. Thus, the diagrams were used to build information and allow for issues to be probed in greater depth.

Source: Adapted from Punch, 2002

Activity 9.5

Consider the following questions in relation to Case Study 9.2:

1 Why were the interviews conducted with single sex friendship groups?
2 In developing a simple protocol that you could use for each of the above activities, how would you explain each activity, and how would you provide the necessary reassurances?

Suggested answers are provided at the end of the chapter.

TELEPHONE INTERVIEWS

We looked briefly at telephone interviews in Chapter 5 in the context of conducting telephone surveys. One of the main advantages of conducting interviews by telephone is the low cost. They also tend to be conducted faster, another important benefit. A potential disadvantage of telephone interviews is the fear that the refusal rate may be higher. Oppenheim (1992), however, provides some comfort here, suggesting that refusals are sometimes actually lower because of 'interviewer invisibility' to some respondents. But interviewers will need to adopt a professional telephone manner, especially to strike up a rapport. For a long interview, though, it is usually best to make a preliminary call to set up a time for the interview.

In terms of questions, all but the most complex kinds can be asked over the telephone. Indeed, as Arksey and Knight (1999) point out, one of the strengths of telephone interviews over questionnaires is that the interviewer can help respondents with any misunderstandings or difficulties they have. Response rates can also be raised if the interviewer has a slick, persuasive manner and can give encouragement. Table 9.4 provides a summary of the kinds of responses commonly given.

SAFETY ISSUES

Safety is probably not an issue that is uppermost in the minds of most researchers as they plan an interview. Often, respondents are known to the interviewer, or the interview may be conducted over the telephone or in a public place. Occasionally, however, a study may require that interviews are conducted in someone's home or isolated work location in circumstances where the respondent is not known to the researcher. Kenyon and Hawker (1999) raised this issue in an e-mail discussion with fellow researchers (recall Case Study 5.2 in Chapter 5). While most researchers (thankfully) have never experienced any problem, a minority had, and as the authors comment: 'once would be enough'. Their e-mail survey helped them to compile a list of 'best practice' guidelines, presented in Table 9.5.

Once again, it must be emphasized that the majority of interviewers face no significant problems in conducting their research. But as these guidelines make clear, it is better to be safe than sorry.

TABLE 9.4   EXAMPLE OF EXPLANATIONS GIVEN BY TELEPHONE INTERVIEWERS

Respondent's comments	Typical interviewer's replies
What's the purpose of the survey?	The questions are about your attitude to [*give name of topic*]
	It will give us a better idea of [*what to do/how to improve things/what the firm, department, etc. should concentrate on in the future*]
	I'm doing this as part of my work for [*name your institution*]
	All your replies will be treated in confidence
How will the survey be used?	A summary of the findings will go to [*add name of sponsor*]
	A short version of the survey will be available to our respondents at [*give Web address*]
How did you get my number?	Your number was chosen by a computer which randomly generates a list of numbers
	Your name was provided by a professional association/club [*name association/club*]
Why don't you want to talk to [*someone of the opposite sex, someone older or younger*] rather than me?	I need to make sure I have a good mix of men and women, younger and older people. You have been chosen because this helps us to achieve this mix
Hmm. I'm still not sure	If you want to check [*our/my*] credentials, why not call [*give name and number of sponsor*] and I'll call back later

Source: Adapted from Arksey and Knight, 1999

TABLE 9.5   BEST PRACTICE GUIDELINES FOR RESEARCHER SAFETY

Equipment	Carry a mobile phone. This helps researchers to check 'in and out' of interviews and provides a means of summoning help if needed.
	Use official stationary to arrange and confirm interviews and show an identity card if you possess one, as these can help to confirm a professional identity and show that you are affiliated to an institution.
Personal demeanour	Develop an awareness of body language (both your own and that of your respondents).
	Be honest, but not over friendly, dress in an appropriate manner and avoid carrying or wearing valuables.
Knowledge and accountability	Have a good knowledge of the working environment both in terms of the research venue and the geographical area in which it is situated.
	Record and report any doubts or incidents, however trivial they may seem.
	Advise others (particularly friends or relatives) of your whereabouts and movements at all times during fieldwork.
Avoidance strategies	Use daylight hours for interviews if possible.
	If interviewing someone in their home, take along a second interviewer as a 'minder'.
	Avoid potentially dangerous areas such as unlit stairwells, lifts and empty buildings.
	Try to use informants that are 'known' in some way, for example, through a third party or through a network. Male respondents should be accessed through female friends or partners.
	Avoid pressurizing anyone to become involved in the research.

Source: Adapted from Kenyon and Hawker, 1999

CONSENT FORM		
Beechwood Academy		
Evaluation of anti-bullying policy		
This consent form is designed to check that you understand the purposes of the study, that you are aware of your rights as a participant and to confirm that you are willing to take part		

Please tick as appropriate		
	YES	NO
1 I have read the leaflet describing the study		
2 I have received sufficient information about the study for me to decide whether to take part		
3 I understand that I am free to refuse to take part if I wish		
4 I understand that I may withdraw from the study at any time without having to provide a reason		
5 I know that I can ask for further information about the study from the research team		
6 I understand that all information arising from the study will be treated as confidential		
7 I know that it will not be possible to identify any individual respondent in the study report, including myself		
8 I agree to take part in the study		

Signature:	Date:
Name in block letters, please:	

I confirm that quotations from the interview can be used in the final research report and other publications. I understand that these will be used anonymously and that no individual respondent will be identified in such report.	
Signature:	Date:
Name in block letters, please:	

FIGURE 9.1   EXAMPLE OF AN INFORMED CONSENT FORM (ADAPTED FROM ARKSEY AND KNIGHT, 1999)

TABLE 9.6   ACTION THAT CAN BE TAKEN FOR CONDUCTING AN ETHICAL
              INTERVIEW

Ethical issue	Actions
Promises and guarantees	State what the interviewee will gain Ensure that if a copy of the report is promised, it is delivered
Risk assessment	Consider in what ways might the interview put people at risk in terms of: Stress Hostility from line-managers, peers, etc
Confidentiality	Reflect on the extent to which promises of confidentiality can *actually* be met.
Organizational permissions	Consider whether you have the 'right' to interview respondents Are permissions necessary?
Data access and ownership	Evaluate who has the right to access data and for what purpose. Who 'owns' the final report in terms of intellectual property rights?
Mental health	Consider how interviewer and interviewee mental health may be affected by conducting the interview
Advice	Appoint an adviser on ethical matters during the course of the study

Source: Adapted from Patton, 1990

ETHICAL ISSUES

The central ethical issue surrounding data collection through interviews is that participants should not be harmed or damaged in any way by the research. If a respondent becomes anxious or upset during the course of an interview, the session should be immediately abandoned. We have already seen that confidentiality should be offered to respondents when completing questionnaires, so, clearly, the same respect should be afforded those participating in interviews. Furthermore, interviewees have the right not to answer individual questions or to terminate the interview before its completion. It is also important that interviews are not used as a devious means of selling something to the respondent.

One of the problems is that, as Patton (1990) states:

> A good interview lays open thoughts, feelings, knowledge, and experience not only to the interviewer but also to the interviewee. (Patton, 1990: 353)

After a good interview, the interviewees know more about themselves and their situation than they did before. This, in itself, may be quite therapeutic (or not as the case may be), but the purpose of research is to collect data, not to change people or opinions. A key ethical consideration is that of informed consent. In some countries, for example the USA, written consent is required even when the research is small scale or only involves structured, closed–question interviews. An example of an informed consent form is given in Figure 9.1.

Having taken steps to ensure informed consent, what are the practical considerations that help to ensure that an interview is ethically conducted? Table 9.6 sets out some issues and suggested ethical solutions.

Ethical issues might arise in any number of unexpected ways. For example, in dealing with particularly difficult or sensitive topics, the respondent might ask for practical guidance or advice. It should be noted that the interviewer is not a counsellor, and should avoid being drawn into this type of discussion. The proper course of action would be to offer contact details for those kinds of organization that could provide help. These would include advice bureaux, voluntary organizations, support networks and telephone helplines.

SUMMARY

- Interviews can be divided into five categories ranging from the informal conversational to the completely structured.
- The choice of approach will depend on the objectives of the research, with structured interviews eliciting more quantitative data and unstructured or focused interviews, qualitative.
- The danger of bias in interviews stems not only from the type of questions asked but the way in which they are articulated by the interviewer.
- Interviewing is a skill and includes the ability to build rapport with respondents while maintaining detachment, and observing and listening in order to keep control of the interview.
- Be aware of some of the safety issues involved in interviewing, particularly interviewing people in their own homes or in isolated work situations. Use common-sense to avoid potentially dangerous situations. Carry a mobile phone and always let close confidants know where you are.
- Ethical issues are of paramount importance since confidentiality may be more difficult to maintain than in other forms of data gathering, such as postal questionnaires.

Further reading

Arksey, H. and Knight, P. (1999) *Interviewing for Social Scientists*. London: Sage. Easy to read, but detailed and comprehensive. This book shows how to design an interview study and provides essential advice on how to conduct a successful interview.

Keats, D.M. (2000) *Interviewing: A Practical Guide for Students and Professionals*. Buckingham: Open University Press. A simple but practical guide to interviewing skills that includes the structure of interviews, interpreting responses, and chapters on interviewing children, adolescents, the aged and people with disabilities.

Suggested answers for Activity 9.2

While the response does offer factual information, the question is probing for the respondent's *feelings*, and so the response received is inappropriate.

Suggested answers for Activity 9.5

1   Clearly, because of the often personal nature of some of the discussions, single sex groups are more appropriate for the interviews.
2   Any research protocol should be simple and easy to use. It could, perhaps, take the form of a single side of A4 paper to be given to the respondent, containing the purpose of the research and a short list of instructions. Assurances of confidentiality could be given at the top of the proforma and at the end (as reinforcement). The researcher could repeat these assurances orally.

Collecting Primary Data: Observation

Chapter objectives

After reading this chapter you will be able to:

- **Describe some of the advantages and disadvantages of the observational approach.**
- **Select an observational approach appropriate to a given research objective.**
- **Analyse and interpret observational data.**
- **Produce observational data that are valid and reliable.**
- **Use observational methods in an ethical manner.**

Observation is not simply a question of looking at something and then noting down 'the facts'. Observation is a complex combination of sensation (sight, sound, touch, smell and even taste) and perception. A ringing sound in the office might be a telephone, an error signal from the new fax machine or the fire alarm! On hearing such a sound, we would have to use some experience from the past as a guide to interpreting it, and to give it meaning. Think of those people who have, say, lost their memories as a result of an accident, and the problems they face in their lives, re-interpreting sensations from scratch. Meanings (concepts) are stored in memory, are in people's minds and are individual interpretations of 'reality'. Hence, when a door is left open in the corridor, one worker may see this as a welcome way of improving air circulation in the office, while another worker (the safety representative) sees this as a safety hazard if it is a fire door!

The interpretation of 'meaning' is one of the benefits but also potentially one of the drawbacks of the observation method. On the positive side, observation provides an opportunity to get beyond people's opinions and self-interpretations of their attitudes and behaviours towards an evaluation of their actions in practice. For example, we might ask people their views about working with the opposite sex and find that, through a questionnaire and a set of interviews, most state that they find this constructive and rewarding. A researcher, however, spends a month in the organization listening to conversations and observing behaviour and finds barely concealed hostility and 'backbiting' among quite a significant proportion of male shopfloor workers against their female counterparts.

As we shall see, one of the drawbacks of observation is that the interpretation of what is observed may be influenced by the mental constructs of the researcher (including their values, motivations, prejudices and emotions). We often 'see' what we want to see and disregard other phenomena that could prove important. Secondly, if stationed among those who are being observed, the researcher may begin actually to influence events. Furthermore, while the data gathered from observation are often rich in evidence, extracting themes and concepts from the data can be quite challenging.

The observational method is often associated with ethnographic methodology in that it studies people in their natural settings or 'fields'. Ethnography, however, can also entail the use of other methods such as in-depth interviewing, and the analysis of personal documents.

APPROACHES TO OBSERVATION

Observation involves the systematic viewing of people's actions and the recording, analysis and interpretation of their behaviour. Saunders et al. (2000) differentiate between *participant* and *structured* observation. Participant observation is largely qualitative and emphasizes the meanings that people give to their actions, while structured observation is largely quantitative and focuses on the frequency of their actions. Within each of these categories the researcher can collect the data covertly by hiding their identity, or collect the data overtly (see Figure 10.1).

Overt and covert observation

Overt observation is where those being observed are aware that the observation is taking place. By contrast, covert observation is where they are unaware of this. One of the arguments in favour of covert observation is that people may change their behaviour when they know they are being observed, thus threatening the validity of the results. The problem with covert observation, of course, is that it can be construed as unethical. Consider your own feelings – how would you feel if you discovered that someone, perhaps in your own organization, and, say, with the approval of management, had been observing you performing some element of your work. Douglas (1976), however, considers it legitimate to conduct covert observations since people try to obscure the truth through misinformation, evasions, lies and 'fronts'. In practice, the extent to which participants in a research project are informed that they are being observed ranges from full disclosure to no disclosure at all, with many projects somewhere in the middle. As Berg (1995) comments, some subjects are so sensitive that it might be impossible to carry out research by any other means. It is worth noting that most communication within organizations today takes place via e-mail and that all these messages are stored and can be analysed. The laws on how this is done, and what consequences result, vary between countries, but, in a sense, covert observation is now part of our everyday lives.

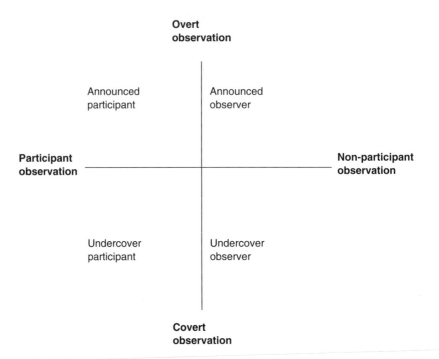

FIGURE 10.1 OBSERVATION RESEARCH ROLES

If covert observation is undertaken, it is essential that confidentiality is still respected. Hence, the names and locations of those being observed should not be revealed to any sponsor of the research. Case Study 10.1 provides an illustration of how covert observation can produce unexpected findings.

Case Study 10.1   How smart is covert observation?

A company running a Holiday Village has just introduced a smart card for its customers so that the customer can:

- Check in on arrival using the smart card without having to get out of the car.
- Pre-book facilities such as bicycle hire and the hire of tennis courts.
- Open their lodge door.
- Use the card instead of making credit card or cash transactions.

A covert participant researcher with knowledge and expertise in smart card technology enters the Village as a 'guest' to observe the 'customer experience' in using the cards. As a covert observer she is able to note some of the problems guests experience with the system including:

(Continued)

- A court booking system that does not use real time updating, thus allowing double booking of the system.
- Aspects of the system failing to be fully functional when the volume of customers exceeds capacity.

The full interpretation of systems failures depends on the researcher's knowledge of computer systems and, at times, her ability to phrase questions that are deemed as acceptable coming from a fellow customer.

Source: Slack and Rowley, 2001

Activity 10.1

Examine Case Study 10.1. Is covert observation justified here? Could the study have been conducted using overt observation with the same success?

Suggested answers are provided at the end of the chapter.

Participant and non-participant observation

Participant observation is a research method most closely associated with ethnographic methodology, and has its origins in British anthropology and the Chicago School of sociology. The central intent of this method is to generate data through observing and listening to people in their natural setting, and to discover their social meanings and interpretations of their own activities. Part of this process is the reporting of the researcher's own experiences, feelings, fears, anxieties and social meanings when engaged with people in the field. With participant observation, the researcher becomes a member of the group being researched and so begins to understand their situation by experiencing it. The researcher becomes 'immersed' in the research setting with the objective of sharing and experiencing people's lives in order to learn about their symbolic world. This symbolic framework was first developed within a school of sociology known as symbolic interactionism (recall Chapter 2).

The principle behind symbolic interactionism is that people develop a sense of identity through their interaction and communication with others. Through this interaction, a process of negotiation takes place through which they respond to others and adjust their understanding and behaviours to create a shared sense of reality. This theory stresses the dynamic nature of social interaction in which people continually change through their interaction with their environment. A person's identity is not something that is given, but is being continually reconstructed as he or she moves through different social settings. Participant observation, then, involves working or acting alongside people in order to observe their interactions with their social environment to explore how it changes their ideas and behaviour, and even their own reflexive awareness of these changes. As Gans (1999) warns, ethnographic research of this kind usually involves months or even years of research. It is therefore costly. Hence, much participant observation tends to be in public health and medical institutions that are often supported by some of the larger funding agencies.

In undertaking participant observation one of the challenges is to maintain a balance between 'insider' and 'outsider' status. To gain a deep understanding of people's lives it is essential that the researcher gets both physically but also emotionally close to them – but how then does the researcher maintain a professional 'distance'? Achieving this is often affected by issues such as the gender, race, social class and the education of the researcher compared to that of the people being researched. Burgess (1984) also adds that age can sometimes be an issue – is it practical for researchers of more advanced years to observe youth gangs, for example? As one set of researchers put it:

> *The more one is like the participants in terms of culture, gender, race, socio-economic class and so on, the more it is assumed that access will be granted, meanings shared, and validity of findings assured.* (Merriam et al., 2001: 406)

To remain an 'outsider' would be to fail to gain the kind of rapport that is needed to make this method a success. The participant observer, in a sense, needs to be both inside and outside the setting. Indeed, Merriam et al. (2001) argue that the boundaries between the two positions are not simple or clearly delineated. Being inside or outside is relative to a whole host of cultural and social characteristics and is a position that can shift over time. According to Hall (2000), the best the ethnographer can achieve is to negotiate a position in which one is in some way 'at home' and considered as 'one of us' without becoming completely immersed.

Participant observation can be contrasted with research using a questionnaire where it is often not possible to verify whether people are telling the truth, or if their perceptions of their own behaviour or attitudes are accurate. In contrast, with participant observation it can be possible to interpret some of the subtleties of meaning in the data. Most organizations, for example, and particularly large ones, will contain a variety of social groups, each of which has, to a certain extent, its own norms, standards, attitudes and even culture and language. Contrast the cultures of those who work in the human resources department with those who work in security. Working amongst groups may reveal a whole set of norms and attitudes that would simply not emerge from more traditional research methods.

Cohen and Manion (1997), referring to the work of Bailey, suggest that participant studies are of value in that they:

- Are effective at observing non-verbal behaviour.
- Are immediate in the sense that they elicit data on events as they happen.
- Allow for a more natural relationship to develop over time between the researcher and respondent.

But, clearly, such methods are also open to criticism of bias and subjectivity.

On a slightly divergent note, the increasingly modern phenomenon of the organizational 'whistleblower' can also be regarded as a form of participant observation. The persons who seek to investigate or publicize illegal or unethical acts may not regard themselves as such, but their aims drive them to systematically seek out information – thereby joining themselves to the research community (Vinten, 1994: 34).

The practitioner–researcher

A practitioner–researcher is someone who undertakes research within and often on behalf of their organization. As a researcher, then, they are in an ideal position to understand the culture, strengths and weaknesses of the organization, as well as its developing needs. If the research is sponsored by the organization, and especially if sponsored by senior management, then the practitioner researcher may often have good access to records and other information. Above all, the practitioner–researcher may have fairly open access to key decision makers in the organization. However, one of the limitations of using practitioner–researchers is the fact that they may be imbued with the organization's ethos and attitudes and so have difficulty in adopting fresh perspectives and approaches.

One element of the practitioner–researcher approach is *action research* (see Chapter 15). Today, it has a number of different connotations, but is mainly concerned with the promotion of organizational change, and the active involvement of practitioners in the research process. In a business context, it may involve managers in the sponsorship of research or their own participation in a research project, the aim of which is to initiate change, to learn from this process and to transfer this knowledge more generally within the organization.

Variations in duration

In truly ethnographic studies, social science researchers have spent, literally, years living among the people they are studying. Clearly, this is neither practical nor necessary for most business research. So, over what kind of time period should the observation take place? Patton (1990) states the obvious, that fieldwork should take as long as is necessary to get the job done. A study, for example, that set out to measure changes in staff attitudes to corporate re-structuring would have to allow for observation before, during and after the reorganization, thus taking many months, if not a number of years.

DATA GATHERING AND RECORDING

Before examining how researchers can gather observational data, we should first ask: what actually constitutes data? Burgess (1984), using the example of a study

TABLE 10.1   FEATURES OF SOCIAL SITUATIONS AS A BASIS FOR OBSERVATIONAL DATA SOURCES

Data features	Features of a school
Space	Layout of classrooms and offices
Actors	The people involved in the situation and their names
Activities	The various activities of people in the setting
Objects	The physical elements present such as furniture and its position in the room
Acts	The actions of individuals
Events	Activities such as school assemblies
Time	The time sequence of the school such as lessons, breaks and lunch hours
Goals	The activities people are attempting to accomplish
Feelings	Emotions in particular contexts

Source: Adapted from Burgess, 1984

in a school, provides a list of potential data sources (see Table 10.1). Any of these data features could be followed up by more focused questions dealing with each area in more detail. While there are a variety of ways in which observational data are collected, two of the most widely used are the writing of field notes and the use of more structured data collection methods.

Field notes

According to Bailey, field notes are 'the backbone of collecting and analyzing field data' (1996: 80). They are absolutely essential to the success of fieldwork, and comprise everything the fieldworker believes to be of importance. The danger of taking field notes is to fail to note a situation in the belief that it will always be recalled at a later date. The field researcher should guard against this kind of optimism. In general, field notes should be written up immediately following the observation. Bailey (1996) suggests that field notes develop out of an analytic process. First, the researcher must attempt to mentally capture and remember as much detail as possible: who was in the field setting, what did they look like, what did they say, how did you feel about them, etc. These constitute *mental notes*, which can be recalled latter to aid the production of *jotted notes*. Jotted notes comprise observations taken in the field that act as a kind of *aide-mémoire* for the later production of more comprehensive *field notes,* of which there are several components (as illustrated in Figure 10.2):

- *Primary observation: chronological log.* Raw data (i.e., no explanations or analysis) of observations on people, their surroundings, behaviours and conversations. Each set of field notes is dated and the time of occurrence noted. It is important to distinguish between actual verbatim quotations and approximate recall of conversations. You could, for example, put all real quotations in quotation marks and leave the general paraphrasing of conversations without such quotations.
- *Reflection and recall.* Some of these will be stimulated from jotted notes and some recalled during the process of writing up field notes. Sometimes objects or events do not seem important at the time but are then recalled when they occur again.

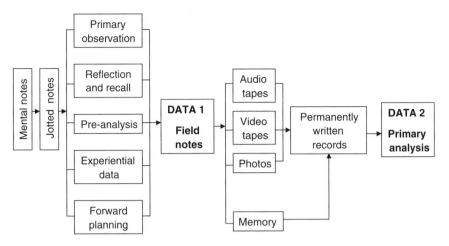

FIGURE 10.2 THE DATA GATHERING PROCESS (ADAPTED FROM ELLEN, 1984)

- *Pre-analysis data: ideas and inferences.* Themes and insights may start to emerge. Do not try to censor yourself at this stage, but write down anything that occurs to you – even when in the field. Indeed, Burgess (1984) advises the use of wide margins for field notes so that there is space to add preliminary categories. Make sure that a distinction is maintained between observational and analytical notes, even though they may be written at virtually the same time.
- *Experiential data: impressions and personal feelings.* These can often be a useful source of analytic insights at a later stage. So write down everything you can think of, including your feelings about events, people, conversations and your interpretations of your emotional reactions. These kinds of notes might be kept in the form of a diary.
- *Forward planning.* This might involve planning to revisit the field to collect missing data or to plan the next stage of the research project.

Once the field notes are completed, they can be written up along with any visual media that have been collected, such as photographs or audio tapes, and held as a permanent record. Burgess (1984) also recommends the drawing of diagrams to show, for example, the arrangements of furniture and people's sitting positions (especially for the recording of groups). Even at this stage, people, events or instances might be recalled that did not appear in the field notes, but which can now be recorded. This permanent written record (Figure 10.2) provides the basis for the primary analysis of the data.

What do field notes actually look like? Obviously, there are no rigid rules that define the answer. But it should be noted that too much data is better than too little. It is also usually far from clear when in the field as to which data are going to be relevant and which of little value. Hence, try to be as comprehensive as possible. Presented in Figure 10.3 is an example of inadequate field notes (left column) against a set of more detailed, descriptive notes.

Inadequate field notes	Improved field notes
The till worker served a customer but gave her scant attention.	**Date:** May 4th 2002 **Location:** Cafe Talk **Time in:** 11.15 **Time out:** 11.30 **Description:** There was a smell of fried food mixed with disinfectant. Young, white male (about 20 years of age), medium height and build, wearing staff canteen smock, short, neat, brown hair. Right ear pierced. The till worker looked up at the customer as she approached the till, but then looked away. He adjusted the till roll and opened and closed the cash till twice. He made no eye contact with the customer when she arrived at the till, and smoothed his hand through his hair. I felt that this was an unhygienic thing to do. I felt a sudden rush of antagonism towards him that I then tried to repress. He began entering the price of the coffee, soup and cake into the till, stated the price and held out his hand (again no eye contact made). He gave the customer some change, said 'Cheers' and closed the till. He turned away from the customer before she walked away, and shouted for more change from the adjacent till. **Things to do:** Return to Cafe Talk tomorrow to make observations of other staff and to observe their interactions with customers.

FIGURE 10.3 OBSERVATION OF TILL SERVICE IN A BUSY STAFF CANTEEN, ILLUSTRATING INADEQUATE NOTES (LEFT) AND MORE COMPREHENSIVE NOTES (RIGHT)

Activity 10.2

Looking at Figure 10.3, what evidence can you find of:

1   A chronological log (raw data).
2   Experiential data.
3   Forward planning.

Suggested answers are provided at the end of the chapter.

Like all note-taking, the way in which field notes are written up will depend on the researcher. Some wait until they have left the observational setting and write up their notes immediately. Others make cryptic notes during the observation and translate these later into field notes, usually as a computer file. In terms of content, field notes should contain:

- Key quotations, reproduced verbatim.
- Details of the physical appearance of inhabitants: gender, height, physical build, age, ethnicity, clothes, style of hair, appearance of jewellery, etc.
- Observation of verbal behaviours such as the verbatim text of conversations, the characteristics of the speech and the speaker (use of slang or technical language); who does most of the talking and whose suggestions are followed and whose ignored; who interrupts and who does not; the tone of the conversation (polite, bored, hostile, formal, indifferent, etc.)
- Observation of non-verbal behaviours such as body language – facial expressions, body posture (arms folded in front is usually a defensive posture), how they move (confident or diffident?), length and frequency of eye contact.
- The time of events and activities.
- The alteration of names and places to assist in the promotion of confidentiality (but a list of pseudonyms should be kept so the same name can be allocated to each term used).
- The researcher's views and feelings at the time of the observation.

In making field notes, Berg (1995) also suggests that the researcher:

- Records key words and phrases while in the field.
- Makes notes about the *sequence* of events.
- Limits the time spent in the field, since every hour will take 4 hours to write up (at least).
- Writes up full notes immediately on exiting the field. It is not worth undertaking any further observation until this is done.

The reproduction of field notes can be accomplished quite simply using a word processing program. Alternatively, you might consider using a specifically designed software program that provides facilities for data storage and later content analysis.

Having described in some detail the process of observing and writing up field notes, it is worth heeding de Laine's (2000) words of caution. She argues that in producing field notes, the researcher brings personal meaning to the account created. In other words, field notes are not 'raw data' in the simple sense, but details that are sieved from all the possible data through the researcher's mental constructs, understandings and interpretations.

> **Activity 10.3**
>
> Go to a busy environment (such as a train station or supermarket) and spend ten minutes observing people in action, and listening to their conversations. During the observation make as comprehensive a set of field notes as you can, and write these up as soon as is practicable. Examine your completed field notes. Do they accurately reflect what you observed? What was the ratio between time observing and time taken to write up?

Structured observation

The advantages of structured observation

In contrast to the use of field notes, structured observation is more quantitative in nature. A typical example in the workplace would be a time-and-motion study where someone is observed performing a task and their actions noted on a pre-designed proforma. Structured observation has a number of distinct advantages:

- It should result in more reliable data because the results can be replicated either by the same researcher at a different time, or by other researchers.
- It allows data to be collected at the time they occur and does not have to rely on the recall of participants or their interpretation of events.
- It collects data that participants themselves may not realize are important.

Against this must be set the disadvantages that:

- The researcher must be at the place where the events are occurring and at the appropriate time.
- Only overt actions can be observed, from which often subtle inferences have to be made.

Coding schedules

Coding schedules are structured schemes using predetermined categories for recording observable events. They range from quite simple approaches such as a system based upon *time*, to quite complex *event* systems. Robson (1993) suggests that before a coding schedule is selected, the first phase of a structured observation approach will be an exploratory one, often using other techniques such as interviews or questionnaires.

Coding schedules can be developed by the researcher (an onerous task) or use made of existing schedules. A common time scheme, the Flanders interaction analysis (IA) system, has been widely used in educational research for many years to illustrate the interaction between teachers and pupils. In Table 10.2 the Flanders system has been adapted for a situation where interaction is taking place between

TABLE 10.2 FLANDERS INTERACTION ANALYSIS SYSTEM

Categories	
1	**Manager accepts subordinate's feelings**. Accepts and clarifies an attitude or the feeling tone of a subordinate in a non-threatening manner. Feelings may be positive or negative. Predicting and recalling feelings are included
2	**Manager praises subordinate**. Praises or encourages subordinate's action or behaviour. Jokes that release tension, but not at the expense of another individual; nodding head, or saying 'mm hm?' or 'Go on' are included
3	**Manager uses subordinate's ideas**. Clarifying, building or developing ideas suggested by subordinate. Manager's extensions of subordinate's ideas are included but as the manager brings more of his/her ideas into play, switch to category 5
4	**Manager questions**. Asking a question about content or procedure, based on manager's ideas, with the intention that the subordinate will answer
5	**Manager discusses**. Manager gives facts or opinions about content or procedures; expresses own ideas, gives own explanations, or cites an authority other than the subordinate
6	**Manager gives directions**. Directions, commands or orders with which the subordinate is expected to comply
7	**Manager criticizes subordinate**. Statements intended to change subordinate's behaviour from non-acceptable to acceptable patterns; bawling someone out; stating why the manager is doing what she/he is doing; extreme self-reference
8	**Subordinate response**. Talk by subordinate in response to manager. Manager initiates the contact or solicits subordinate's statement or structures the situation. Freedom for subordinate to express own ideas is limited
9	**Subordinate-initiated response**. Talk by subordinate that they initiate. Expressing own ideas; initiating topic; freedom to develop opinions
10	**Silence and confusion**. Pauses, short periods of silence and periods of confusion which cannot be understood by the observer

Source: Adapted from Flanders, 1970: 34

work-based employees. This could be on the basis of peer group interaction, for example, a project team working on the development of a new software system, or a manager–subordinate interaction. Table 10.2 provides an example of the latter.

In using the Flanders system an interval coding system is used where a code is selected for every three seconds of interaction. Figure 10.4 illustrates a typical coding sheet, showing that, so far, three minutes of interaction have been logged, with a code number noted for every three seconds. In the first minute, it can be seen that most of the conversation is led by the manager either making comments (5) or giving directions (6). In the third minute, the manager asks a question (4), the subordinate responds (8), and the manager criticizes this response (7).

The Flanders interaction analysis system is an example of an *interval* coding scheme since data are collected at pre-determined time periods. Other categories

1	5	5	5	5	5	9	9	9	9	5	5	5	5	6	6	6	5	5	9	9
2	7	7	7	4	4	4	7	7	7	7	7	7	7	7	5	5	5	5	5	5
3	4	4	4	8	8	8	8	7	7	7	7	5	5	5	5	9	9	9	7	7
4																				
5																				

FIGURE 10.4 ANALYSIS OF DIALOGUE BETWEEN MANAGER AND SUBORDINATE USING THE FLANDERS INTERACTION ANALYSIS SYSTEM

of coding scheme include *event* coding when a tally is made only when an event occurs. Figure 10.5 illustrates alternative ways in which this can be done. In (*a*) we have a simple array of events labelled 1 to 3. When each event occurs, it is tallied. Hence, we can see that event 2 occurred more frequently than event 3. Knowing the number of times an event occurred is often enough. In (*b*) the sequence record gives us not only how often an event occurred, but the sequence of events. This can often be more useful at the analysis stage than knowing the simple frequency. The sequence record on timescale (*c*) adds a further layer of detail, showing not only how often events occurred and their frequency, but also the time intervals between these events.

THE PROCESS OF OBSERVATION

Getting in

One of the greatest problems with the observational method is that of actually *getting into* the research setting. Bailey (1996) argues that one of the ways to gain entry is through building relationships with gatekeepers, individuals who play a key role in either granting or denying access. Formal gatekeepers include managers, directors, head teachers, chief administrators, etc., while informal gatekeepers do not have institutional power, as such, but exert an influence over the research setting. Gatekeepers dictate when the researcher can enter the setting, who is talked to and what can be observed. The gatekeeper is not necessarily the highest person in authority. Indeed, relying on such a person might negatively influence the attitude of the real gatekeepers lower down in the social hierarchy of an organization.

Negotiating access with gatekeepers is a vitally important process and one that affects the rest of the study. It will often be necessary to negotiate collaboration with more than one gatekeeper and to re-negotiate access on a continual

(a) Simple checklist

Event	1	2	3
	///	////	/

(b) Sequence record

Event	2	2	1	3	1	1	1	2	3

(c) Sequence record on timescale

Elapsed time (min)	0	5	10	15	20	25	30
Event	1	2	3 2 2	1	1 2	2	1

FIGURE 10.5 ALTERNATIVE WAYS OF EVENT CODING

basis. Bailey (1996) warns that these negotiations can often be affected by issues of gender, race, age or sexual orientation. For example, a heterosexual woman who wants to observe a lesbian reading group might be welcomed by some groups but not by others. It will certainly be easier to gain entry if the researcher has empathy with those being studied. This does not mean necessarily agreeing or disagreeing with them, but it does mean avoiding the adoption of judgemental attitudes. Patton (1990) suggests that a reciprocity model of gaining entry is valuable, where both researcher and participants come to see mutual advantages emerging from the observational process. This, of course, may be a pious hope. As Hall (2000) points out, especially when working with disadvantaged groups, an outsider's curiosity might be construed as objectionable and patronizing – the first few weeks of fieldwork can sometimes be a miserable experience for the researcher.

Getting in, though, is helped by getting to know the routines and rituals of the target audience. For example, sometimes 'guides' can help to smooth the passage of the researcher into the organization or group. Guides are indigenous workers within the location to be studied or are people who can vouch for the trustworthiness of the researcher and the value of the research. If the guide's role turns out to be rejected by the hostile attitudes of the group, then this role can be snowballed to another person, recommended by the original guide.

Informed consent

Informing people in the research setting of what you are doing, and eliciting their consent, is seen as good practice by most researchers. Diener and Crandall (1978) suggest that fully informed consent should include:

- Describing the overall purpose of the research.
- Telling the participants about their role in the study.
- Stating why they have been chosen.
- Explaining the procedures, including the amount of time required.
- Clearly stating the risks and discomforts.
- Stating that the participants may withdraw at any time.

As we saw in Chapter 9 (recall Figure 9.1), getting participants to sign a consent form is also prudent. This, of course, implies that covert observation cannot be undertaken. Bailey (1996) argues that achieving a cooperative relationship with a group more than compensates for what is lost through reactivity (between researcher and those being researched). However, the impact of the researcher's presence and interactions needs to be reflected in field notes and analysis. Note that even after permission has been granted it can be withdrawn at any time and that this must be respected. Of course, there are often circumstances when informed consent is simply impractical. Burgess (1984) notes that in research in public settings (sports events, parents' evenings, church services, etc.) access cannot be negotiated with every participant.

Becoming invisible

The researcher may become 'invisible' due to the length of time they are involved in the project, by immersing themselves into the norms and behaviours of the group being studied, or simply by hiding the fact that they are researchers. As Berg (1995) points out, however, there are reasons why invisibility is a danger. If, for example, you go 'undercover' to research, say, criminal activities within an organization, you need to ensure that you do not become implicated yourself! On the whole, though, invisibility means that participants cease to be consciously aware of the researcher's presence, and therefore act more naturally.

Building rapport

Assuming that you adopt an overt observation strategy, then it is important that you begin to build rapport, established on 'relationships that ideally are emotional and personal, not formal and hierarchical' (Bailey 1996: 60). There can be no hard and fast rules about how rapport is established since this very much depends on the interactions between the researcher and those in the field setting. But being honest, friendly and open is probably the best place to start. People tend to respond when interest is shown in them. Of course, the opposite also applies. The moment people believe that the researcher has been dishonest or manipulative all trust will evaporate and will be almost impossible to re-establish.

Handling identity

In all aspects of research where the researcher is in direct contact with informants, the personal identity of the researcher will affect research practice. Given the close proximity and often the length of time spent in the field, this is particularly true of participant observation. Elements such as gender (often the main focus of concern), age, social class, race and religion are all important identifying factors. A problem, for example, of being a female researcher in male-dominated environments is that the researcher sometimes becomes treated as a sex object. In ethnographic research

> *young female ethnographers can be subject to sexual hustling, fraternity and paternalistic attitudes from male respondents, and treated as gofers, mascots or surrogate daughters.* (Brewer, 2000: 100)

One of the advantages of being a female participant observer is that women often tend to explore issues, including gender issues, that would often be glossed over by their male counterparts. Similarly, it may be easier for a young researcher to work with youth gangs, although this is not to rule out the possibility of older researchers managing to build rapport.

Observing and learning

It is impossible to observe everything that takes place in a situation, so it helps if the researcher is able to partition activities to focus on key areas. For example, in researching customer behaviour at an international airport, the researcher might select particular locations or subgroups of customers for study. Observation might be conducted by personally mingling with the subjects, but, equally, might occur through filming or videoing activities or viewing the results of closed circuit television monitoring. If the observation is 'live', Berg (1995) suggests some strategies for collecting data:

- Take in the physical setting by visiting the environment that people will be observed in. This allows an opportunity to get acquainted with the target group, and drawing up first impressions and points of reference. Fetterman (1989) refers to *outcropping*, the unobtrusive measures that protrude or are visible in the field setting. These could include buildings, graffiti, the smell of urine in city streets, litter or a park full of trees in blossom.
- Develop relationships with inhabitants. We have seen that guides may help here, but whether they are available or not, it is important to strike up a rapport with the inhabitants. If the observation is announced, it is sensible to provide a brief description of the purpose of the research, but it is best to avoid technical details. It is also wise to provide assurances of confidentiality at an early stage, and perhaps to possess a letter of introduction supporting the project. A key objective will be to quickly establish relations beyond that with the guides.
- Track, observe, eavesdrop and ask questions. Tracking comprises following guides around their daily tasks, and watching their activities and interactions with others. Eavesdropping can offer opportunities for picking up vital new

TABLE 10.3 EXAMPLES OF WHAT TO OBSERVE WHEN ENTERING FIELD SETTINGS

Subject	Comments
Lighting	Lighting conveys social meaning, and may influence the way in which individuals interact with the setting and with each other. For example, loving couples prefer subdued lighting, sports people usually bright, specialist lights
Colour	Colours help create a mood. Are they garish, bold, soft, well coordinated? What purpose might they serve?
Smell	What does the smell convey: food, pets, children, cars, chemicals, cleaning fluids? Does it have the scent of a family home, business, hospital? Sense for smells early on entry to the setting because people adjust to smells after time
Sound	What sort of sounds are there: machinery, cars, crying babies, bird song, music? Do people react to the sounds or are they ignored? Are the sounds used to convey information? Does the volume of sound rise, fall or stay constant? Like smell, be aware of sound early on entry as the ability to detect sounds falls with exposure
Objects	Pay attention to objects such as: furniture, computers, machinery, tools, books, pictures and other decorations. Are the objects in good or poor condition? What sort of 'statement' do the objects make? What do they convey in terms of status?
Weather and temperature	Note any relationship between temperature and moods and behaviours. Are there more people on the neighbourhood streets when it is hot?

Source: Adapted from Bailey, 1996

data, but one problem may be understanding the language used, especially if the information is couched in the jargon or technical language of the organization, location, or neighbourhood.

- Locate sub-groups and 'stars'. Sub-groups may exist on the basis of personal relationships, job roles, or mutual interests, and may contain central figures or stars. Locating stars and establishing good relationships with them may be important in opening doors and soliciting the cooperation of the group. However, as Patton (1990) points out, organizations may be rife with political conflicts between various groups and sub-groups. This may sometimes lead to a group trying to align itself with the researcher as part of its conflict with other groups.

But it is not just a question of how to conduct an observation but *what* to observe. Table 10.3 offers some suggestions.

You will probably have noted when looking at Table 10.3 that a considerable amount of observation also includes interpretation. If, for example, you notice a particularly high specification desktop computer, you might assume that the person sitting behind it was of a high status. But there again, you might be entirely wrong. The owner might be off sick and the person sitting at the desk, a temporary worker. The next Case Study illustrates this point.

Case Study 10.2 The impact of gaudy colours

A researcher conducted some observational research in a home for elderly people. One of her strong initial impressions was the paint-work – lots of strong colours such as red, black and orange. She found the colours gaudy and reported in her field notes that they made her feel 'jumpy'. However, as she spent some time in the home she learned that the ageing process means that we become less able to distinguish softer colours. Hence, the bright colours were needed by the elderly residents for them to be able to see and enjoy them. When interviewed, the residents stated that they liked the colours. The researcher was able to reflect that it is important not to base interpretations only on her own reactions to phenomena.

Source: Adapted from Bailey, 1996

Activity 10.4

Carry out a small-scale exercise with a fellow researcher. Select a place to conduct an observation. It could be a restaurant, library, park, etc. Spend about 20 minutes during which time you both take field notes using the criteria in Tables 10.1 and 10.3. Leave the field setting and complete your field notes. Working independently, begin to interpret your notes. When you are both ready, compare your interpretations. How similar are they? What do you disagree about? What has caused this difference in interpretation? Are either of you willing to re-interpret your data on the basis of the discussion? What evidence would you base this re-interpretation on?

Getting out

When to leave may have been planned early on in the project or it might result from the 'things to do' portion of field notes getting ever smaller, or when fewer insights are emerging. Leaving the field of observation involves both the physical and emotional disengagement of the researcher. This is particularly the case if the observation has been conducted over a lengthy period of time and the researcher has developed empathy and commitment to the inhabitants. Prior to disengagement, the researcher should warn the community of members that this exit is imminent. The withdrawal is probably best handled in a series of stages.

VALIDITY AND RELIABILITY ISSUES

Validity

With internal validity, given the often high degree of personal interpretation in observation, it may be difficult to prove conclusively that the data gathered are sufficiently objective to represent a true reflection of events. This, however, may be assisted if the researcher is able to display a sound understanding of the organization or context being researched because she or he actually works in it. In other words, they are a practitioner–researcher (see Chapter 15).

In the case of external validity, the very individuality of some observations may make it difficult to generalize the findings to other situations. Many observational research projects take the form of case studies and, as such, suffer from all the problems of generalization normally associated with the case study approach, one being small sample size. While Brewer (2000) concedes that it is essential not to exaggerate the generalizability of findings obtained from one or two fields, this does not mean that generalization should be ruled out. Cases, for example, can be carefully selected on the basis of their potential for being representative of the population (so the researcher must be aware of, and have access to, multiple field sites). Secondly, cases can be studied in one field that are similar to cases in another, or a series of longitudinal studies can be taken to build up a historical, comparative perspective.

Claims for generalizability are also strengthened if the researcher is able to stay in the field long enough to observe or experience the full range of routines and behaviours that typify the case. If this is not practically possible, then time sampling becomes necessary, in which all activities are recorded during a specified period. This should allow the observer to identify frequent routine activities, and irregular events that are special or abnormal.

Brewer (2000), however, argues that ethnographic research (which includes participant observation as a prime data gathering method) needs to go beyond issues of validity. It must also be relevant to issues of public concern.

> *Ethnographic research could be judged on whether and how well it resolves some social problem, or achieves emancipation for some oppressed group (such as women) or release from some constraining situation or setting (such as discrimination experienced by ethnic minorities).* (Brewer, 2000: 49)

Hammersley (1992) also argues that, while validity and reliability are important issues, they are not sufficient. In considering the value of a study, plausibility and credibility must also be taken into account. In writing reports, researchers have the duty to present sufficient evidence that may convince an audience – given the existing state of knowledge. The more central a claim is to the core arguments of the research, the greater the breadth and depth of evidence that must be provided.

Reliability

As we have seen, one of the problems with observation is that different researchers may see different objects, phenomena and human behaviours when observing the same event. Similarly, each researcher may give different interpretations of an event when seeing it on different occasions. One way of reducing this unreliability is to record the observed events in some way so that the data can be reviewed and, if necessary, re-interpreted. The recording of data through an exact notation system is important here because it reduces the danger of human error in the recall of events. Experienced researchers tend to keep very comprehensive notes, as some details that appeared hardly relevant at the time of the observation may later prove to be crucial. Again, reliability will be increased by this more structured process.

Another way of improving the reliability of a study is through the process of *triangulation*, that is, the use of multiple methods of data collection. Triangulation is a word drawn from the world of surveying where measurement is taken from three or more different points in order to identify a particular area with accuracy. According to Begley (1996) triangulation comes from a positivist frame of reference, which assumes, as we have seen, that a single reality or 'truth' can be found. But this does not mean that only quantitative data are relevant. Both quantitative and qualitative data can be combined to form a coherent picture.

In principle, then, triangulation reduces sources of error by gathering data from multiple sources, or using a variety of methods or theoretical approaches. But while it may reduce the chance of error, it does not eliminate it. Indeed, using a number of inappropriate data gathering methods, or using more than one badly trained observer, does not improve research reliability! So, just as in the selection of one research approach or method, using multiple methods still requires making them congruent with the research questions being asked. As Begley (1996) puts it:

Unfortunately, many neophyte researchers 'use triangulation' without either explaining or rationalizing their decisions, seeming to expect that the mere fact that they are utilizing this approach will magically solve all problems of bias, error and invalidity. (Begley, 1996: 127)

DATA PRESENTATION

In contrast to other research approaches, observational research (particularly if it is ethnographic) does not leave the writing up of results to a later stage – it is an ongoing process right from the start. This permits the researcher to interact with the data, to expose gaps in knowledge and identify where further investigation is required. Important issues in the presentation of data include: what to write, how to write it and what kinds of claim can be made for the status of the account.

What to write

There can be no prescriptive rules on this, but accounts could include:

* The context of the study (physical setting, history, etc.).
* The number of participants.
* The activities taking place.
* The division of labour and hierarchies.

- Significant events.
- Member's perspectives and meanings.
- Social rules and basic patterns of order.

Quotations should be used to provide the reader with an opportunity to verify some of the claims made in the report, but should not be too numerous as to be intrusive. Reports can also include photographs, charts, leaflets and other visual media.

Writing for the audience

We will look at some of the essential skills of report writing in Chapter 14, so these will not be examined in any detail here. For reporting on observational research, all the basic rules of report writing stand: use language that the audience understands, engage the reader's interest through the use of rich, vivid descriptions, and make connections from data analysis to the theory clear.

Determine the status of the writing

Researchers, and particularly ethnographic researchers, are divided as to the level of credibility they should assign to their report. Those who adhere to more positivistic traditions tend to argue for the authenticity of their research as a reflection of 'how it really is' in the field. Postmodernists, of course, challenge this view, arguing that any version of events is just one amongst multiple perspectives and interpretations. In extreme postmodern accounts, ethnographers even hold back from interpretation, allowing the text to 'speak for itself'.

ETHICS IN OBSERVATIONAL STUDIES

While we have raised ethical concerns in looking at the use of other research methods and instruments, ethical issues are certainly no less important here. For one reason, researchers are in much closer proximity with the subjects of the research – the 'moral community of their hosts' (Ellen, 1984: 138) – and often for longer periods than with most other approaches. In the case of ethnographic observation, researchers are unique in actually sharing the lives of those they are researching. In the case where this observation is being conducted covertly, some quite acute problems and issues can arise.

One of the justifications for covert observation is that, by omitting informed consent, it 'protects' subjects from any of the potentially negative effects of knowing that they are being observed. This might include apprehension or nervousness. Another argument is that all researchers assume a 'variety of masks' depending on where they find themselves, so covert observation is no different. The notion of 'net gain' is cited, whereby the benefits of the research outweigh the risks of the covert method. Diener and Crandall (1978), however, point out that the costs and benefits of research are often both impossible to predict and difficult to measure. Herrera (1999) also has little sympathy with the net gain argument, suggesting that some subjects may discover their involvement and might be disturbed by the revelation – not least that they learn of their own naivete. It is probably best if covert methods are only used where there is no alternative, such as where gatekeepers impose impossible barriers or where access is closed.

To advise and guide researchers through this ethical and moral maze, most professional associations that concern themselves with research draw up ethical codes of conduct. If a researcher is commissioned, sponsored or provided with access to a site through one of these associations, then she or he will be required actually to sign up to the code. The British Sociological Association's statement of ethics, for example, provides guidelines on:

- *Professional integrity.* Members should seek to safeguard the interests of those involved or affected by their work. They should recognize the boundaries of their own competence and not accept work they are not qualified to carry out.
- *Relations with and responsibility to research participants.* The physical, social and psychological well-being of participants should not be adversely affected. Participation should be on the basis of informed consent, and participants should understand how far they will be afforded anonymity and confidentiality. Special care must be taken when dealing with groups that are vulnerable by virtue of age, social status or powerlessness. If research is covert, anonymity of participants must be protected and, if possible, informed consent obtained post hoc.
- *Relations with and responsibility towards sponsors and funders.* The obligations of sponsors and researchers should be clarified in advance of the research. Researchers should not accept conditions that are contrary to their professional ethics or competence. During the research, sponsors or funders should be informed of any departure from the terms of reference.

Activity 10.5

For a more detailed description of ethical guidelines see the British Sociological Association's website at:
   http://www.britsoc.org.uk/about/ethic.htm
Also take a look at the ethical guidelines on covert observation for the National Health and Medical Research Council of Australia at:
   http://www.nhmrc.gov.au/publications/humans/part17.htm

Our final Case Study illustrates an actual use of covert observation (both participative and non-participative within the same study) and the uses of multiple sources of evidence.

Case Study 10.3   The role of observation in market research

In certain situations, observation is the only way of obtaining information on customer behaviour, especially where the influences on that behaviour are sub-conscious. A study was undertaken to develop guidelines for the siting of middle-market restaurant outlets, in order to maximize the number of potential consumers passing by at lunch-times. The location was three interconnecting streets in a sub-urb of South London. The study was in two stages. First, an observation of con-sumer movements around the high street. Secondly, a series of visits to the restaurants as covert observers during the lunch period.

In Phase 1, a range of factors was assessed to see if they had any influence on consumer traffic flows in general and on restaurant usage. These included: the curve of the road, the sunny side of the street, pedestrian crossings, public transport sites, the gradient of the street, and the types of shops in the vicinity of the restaurant. Counts of consumer traffic were conducted for 15 minute periods, focusing on strategic areas such as those near pedestrian crossings, the top and the bottom of the hill, near banks with cash withdrawal facilities, etc.

During Phase 2 the restaurants in the study were visited four times at lunch-time and detailed notes taken of customers using classifications such as: types of customer (individuals, couples, families, similar age groups), dining purpose (busi-ness, family treat, celebration, romantic one-to-one); style of dress (formal or casual); mode of transport (walk, taxi, car, bus, etc.). By analysing the types of cus-tomer in the restaurant, it was then possible to assess if there was a positive rela-tionship between the type of customer on the streets and the type of customer in the restaurants. In other words, the study was assessing whether the restaurant was situated in the right place.

It was found that, to maximize the flow of potential customers going past the restaurant at lunch-times, the outlet ought to be situated: on a central site rather than at the far end of the high street, on the sunny side of the street, on the inner rather than the outer curve of the street, and near transport links appropriate to the outlet's key market segments (customers).

Source: Adapted from Boote and Mathews, 1999

Activity 10.6

Examine the observational design in Case Study 10.3. Could the data gather-ing have been done in any other way? How effective would this alternative method have been in terms of the validity of the data. What dangers are there of observer bias in the study and how could they be controlled for?

Suggested answers are provided at the end of the chapter.

SUMMARY

- Observation is more than just 'seeing'; it also involves complex combinations of all the senses and the interpretation of observed events.
- Observation can be overt or covert and involve the active participation of the observer or non-participation.
- One of the challenges of the observational approach is the gathering of data, particularly if the observer is a covert participant.
- Field notes should be as comprehensive as possible and should be taken either as events are observed or as soon as possible afterwards.
- Observational methods will often be triangulated with other research approaches, such as interviews and questionnaires.
- For structured observation, coding schedules will be used based on the principle of either noting events over a period of time or noting when an event occurs.
- Ethical issues arise, particularly where covert observation is being used. Researchers may do well to make use of a code of ethics drawn up by the relevant professional body, if such a code exists.

SUMMARY OF WEB LINKS

http://www.britsoc.org.uk/about/ethic.htm
http://www.nhmrc.gov.au/publications/humans/part17.htm

Further reading

Bailey, C.A. (1996) *A Guide to Field Research.* Thousand Oaks, CA: Pine Forge Press. Not only is it clearly written, this book contains a host of valid and informative examples of practical experiences in the field.

Brewer, J.D. (2000) *Ethnography.* Buckingham, Philadelphia: Open University Press. Although the focus is on ethnography, this book provides plentiful advice and comment on designing observational studies, data collection and ethics.

Pink, S. (2001) *Doing Visual Ethnography.* London: Sage. Explores the potential of photography, video and hypermedia in ethnography and social research. Provides a reflexive approach to practical, theoretical and methodological issues.

Suggested answers for Activity 10.1

Covert observation can be justified because it allows the researcher to 'get close' to the situation and to identify where customers are really having difficulties. If the observation was overt, then customers might act in ways that might hide or obscure their inability to cope with some aspects of the system.

Suggested answers for Activity 10.2

1 Most of the data here take the form of a chronological log, that is, direct observations.
2 The experiential data comprise the more personal reflections of the researcher, beginning with 'I felt ...'.
3 Forward planning is contained in the 'Things to do' section.

Suggested answers for Activity 10.6

Certainly, data could have been collected in other ways – for example, through a market research survey of customer attitudes to the sighting of the new restaurant. But would the return rate be adequate? Would the responses be honest? With observations, however, one of the dangers is observer bias. One way of controlling for this is through the use of multiple observers, who would each observe independently and then compare both their raw data and analysis.

Collecting Primary Data: Unobtrusive Measures

Chapter objectives

After reading this chapter you will be able to:

- **Distinguish between unobtrusive measures and other research approaches.**
- **Describe the advantages of unobtrusive measures over more interactive methods.**
- **Select between different unobtrusive measures for conducting research.**
- **Demonstrate how to access data archives on the Internet.**

So far, we have concentrated on interactive research methods such as surveys, case studies, interviews and observations. Unobtrusive measures, however, involve the use of non-reactive sources, independent of the presence of the researcher, and include documentary evidence, physical evidence and archival analysis. The term archive derives from the ancient Greek *aekheion*, which means a house that is the residence of the superior magistrates, the *archons*, those that command. This house was where official documents were stored and where the *archons* acted as both guardians and interpreters of the documents. Here, the principle was created that archives require that documents are stored in one place (Featherstone, 2000).

These archives exist in a wide variety of formats and can consist of files, maps, drawings, films, sound recordings and photographs. While libraries tend to provide access to published materials, archives hold unique unpublished records. But, as Sleeman (2002) points out, with the growth of electronic environments such as the Internet, what is 'unique' and 'published' or 'unpublished' is increasingly blurred. Web pages, for example, can contain links to many other sites or pages, challenging the notion of a document as an integral and independent record.

As we have seen, interactive measures carry with them various inherent problems, such as the dangers of interviewer bias, the possibility of research tools of questionable validity and reliability, or reactivity between the interviewer and interviewee. Unobtrusive measures, because they are dealing with 'dead' data, in principle, are unlikely to face the risk of reactive measurement effects.

But, as we shall see, unobtrusive measures pose other risks if used on their own. Some materials, for example, tend to survive better than others, so their representativeness is open to question. To ensure reliability, it is often prudent to use unobtrusive measures in conjunction with other approaches.

In this chapter we will look at various kinds of unobtrusive measures and how they can be of value to the researcher. We will then examine a number of typical sources of unobtrusive measures.

PHYSICAL MEASURES

From the prehistoric cave paintings of early man to the Great Wall of China, medieval cathedrals or the discarded fast food containers of modern times, human beings have left behind physical evidence of their existence. According to Webb et al. (1966), these physical or *trace* measures can be divided into four broad categories: natural and controlled accretion measures, and natural and controlled erosion measures.

Natural accretion measures

Accretion takes place where there is a build up of deposits of materials or evidence. Within the context of ancient worlds, for example, this could include the accumulation of shards of pottery. In a more modern context, it could include the build up of piles of litter, or, say, the amount of dust gathering on some files or equipment, showing how little they are being used. An often-quoted example is that of graffiti appearing on the surfaces of (usually) urban features such as walls or buildings. Lee (2000) provides examples of research where graffiti have been used to analyse relationships and attitudes between different ethnic gangs, and how the graffiti delineated certain 'zones of tension' between groups.

But accretion measures could also include more innocent examples, such as the number of plastic cups accumulating in waste bins around an office. We are not interested, however, in these materials for themselves, but for what they might reveal about aspects of human behaviour. In the case of the plastic cups, we could use them to come to a tentative estimate of the number of breaks taken by office workers, as the following Case Study shows.

Case Study 11.1 Natural accretion measures – cold coffee!

After trades union pressure, an office manager agrees to install a vending machine for hot and cold drinks. After only a month, through casual observation, he becomes concerned that the vending machine is encouraging a 'take a break' mentality, and that too many staff are losing focus on their work. He decides to carry out a short study to see if his hypothesis is correct.

(Continued)

He first of all notes where people consume their drinks, and finds that there are two areas: at the vending machine itself, which has now become a sort of social area, and at people's personal desks. Using unobtrusive measures, once staff have left work at the end of the day, he goes around the office, collecting used plastic cups from the waste bins. He finds over 50 cups in the bin next to the vending machine, but a total of over 200 in individual staff bins.

The next day, he covertly observes six members of staff consuming their drinks to make an average estimate of the time they spend on each break. In doing this, however, he finds that it is only those people who congregate around the vending machine who actually stop to talk. Those who take their drinks back to their desks continue immediately with work, taking a drink when they can. Indeed, he now recalls that when he delved into individual waste bins the previous evening, many contained grey-brown slops in the bottom. This is another unobtrusive measure – the fact that many staff had been so busy, their tea or coffee had gone cold and had to be poured into the bin! Since these people are clearly working rather than taking a break, the manager concludes that the vending machine is probably increasing productivity, not reducing it.

Activity 11.1

Take another look at Case Study 11.1.

1 What evidence is there that the manager used a triangulation of methods?
2 How accurate would the study have been if the manager had only used unobtrusive measures? Would the data have been reliable if he had conducted the research using, say, an interview schedule?

Suggested answers are provided at the end of the chapter.

Another example of natural accretion measures comes from Patton (1990), who refers to Palmer's study of letters and remembrances laid at the Vietnam Veterans Memorial. She took samples of material left at the memorial and then located and interviewed the people who had left it. The combination of both the materials and the interviews allowed a powerful analysis to be written of the effects of the Vietnam War on the veterans who had survived it.

Controlled accretion measures

This is where the researcher tampers with the materials that are connected to the accretion comparison. Webb et al. (1966) give the example of researchers who tested advertising exposure using the 'glue-seal method'. Here, a small glue spot was inconspicuously placed between the pages of a magazine close to the binding. After the magazine had been read, the researchers could detect, by noting whether the seals had been broken, which pages had been opened fully and looked at and which had not. This method was developed because of the tendency in question-naire surveys for respondents to falsely claim they had read or viewed an adver-tisement. But as Webb et al. note, this controlled accretion measure is rather limited in its effectiveness. It does not, for example, allow researchers to determine precisely which advertisement was seen, only which pair of pages. It also yields no data on how long an advertisement was looked at, or indeed, if it was actually viewed at all.

A more modern example of controlled accretion is the use of the Web. Many organizations make use of a web counter to keep a tally of how many 'hits' they are receiving on their website. Sophisticated software is also now available to provide data on how long a person stayed on the site, which pages they viewed, and whether the hit came from inside or outside the organization. Where a com-pany has a website that contains information that people may genuinely want (reports, articles, economic or business data, etc.), then it can grant access to the site only through visitors having to complete an online proforma about them-selves. The company can now develop a detailed profile of its potential customers that it then targets with its marketing materials.

Natural erosion measures

Here, there is a degree of selective wear or deterioration on the material being studied. For example, examining the wear and tear on office carpet tiles may reveal the density of human 'traffic' in a particular section of a library. Similar deteriora-tion in a department store might reveal the location of the most popular goods. Observation (see Chapter 10) might also be used to confirm these findings.

If, for example, you wanted to discover the most popular resources used by learners in an organization's Open Learning Centre, a sensible approach would be to check the records of how often a book, video or CD-ROM had been bor-rowed. But this is only an indirect measure, since it tells us nothing about the extent to which the resource has actually been used. Here, unobtrusive natural erosion measures could be used, checking the wear and tear on the learning mate-rials. So, we could compare how many times page corners had been turned down on different study guides and handbooks. Playing some of the Centre's training videos might soon reveal which ones seem rather worn out. One problem, of course, is that with the move towards digital technology, such signs of wear and tear will be virtually impossible to detect.

Controlled erosion measures

In this case, it is possible to use or manipulate the extent to which something wears out against some other experimental variable. Say, for example, a company hired people to distribute its leaflets door-to-door around neighbourhoods. How does it know that the leaflets are being delivered? Using controlled erosion measures it could estimate the rate at which the distributors' shoes wore out, by taking a measurement of sole depth before they started the job and, say, after 3 months. Of course, there are many potential intervening variables here, not least of which is the extent to which staff used their shoes during their leisure time. The answer here would be to issue 'company' shoes so that this could be controlled for.

DOCUMENTS: RUNNING RECORDS

Documents are some of the most frequently used unobtrusive measures and include a wide variety of organizational and institutional documents, and state financial, political and legal records.

Organizational documents

Running records are described by Webb el al. (1966) as the records of society, such as actuarial records, voting records, city budgets and communication media. Hakim (1993) also points to health service records, school records, membership records of trade unions and voluntary associations, records of births, deaths and marriages, police, court and prison records. Such records tend to be updated over time. Hakim also suggests that these types of records are expanding with the spread of computerized management information systems. One of the distinct advantages of using them is their non-reactivity. While the information may sometimes be inaccurate or incomplete, at least it is not usually manipulated by the producer of the data in the knowledge that the material is going to be studied. Hakim (1993) suggests that administrative records can provide the basis for longitudinal studies, quasi-experimental designs, international comparisons and studies of organizations and their development of policy.

On the negative side, there are at least two sources of potential bias: *selective deposit* and *selective survival*. Hence, which records, documents or materials are archived by an organization will depend both on the policy of that organization but also on the extent to which that policy is implemented by its employees. In most modern organizations there exists a store of 'official' records, such as legal and financial documents, company reports, rules and regulations, staff handbooks and human resource records. But in addition, there will exist a wealth of less official 'grey' materials, such as e-mails, memoranda, minutes of meetings, team plans, marketing ideas, etc. that are an integral part of the knowledge base and thinking of the organization. Many of these will be stored on the computer hard disc of designated employees (company secretary, HR manager, Director of Marketing, etc.) or shared networks or are created and stored by individuals. What is stored or shared (often via e-mail attachments) and what is discarded will often be a matter of individual choice, rather than organizational policy. Hakim (1993) warns that researchers who use organizational records will often find that vital data are missing, or that they have to contact employees to have the data interpreted or explained to them, to avoid erroneous assumptions.

Developments in computer technology have made the chances of records surviving both better and worse. We are all familiar with how the ravages of time have destroyed many ancient records. Those artefacts that we can see in museums have survived because of their composition (stone or clay rather than paper or wood, for example), or just by luck. Computers allow us to store vast amounts of data efficiently – or do they? There are many ways in which computers hinder the survival of data and records. First, there is plentiful evidence of computer failure – systems crash and backups fail. Secondly, there is the problem of incompatible computer systems; if, say, an organization moves to a single computer platform, what happens to the data on the discontinued system? Thirdly, there is technical obsolescence. In theory, computer systems are upwardly compatible, so that upgraded computers can read the data on older systems. But in the case of the original 5½ inch floppy disk, this data can only be read if it was copied to a hard drive. Similarly, how many of today's videos will be available for viewing in ten year's time when all transmission equipment is digital and most VCRs have broken down?

Apart from the impact of computers on data survival, organizations themselves are subject to mergers, takeovers and closures, all of which impact on whether data survive or are discarded. For example, if a company is taken over by another, which of its records would the new owner want to retain? Since the aggressor company already has its own legal, financial, operational and HR set up, it would probably not want to retain all of the captured company's records. It is not only large companies where data and documents are destroyed. Many small organizations fail to survive beyond their first few years of existence. In addition to the casual destruction of records as organizations move or merge, there is also the risk of the deliberate destruction of material where this highlights the errors that organizations have made.

In exploring organizational archives, reliability can be improved by comparing the data with that from other sources, such as newspaper or other media reports, customers or suppliers. This does not eliminate the risk that records are biased through selectivity, but it does at least reduce it.

Actuarial records

These include the data on births, deaths and marriages that most societies maintain as a matter of course. They also include a wealth of other statistical, economic, social and political data. Such records are essential for providing governments and other agencies with data for planning purposes. The potential power of actuarial records is demonstrated by Webb et al. (1966), who refer to the study by Durkheim in 1951. In this, using government records, he showed how suicide rates were linked not so much to individual clinical depression but to religion, season of the year, time of day, race, sex, education and marital status.

One of the problems in comparing time-sets of data, that is, data across different periods of time, is the influence of economic depressions, wars and other intervening factors. Data sets may also be difficult to compare across countries, since there may be different criteria for recording data. For example, how do we compare commitment to marriage between countries in which monogamy and multiple marriage is practised?

Political and judicial records

The study of voting statistics and opinion polls is now almost an element of popular culture, and certainly one that is common in the mass media. Political pundits and researchers are interested not only with voting intentions, or the total votes cast for a particular party or candidate, but also with a breakdown of votes cast by region, locality, age group and social class. Voting behaviour is studied because it is seen by some as a 'window' into the hearts and minds of people as electors, citizens, workers and consumers. This assumes, of course, that people do not vote tactically, that is, they vote for the party of their genuine political choice, and not for another party to keep the party they dislike most out of office.

Other political records include the voting behaviour of members of the government legislature. These are of interest not only to political commentators but also to professional lobbyists hired as consultants by businesses, interest groups and campaigning organizations. Another source for gauging the views of politicians is interviews or comments in the media through television programmes and the press. Particularly if a source is an article written by a journalist, one has to be especially conscious of the threats to validity through biased reporting and hidden agendas.

DOCUMENTS: EPISODIC RECORDS

In contrast to running records that tend to be in the public domain, episodic records are discontinuous and tend to be private. Hence, they are often more difficult to access. Webb et al. (1966) suggest three main classes: sales records, industrial and institutional records, and personal documents. To these we can add: visual and mass media records, and institutional investigations.

Sales records

Sales records do not just tell us how a company is doing in terms of successfully selling products or services, they can be used as indicators of social, business or other trends. Take, for example, a rise in the sale of beer and spirits at a company's staff social club. This could be an indicator of a rise in gregarious activity, of contented employees choosing to mingle and socialize with each other. On the other hand, it could also be an indication of rising levels of stress and anxiety amongst the staff, leading to levels of alcohol abuse. Clearly, as is often the case, unobtrusive measures have to be used with other indicators (such as observation or interviews) before an accurate picture emerges.

Activity 11.2

Think of what each of the following sales records might indicate and what events they might be linked to:

- Increased sale of personal insurance.
- A fall in the sale of personal handguns.
- A rise in the sale of cuddly toys.

Industrial and institutional records

These include the records kept by companies, schools, hospitals, prisons and the military and can cover a multiplicity of subjects. A company, for example, might collect data on employee headcount, employee turnover, promotions and absenteeism. In terms of finance, many organizations are interested in knowing the size of their borrowing and the costs of financing it, turnover compared to profits and share price movements.

Examples of other kinds of institutional record include those organizations responsible for monitoring sex and race discrimination. In the latter case, organizations might collect data on the type and location of reported racial incidents, police responses and the actions, if any, of the judicial authorities. The episodes of racial 'hotspots' might be compared against other independent variables such as inflammatory speeches by certain politicians, media commentary, or the passing of equal opportunities legislation.

Personal records

Personal records include letters, diaries, autobiographies, biographies and oral histories. Brewer (2000) suggests a way of classifying personal records across two dimensions. The first is whether the records are primary (compiled by the author) or secondary (containing data obtained from someone else's primary document). A second dimension is contemporary (compiled as a document at the time) or secondary (produced as a document after the event). Using these dimensions, we get four categories, as illustrated in Figure 11. 1.

As Brewer warns, making generalizations from such documents can be problematic, especially if they are personal documents about one individual. There may be more possibility of generalizations if the documents can be shown to be representative or typical of a group. The contents of personal documents should also be evaluated for distortion, misrepresentation, exaggeration and omission.

Visual and mass media records

Industrial societies are now awash with visual images in the mass communication media, many of which can provide a novel source of data, worthy of investigation and analysis. These include advertisements, newspaper photographs, textbooks,

Contemporary primary		Contemporary secondary	
Personal	*Official*	*Personal*	*Official*
Letters Suicide notes	Court record Minutes of meetings	Edited transcripts of letters, talks, etc	Research using census data
Retrospective primary		Retrospective primary	
Personal	*Official*	*Personal*	*Official*
Diary Autobiography Oral history	Novels Historical archives	Research using diaries	Medical records Newspaper reports

FIGURE 11.1   SOURCES OF PERSONAL RECORDS (ADAPTED FROM
BREWER, 2000)

comics and magazines, postcards and product packaging. If we take advertisements first, consider whether groups such as ethnic minorities or women are depicted in ways that are obviously different. Lee (2000) refers to the work of several researchers that suggests that real differences do exist. In some countries, visual images of black people, for example, are under-represented in advertisements, and where they appear, this is often in stereotypical roles as sportspeople or musicians. When black and white people appear in the same advertisement, they are rarely interacting with one another (Lee, 2000).

Institutional investigations

One potentially useful source of data that justifies more consideration is the use of evidence from legal and judicial investigations. Many governments, for example, set up special commissions to investigate large-scale disasters (such as rail crashes) or public inquiries into the siting of a new airport. It is not so much the subject focus of these inquiries that is of interest, but what the debate and dialogue reveals about the roles of organizations, institutions and pressure groups that attempt to influence the state. Of course, one of the dangers is not knowing the extent to which witnesses have been screened or specially selected, and what evidence has been submitted and what withheld.

THE NEW DIGITAL ARCHIVES

So far, we have looked at quite traditional forms of unobtrusive measures, many of which include the collection of documents (of various descriptions), usually located in one place. But because of problems of access, many document archives are under-utilized by researchers. After all, if the archive that you need is hundreds or even thousands of kilometres away, you are going to have to do some serious personal planning to see it. The growth of the Internet and the World Wide Web, however, is changing this. It is also worth considering another new and digital source of information, closed circuit television, as yet another modern source of unobtrusive information.

The Internet

The Internet and World Wide Web are already making an impact on how archives are accessed.

> *In the long term it may well be that the greatest contribution which the Internet makes to research is to provide easier access to archives.* (Sleeman, in Dochartaigh, 2002: 220)

Archives were once one of the most inaccessible research resources, and just discovering which resources were held in which archive could be a major research activity in itself. Today, however, the Internet allows archivists to put information about their collections into the public arena. The next stage, which is happening with many archives already, is then to put the collection itself onto the Web. With the provision of a search facility, it becomes possible to search for archival information from your work desk. Activity 11.3 provides some useful examples.

One factor that distinguishes archives from published sources, is that collections are presented so that the context and original order of the materials is maintained. This is an attempt to preserve the authenticity of the archive and its value to researchers. One of the dangers of the Web is that it can allow the user multiple access to documents at different levels. Archivists are conscious of this danger, hence, they often show the researcher how a holding was created. The use of Web links also allows for documents to be linked to one another in a variety of ways, each of which demonstrates different relationships and contexts.

Activity 11.3

Take a look at the following websites, each of which provides you with access to archives of government and business information.

Euromonitor (http://www.euromonitor.com/default.asp)   This site is a global information provider of strategic analysis and market statistics for dozens of global industries.

National Archives and Records Administration of the United States (NARA) (http://www.nara.gov)   This site provides a research room that gives details of its records, plus a search tool, NARA Archival Retrieval Locator (NAIL), for locating archival sources across the USA.

(Continued)

Public Records Office, England (PRO) (http://www.pro.gov.uk) A site that contains over 9 million files that are searchable through a multi-level catalogue. The database includes legal and government archives.

The National Archives of Australia (http://www.aa.gov.au) This site holds federal government records on defence, immigration, security and intelligence, naturalization and other issues.

EAN (European Archival Network) (http://www.european-archival.net) A site, organized alphabetically and geographically, for searching for European archives.

As well as websites dealing with general government and business information, there are a growing number of sites that offer access to statistics. Sleeman (2002) distinguishes between two kinds of site:

- *Statistics websites.* These are the websites of agencies (often government agencies) that collect statistics and make them available online. Not only can data tables be viewed, the sites often provide tools with which the data can be manipulated and analysed.
- *Data archives.* These provide indexes to datasets gathered from a wide variety of research projects and organizations, often allowing users to download full datasets for analysis on their own computers.

Activity 11.4 provides you with an opportunity to explore examples of each type of website.

Activity 11.4

Statistics websites
National Statistics: the official UK statistics site (http://www.statistics.gov.uk) A site that contains UK government economics statistics as well as statistics on education and migration.

US Census Bureau (http://www.census.gov) Provides data on the US population, income, housing, and economic and government statistics.

Statistical Resources on the Web (http://www.lib.umich.edu/libhome/documents.center/stats.html) A vast guide with links to economics, politics and sociology sources.

Data archives
National Digital Archive of Datasets (NDAD) (http://www.ndad.ulcc.ac.uk) Provides access to computer datasets of UK government departments and agencies.

ICPSR (The Inter-university Consortium for Political and Social Research) (http://www. icpsr.umich.edu) Provides access to the world's largest archive of computerized social science data.

Monitoring technology

Many workplaces are now becoming penetrated by a growing infrastructure of technology capable of monitoring work performance. Leaving aside, for a moment, any ethical issues, the data generated from such technology are not only of value to the organizations that had it installed, but also to researchers – if they are able to gain access to it. Davies (2001) discusses both the range and power of the emerging technologies, including miniature cameras that monitor employee behaviour, 'smart' ID badges that track an employee's movements in a building, and telephone management systems analysing the patterns of telephone use and the destination of calls.

Advances in location tracking now mean that geostationary satellite-based systems can send information on the precise location of an employee or vehicle back to a tracking centre. In the growing IT industry, employee use of their computer can also be monitored and measured, including the number of keystrokes they have been making, which websites they have accessed and the amount of time the computer was idle during the day. Many businesses routinely analyse their employees' e-mail. Software can be used for analysing an organization's entire e-mail traffic phrase by phrase, including a look for specific key words. In telephone call centres, software monitors the length and content of calls and the timing and duration of employee toilet and lunch breaks. Software can also monitor how often a call worker uses a customer's name and how often they try to overcome a potential customer's initial objection to a sale.

Closed circuit television (CCTV) equipment is also now becoming commonplace where people travel, shop, socialize and even work. According to Davies:

> Once viewed as a blunt tool of surveillance, CCTV in the space of fifteen years is now seen as an integral design component of the urban and the work environment. (Davies, 2001: 13)

Certainly CCTV is now becoming an integral component in modern retailing. Kirkup and Carrigan (2000) relate how CCTV is being used for:

- *Security:* to deter shoplifters and pickpockets and also to detect fraudulent activities among staff.
- *Safety:* to see who is still in a building after a fire or security alert.
- *Training:* allowing a retailer to capture the behaviour of both staff and customers that can then be used in staff development programmes.

But it is the research dimension where CCTV can provide a valuable mechanism for understanding consumer behaviour. For example, it can help retailers (or the researchers they commission) to:

- Analyse customer flows.
- Evaluate the impact of store refits.
- Identify ways of increasing store penetration.

- Measure dwell-time in different departments or on specific displays.
- Understand the nature of interactions between staff and customers.

In short, CCTV allows the retailer to explore the relationships between the profile of shoppers, their level of involvement in browsing and trialling, and the nature of their response to different stimuli (Kirkup and Carrigan, 2000). Digital technology can now be used both to gather and to analyse data. Software called 'The Observer', for example, allows for the computerized coding of observations, and the production of video 'highlights' (see Activity 11.5).

Activity 11.5

Take a look at the specifications for The Observer software and what you can do with it at:
    http://www.noldus.com/products/index.html

ETHICAL ISSUES IN USING THE DIGITAL TECHNOLOGY

Ethics and the Internet

Once e-mail communication has occurred between people, it remains available for other people to access in the future. In the case of newsgroups this can be for days or weeks, but for mailing lists it can be for as much as two years. These posts and archives, then, can be used by researchers as documents for analysis, and form a potentially rich source of data. Sixsmith and Murray (2001), however, raise some intriguing ethical issues linked specifically to research using the Internet.

Accessing voices

The ethical obligations of researchers go beyond the need merely to protect participants. It is also necessary to involve those in the research process whose voices are rarely heard in research, and for whom the new digital media provide a unique opportunity for communication. This could include socially disadvantaged groups, people with disabilities or children. For Flietas (referenced in Sixsmith and Murray, 2001), e-mail and Internet chatrooms may be perfect communication tools to address this problem.

Consent

As we saw in Chapter 10, an important feature of ethical considerations is that participants give their fully informed consent. An exception to this principle is observational research in which behaviour in the public domain may be observed without consent, so that natural behaviour can be observed in its context. But in 'observing' e-mail and Internet communications, are researchers similarly free from seeking consent? As Sixsmith and Murray (2001) comment, this is a highly contentious issue. Some researchers believe that all posts on the Internet are in the public domain and are, therefore, available for research purposes without the need for consent. But as Sixsmith and Murray warn, such a practice could lead to distrust and anger amongst discussion forum participants and would be highly damaging. Yet, if researchers do consult the discussion group, they run the risk of alerting participants to the fact that they are being observed and this may alter the dynamics of the group interaction. The observation would no longer be unobtrusive in the strictest sense. But Sixsmith and Murray conclude that the best course of ethical action is for researchers to consult the introductory notes or charters of electronic forums.

Even when following these kinds of guidelines, if undertaking research through a discussion list it is prudent to contact the list moderator to gain permission for the research. Even if permission is granted, researchers need to be aware that their activities may not be greeted with approval by all members of the list. In joining a discussion group, researchers should announce their presence *as* researchers. But later on, other new members will be unaware of this intrusion unless researchers post reminders of their presence. Of course, they will also have access to the posts of those who left messages but subsequently left the group. These people will be unaware that their comments are being used by researchers.

Privacy

The ethics of research stipulate that the privacy and anonymity of participants must be respected during the research process (American Psychology Association, 1992). However, in practical terms, distinguishing between what is private and public behaviour can be difficult, since some private behaviour (for example, private conversations, intimate behaviour, etc.) can be observed in public places. Hence, the concept of privacy needs to be understood within its specific social setting.

In the case of discussion list posts, the researcher has to establish whether these are made in a public or private context. The problem here is that participants may tend to regard their posts as public (to the group) but private as far as outsiders are concerned. Since many posts are made from home-based computers, participants may tend to assume that their privacy will be respected. It may be useful, then, to distinguish between discussion groups, where privacy is probably assumed, and mailing lists where posts may be transmitted to hundreds or thousands of subscribers. Since the latter are available to everyone on the Internet, it is fairly safe to assume that they can be regarded as being in the public domain.

Anonymity

In using archived posts for research analysis, the anonymity of participants should be preserved. Any information that could identify the originators of the post should be removed, including names or pseudonyms used, as well as the names and locations of lists and newsgroups. The problem here, however, is that the removal of this kind of information also limits the possibilities of thick description, that is, relating the research data with features such as the age, nationality and occupation of participants. Despite this problem, it is respect for ethical principles that should take priority.

Interpretation

In analysing data, it is important that the researcher does not misrepresent the participant's meaning or views. This can be a particular danger when using data from discussion forums or archives because the data available may be incomplete (often old posts are deleted by the moderator or writers themselves). Another problem is that the discussion group data may not represent the entire communication process, since some participants will exchange e-mails privately.

To reduce the danger of misinterpretation, tracts of related messages need to be considered as a group, especially since messages are often related to each other in a thread. This allows for the discursive context of a message to be considered through a more grounded interpretation.

Ownership

This is a complex issue. Do posts or archives belong to the poster (author), the discussion group or the observer (who may be a researcher)? Issues of intellectual property rights and the Internet are contentious and, as yet, still largely unresolved.

Mailbase (2002), for example, a UK discussion list for the academic community, argues that e-mail messages are creative works and are therefore subject to copyright. Copyright exists automatically from the moment the e-mail is created – it does not have to be registered anywhere. The first owner of the copyright is the author, except when the e-mail has been created in the course of employment, in which case it is owned by the employer. When a message is posted to a public list, this does not mean that the author loses this copyright, but should accept that the message may be archived, forwarded to other lists or quoted by others. What is important is that the message should not be quoted out of context, the wording changed or be mis-attributed. It is usual practice, then, that:

- Messages sent to a closed mailing list or individual should not be forwarded without the author's permission.
- Messages sent to a public mailing list can be forwarded provided that:

    The message is not changed or reworded.
    Attribution is given to the author.
    Any appended copyright notice is respected.

Authorship

It is the convention always to attribute authorship when making a direct quotation from someone's work. But what if the source is a discussion group? We have seen that Mailbase (2002) regards e-mails as similar to published works so that any quotation should include a credit to its source. However, as we have seen, this contradicts people's right to anonymity. The solution here is to request the author's permission before making long quotations.

Ethics and monitoring technology

Many of the above issues, particularly those relating to privacy, are also raised by the growth of monitoring technology, such as CCTV cameras and other surveillance media. Carrigan and Kirkup (2001) argue that the researcher's main responsibility is to those that are observed, but there are also responsibilities to other groups, namely:

- The client who has commissioned the research.
- The general public who may not want to be filmed in certain shops (for example, chemists, opticians or lingerie stores).
- Innocent bystanders, since modern surveillance cameras have a 360° field of vision and are capable of filming well beyond their intended zone.
- The police or legal system if criminal activities are observed.
- Employees who may be concerned that recordings of their good or bad behaviour will affect their pay or promotional prospects.

The challenge is in reconciling the interests of these disparate groups. The objective of the research might be monitoring flows of customer traffic within the store to observe interest in particular displays. But later, the store management (clients) might request the tapes to examine employee behaviour. This abuses the privacy rights of the employee and reneges on the purpose of the research. If employees become aware of this kind of potential for abuse, they may become uncooperative, which then threatens the reliability and validity of subsequent research. However, the wishes of clients are difficult to ignore since they are the financial sponsors of the research. One way out of these difficulties is through the design of ethical frameworks.

Ethical frameworks
Laczniak (cited in Carrigan and Kirkup, 2001) suggests an ethical framework through which, if any of the following questions can be answered negatively, then the action is probably unethical:

- Does action A violate the law?
- Does action A violate any general moral obligations: justice, beneficence, self-improvement, etc?
- Is the intent of action A evil?
- Are any major evils likely to result from action A?
- Is a satisfactory alternative, action B, which produces equal or more good with less evil than action A, being knowingly rejected?

- Does action A infringe the inalienable rights of the participant?
- Does action A leave another person or group less well off, and is this person or group already relatively under-privileged?

The purpose of this framework is to sensitize researchers to the factors that are important in dealing with ethical issues. For example, if employees are recorded while customer behaviour is being taped, is the framework being violated? The answer is 'Yes'. While no evil is being intended, we cannot be assured that no evils will arise from the action because there is no way of knowing whether employers will use the video evidence against employees. Hence, it becomes important to look for other defence mechanisms.

Professional codes of conduct

We have seen in previous chapters that many professional associations that rely on research have put in place their own professional codes of conduct. In the case of market research, for example, this is provided by the Market Research Society's (MRS) Code of Conduct which in turn is based upon the International Code of Marketing and Social Research Practice. In terms of establishing rules on the uses of video and other recording equipment, the MRS stipulates that:

- The researcher *must* [original emphasis] inform employees about any recording or monitoring methods (e.g. tape recording video recording and presence of a mirror or a camera) both at recruitment and at the beginning of an interview, giving the employee the option not to proceed. This also applies to instances where remote monitoring is used.
- Any audio or video recordings *must* [original emphasis] not be released by a researcher or research agency unless explicit permission has previously been obtained from all the employees involved. Where such permission is to be obtained the researcher must ensure that employees are given as much relevant information as possible about the future use of the data, in particular:

  To whom they are to be given.
  To whom they are likely to be shown.
  For what purposes they are likely to be used.

- Any recorded data collected for research purposes *must* [original emphasis] not be used for any non-research purpose (Market Research Society, 2002)

However, as Carrigan and Kirkup (2001) note, as yet, many professional codes contain few specific references to the use of CCTV in retail settings. They also exclude the need to inform individuals where observation techniques or recording equipment are being used in a public place. Unfortunately, one of the difficulties is in the definition of a 'public place', with some organizations arguing that this includes the workplace, thereby gaining exclusion from codes of conduct. Conversely, employees and their trade unions or professional associations may disagree with this broad definition.

The codes of conduct of some television companies suggest that when filming in an institution there is no obligation to seek agreement when people are shown incidentally, randomly or anonymously. However, Carrigan and Kirkup (2001) argue that employees are not anonymous in this sense and so deserve equal rights of privacy. Where employees are the specific subject of the surveillance where standards of service are being evaluated, further safeguards are needed. For example, the video material should not subsequently be used for purposes other than the original objective (hence, it should not be used for disciplinary purposes). Staff should also be informed that filming is going to take place. The professional code of the European Society for Opinion and Market Research (ESOMAR) stipulates that participants must be asked to give their permission for the use of video tapes for non-research purposes and should be given the opportunity to have the tapes deleted. If researchers pass a video on to a client it must be labelled with appropriate restrictions.

Activity 11.6

Take a look at the Market Research Society's Code of Conduct at:
  http://www.mrs.org.uk/
Click on Code/Guidelines, and look in particular for guidelines dealing with employees.

See also the website of the European Society for Opinion and Market Research at:
  http://www.esomar.nl/guidelines/Tapeandvideo.htm

Ethical contracts

Since many professional codes are still trying to catch up with the ever-changing developments in technology, Carrigan and Kirkup (2001) suggest that an important safety-net can be provided by ethical contracts. These make transparent the roles and responsibilities of all stakeholders, including the researcher, before any research is undertaken through:

- Clarifying the aims and nature of the research.
- Identifying, with stakeholders, any potential conflicts that may arise.
- Drafting resolutions to these problems.
- Seeking the explicit agreement of all those affected.

If, at any point, a stakeholder wishes to act outside of the contract, the agreement of all other stakeholders must be sought.

There are, however, differences between employees and customers as subjects of surveillance research in that employees can be identified by researchers or by their client. As such, the researcher has a particular responsibility to ensure anonymity for these individuals, or at least informed consent. Staff should be given assurance about the objectives of the research and should be allowed open access at all times to the CCTV control room. These objectives should not include using surveillance for non-research purposes such as disciplinary action, and permission for filming (although not necessarily its timing) should be sought.

Seeking the permission of customers is much more problematic. First, it would be simply impractical to ask all customers individually for their agreement. Secondly, there might be circumstances when the researcher might not want customers to know that they were being filmed since this might affect their subsequent behaviour. Most market research codes of practice allow researchers to withhold this information to reduce the risk of bias. But permission would have to be obtained if the researcher wished to pass on video-footage to any third party. If a tape is passed on to a client, it should be labelled with appropriate restrictions that the recipient should be made aware of. It is also important that the video data are not held for longer than the purposes for which they were collected. Kirkup and Carrigan (2000) suggest a maximum time period of 31 days for CCTV footage, after which it should be destroyed.

SUMMARY

- Unobtrusive measures involve the use of non-reactive sources such as files, photographs, videos, sound recordings and drawings and now the Internet.
- Unobtrusive measures include the analysis of physical accretion and erosion measures, and the use of documents that include a wide range of organizational, business and personal records.
- One of the advantages of using unobtrusive records is that they deal with 'dead' data, they do not pose the risk faced by many other research methods, of reactive measurement effects such as interviewer bias, or socially conditioned responses by participants.
- An important source of unobtrusive measures are documents that include running records (such as actuarial, political and judicial records) and episodic records (such as sales records and personal records).
- Unobtrusive measures carry with them their own inherent problems in that documents, for example, may be stored selectively, survive selectively and be inaccurate and incomplete.
- The growth of the Internet and monitoring technology such as CCTV means that the scope for research using unobtrusive measures is increasing at a rapid rate. However, the new technology also brings with it new ethical challenges which require recognizing the interests of disparate groups. The use of ethical contracts may be one way of reconciling these different interests.

(Continued)

Summary of web links

http://www.aa.gov.au
http://www.census.gov
http://www.esomar.nl/guidelines/Tapeandvideo.htm
http://www.euromonitor.com/default.asp
http://www.european-archival.net
http://www.icpsr.umich.edu
http://www.lib.umich.edu/libhome/documents.center/stats.html
http://www.nara.gov
http://www.ndad.ulcc.ac.uk
http://www.noldus.com/products/index.html
http://www.mrs.org.uk/
http://www.pro.gov.uk
http://www.statistics.gov.uk)

Further Reading

Webb, E.J., Campbell, D.T., Schwartz, R.D. and Sechrest, L. (1966) *Unobtrusive Measures: Nonreactive Research in the Social Sciences*. Chicago: Rand McNally. Something of a classic, it was in this book that the term unobtrusive measures was originally coined and described with elegance, clarity and intriguing examples.

Lee, R.M. (2000) *Unobtrusive Measures in Social Research*. Buckingham: Open University Press. Given that the pioneering work of Webb et al. was written in 1966, this is a welcome and very much updated discussion of the subject. It also contains a useful chapter on unobtrusive measures and the Internet.

Suggested answers for Activity 11.1

1 Triangulation of methods is evidenced by the fact that the researcher uses observation (of where people consume their drinks), as well as using the unobtrusive indicators. This, certainly, helps towards the reliability of the study.
2 Using an interview method would probably not have worked here because the honesty of replies could not be assured – and would the manager have believed them?!

PART D

Analysis and Report Writing

12 Analysing and Presenting Quantitative Data

Chapter objectives

After reading this chapter you will be able to:

- **Prepare data for analysis.**
- **Select appropriate formats for the presentation of data.**
- **Choose the most appropriate techniques for describing data (descriptive statistics).**
- **Choose the most appropriate techniques for exploring relationships and trends in data (correlation and inferential statistics).**

As we have seen in previous chapters, the distinction between quantitative and qualitative research methods is often blurred. Take, for example, survey methods. These can be purely descriptive in design, but on the other hand, the gathering of respondent profile data provides an opportunity for finding associations between classifications of respondents and their attitudes or behaviour, providing the potential for quantitative analysis.

One of the essential features of quantitative analysis is that, if you have planned your research tool, collected your data and *now* you are thinking of how to analyse it – you are too late! The process of selecting statistical tests should take place at the *planning* stage of research, not at implementation. This is because it is so easy to end up with data for which there is no meaningful statistical test. Robson (1993) also provides an astute warning that, particularly with the aid of the modern computer, 'it becomes that much easier to generate elegantly presented rubbish (remember GIGO – Garbage In, Garbage Out)' (Robson, 1993: 310).

The aim of this chapter is to introduce you to some of the basic statistical techniques. It does not pretend to provide you with an in-depth analysis of more complex statistics, since there are specialized textbooks for this purpose. It is assumed that you will have access to a computer and an appropriate software application for statistical analysis, such as Microsoft Excel or SPSS. Again, detailed advice is not provided on how to actually use these programs since there are already textbooks available. It is also suggested that, especially if you are relatively new to statistics, you obtain access to someone more experienced than yourself to act as a guide or mentor. Note that in this chapter, rather than offer you Activities, Worked Examples using statistical formulae will be provided.

CATEGORIZING DATA

The process of categorizing data is important because, as was noted in Chapter 4, the statistical tests that are used for data analysis will depend on the type of data being collected. Hence, the first step is to classify your data into one of two categories, *categorical* or *quantifiable* (see Figure 12.1). Categorical data cannot be quantified numerically but are either placed into sets or categories (*nominal* data) or ranked in some way (*ordinal* data). Quantifiable data can be measured numerically, which means that it is more precise. Within the quantifiable classification there are two additional categories of *interval* and *ratio* data. All of these categories are described in more detail next. Saunders et al. (2000) warn that if you are not sure about the level of detail you need in your research study, it is safest to collect data at the highest level of precision possible.

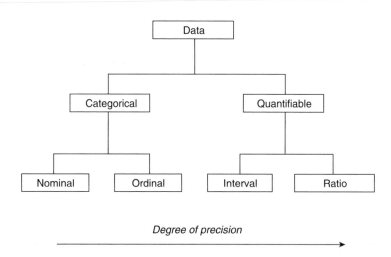

FIGURE 12.1 TYPES OF CATEGORICAL AND QUANTIFIABLE DATA

In simple terms, these data are used for different analysis purposes. Table 12.1 suggests some typical uses and the kinds of statistical tests that are appropriate.

As Diamantopoulos and Schlegelmilch (1997) point out, the four kinds of measurement scale are nested within one another: as we move from a lower level

TABLE 12.1 MEASUREMENT SCALES AND THEIR USES

	Nominal	Ordinal	Interval	Ratio
Example of usage	Type of firm	Customer preference	Temperature	Sales
	Type of product	Organizational hierarchy	Weight	Costs
	Location of organization		Blood pressure	Number of customers
		Attitudes		Age of workforce
Statistical tests	Non-parametric tests		Parametric tests	

Which category describes where the employee works? (Tick one)	
Retail department	❏
Warehouse	❏
Accounts	❏
Personnel	❏

FIGURE 12.2 TYPES OF QUESTION THAT YIELD NOMINAL DATA

of measurement to a higher one, the properties of the lower type are retained. Thus, all the statistical tests appropriate to the lower type of data can be used with the higher types as well as additional, more powerful tests. But this does not work in reverse: as we move from, say, interval data to ordinal, the tests appropriate for the former cannot be applied to the latter. For categorical data only, non-parametric statistical tests can be used, but for quantifiable data (see Figure 12.1), more powerful parametric tests need to be applied. Hence, in planning data collection it is better to design data gathering instruments that yield interval and ratio data, if this is appropriate to the research objectives. Let us look at each of the four data categories in turn.

Nominal data

Nominal data constitute a name value or category with no order or ranking implied (for example, sales departments, occupational descriptors of employees, etc.). A typical question that yields nominal data is presented in Figure 12.2, with a set of data that results from this presented in Table 12.2. Thus, we can see that with nominal data, we build up a simple frequency count of how often the nominal category occurs.

TABLE 12.2   NUMBER OF EMPLOYEES PER
DEPARTMENT (NOMINAL SCALE)

Department/location	Frequency
Retail	67
Warehouse	62
Accounts	15
Personnel	16

Ordinal data

Ordinal data comprises an ordering or ranking of values, although the intervals between the ranks are not intended to be equal (for example, an attitude questionnaire). A type of question that yields ordinal data is presented in Figure 12.3. Here there is a ranking of views (Sometimes, Never, etc.) where the order of such views is important but there is no suggestion that the differences between each scale are identical. Ordinal scales are also used for questions that rate the quality of something (for example, very good, good, fair, poor, etc.) and agreements (for example, Strongly agree, Agree, Disagree, etc.). The typical results of gathering ordinal data are taken from Figure 12.3 and presented in Table 12.3.

How often have you felt like insulting a customer? (Tick one)	
Every day	❏
Once a week	❏
Sometimes	❏
Never	❏

FIGURE 12.3   TYPES OF QUESTION THAT YIELD ORDINAL DATA

Interval data

With quantifiable measures such as interval data, numerical values are assigned along an interval scale with equal intervals, but there is no zero point where the trait being measured does not exist. For example, a score of zero on a traditional IQ test would have no meaning. This is because the traditional IQ score is the raw (actual) score converted into a mental age divided by chronological age. Another characteristic of interval data, is that the difference between a score of 14 and 15 would be the same as the difference between a score of 91 and 92. Hence, in contrast to ordinal data, the differences between categories *are* identical. The kinds of results from interval data are illustrated in Table 12.4, showing quite a normal distribution of scores on an IQ test, delivered as part of a company's aptitude assessment of staff.

TABLE 12.3 FREQUENCY TABLE SHOWING NUMBER OF RESPONSES ON ATTITUDE QUESTIONNAIRE (ORDINAL)

Staff tendency to insult customers	Number of responses
Every day	10
Once a week	15
Sometimes	11
Never	4

TABLE 12.4 FREQUENCY TABLE SHOWING NUMBER OF EMPLOYEES SCORING WITHIN VARIOUS RANGES ON IQ TEST

Scores	Frequency
76–80	1
81–85	0
86–90	4
91–95	10
96–100	21
101–105	25
106–110	48
111–115	18
116–120	11
121–125	4
126–130	1
131–135	2
136–140	1

Ratio data

Ratio data are a subset of interval data, and the scale is again interval, but there is an absolute zero that represents some meaning, for example, scores on an achievement test. If an employee, for example, undertakes a work-related test and scores zero, this would indicate a complete lack of knowledge or ability in this subject! An example of ratio data is presented in Table 12.5.

This sort of classification scheme is important because it influences the ways in which data are analysed and what kind of statistical tests can be applied. Having incorporated variables into a classification scheme, the next stage is to look at how data should be captured and laid out, prior to analysis and presentation.

DATA ENTRY, LAYOUT AND QUALITY

Data entry involves a number of stages, beginning with 'cleaning' the data, planning and implementing the actual input of the data, and dealing with the thorny problem of missing data. Ways of avoiding the degradation of data will also be discussed.

TABLE 12.5 FREQUENCY DISTRIBUTION OF
EMPLOYEE SCORES ON AN
IN-HOUSE WORK-RELATED TEST

Scores range	Frequency
0–4	4
5–9	13
10–14	15
15–19	12
20–24	8

Cleaning the data

Data analysis will only be reliable if it is built upon the foundations of 'clean' data, that is, data that have been entered into the computer accurately. When entering data containing a large number of variables and many individual records, it is easy to enter a wrong figure or to miss an entry. One solution is for two people to enter data separately and to compare the results, but this is expensive. Another approach is to use frequency analysis on a column of data that will throw up any spurious figures that have been entered. For example, if you are using numbers 1 to 5 to represent individual codes for each of five variables, the frequency analysis might show that you had also entered the number 8 – clearly a mistake. Where there are branching or skip questions (recall Chapter 8) it may also be necessary to check that respondents are going through the questions carefully. For example, they may be completing sections that do not apply to them or missing other sections.

Data coding and layout

Coding usually involves allocating a number to data. Take care, however, not to make the mistake of subsequently analysing the codes as raw data! The codes are merely shorthand ways of describing the data. Once the coding is completed, it is possible to collate the data into groups of less detailed categories. So, in Case Study 12.1 the categories could be re-coded to form the groups Legal and Financial and then Health and Safety.

The most obvious approach to data layout is the use of tables in the form of a *data matrix*. Within each data matrix, columns will represent a single variable while each row presents a case or profile. Hence, Table 12.6 illustrates an example of data from a survey of employee attitudes. The second column, labelled 'Id', is the *survey form identifier*, allowing the researcher to check back to the original survey form when checking for errors. The next column contains numbers, each of which signifies a particular department. Length of service is quantifiable data representing actual years spent in the organization, while seniority is again coded data signifying different scales of seniority. Thus, the numerical values have different meanings for different variables. Note that Table 12.6 is typical of the kind of data

TABLE 12.6 DATA MATRIX FROM SURVEY SHOWING DATA CODING FOR EACH VARIABLE

Case	Id	Department	Length of service	Seniority
Case 1	1	5	3	2
Case 2	2	2	1	3
Case 3	3	3	12	2

matrix that can be set up in a software program such as Excel, ready for the application of statistical formulae.

Case Study 12.1 illustrates the kind of survey layout and structure that yields data suitable for a data matrix (presented at the end of the Case Study). Hence, we have a range of variables and structured responses, each of which can be coded.

Case Study 12.1 From survey instrument to data matrix

A voluntary association that provides free advice to the public, seeks to discover which of its services are most utilized. A survey form is designed dealing with four potential areas, namely the law, finance, health, and safety in the home.

Question: Please look at the following services and indicate whether you have used any of them in the last 12 months.

	Yes	No	Not sure
Legal advice	❏	❏	❏
Financial advice	❏	❏	❏
Health advice	❏	❏	❏
Advice on safety in the home	❏	❏	❏

The data are collected from 100 respondents and input into the following data matrix using the numerical codes: 1 = Yes; 2 = No; 3 = Not sure; 0 = No data/no response.

Id	Legal	Finance	Health	Safety
Respondent 1	1	2	2	2
Respondent 2	2	1	1	1
Respondent 3	1	0	0	0

Note that in Case Study 12.1 Respondent 3 has ticked the box for 'Legal advice' but has failed to complete any of the others – hence, a '0' for no data has to be put in the matrix.

Dealing with missing data

Oppenheim (1992) notes that the best approach to dealing with missing data is not to have any! Hence, steps should be taken to ensure that data are collected from all of the intended sample and that non-response is kept to a minimum. But in practice, we know that there will be cases where either a respondent has not replied or has not answered all the questions. The issue here is one of potential bias – has the respondent omitted those questions they feel uneasy about or hostile to answering? For example, in answering a staff survey on working practices, are those with the worst records on absenteeism more likely to omit the questions on this (hence, potentially biasing the analysis)?

It might be useful to distinguish between four different types of missing values: 'Not applicable' (NA), 'Refused (RF), 'Did not know' (DK) and 'Forgot to answer' (FA). Making this distinction may help you to adopt strategies for coping with this data loss. Table 12.7 illustrates examples of these responses.

TABLE 12.7   DISTINGUISHING BETWEEN DIFFERENT TYPES OF
NON-RESPONSE

Response	Recorded for value
Question answered by wrong or inappropriate person, e.g. line manager of intended respondent	Not applicable
Rude message instead of response	Refused
All questions answered except one	Forgot to answer
All questions answered accurately but one left blank	Did not know

You may note that the categories for non-response chosen may depend largely on the researcher's inferences or guesswork. How do we know that someone forgot to answer or simply did not know how to respond? Of course, if many people fail to answer the same question, this might suggest there is something about the question they do not like – in which case, this could be construed as 'Refusal'. You may decide to ignore these separate categories and just use one 'No answer' label. Alternatively, you might put in a value if this is possible by taking the average of other people's responses. There are dangers, however, in this approach, particularly for single item questions. Note that some statisticians have spent almost a lifetime pondering issues of this kind! It would be safer if missing data were entered for a sub-question that comprised just one of a number of sub-questions (for which data *was* available). Note, also, that this becomes unfeasible if there are many non-responses to the same question, since it would leave the calculation based on a small sample.

Please indicate your age by ticking the appropriate box:	
18–24	[ ]
25–34	[ ]
35–44	[ ]
45–54	[ ]
55–64	[ ]
65+	[ ]

FIGURE 12.4 SECTION OF QUESTIONNAIRE COMPRISING AN AGE PROFILE

Avoiding the degradation of data

It is fairly clear when non-response has occurred, but it is also possible to compromise the quality of data by the process of degradation. Say, we were interested in measuring the age profile of the workforce and drew up a questionnaire, as illustrated in Figure 12.4. One problem here is that the age categories are unequal (for example, 18–24 compared with 25–34). But a further difficulty is the loss of information that comes with collecting the data in this way. We have ended up with an ordinal measure of what should be ratio data and cannot even calculate the average age of the workforce. Far better would have been simply to ask for each person's exact age (for example, by requesting their date of birth) and the date the questionnaire was completed. After this, we could calculate the average age (mean), the modal (most frequently occurring) age, identify both the oldest and youngest worker, etc.

PRESENTING DATA USING DESCRIPTIVE STATISTICS

One of the aims of descriptive statistics is to describe the basic features of a study, often through the use of graphical analysis. Descriptive statistics are distinguished from *inferential* statistics in that they attempt to show what the data *is*, while inferential statistics try to draw conclusions beyond the data – for example, inferring what a population may think on the basis of sample data.

Descriptive statistics, and in particular the use of charts or graphs, certainly provide the potential for the communication of data in readily accessible formats, but the kinds of graphics used will depend on the types of data being presented. This is why the start of this chapter focused on classifying data into nominal, ordinal, interval and ratio categories, since not all types of graph are appropriate for all kinds of data. Black (1999) provides a neat summary of what is appropriate (see Table 12.8).

TABLE 12.8   APPROPRIATE USE OF CHARTS AND
GRAPHS FOR FREQUENCY DATA

	Bar chart	Pie chart	Histogram	Frequency polygon
Nominal	+	+		
Ordinal	+			
Interval			+	+
Ratio			+	+

Source: Adapted from Black, 1999: 306

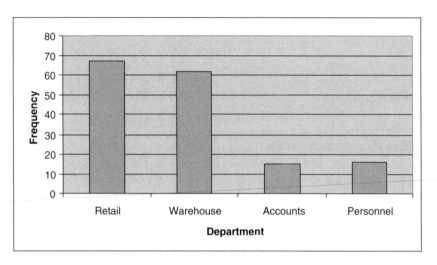

FIGURE 12.5   BAR CHART FOR THE NOMINAL DATA IN FIGURE 12.2

Nominal and ordinal data – single groups

As we saw earlier, nominal data are a record of categories or names, with no intended order or ranking, while ordinal data do assume some intended ordering of categories. Taking the nominal data in Table 12.2, we can present a bar chart (Figure 12.5) for the frequency count of staff in different departments.

   Figure 12.6 shows that this same set of data can also be presented in the form of a pie chart. Note that pie charts are suitable for illustrating nominal data but are not appropriate for ordinal data – obviously, because it presents proportions of a total, not the ordering of categories.

Interval and ratio data – single groups

Interval and ratio data describe scores on tests, age, weight, annual income, etc., for a group of individuals. These numbers are then, usually, translated into a frequency table, such as in Tables 12.2 and 12.3. The first stage is to decide on the number of intervals in the data. Black (1999) recommends between 10 and 20 as

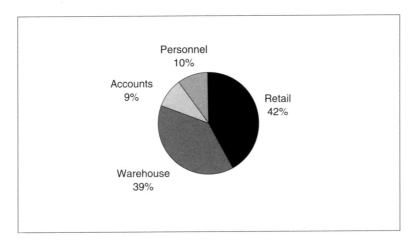

FIGURE 12.6   PIE CHART OF THE NOMINAL DATA IN FIGURE 12.2

TABLE 12.9   AGE PROFILE OF E-COMMERCE
DEVELOPMENT COMPANY

Age	Frequency	Age	Frequency
22	1	33	10
23	2	34	4
24	3	35	3
25	6	36	2
26	5	37	4
27	11	38	2
28	15	39	2
29	7	40	0
30	9	41	0
31	3	42	1
32	4	43	0

acceptable, since going outside this range would tend to distort the shape of the histogram or frequency polygon. Take a look at the data on an age profile of the entire workforce in an e-commerce development organization, presented in Table 12.9. The age range is from 22 to 43, a difference of 21. If we selected an interval range of 3, this would only give us a set of seven age ranges and conflict with Black's (1999) recommendation that only a minimum of 10 ranges is acceptable. If, however, we took two as the interval range, we would end up with 11 sets of intervals, as in Table 12.10, which is acceptable. We then take this data for graphical presentation in the form of a histogram, as in Figure 12.7.

Nominal data – comparing groups

So far, we have looked at presenting single sets of data. But often research will require us to gather data on a number of related characteristics and it is useful to

TABLE 12.10 FREQUENCY TABLE FOR AGE RANGE
(INTERVAL) DATA

Age range	Frequency	Age range	Frequency
22–23	3	34–35	7
24–25	9	36–37	6
26–27	16	38–39	4
28–29	22	40–41	0
30–31	12	42–43	1
32–33	14		

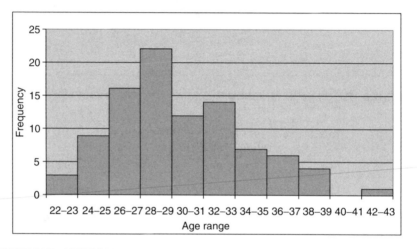

FIGURE 12.7 HISTOGRAM ILLUSTRATING INTERVAL DATA IN TABLE 12.10

be able to compare these graphically. For example, returning to Table 12.2 and the number of employees per department, these may be aggregate frequencies, based on the spread of both male and female workers per department, as in Figure 12.8.

Another way of presenting these kind of data is where it is useful to show not only the distribution between groups, but the total size of each group, as in Figure 12.9.

Interval and ratio data – comparing groups

It is sometimes necessary to compare two groups for traits that are measured as continuous data. While this exercise is, as we have seen, relatively easy for nominal data that is discreet, interval and ratio data are continuous, so the two sets of data may overlap and one hide the other. The solution is to use a frequency polygon. As we can see in Figure 12.10, we have two sets of continuous data of test scores, one set for a group of employees who have received training and another for those who have not. The frequency polygon enables us to see both sets of results simultaneously and to compare the trends.

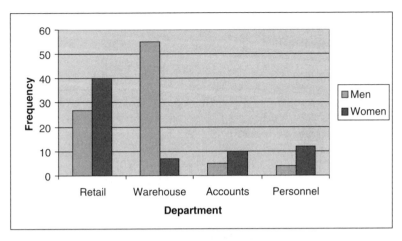

FIGURE 12.8   BAR CHART FOR NOMINAL DATA WITH COMPARISON BETWEEN GROUPS

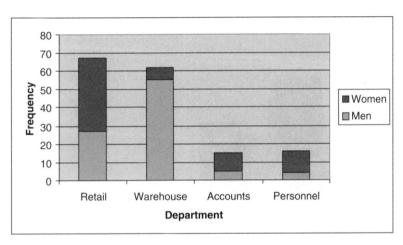

FIGURE 12.9   STACKED BAR CHART FOR NOMINAL DATA WITH COMPARISON BETWEEN GROUPS

Two variables for a single group

You may also want to compare two variables for a single group. Returning once more to our example of departments, we might look at the age profiles of the workers in each of them. Figure 12.11 shows the result.

ANALYSING DATA USING DESCRIPTIVE STATISTICS

A descriptive focus involves the creation of a summary picture of a sample or population in terms of key variables being researched. This may involve the

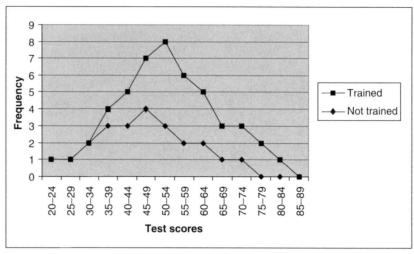

FIGURE 12.10   FREQUENCY POLYGONS FOR TWO SETS OF CONTINUOUS
DATA SHOWING TEST SCORES

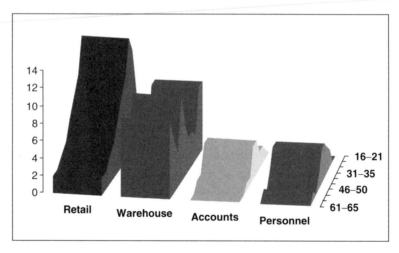

FIGURE 12.11   SOLID POLYGON SHOWING DATA FOR TWO VARIABLES:
DEPARTMENT AND AGE

presentation of data in graphical form (as in the previous section) or the use of
descriptive statistics, as discussed here.

Frequency distribution and central tendency

Frequency distribution is one of the most common methods of data analysis,
particularly for analysing survey data. Frequency simply means the number of

TABLE 12.11 PERCENTAGE OF RESPONDENTS ANSWERING FOR EACH
ATTITUDE CATEGORY OVER A TWO-YEAR PERIOD

	Strongly Agree	Agree	Disagree	Strongly Disagree	Total
2002	14	40	32	14	100
2003	21	33	26	20	100

TABLE 12.12 METHOD OF SCORING EACH RESPONSE CATEGORY IN ORDER
TO CALCULATE THE MEAN SCORE

	Strongly Agree	Agree	Disagree	Strongly Disagree
Score	4	3	2	1

instances in a class, and in surveys it is often associated with the use of Likert scales. So, for example, a survey might measure customer satisfaction for a particular product over a two-year period. Table 12.11 presents a typical set of results, showing what percentage of customers answered for each attitude category to the statement: 'We think that the Squeezy floor cleaner is good value for money'.

Comparing the data between the two years, it appears that there has been a 7 per cent rise in the number of customers who 'Strongly Agree' that the floor cleaner is good value for money. Unfortunately, just to report this result would be misleading because, as we can see, there has also been a 6 per cent rise in those who 'Strongly Disagree' with the statement. So what are we to make of the results? Given that the 'Agree' category has fallen by 7 per cent and the 'Disagree' category by 6 per cent, have attitudes moved for or against the product? To make sense of the data, two approaches need to be adopted.

- The use of *all* the data, not just selected figures that meet the researcher's agendas.
- A way of quantifying the results using a single, representative figure.

This scoring method involves the calculation of a *mean score* for each set of data. Hence, the categories could be given a score, as illustrated in Table 12.12.

All respondents' scores can then be added up, yielding the set of scores presented in Table 12.13, and the *mean*, showing that, overall, attitudes have moved very slightly in favour of the product.

Since the data can be described by the mean, a single figure, it becomes possible to make comparisons between different parts of the data or, if, say, two surveys are carried out at different periods, across time. Of course, there are also dangers in this approach. There is an assumption (possibly a mistaken one) that the differences between these ordinal categories are identical. Furthermore, the mean is only one measure of central tendency, others including the median and the mode. The *median* is the central value when all the scores are arranged in order. The *mode* is simply the most frequently occurring value. If the median and mode scores are less than the mean, the distribution of scores will be skewed to the left (positive skew); if they are greater than the mean, the scores are said to be skewed

TABLE 12.13   CALCULATION OF MEAN SCORES FOR ATTITUDE CATEGORIES
TO DISCOVER ATTITUDE TRENDS OVER A TWO-YEAR PERIOD

	Strongly Agree (4)	Agree (3)	Disagree (2)	Strongly Disagree (1)	Total	Mean
2002	56	120	64	14	254	2.86
2003	84	99	52	20	255	2.97

to the right (negative skew). So, while two mean scores could be identical, this need not imply that two sets of scores were the same, since each might have a different *distribution* of scores.

Having made these qualifications, this scoring method can still be used, but is probably best utilized over a multiple set of scores rather than just a single set. It is also safest used for descriptive rather than for inferential statistics.

Measuring dispersion

In addition to measuring central tendency, it may also be important to measure the *spread* of responses around the mean to show whether the mean is representative of the responses or not. There are a number of ways of measuring this:

- The *range:* the difference between the highest and the lowest scores.
- The *inter-quartile range:* the difference between the score that has a quarter of the scores below it (often known as the first quartile or the 25th percentile) and the score that has three-quarters of the scores below it (the 75th percentile).
- The *variance:* a measure of the average of the squared deviations of individual scores from the mean.
- The *standard deviation:* a measure of the extent to which responses vary from the mean, and is derived by calculating the variances from the mean, squaring them, adding them and calculating the square root. Like the mean, because you are able to calculate a single figure, it allows comparisons to be made between different parts of a survey and across time periods.

The normal distribution

The normal distribution curve is bell-shaped, that is symmetrical around the mean, which means that there are an equal number of subjects above as below the mean (X). The shape of the curve also indicates the proportion of subjects at each of the standard deviations (S, 1S, etc.) above and below the mean. Thus in Figure 12.12, 34.13 per cent of the subjects are one standard deviation above the mean and another 34.13 per cent below it.

In the real world, however it is often the case that distributions are not normal, but skewed, and this will have implications for the relationship between

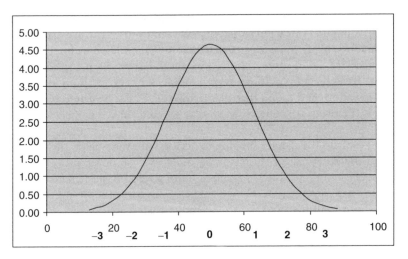

FIGURE 12.12 THE THEORETICAL 'NORMAL' DISTRIBUTION WITH MEAN = 0

the mean, the mode and the median. Where the distribution is positively skewed, the majority of the subjects are above the mean in terms of the trait or attitude being measured; for a distribution that is negatively skewed, the majority are below the mean.

THE PROCESS OF HYPOTHESIS TESTING: INFERENTIAL STATISTICS

We saw in Chapter 4 that the research process may involve the formulation of a hypothesis or hypotheses that describe the relationship between two variables. In this section we will re-examine hypothesis testing in a number of stages, which comprise:

- Hypothesis formulation.
- Specification of significance level (to see how safe it is to accept or reject the hypothesis).
- Identification of the probability distribution and definition of the region of rejection.
- Selection of appropriate statistical tests.
- Calculation of the test statistic and acceptance or rejection of the hypothesis.

Hypothesis formulation

As we saw in Chapter 4, a hypothesis is a statement concerning a population (or populations) that may or may not be true, and constitutes an inference or inferences about a population, drawn from sample information. Let us say, for example, that we work for a marketing company conducting some research on the ownership of palmtop computers in western Europe. We conjecture that per capita ownership in the UK is likely to be greater than that in France. If we had unlimited time and resources, we could survey both populations. For practical considerations, of course, we have to sample. If we took random samples for both the UK and French populations and found that ownership was 18 per cent in the UK and 12 per cent in France, our conjecture would be confirmed by the evidence. Or would it?

First, we run the danger of sampling error, with the smaller the sample size the greater the potential for this error. Secondly, we can never 'prove' something to be true, because there always remains a finite possibility that one day someone will emerge with a refutation. Hence, for research purposes, we usually phrase a hypothesis in its null (negative) form. So, rather than state:

The ownership of palmtop computers will be greater in the UK than in France.

We say:

The ownership of palmtop computers will not *be greater in the UK than in France.*

Then, if we find that the data for ownership is greater for the UK than in France, we can reject the null hypothesis.

Hypotheses come in essentially three forms. Those that:

- Examine the characteristics of a single population (and may involve calculating the mean, median and standard deviation and the shape of the distribution).
- Explore contrasts and comparisons between groups.
- Examine associations and relationships between groups.

For one research study, it may be necessary to formulate a number of null hypotheses incorporating statements about distributions, scores, frequencies, associations and correlations.

Specification of significance level

Having formulated the null hypothesis, we must next decide on the circumstances in which it will be accepted or rejected. Since we do not know with absolute certainty whether the hypothesis is true or false, ideally, we would want to reject the null hypothesis when it is false, and to accept it when it is true. However, since there is no such thing as an absolute certainty (especially in the real world!), there is always a chance of rejecting the null hypothesis when in fact it is true (called a Type I error) and accepting it when it is in fact false (a Type II error). Table 12.14 presents a summary of possible outcomes.

TABLE 12.14   POTENTIAL ERRORS IN HYPOTHESIS TESTING

	Situation in the population	
Decision made on null hypothesis	**Hypothesis is true**	**Hypothesis is false**
Hypothesis is rejected	Type I error	Correct decision
Hypothesis is not rejected	Correct decision	Type II error

What is the potential impact of these errors? Say, for example, we measure whether a new training programme improves staff attitudes to customers, and we express this in null terms (the training will have no effect). If we made a Type I error then we are rejecting the null hypothesis, and therefore claim that the training *does* have an effect when, in fact, this is not true. You will, no doubt, recognize that we do *not* want to make claims for the impact of independent variables that are actually false. Think of the implications if we made a Type I error when testing a new drug! We also want to avoid Type II errors, since here we would be accepting the null hypothesis and therefore failing to notice the impact that an independent variable was having.

Type I and Type II errors are the converse of each other. As Fielding and Gilbert (2000) observe, anything we do to reduce a Type I error will increase the likelihood of a Type II error, and vice versa. Whichever error is the most likely depends on how we set the significance level (see next).

Identification of the probability distribution

What are the chances of making a Type I error? This is measured by what is called the *significance level,* which measures the probability of making a mistake. The significance level is always set before a test is carried out, and is traditionally set at either 0.05, 0.01, or 0.001. Thus, if we set our significance level at 5 per cent (p = 0.05), we are willing to take the risk of rejecting the null hypothesis when in fact it is correct 5 times out of 100.

All statistical tests are based on an area of acceptance and an area of rejection. For what is termed a one-tailed test, the rejection area is either the upper or lower tail of the distribution. A one-tailed test is used when the hypothesis is directional, that is, it predicts an outcome at either the higher or lower end of the distribution. But there may be cases when it is not possible to make such a prediction. In these circumstances, a two-tailed test is used, for which there are two areas of rejection – both the upper and lower tails. For example, for the z distribution where p = 0.05 and a two-tailed test, statistical tables show that the area of acceptance for the null hypothesis is the central 95 per cent of the distribution and the areas of rejection are the 2.5 per cent of each tail (see Figure 12.13). Hence, if the test statistic is less than 1.96 or greater than 1.96 the null hypothesis will be rejected.

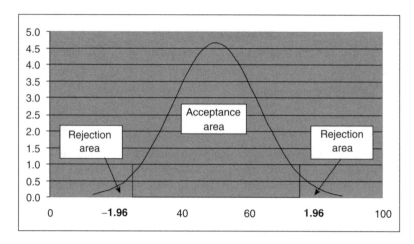

FIGURE 12.13   AREAS OF ACCEPTANCE AND REJECTION IN A STANDARD
NORMAL DISTRIBUTION WITH $\alpha = 0.05$

Selection of appropriate statistical tests

The selection of statistical tests appropriate for each hypothesis is perhaps the most challenging feature of using statistics but also the most necessary. It is all too easy to formulate a valid hypothesis only to choose an inappropriate test, with the result – statistical nonsense! The type of statistical test used will depend on quite a broad range of factors.

First, the type of hypothesis – for example, hypotheses concerned with the characteristics of groups, compared with relationships between variables. Even within these broad groups of hypotheses different tests may be needed. So a test for comparing differences between group means will be different to one comparing differences between medians. Even for the same sample, different tests may be used depending on the size of the sample.

Secondly, assumptions about the distribution of populations will affect the type of statistical test used. For example, different tests will be used for populations for which the data are evenly distributed compared with those that are not.

A third consideration is the level of measurement of the variables in the hypothesis. As we saw earlier, different tests are appropriate for nominal, ordinal, interval and ratio data, and only non-parametric tests are suitable for nominal and ordinal data, but parametric tests can be used with interval and ratio data. Parametric tests also work best with large sample sizes (that is, at least 30 observations per variable or group) and are more powerful than non-parametric tests. This simply means that they are more likely to reject the null hypothesis when it should be rejected, avoiding Type I errors. Motulsky (1995) advises that parametric tests should usually be selected if you are sure that the population is normally distributed. Table 12.15 provides a summary of the kinds of statistical test available in the variety of circumstances just described.

TABLE 12.15   GUIDE TO SELECTION OF STATISTICAL TESTS

Survey objectives	Type of Data Independent variable	Dependent variable	Potential statistical test
For objectives with one dependent and one independent variable			
Compare departments in frequency of issue of written warnings	Nominal: groups (departments)	Nominal (number of written warnings)	Chi-square, Fisher's exact test
Compare an experimental and control group in their attitudes after 'anti-smoking' campaign	Nominal (dichotomous): groups (experimental and control)	Quantifiable (attitude scores)	One-sample *t*-test, dependent *t*-test and independent *t*-test; Wilcoxon signed-ranks test; Wilcoxon rank-sum test
Compare attitudes across five company departments to new working practices	Nominal: more than two values	Quantifiable (attitude scores)	One-way analysis of variance (using the *F*-test)
Determine if high scores on measurement of confidence predict high scores on test of ability	Quantifiable (attitude scores)	Quantifiable (knowledge scores)	Regression (when neither variable is dependent or independent, use correlation)
For objectives with two or more independent variables			
Compare manual and white collar staff in experiment and control groups with respect to attitudes	Nominal (manual and white collar)	Quantifiable (attitude scores)	Analysis of variance (ANOVA)
Determine if length of service and salary level relate to attitudes	Quantifiable (length of service and salary level)	Quantifiable (attitude scores)	Multiple regression
Compare men and women in experimental and control groups in their attitudes when their salary level is controlled	Nominal (gender and group) with confounding factors (salary level)	Quantifiable (attitude scores)	Analysis of covariance (ANCOVA)
For objectives with two or more independent and dependent variables			
Compare men and women in experimental and control groups in their attitude and knowledge scores	Nominal (gender and group)	Quantifiable (scores on two measures: attitudes and knowledge)	Multivariate analysis of variance (MANOVA)

Source: Adapted from Fink, 1995c

Calculation of the test statistic and acceptance or rejection of the hypothesis

Provided that the above stages have been performed accurately, the final stage, using an appropriate statistical software program, should be relatively straight-forward. Once the test statistic is calculated, the final task is to compare this with the hypothesized value. If the test statistic does not reach this value, then the null hypothesis must be accepted.

Worked Example 12.1

A government department sets up a research study to examine a possible relationship between personality traits and absenteeism. Using a sample of 22 employees, it sets the significance level at $p \leq 0.05$. Analysing the data using the Pearson product moment correlation attains a value for this association of $r = 0.287$. This value is looked up in a special table of critical values for this particular test. (NB: Critical value tables can be found in many statistics text-books.) The critical value for a one-tailed test with 20 degrees of freedom (i.e. $n - 2$) is found to be 0.360. Hence, the correlation between personality traits and absenteeism is not found to be significant.

In the sections that follow, we will take some examples from Table 12.15 and describe them for the purpose of illustration.

STATISTICAL ANALYSIS: COMPARING VARIABLES

In this section and the one that follows, we will be performing a number of statistical tests. It will be assumed that most readers will have access to Excel, so this, rather than other programs such as SPSS, will be used. However, sometimes even using Excel calculations can get quite complicated, so in these cases the calculations will be illustrated for you in the text.

Nominal data – one sample

In the following section we will look at comparing relationships *between* variables, but here we will confine ourselves to exploring the distribution *of* a variable. First, if we assume a pre-specified distribution (such as a normal distribution), we can compare the observed (actual data) frequencies against expected (theoretical) frequencies, to measure the *goodness-of-fit*.

Let us say that a company is interested in comparing disciplinary records across its four production sites by measuring the number of written warnings issued in the past two years. We might assume that, since the sites are of broadly equal size in terms of people employed, the warnings might be evenly spread across these sites, that is, 25 per cent for each. Since the total number of recorded

TABLE 12.16 CONTINGENCY TABLE OF DATA FOR ANALYSIS

	Cases	
Site	Observed O_i	Expected E_i
A	12	29
B	68	29
C	14	29
D	22	29
Total	116	116

TABLE 12.17 ANALYSIS OF DATA IN TABLE 12.16

Site	Observed O_i	Expected E_i	$\dfrac{(O_i - E_i)^2}{E_i}$
A	12	29	9.97
B	68	29	52.45
C	14	29	7.76
D	22	29	1.69
Total	116	116	71.86

written warnings is 116 (see Table 12.16), this represents 29 expected warnings per site. Data are gathered (observed frequencies) to see if they match the expected frequencies. The null hypothesis is that there will be no difference between the observed and expected frequencies. Following our earlier advice, we set the level of significance in advance. In this case let us say that we set it at $p = 0.05$. If any significant difference is found, then the null hypothesis will be rejected. Table 12.16 presents the data in what is called a contingency table.

The appropriate test here is the chi-square statistic. For each case we deduct the expected frequency from the observed frequency and square the result and divide by the expected frequency; the chi-square statistic is the sum of the totals (see Table 12.17).

Is the chi-square statistic of 71.86 significant? To find out, we look the figure up in an appropriate statistical table for the chi-square statistic. The value to use will be in the column for $p = 0.05$ and for 3 degrees of freedom (the number of categories minus one). This figure turns out to be 7.81, which is far exceeded by our chi-square figure. Hence, we can say that the difference is significant and we can reject the null hypothesis that there is no difference between the issue of written warnings between the sites.

Note, however, that the expected frequencies do not have to be equal. Say, we know through some prior research that site B is three times as likely to issue warnings as the other sites. Table 12.18 presents the new data.

Here we find that the new chi-square statistic is only 6.34, which is not significant. Diamantopoulos and Schlegelmilch (1997) warn that when the number of categories in the variable is greater than two, the chi-square test should not be used where:

TABLE 12.18   EXAMPLE OF A ONE-SAMPLE CHI-SQUARE TEST WITH UNEVEN
EXPECTED FREQUENCY

Site	Observed O_i	Expected E_i	$\dfrac{(O_i - E_i)^2}{E_i}$
A	12	19.33	2.78
B	68	58.00	1.72
C	14	19.33	1.47
D	22	19.33	0.37
Total	116	116.00	6.34

- More than 20 per cent of the expected frequencies are smaller than 5.
- Any expected frequency is less than one.

If the numbers within cells are small, and it is possible to combine adjacent categories, then it is advisable to do so. For example, if some of our expected frequencies in Table 12.14 were rather small but sites A and B were in England and site C and D in Germany, we might sensibly combine A with B and C with D in order to make an international comparison study.

Nominal groups and quantifiable data (normally distributed)

Let us say that you want to compare the performance of two groups, or to compare the performance of one group over a period of time using quantifiable variables such as scores. In these circumstances we can use a paired *t*-test. *T*-tests assume that the data are normally distributed, and that the two groups have the same variance (the standard deviation squared). If the data are not normally distributed then usually a non-parametric test, the Wilcoxon signed-ranks test, can be used. The *t*-test compares the means of the two groups to see if any differences between them are significant. If the p-value associated with *t* is low (< 0.05), then there is evidence to reject the null hypothesis.

Say that we want to examine the effectiveness of a stress counselling programme. Recall Chapter 4 on research design where we saw that we should avoid using a pre-test/post-test design due to the danger of confounding variables. Table 12.19, therefore, shows that we have randomly divided our sample of employees into two groups, an experimental and control, and assessed the stress levels of each group before and after the programme. Of course, only the experimental group receives the stress counselling. Each worker in the sample provides a self-assessed score of their stress levels on a scale of 1–20, with 20 being the maximum.

We can see from Table 12.19 that in a number of cases the levels of stress have actually increased! But in most cases, particularly in the experimental group, stress levels have fallen, in some cases quite sharply. Worked Example 12.2 shows how we can use Excel to see if this is statistically significant.

TABLE 12.19 STRESS SCORE DATA FOR EXPERIMENTAL AND CONTROL GROUPS BEFORE AND AFTER A STRESS COUNSELLING PROGRAMME

	Stress score: A_1 (pre-counselling)	Stress score: A_2 (post-counselling)	Gain scores: $A_2 - A_1$
Experimental group (receiving the counselling)			
Employee A	15	9	−6
Employee B	18	14	−4
Employee C	4	6	2
Employee D	8	7	−1
Employee E	16	8	−8
Employee F	15	4	−11
Employee G	20	10	−10
Employee H	17	10	−7
Control group (not receiving counselling)			
Employee J	13	11	−2
Employee K	16	17	1
Employee L	7	9	2
Employee M	4	4	0
Employee N	14	11	−3
Employee O	16	15	−1
Employee P	9	8	−1
Employee Q	8	9	1

Worked Example 12.2

Cut and paste the gain scores for both the experimental and control groups into an Excel spreadsheet, making sure that each set of figures is in a sepa-

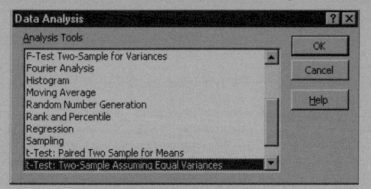

rate column. Under Tools/Data Analysis, select the *t*-Test: Two Samples Assuming Equal Variances (as in the graphic).

Place your cursor in the Variable 1 range, then sweep across your first column of gain scores data. Repeat the process for Variable 2 for your second column (the control group data). For Output options, select Output range. After clicking on [OK] you should see the following data:

(Continued)

t-Test: Two-Sample Assuming Equal Variances		
	Variable 1	*Variable 2*
Mean	5.625	0.375
Variance	19.696	2.839
Observations	8.000	8.000
Pooled Variance	11.268	
Hypothesised Mean Difference	0.000	
df	14.000	
t Stat	3.128	
P(T<=t) one-tail	0.004	
t Critical one-tail	1.761	
P(T<=t) two-tail	0.007	
t Critical two-tail	2.145	

Notice that the mean scores of the two groups are quite different – always a good sign that there may be statistical significance. To check whether this is true, take the *t*-statistic, in this case 3.128, and compare it with the *t*-value for a two-tailed test at a specified level (0.01, 0.05) of statistical significance. We can see that the *t*-statistic is greater so we can conclude that the change in gain scores *is* significant. The stress counselling worked!

Nominal groups and quantifiable data (not normally distributed)

In the section above we looked at differences in normally distributed data between groups. But what if the data do not satisfy the assumptions required for statistical tests based on normal distribution? Let us say that we work for a retail store that wants to evaluate the impact of two alternative layouts for its clothing departments. Two sections of the department are re-designed and, over a two-week period, a random sample of customers purchasing goods in each section is asked to award a score out of 100 for the quality of layout. Table 12.20 presents the findings, with each set of data awarded a ranking. These rankings were automatically generated in Excel using the Tools/Data Analysis/Rank and Percentile feature. Note that where scores are tied (a common feature of ordinal data) the program automatically allocates them the same rank – in this case, both scores of

TABLE 12.20 RANKING OF TWO RETAIL STORE FEATURES BASED ON
CUSTOMER SCORING

Scores for Section A	Ranking	Scores for Section B	Ranking
60	5	42	10
92	1	50	8
50	8	38	11
35	12	58	6
75	4	55	7
84	3	26	13
88	2		
Totals	35		55

50 are given an 8th position. The null hypothesis is that there will be no difference
between the two sets of scores.

For data of this type the Mann Witney U-test is valid.

Worked Example 12.3

We work out the values for U_1 for one group and U2 for the other, which is
calculated by the formula for the Mann Witney U-test:

$$U_1 = n_1\, n_2 + \frac{n_1\, (n_1 + 1)}{2} - R_1$$

$$U_2 = n_1\, n_2 + \frac{n_2\, (n_2 + 1)}{2} - R_2$$

Here n_1 (7) and n_2 (6) are the size of the two groups, R_1 (35) and R_2 (55) the
sum of the rankings. Therefore, we have:

$$U_1 = 6 \times 7 + \frac{7\, (7 + 1)}{2} - 35 = 35$$

$$U_2 = 6 \times 7 + \frac{6\, (6 + 1)}{2} - 55 = 8$$

We then check the values for U_1 and U_2 in the relevant statistical table and find
that for a two-tailed test with n_1 equal to 7 and n_2 equal to 6, at the $p = 0.05$
level, the critical values of U are 6 and 36. Hence, to reject the null hypothesis, the value of U in one case must be less than 6 and in the other greater
than 36. Our data reveal that this is not the case, so the null hypothesis
cannot be rejected. Back to the drawing board for that store layout!

TABLE 12.21 SUMMARY OF STATISTICAL TESTS AVAILABLE FOR MEASURING ASSOCIATION BETWEEN TWO VARIABLES

Association	Measure
Between two nominal variables	Cramer's V
Between two ordinal variables	Spearman rank-order correlation (where the relationship is non-linear)
Between interval and/or ratio scale variables	Pearson's product moment correlation (where the relationship is linear)

Note that the Mann Witney U-test is also useful in other situations. Say, for example, we employ two different training programmes that teach the same topic and want to see which is the most effective. If it cannot be assumed that the data come from a normal distribution, we would use the Mann Witney U-test to compare the test scores of the two sets of learners.

STATISTICAL ANALYSIS: ASSOCIATIONS BETWEEN VARIABLES

This section examines situations where the study contains two independent variables of the same type (nominal, ordinal, interval/ratio). Table 12.21 illustrates the different kinds of measurement of association between two variables, depending on the type of variable involved.

Associations between two nominal variables

Sometimes we may want to investigate relationships between two nominal variables – for example:

- Educational attainment and choice of career.
- Type of recruit (graduate/non-graduate) and level of responsibility in an organization.

You will recall in the discussions about chi-square, above, that we used the statistic to see whether the distribution of a variable occurred by chance or not. Cramer's V (which is an extension of the chi-square statistic) takes this a stage further and determines the *strength* of the relationship.

The value of Cramer's V ranges from 0 to 1, and is represented by the formula:

$$V = \sqrt{\frac{\chi^2}{n\,(k-1)}}$$

TABLE 12.22 OBSERVED AND EXPECTED VALUES OF GRADUATE AND
NON-GRADUATE EMPLOYMENT AGAINST RESPONSIBILITY LEVEL
WITHIN AN ORGANISATION

| | Educational attainment | | |
	Non-graduate	Graduate	Total
Actual			
Executive	2	10	12
Managerial	20	80	100
Administrative	70	64	134
Manual	240	4	244
Total	332	158	490
Expected			
Executive	8.13	3.87	12
Managerial	67.76	32.24	100
Administrative	90.79	43.21	134
Manual	165.32	78.68	244
Total	332	158	490

Here, you divide the chi-square value by n (the sample size) multiplied by $(k - 1)$
where k is the smaller of the number of columns or rows in the original contingency table. You then take the square root of this figure.

Let us say that a company wishes to evaluate its graduate recruitment
policy by comparing how well its graduates do compared with non-graduates in
terms of the levels of responsibility that they reach in the organization. The null
hypothesis is that there will be no difference between the levels of seniority of
graduates compared to non-graduates. Table 12.22 provides data on both the
observed and expected values. The expected values are calculated by dividing the
column total by the grand total then multiplying by the row total. Hence, for
executive, non-graduates, the calculation is $332/490 \times 12 = 8.13$.

Worked Example 12.4

We calculate chi-square in the same way as a one-sample and find that $\chi^2 =$
238.1. This gives us:

$$0.49 = \sqrt{\frac{238.1}{490 (2 - 1)}}$$

The number of degrees of freedom for a 4×2 contingency table is $v = (4 - 1)$
$\times (2 - 1) = 3$. For an significance level where $p = 0.05$ at 3 degrees of freedom,
we find that the chi-square statistic is highly significant. Thus, we can reject the
null hypothesis that 'graduateness' makes no difference to seniority in the
organization. Maybe we should recruit more people with degrees!

Correlation analysis: principles of measurement

Correlation analysis is concerned with *associations* between variables. Correlations are sometimes confused with regression. As Fink (1995c) makes clear, however, correlation is concerned with describing relationships (for example, between X and Y), while regression predicts a value (say, X based on a value of Y). When an association is measured numerically, we get a correlation coefficient that gives the strength and the direction of the relationship between two variables. In addition to the strength of a relationship, we might also be interested in the *direction* of an association. Such relationships can be the basis of some very important questions in organizational analysis. For example,

- Does the introduction of performance management techniques to specific groups of workers improve morale compared to other groups? (Relationship: performance management/morale)
- Is there a relationship between size of company (measured by size of workforce) and efficiency (measured by output per worker)? (Relationship: company size/efficiency)
- Do measures to improve health and safety inevitably reduce output? (Relationship: health and safety procedures/output)

The most commonly used coefficients assume a *linear* relationship between the variables, with Figure 12.14 illustrating an idealized form of 'perfect' linear correlation. Measured numerically, this would give a perfectly positive correlation coefficient of +1.0 for (a) and perfectly negative correlation of −1.0 for (b). Very crudely, if an association is between 0 and 0.4 it is said to be 'weak', between 0.4 and 0.8 'moderate' and above 0.8, 'strong'. Figure 12.15, however, shows a much more likely type of correlation where the variables are highly positively correlated. The points shown all fall close to a cigar-shaped envelope. The thinner this envelope, the stronger the correlation, while the broader the envelope, the weaker the correlation. Where the points are scattered so much as to appear entirely random, then the correlation is likely to be zero, or close to it.

The correlation coefficient is calculated in a number of ways, depending on the type of data being used. This section focuses on bivariate relationships, that is, associations between just two variables. Calculating a correlation for a set of data should only be done when:

- The subjects are independent and not chosen from the same group.
- The values for X and Y are measured independently.
- X and Y values are sampled from populations that are normally distributed.
- Neither of the values for X or Y is controlled (in which case, linear regression, not correlation, should be calculated).

Associations between two ordinal variables

Sometimes it is not possible to give values to variables, only ranks (1st, 2nd, 3rd, etc.). Let us take the example of a case where we are judging the performance of

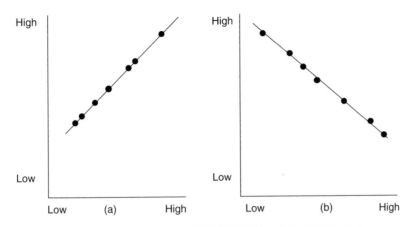

FIGURE 12.14   PERFECT POSITIVE CORRELATION (LEFT) AND PERFECT
NEGATIVE RELATIONSHIP (RIGHT)

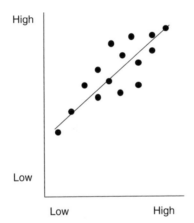

FIGURE 12.15   EXAMPLE OF A HIGHLY POSITIVE CORRELATION WITH
CIGAR-SHAPED ENVELOPE

five new office administrators. Two supervisors are asked to rank the performance
of the administrators with the results presented in Table 12.23.

For data that is ranked, or in circumstances where relationships are non-
linear, Spearman's rank-order correlation, often known as Spearman's rho, can be
used, calculated by the following formula, where D is the rank difference for any
member.

$$p = 1 - \frac{6\Sigma D^2}{n\,(n^2 - 1)}$$

Taking the data in Table 12.23 we can obtain values for D^2, as presented in Table 12.24.

TABLE 12.23 RANKINGS OF JUDGEMENTS MADE BY SUPERVISORS ON THE PERFORMANCE OF FIVE ADMINISTRATORS

Supervisor	Alice	Raj	Jo	Beth	Sid
Mr Jones	5	2	4	3	1
Mrs Smith	4	1	3	5	2

TABLE 12.24 COMPARISON OF RANKING DIFFERENCES BETWEEN THE TWO JUDGES

Supervisor	Alice	Raj	Jo	Beth	Sid
Mr Jones	5	2	4	3	1
Mrs Smith	4	1	3	5	2
D	1	1	1	-2	-1
D^2	1	1	1	4	1

Worked Example 12.5

The value of D is obtained by subtracting the ranks of Mrs Smith from those of Mr Jones, after which we obtain D^2 by squaring the results. Thus, $\sum D^2 = 1 + 1 + 1 + 4 + 1 = 8$, with $n = 5$ (the number of people being ranked). This give us:

$$p = 1 - \frac{6 \times 8}{5(25-1)} = 0.6$$

To interpret this figure, we look at the appropriate statistical table for Spearman's rho. We find that for a two-tailed test with 3 degrees of freedom ($v = n-2$), we would need to obtain a coefficient of 0.805 to achieve statistical significance at the 10 per cent level ($\alpha = 0.1$). We have, therefore, to accept the null hypothesis that there is no significant correlation between the two judgements.

Associations between numerical variables

It is often the case that organizational researchers want to explore potential associations between variables such as income or age and various human activities such as spending patterns. Another use would be comparing sales figures against the number of sales representatives a company employs – do sales rise as more representatives are used? When exploring relationships between numerical data (interval and/or ratio) such as sales figures, age or income, then we can use the Pearson product moment correlation. Note, however, that this statistical test is only appropriate if the relationships between variables are linear. In some circumstances there my be strong associations between variables but the relationship may be ∩ or ∪-shaped. The Pearson product moment correlation would not be able to detect this. For non-linear associations it is best to use the Spearman's rho calculation.

Worked Example 12.6

Let us take the example of a cosmetics company that wants to know if there is any association between the sales of one of its face creams and the weather. Are people put off from using face cream if the weather is wet? To discover if there is a relationship, the company looks at sales figures and annual rainfall patterns over the past five years and produces the data presented in Table 12.25.

TABLE 12.25 ASSOCIATION BETWEEN ANNUAL RAINFALL AND ANNUAL SALES OF FACE CREAM OVER A TEN-YEAR PERIOD

Year	Rainfall (cm)	Sales (£000s)
2002	50	92
2001	43	155
2000	48	120
1999	30	162
1998	35	150
1997	62	100
1996	40	130
1995	29	160
1994	31	155
1993	65	82

Paste the data into an Excel spreadsheet, then click on the Function wizard [*f*ₓ]. Under Statistical, select CORREL for correlation.
With the cursor in the Array 1 box, sweep the first column or row of data, and repeat this process for Array 2 and the second column or row of data. Click on [OK] and you should be given a value of –0.91715, which means that the association is strongly negatively correlated. So, as it rains, people make less use of our face cream – maybe there is something wrong with it!

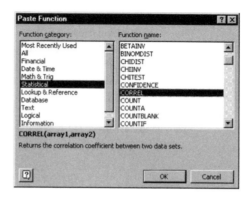

SUMMARY

- The selection of statistical tests should be made at the design stage of the research and not as an afterthought.
- Data can be classified into categorical data (which includes nominal and ordinal) and quantifiable data (which includes interval and ratio). The types of data yielded by a study will determine the kinds of analysis and statistical tests applied to them.
- Data may be presented descriptively through the use of pie charts, bar charts and histograms or through the use of descriptive statistics. The latter focus on themes such as the distribution of the data and its dispersion.
- Inferential statistics are used to draw conclusions from the data and involve the specification of a hypothesis and the selection of appropriate statistical tests.
- Some of the inherent danger in hypothesis testing is in making Type I errors (rejecting a hypothesis when it is, in fact, true) and Type II errors (accepting a hypothesis when it is false).
- For categorical data, non-parametric statistical tests can be used, but for quantifiable data, more powerful parametric tests need to be applied. Parametric tests usually require that the data are normally distributed.

Further reading

Black, T. (2001) *Evaluating Social Science Research,* 2nd edn.London: Sage. Provides an clearly written introduction to evaluating research projects. The last chapter (in the second edition) contains a very useful introduction to using Excel as a data analysis tool.

Fielding, J. and Gilbert, N. (2000) *Understanding Social Statistics.* London: Sage. Comprehensive and clearly articulated. Illustrates how to perform statistical calculations using SPSS, one of the most popular statistical programs.

Hosker, I. (2002) *Social Statistics: Data Analysis in Social Science Explained.* Taunton: Studymates. A very short and simple text for those truly terrified by statistics!

13

Collecting and analysing qualitative data

Chapter objectives

After reading this chapter you will be able to:

- **Distinguish between the aims and methods used in qualitative and quantitative research.**
- **Select appropriate qualitative methods, including content analysis and grounded theory approaches.**
- **Apply qualitative methods to produce valid, reliable and trustworthy data.**

We saw in Chapter 2 that while some research methodologies tend to utilize either quantitative *or* qualitative methods, very often both are used. This is because qualitative data can provide rich descriptions and explanations that demonstrate the chronological flow of events as well as often leading to serendipitous (chance) findings. According to Miles and Huberman (1994) qualitative studies have a quality of 'undeniability' because words have a more concrete and vivid flavour that is more convincing to the reader than pages of numbers. However, qualitative analysis has been criticized for being lacking in methodological rigour, prone to researcher subjectivity and based on small cases or limited evidence. We will explore how qualitative analysis addresses such problems later in this chapter.

Qualitative analysis is (or should be) a rigorous and logical process through which data are given meaning. Through analysis, we can progress through an initial description of the data then, through a process of disaggregating the data into smaller parts, see how these connect into new concepts, providing the basis for a fresh description. As we saw in Chapter 2, there are different approaches to qualitative research, including grounded theory, ethnography and phenomenology, researchers often using a combination of approaches in one research project. One of the major issues in qualitative research is the extent to which data should be analysed. As Strauss and Corbin (1998) point out, some researchers believe that the data should not be analysed at all, but should merely be presented. This allows the data to 'speak for themselves', untainted by the potential subjective interpretations

319

of the researcher. Other qualitative researchers are concerned, however, with accurate selection, synthesis and description of the data, but in as detached and objective a way as possible. Other researchers are more concerned with theory building, interpreting the data to build concepts and categories that can be brought together into theoretical frameworks. In contrast, some researchers see qualitative research as primarily being about storytelling and description (Wolcott, 1994).

In this chapter we will look at the possible sources of qualitative data and approaches to how data can by analysed, looking particularly at content analysis and grounded theory methods and also including some increasingly influential approaches such as the use of narratives, conversational analysis and discourse analysis. The important issues of reliability and validity will also be addressed, but more from the stance of those who favour interpretivist and naturalistic approaches.

CHARACTERISTICS OF QUALITATIVE RESEARCH

Qualitative research can take many forms and results from the use of data gathering instruments such as observations, interviews, questionnaires and document analysis. While, even today, qualitative research is often regarded in some quarters as less valid and reliable as its quantitative cousin, qualitative data can be a powerful source of analysis. First, qualitative research is highly contextual, being collected in a natural 'real life' setting, often over long periods of time. Hence, it goes beyond giving a mere snapshot of events and can show how and why things happen – also incorporating people's own motivation, emotions, prejudices and incidents of interpersonal cooperation and conflict (Charmaz, 1995). Far from lacking scientific rigour, qualitative research can even be used for testing hypotheses to see if theoretical propositions can be supported by the evidence.

As Miles and Huberman (1994) show, most qualitative research involves a number of characteristics:

- It is conducted through intense contact within a 'field' or real life setting.
- The researcher's role is to gain a 'holistic' or integrated overview of the study, including the perceptions of participants.
- Themes that emerge from the data are often reviewed with informants for verification.
- The main focus of research is to understand the ways in which people act and account for these actions.
- Qualitative data are open to multiple interpretations (but some are more compelling than others either on theoretical grounds or because of internal consistency).

Unlike more quantitative data, qualitative data are rarely accessible for immediate analysis, but require a processing stage often involving the editing of notes and transcribing of tape recordings. An important first step is to codify notes that

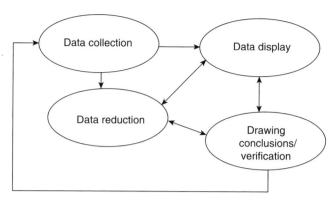

FIGURE 13.1   AN INTERACTIVE MODEL OF QUALITATIVE DATA ANALYSIS
(ADAPTED FROM MILES AND HUBERMAN, 1994)

are taken in the field (recall Chapter 10 and the taking of field notes as part of observation). Such field notes may also often contain remarks or reflections of the researcher, taken whilst in the field. Analysis does not necessarily occur sequentially after data collection, but simultaneously with it and involves the teasing out of patterns, themes and groupings in the data. This is part of the process of *data reduction* through which the sheer volume of data is reduced and made not only more manageable but more coherent. Further data gathering may then ensue where more evidence of these patterns and themes is sought. Finally, in drawing conclusions, attempts are made to find consistencies in these themes and patterns so that generalizations can be drawn and compared with the relevant body of constructs and theories for verification. The relationships between data collection, data reduction, data display and the drawing of conclusions and the verifying of data are illustrated in Figure 13.1. Presented here is not so much a sequential process but an interactive one, where, even at the final stage of writing up, gaps or inconsistencies may trigger the need for further data collection.

QUALITATIVE RESEARCH DESIGN

We saw in Chapter 1 that qualitative research is often associated with inductive research designs. But it would be wrong to assume that qualitative researchers always enter a field of study with no prior theoretical assumptions or research questions. For highly ethnographic studies this may be the case. But often, qualitative researchers will wish to impose at least some structure on the study in terms of the kinds of questions that are being asked, the focus of the research and the selection of field sites. The amount of structure required will depend on factors such as the time available and how much is already known about the phenomenon. Other decisions then have to be made about what is going to be researched (including the units of analysis and the sampling frame).

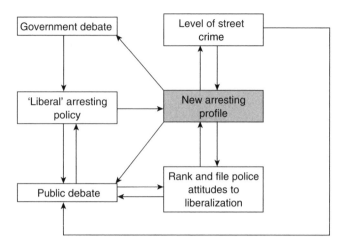

FIGURE 13.2 CONCEPTUAL FRAMEWORK FOR A RESEARCH PROJECT ON DRUG LIBERALIZATION AND POLICING

Conceptual frameworks

Miles and Huberman (1994) talk about the structure of research being formulated as a *conceptual framework* that describes in narrative, but often in graphical format, the key factors, constructs and variables being studied – and the presumed relationship between them. Of course, whether this relationship really exists is one of the elements of the study. Miles and Huberman conceive of this conceptual framework as a series of intellectual 'bins' containing key events and behaviours. Hence, Figure 13.2 shows a study of new 'liberal' policing policies which have de-criminalized possession of 'soft' drugs, and a hypothesized conceptual framework containing inter-related bins. For example, it is believed that the new policy will change the profile of arrests, with fewer people being arrested for possession of soft drugs (that is, the policy is being effectively implemented by officers on the street) and that this will reduce the level of street crime. Producing a conceptual framework forces the researcher to specify what it is that is going to be studied and what is going to be omitted, and hypothesized relationships between key variables. This, of course, is not a hypothesis in the positivistic sense, but a way of alerting the researcher to the possible relationships that exist and which can be explored.

Activity 13.1

Examine Figure 13.2. Do you agree with its hypotheses? Draw an alternative conceptual framework adding new bins and relationships.

TABLE 13.1   ORIENTATION OF RESEARCH QUESTIONS

Orientation	Resulting questions
States	Which type of object, event or behaviour is this? How often does this event occur? What caused it? How is it maintained?
Processes	How is the object, event or behaviour changing over time? What are the consequences of this process? What strategies are being used?

Research questions

Of course, if the research design is entirely inductive, there may be no formulation of a priori questions for study. With most qualitative designs, however, there will be, at least, a set of tentative issues that require addressing. As Flick (1998) notes, the less clearly research questions are formulated, the greater the chance that researchers will find themselves confronted with mountains of data. If issues are formulated as a conceptual framework, this in turn leads naturally to the design of research questions. Again using Figure 13.2 as an illustration, we might ask about the actual impact of policy changes on practice (the number and profile of drug-related arrests), and how rank and file police attitudes have mediated between policy and practice. Like the conceptual framework, research questions allow the researcher to see where the boundaries of the study lie.

Of course, having established the research questions, the researcher still has to remain open to new and perhaps unexpected results (Flick, 1998). Research questions can be orientated towards describing states or describing processes, as Table 13.1 shows.

Units of analysis

As in any research approach, in qualitative research decisions have to be taken at the design stage on the unit of analysis to be used. Typically, this might include: individuals, groups, organizations or communities. Using health care as an example, the research might focus on individuals (patients, doctors, nurses and other health care professionals), groups (the hospital management board), organizations (hospitals or professional bodies) and communities (a town and its hospitals and local surgeries).

Sampling

We saw in Chapter 4 that experimental and quasi-experimental research designs are concerned to use samples that are as representative as possible of the population under study – hence the use of random probability sampling. In qualitative research this approach is usually impractical or rejected by researchers on epistemological grounds. Qualitative research, then, often works with small samples of people, cases or phenomena nested in particular contexts. Hence, samples tend to be more *purposive* than random. Again, in contrast to more quantitative approaches, samples may not always be pre-planned in advance, but may evolve once fieldwork has begun. So an initial choice of informants may lead to a decision to select a more contrasting set of deviant subjects (cases) as a comparison (Lincoln and Guba, 1985). A wide range of qualitative sampling strategies suggested by Patton (1990) is presented in Table 13.2.

Activity 13.2

Examine the sampling strategies in Table 13.2. Which of them can be most easily defended for potentially yielding valid results? Which are most susceptible to accusations of invalidity?

Suggested answers are provided at the end of the chapter.

Very often it is not a case of selecting between the various approaches illustrated in Table 13.2 but combining some of them into *multiple case sampling*. By using a number of cases that yield similar findings we can show replication (recall Figure 6.4 in Chapter 6) hence strengthening claims for the validity of findings and the grounds for their generalizability. What is needed, however, is an explicit *sampling frame* where, between them, the cases cover the various issues and variables detailed in the study's research questions. Miles and Huberman (1994) advise that the best strategy is to initially target those cases that are most likely to yield the richest data, leaving more peripheral cases until later. But peripheral sampling is still important because it may often yield negative or exceptional cases (those that contradict the initial case findings).

COLLECTING QUALITATIVE DATA

We have seen in a number of previous chapters that qualitative data emerge from a wide spectrum of sources. One of the most common is field studies where the researcher enters a selected setting to gather data, often through the use of observations or interviews. While observation is likely to elicit qualitative data (such as field notes and analysis) interviews may be used to collect both qualitative and quantitative information. Similarly, case studies might involve the use of research instruments such as questionnaires, interview schedules and observations, all of which might yield data that is qualitative in nature.

Field notes

As we saw in Chapter 10, field notes remain one of the mainstays of qualitative data collection methods. They can be supplemented by diaries written by

TABLE 13.2   SAMPLING STRATEGIES IN QUALITATIVE RESEARCH

Sampling strategy	Description
Comprehensive sampling	Examines every case or instance in a given population (e.g. suicides amongst insurance salespeople)
Intensity sampling	Looks for information-rich cases, and ones that are more typical than those at the extremes
Deviant case sampling	Selects at two extremes (e.g., punctual and unpunctual staff) and tries to identify factors that influence these predispositions. Can yield focused information but poses dangers in generalizing from extreme cases
Maximum variation sampling	Seeks to look for a wide range of variations and patterns across the sample. Includes examining outlier cases to see if the main pattern still holds
Homogenous sampling	The opposite of maximum variation, seeks homogenous groups of people to be studied in depth. Focus group interviews are typically conducted with such homogenous groups
Typical case sampling	Highlights what is 'normal' or average in order to illuminate the whole population. Since generalizing is involved, it becomes important to substantiate that the sample is typical, using other sources (e.g. statistical data or other findings)
Stratified purposeful sampling	Selecting a strata (e.g. infant schools, secondary schools and colleges) and purposefully choosing cases (schools/colleges) within each
Critical case sampling	Similar to intensity sampling, but the focus is on one case or site that is deemed to be critical or crucial
Snowball sampling	A first group of participants is used to nominate subsequent individuals or groups for study
Criterion sampling	The sample is selected on the basis of the prime focus of the study (e.g. early retirement); hence, all cases would be chosen to meet this criterion
Theory-based sampling	A more formal type of criterion sampling, cases are chosen on the basis that they represent a theoretical construct
Confirming and disconfirming cases	Often a second-stage sampling strategy, where cases are chosen on the basis that they can confirm or disconfirm emerging patterns from the first stage
Purposeful random sampling	From a large possible set of choices, a limited number are selected randomly
Comparable case selection	Individuals, sites and groups representing the same relevant characteristic are chosen over a time period
Politically important cases	A focus on key, politically important cases because these are more likely to be noticed by policy makers and the results of the study more likely to be implemented

Source: Adapted from Patton, 1990

Interviewee data summary	
Date of interview	....
Place of interview	....
Duration of interview	....
Interviewer	....
Identifier number for interviewee	....
Gender of interviewee	....
Age of interviewee	....
Job role of interviewee	....
Qualifications of interviewee	....
Professional training of interviewee undertaken in the past 3 years	....

FIGURE 13.3   EXAMPLE OF A DOCUMENTATION SHEET

researchers, and also by participants, so that triangulation can be performed. Photographs, drawings, maps and other visual material can also be added (see next section). Lofland and Lofland (1984) recommend that if field notes are supplemented by tape recordings, these should be transcribed as quickly as possible, and that at least as much time should be spent studying and analysing the materials as spent in the interview itself. Flick (1998) also recommends the use of documentation sheets that provide useful summary information on the context within which the data were collected (see Figure 13.3).

Document sheets allow for an overview of the data and can provide a guide as to which files and transcripts to consult at the analysis stage.

Photographs and other sources

In addition to text, photographs or other visual data such as video or film recordings are also sources of qualitative data. Photographs in particular have a long history in ethnography and anthropology (Flick, 1998). Photographs allow the detailed recording of facts, including the presentation of lifestyles and living and working conditions. They can also capture processes that are too rapid for the human eye. Sometimes, the subjects of research can be encouraged to take on the role of the photographer, documenting either a subject of their choice, or a theme that the researcher wants them to record. If desired, these photographs can subsequently be used to stimulate an interview or encourage a participant to produce a narrative to accompany and expand upon the photographic evidence. This can be seen as a concretization of the focused interview (Flick, 1998).

But do photographs tell the truth? Of course, what the camera focuses on, and what it leaves out, is selective. There may also be problems of reactivity, with the subjects altering their behaviour in the presence of the photographer. Hence, there are always dangers of bias, and questions about the extent to which photographs help in the social construction of reality.

Unobtrusive data

As we saw in Chapter 11, organizations also contain a rich array of unobtrusive data in the form of documents such as company reports, business plans, written statements by members of staff, accounts and contracts. Most medium and large organizations also have dedicated websites that present a 'public' image to the world. Analysis of such a site may reveal not only the organization's perception of itself and the image it wants to present to the world, but also what it does *not* wish to reveal. The organization's intranet site and evidence from e-mail interactions may also prove of interest.

Atkinson and Coffey (1997) warn that it is not only the content of documents that should be of concern to researchers, but also the way in which they are produced, circulated, read, stored and used for a variety of purposes. This means that they are not necessarily a description of 'reality' nor are they necessarily 'transparent representations of organizational routines, decision-making processes or professional diagnoses' (Atkinson and Coffey, 1997: 47). Although they should be treated seriously, documents should not be taken as factual evidence of what they report. Rather, they should be examined for their place within the organizational setting, and the cultural values attached to them. But conversely, the temptation should be avoided to use only observational or oral data as the primary source and downgrade documentary evidence to a validating role. Atkinson and Coffey (1997) urge that documents should be regarded as valid sources in their own right.

ANALYSING DATA: CONTENT ANALYSIS

Analysis involves the process of breaking data down into smaller units to reveal their characteristic elements and structure (Dey, 1993: 30). Descriptions can lay the basis for analysis, but we need to go beyond description: we want to interpret, to understand and to explain. Through analysis, however, we can also gain new insights into our data. Data can be broken down into their constituent parts, and connections made between these concepts, providing the basis for new descriptions (see Figure 13.4).

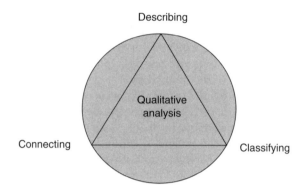

FIGURE 13.4   QUALITATIVE ANALYSIS AS A CIRCULAR PROCESS (DEY, 1993)

One of the most common approaches to analysing qualitative data is through content analysis. Essentially, this involves the making of inferences about data (usually text) by systematically and objectively identifying special characteristics (classes or categories) within them. The attempt to achieve a measure of objectivity in this process is addressed by the creation of specific rules called *criteria of selection* which have to be established before the data can be analysed. In contrast to this, through grounded theory (see next section) no a priori criteria are assumed, these emerging through the process of data collection and analysis itself. Hence, at the risk of over-simplification, grounded theory is more inductive in character, and content analysis more deductive.

In using content analysis, there are three procedures for identifying classes and categories. First, *common classes*, comprising categories in everyday thinking such as age, gender, boss, worker are identified These common classes can be useful in linking or finding associations between the data and important demographic characteristics. Secondly, *special classes* are identified, comprising the kind of labels particular groups or communities use to distinguish amongst things, persons or events. This can include specialist types of language (including slang, the use of acronyms, specialist professional terms, etc.). Thirdly, *theoretical classes*, or those classes that arise in the process of analysing the data, providing the key linkages and patterns. As Flick (1998) points out, however, these categories are themselves often derived from theoretical models. So categories are brought to the empirical data, and not necessarily derived from them. Of course, they will be repeatedly evaluated against the data and modified if necessary.

Having identified categories within the text, the next step is the analysis itself. The key here is to *reduce* the volume of textual material. Using the work of Mayring (1983), Flick (1998) distinguishes three steps in the analysis process:

- *Summarizing content analysis*, where the material is paraphrased with similar paraphrases bundled together and less relevant passages eliminated.
- *Explicating content analysis*, which clarifies ambiguous or contradictory passages by introducing context material in the analysis. This could include dictionary

definitions of terms, statements from the text or outside the text (for example, contextual information, theoretical propositions) that illustrate the passages being analysed. Through this process a clarifying paraphrase is formulated and tested.

- *Structuring content analysis* seeks to identify types of formal structures in the materials. Hence, the analysis might extricate key features in the material and describe them in more detail. Alternatively, the material might be rated according to dimensions on a scale. So, in a passage dealing with, say, 'motivation', the concept could be given a rating scale from 'Highly motivated' to 'Completely demotivated'. The passage is then searched for examples of motivational feelings against the scale, resulting in a frequency count for each of the motivational levels.

Berg (1995) argues that content analysis can also be used with hypothesis testing, that is, a more experimental or quasi-experimental design. With hypothesis testing, he suggests going through the following stages:

- Make a rough hypothesis based upon observations from the data.
- Search the data to find cases that do not fit with the hypothesis.
- If negative cases are found, discard or reformulate the hypothesis to account for the negative cases.

Hence, it is necessary to develop research questions in advance that are linked to previous research (Mayring, 1983 in Flick, 1998). It is because of this insistence on measurement and hypothesis testing that Locke (2001) places content analysis within the modernist, objectivist paradigm.

Content analysis is potentially a very important weapon in the researcher's armoury because it can be highly cost-effective. There may be no need to design and issue costly questionnaires – existing documentation such as company reports, memoranda or e-mails may provide the basis for the data. This, however, could also be construed as a disadvantage since the approach has to rely on 'old' data, rather than gathering fresh information. Another weakness, is that it is incapable of exploring associations and causal relationships between variables. As Flick (1998) also point out, the very conceptual structures that content analysis imposes on the data may obscure some of the interpretations that may have emerged inductively from within it.

ANALYSING DATA: GROUNDED THEORY

One of the most influential qualitative approaches is that of grounded theory, defined as a theory that is: 'discovered, developed and provisionally verified through systematic data collection and analysis of data pertaining to that phenomenon' (Strauss and Corbin, 1998: 23). Locke (2001) suggests that locating grounded theory in a particular research paradigm is difficult, because it has been used in both modernist (objectivist) and interpretivist approaches. There is, however, a clear influence of symbolic interactionism, and this interpretivist paradigm's commitment to studying the social world and the rejection of a priori theorizing.

Grounded theory methods have been extensively used in education, evaluation research, nursing and organizational studies (Charmaz, 1995). Unlike the deductive approach, grounded theory does not begin with prior assumptions about hypotheses, research questions or what literature should underpin the study. This is not to say that grounded theorists embark on a study with no theoretical position. They will have a competent level of knowledge about the area. But, as Strauss and Corbin (1998) warn, grounded researchers should not be so steeped in the literature that their creative efforts become impeded or constrained. The research should commence with a defined purpose, but also with the realization that this purpose may become modified or even radically altered during the research process itself. Through data analysis new theoretical positions or understandings may emerge.

The grounded theory researcher works with his or her participants to actively construct the data, to get beyond static analysis to multiple layers of meaning. According to Charmaz (1995), these layers could include the participant's:

- Stated explanations of her or his actions.
- Unstated assumptions about these actions.
- Intentions and motivation for engaging in the actions.
- The effects of the actions on others.
- The consequences of these actions for interpersonal relations and for further individual actions.

What about the data analysis process itself? Strauss and Corbin (1998) lay down a structured process and one that has become a highly influential way of analysing data comprising:

- *Open coding*: the disaggregation of the data into units.
- *Axial coding*: recognizing relationships between categories.
- *Selective coding*: the integration of categories to produce a theory.

These are pulled together into a framework that is called a *conditional matrix*, a 'complex web of interrelated conditions, action/interaction, and consequences pertaining to a particular phenomenon' (Strauss and Corbin, 1998: 181). These coding processes, however, are not necessarily completely distinct, and do not need to take place in sequence. In a single coding session, the researcher might move quickly from one coding method to another, particularly from open to axial coding. Another point to stress is that data collection and analysis should be an interwoven process with analysis, prompting the sampling of new data. Charmaz (1995) provides advice on the timing of the analysis, also suggesting that the data should be studied as they emerge, making it easier to identify respondents' implicit meanings and taken-for-granted assumptions. Hence, for the novice grounded researcher, it is best to transcribe your own tapes as this gets you into contact with the data at an early stage.

TABLE 13.3   OPEN CODING: DEFINITION OF TERMS

Term	Definition
Concept	Conceptual labels placed on discrete happenings, events and other instances of phenomena
Category	A classification of concepts
Coding	The process of analysing data
Code notes	The products of coding
Open coding	The process of breaking down, examining, comparing, conceptualizing and categorizing data
Properties	Attributes or characteristics pertaining to a category
Dimensions	Location of properties along a continuum
Dimensionalization	The process of breaking a property down into its dimensions

Source: Adapted from Strauss and Corbin, 1998

Before we begin to look at these coding categories in detail, a word of warning. As Dey (1999) discusses, not all advocates of grounded theory agree with Strauss and Corbin's approach. Glaser (1992), for example, accuses their later work of abandoning their earlier, influential, ideas, suggesting that it has evolved into a quite different methodology (the coding paradigm, dealt with next). For Glaser, this smacks too much of rules and structure being imposed upon the data. However, despite these criticisms, the Strauss and Corbin approach is widely used and recognized as a valuable methodology. Given that the methodological advice coming from the grounded theory literature can be 'bewilderingly complex' (Partington, 2002: 138), an attempt is made here to supplement procedural descriptions with illustrative graphics. It must be stressed that this is just one interpretation of how grounded theory can be applied in practice.

Open coding

Open coding is defined as 'the naming and categorizing of phenomena through close examination of the data' (Strauss and Corbin, 1998: 62). Two analytical procedures are involved in the open coding process: the *making of comparisons* and the *asking of questions*, both of which help towards the labelling of phenomena in terms of concepts or categories (see Table 13.3).

According to Strauss (1987), there are four essential guidelines to follow in the data analysis process:

- Ask the data a specific and consistent set of questions, keeping in mind the original objectives of the research study. The intention here is to uncover whether the data fit with these objectives. There may be occasions when new or unanticipated results emerge from the data, an outcome that is entirely valid.

- Analyse the data minutely, but also include as many categories, examples and incidents as possible.
- Frequently interrupt the coding to write a theoretical account. As the data are being coded, ideas or theoretical perspectives may arise. It is essential that these are noted immediately otherwise they may well be forgotten.
- Do not assume the analytical relevance of any traditional variable such as age, gender, social class, etc. until its relevance emerges from the data. This is particularly so if the impact of an expected variable does not emerge – this result must be accepted.

Open coding works through a process of making *constant comparisons*. Each time an instance of a category is found, it is compared with previous instances. If the new instance does not fit the original definition, then either the definition must be modified, or a new category created.

Case Study 13.1 provides a practical example of how the process of asking questions and making comparisons can lead to the generation of concepts and categories.

Case Study 13.1 Developing grounded theory – open coding

A researcher is asked to observe customer behaviour in a large department store. She positions herself in an unobtrusive way, where she can see customers entering and leaving the store, walking down the aisles, looking at merchandise and buying goods, etc. Although the store is very busy and the activity at first appears chaotic, some tentative patterns begin to emerge which she begins to label. Some customers, for example, seem content with examining goods (picking them up, looking at them, putting them down) but then just moving on. She asks herself: why are they doing this? This behaviour she labels *exploring*. Other customers approach counter staff or supervisors walking around and ask them questions. This she labels *questioning*. Still other customers approach the busy tills and seem content to stand in line to be served. The label attached to this is simply *queuing*. Once at the till, they are, of course, *buying*. It is clear, however, that a minority of customers queue for a short time and grow impatient. They can be observed to put the merchandise down on a counter or shelf before leaving the store. This behaviour is labelled as *deserting*. One customer, however, is seen to be arguing with a supervisor. This behaviour is called *remonstrating*.

Later she notices that some customers not only pick up and look at goods they even rub them between their fingers and in some cases smell them! Hence under the category of exploring, she is able to identify three sub-categories: looking, feeling and smelling.

After the observation session our researcher begins the process of *categorizing* the data. In doing this, she is careful to choose categories that are more abstract in nature than the concepts they describe. Hence, she groups exploring and questioning to form the category *information seeking* while queuing and buying are grouped together as *intentional purchasing*.

Activity 13.3

Conduct a detailed observation of an event or phenomenon within a field setting. Analyse your data using open coding, providing your own set of descriptive labels.

Note that the labels given in Case Study 13.1 are original and specific to the researcher. This is important because if she had taken already existing and 'borrowed' categories, these can come with pre-existing meanings that can bias the research. Once categories are produced they still have to be developed so that they can be used in further data collection and analysis. Categories are developed in two ways: by their *properties* and by their *dimensions*. Using Case Study 13.1, we could take the category 'information seeking' and examine it for its properties and dimensions. Table 13.4 illustrates the results, showing that properties are the characteristics or attributes of a category. Dimensions represent the location of a property along a continuum. The development of properties and dimensions is crucially important because they are central in making relationships between categories and sub-categories and later between major categories. They thus provide the basis of the analytical processes of grounded theory.

TABLE 13.4   THE PROPERTIES AND DIMENSIONS OF THE CATEGORY
'INFORMATION SEEKING'

Category	Property	Dimensional range	
Information-seeking	Questioning	Often	Never
	Looking	Up close	From a distance
	Smelling	Repeatedly	Once
	Feeling	Vigorously	Gently

Source: Adapted from Strauss and Corbin, 1998

Axial coding

As we saw in the previous section, open coding disaggregates data so that categories can be located. Axial coding then takes these categories and tries to make connections between categories and subcategories. Essentially, this means specifying:

- A *category* (phenomenon) in terms of the conditions that helped to give rise to it.
- The *context* in which it arises.
- The *actions* and *interactions* that stem from it.
- Its *consequences*.

We are also interested in what caused the phenomenon. Figure 13.5 provides a highly simplified illustration of the relationships between a phenomenon

CONTEXT

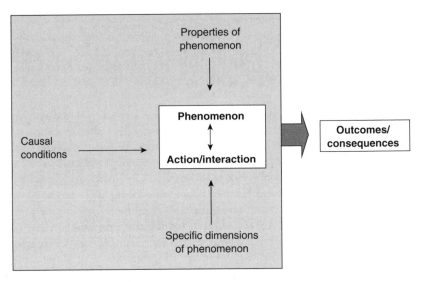

FIGURE 13.5   MAKING CONNECTIONS BETWEEN CATEGORIES AND
SUB-CATEGORIES BY EXAMINING A PHENOMENON IN TERMS OF
ITS PROPERTIES, DIMENSIONS AND CAUSAL CONDITIONS

and its causes, context, actions and consequences. Note that Strauss and Corbin
(1998), referring to the work of Dewey, caution that an initial condition rarely
leads to an action/interaction and then a consequence in a direct manner.

> *Rather, action/interaction may be taken in response to multiple conditions, some of which
> occurred in the past, some of which are happening in the present, and/or some of which are
> anticipated in the future.* (Strauss and Corbin, 1998: 184)

Hence, in Figure 13.5, causal conditions may occur in a variety of different tem-
poral states.

To illustrate the process of linking sub-categories to categories, let us take
the example of our retail store in the previous Case Study. We have seen a customer
remonstrating (phenomenon) with a supervisor. We observe that the reason (causal
condition) for this is the fact that the queues for the tills were very long and that
she could not get served. But the description of this phenomenon, 'remonstration',
does little to fully describe the event. We need more detail. So we are also interested in the specific dimensions of the phenomenon, and discover that this was an
angry remonstration (in terms of volume/language) that lasted 10 minutes (time)
in the middle of the store (location). But we also need to know something about
the properties of the causal condition (the queuing) and discover that the customer
queued for 8 minutes at a till that was shut seconds before she was about to be
served. Next, we take a look at the context in which the phenomenon occurred,
examining issues such as when, how and the type of cause. We discover that some

CONTEXT

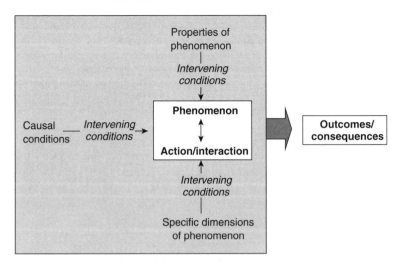

FIGURE 13.6   MAKING CONNECTIONS BETWEEN CATEGORIES AND
SUB-CATEGORIES: THE IMPACT OF INTERVENING CONDITIONS

tills are not operational due to staff shortages and that the till closure happened suddenly because the member of staff was due her lunchbreak.

Yet, there are also *intervening conditions*, or what could be called a 'broader structural context' (Strauss and Corbin, 1998: 103), which act either to constrain or facilitate the actions being taken. For example, again using our illustration, we find that during the angry remonstration, the store manager happens to be passing and intervenes to help. She uses her cellphone to call for more staff and opens a till herself and serves the irate customer. But in general terms, intervening conditions within a context can include a wide range of conditions, including the influence of culture, time, economic status, hierarchical position in an organization, technological status, individual biography, etc. For example, the remonstration is a long one, not just because of the scale of the inconvenience, but because only the previous week the company that owns the store had announced record profits so the customer may be reasoning 'Why haven't they employed more staff?'

We can see from the above analysis that grounded theory is an action/interaction method of theory building which is concerned with the ways in which people manage and respond to phenomena, existing within a specific context or conditions. Recalling the discussion of symbolic interactionism in Chapter 2, people assign meaning to phenomena and then act upon these interpretations, these actions bringing forth fresh interpretations and actions amongst participants. But this action and interaction also has *consequences* that may be predictable or unanticipated. Indeed, the failure to take action also has its consequences. Yet, while axial coding can help us to identify relationships between categories, we still

TABLE 13.5   SELECTIVE CODING: DEFINITION OF TERMS

Term	Definition
Story	A descriptive narrative about the central phenomenon of the study
Story line	The conceptualization of the story around the core category
Selective coding	The process of selecting the core category, systematically relating it to other categories, and validating these relationships
Core category	The central phenomenon around which all the other categories are integrated

Source: Adapted from Strauss and Corbin, 1998

need to see how these categories or classes can be integrated to build theories. This is achieved through selective coding.

Selective coding

This is the process of selecting *core categories* from the data in order to form the grounded theory. In terms of processes, this is not too different to axial coding, the main difference being that it is completed at a much higher level of abstraction. Through axial coding you will have derived a set of phenomena or categories that have been defined in terms of their properties, dimensions, etc. Through selective coding, core categories are sought through which a 'story' can be told. The selective coding process involves a number of stages that illuminate the social processes going on unconsciously among a group of people comprising:

- Finding a story line formulated around core categories.
- Relating sub-categories to the core categories.
- Validating these relationships against the data.
- Filling in categories that need further refinement.

Table 13.5 provides a brief summary of some of these terms, after which we will discuss them in more detail.

One of the key features of grounded theory is *theoretical sampling,* which helps to make the emerging theory more generalizable. This is achieved by seeking to minimize and maximize the selected differences and similarities between core categories and the relationships between them across cases. Hence, finding strong similarities across cases (and minimum differences) helps to build confidence in the validity of the emerging theory. Attempting to find cases that contradict the theory may help to locate unexpected data and perhaps the emergence of new perspectives.

Identifying the story

The best way to start is to describe in a few short sentences the essence of the story to produce a general, descriptive overview. What are the most salient features? What are the main problems being scrutinized? It might be useful to return to the axial coding stage and find an abstract category that in some way summarizes the story. If such a category does not exist, then one will have to be formulated that encapsulates the categories in the study. If more than one category exists, it is necessary to make a choice between them so that only one core category is used. Taking our example of the observation in the retail store, the main story here could be construed as *intentional shopping behaviour*. Whether customers are asking questions, examining goods, leaving the store impatiently or patiently queuing, they behave, or attempt to behave, intentionally – that is, with a specific aim.

Relating sub-categories to the core categories

This involves relating subsidiary categories around the core category by means of the paradigm so that they fit and provide an analytical version of the story. This may mean writing or re-writing the story and rearranging categories until they achieve a better fit with the story. Within these conceptual categories there will be relationships and networks of patterns. Strauss and Corbin (1994) stress how important it is to identify these patterns because it is these that give the theory specificity. Hence, it becomes possible to say that under one set of conditions *this* happens, whereas under another set of conditions *that* happens. Case Study 13.2 takes our retailing research a little further.

Case Study 13.2 Developing grounded theory – selective coding

Although the store is crowded and presents the appearance of chaos, in fact, thanks to the highly intentional behaviour of most customers, there are distinctive patterns of behaviour that become predictable. People do not simply rush into the store, grab the first item they see and then run out with it! They look around (touring) the isles, sometimes leaving this department, but returning later. Our researcher notices that those who examine merchandise closely tend to be with someone else rather than being alone – hence, exploratory behaviour is usually collaborative. Opinions are being shared (the 'second opinion'). People queue, because the alternative, pushing and shoving one's way to the counter, will lead to even more stress. Queuing is a time-consuming activity that is undertaken to *save* time. Customers who approach store staff for information are also attempting to save themselves time by gaining quicker access to information.

Activity 13.4

Returning to your data in Activity 13.3, take your open coding categories through the axial coding process, making connections between categories. Then, using selective coding, identify core categories and formulate a story line.

Validating these relationships against the data

Having found a story and related various categories to it, the relationships uncovered can be validated (grounding the theory) by returning to the data and asking whether the story fits for all those observed in the study. We may find, for example, that a minority of customers do not appear to behave intentionally at all. We noted in Case Study 13.2 that some customers spent some time queuing before losing patience and leaving the store. If their intention was to buy goods, they failed. Yet their behaviour may perhaps still be construed as intentional because leaving the store in this way has saved them time from queuing. They valued their time more highly than the satisfaction to be gained from the purchased commodities. However, for instances that cannot be analysed as intentional, we need to fill in more detail. The researcher needs to trace back to the data to uncover the conditions that might be causing this variation.

Filling in categories that need further refinement

This is necessary to give 'conceptual density' to the theory as well as developing more conceptual specificity. This filling in phase may continue even up to the process of writing up the project, since report writing itself may reveal gaps and inconsistencies that require attention. If this occurs, the researcher may have to return to the field to collect more data (for example, by interviewing some of the shoppers). This illustrates that the task of data collection and analysis is not necessarily sequential but can be an iterative process.

The grounded theory approach just described should be a dynamic one when *process* is built into the analysis. Process means showing the evolving nature of events by noting why and how action/interaction (in the form of events, doings, or happenings) will change, stay the same, or regress (Strauss and Corbin, 1998). In other words, it is a case of not only noticing changes in phenomena but also of explaining *why* they occur. As Strauss and Corbin (1998) concede, however, explanations may not always be obvious, even after additional data have been collected. They suggest, therefore, that a more deductive approach is adopted, in terms of a hypothesis, after which the researcher should return to the data to see if this hypothesis can be supported, modified or rejected.

But how and where do changes occur? There are three potential sources:

- Changes can occur in the causal conditions that led to the phenomenon.
- There may be a change in the intervening conditions.
- The outcomes or consequences of the action/interaction may in turn feed back into new causal conditions (see Figure 13.7).

Theoretical sensitivity

Strauss and Corbin (1998) argue that theoretical sensitivity, keeping an awareness of the subtleties of meaning in data, is an important element of grounded theory. Accordingly, they argue that theoretical sensitivity implies:

CONTEXT

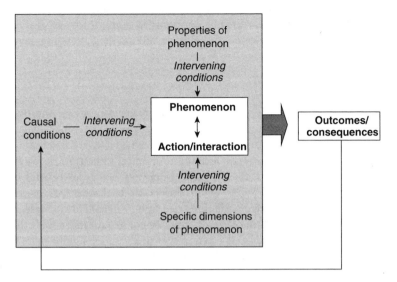

FIGURE 13.7   THE IMPACT OF OUTCOMES AND CONSEQUENCES ON THE
ORIGINAL CAUSAL CONDITIONS

*the ability to give meaning to data, the capacity to understand, and capability to separate the
pertinent from that which isn't.* (Strauss and Corbin, 1998: 42)

Glaser (1992) links this sensitivity more overtly with theory building, arguing that
it is the ability to generate concepts from the data and to relate them, according
to normal models of theory. This sensitivity stems from a number of sources.

- The literature, which helps highlight issues and what might be important and
  unimportant.
- The professional experience of the researcher, showing what is important in
  the field of research chosen, and how things work, allowing events to be more
  clearly understood and interpreted.
- Personal experience, including experience in research, which can facilitate the
  making of comparisons.
- The analytical process itself, which can provide insights into the meaning of
  the data.

Theoretical sensitivity is a way of ensuring that the creativity involved in
qualitative research is harnessed in such a way that the interests of science are not
impeded. The process of scientific inquiry is further facilitated if the researcher is
willing to 'step back from the data' and ask basic questions such as: do the data
really fit the hypothesis? This is part of the process of maintaining a healthy scep-
ticism and realizing that all elements of a study – hypotheses, concepts, questions,

theories, etc. – are provisional. Strauss and Corbin (1998) advise that a sound approach is to alternate between collecting and analysing data. Through this approach, analysis can allow for further questions to emerge, for sample selection and data collection, and the verification of hypotheses as they are being developed.

Concluding grounded research

As we have seen, grounded theory research can involve a fairly continuous iteration between data collection and analysis and between the different levels of coding. So, when is the research completed? When is it time to stop? Glaser and Strauss (1967) suggest that this is when the level of 'theoretical saturation' is reached. By this they mean the non-emergence of new properties, classes, categories or relationships from the data. Knowing when this point is reached, of course, is a matter of experience and judgement. This decision is helped if the research has moved towards the clear identification of core categories (around which the main story line is woven) and peripheral categories of less central significance. Hence, once the analysis has been integrated around the core categories and an adequate theory has emerged, the research could be said to be complete. Note that Bryman (1988) cautions that grounded theory may be effective in the generation of concepts, but he questions whether it actually produces theory itself.

Before finishing this section, it might be useful to look at grounded theory in relation to other research approaches. Locke (2001), for example, suggests that grounded theory has much in common with:

- Ethnography, in that data collection and theory building are woven together as the researcher progresses (although grounded theorists are less interested in the cultural aspects of contexts).
- Case studies, in that grounded theory may be incorporated into a case study as a means of handling and interpreting data.
- Action research (see Chapter 15), in that both seek to develop theoretical elements that are useful to practitioners within the research setting (although grounded theorists are less concerned with organizational transformation).

APPROACHES TO ANALYSING DATA

In a sense, having discussed two of the main analytical approaches, content analysis and grounded theory, we are left with the category of 'other' in which there are a considerable number of competing approaches. Three of the most significant, the use of narratives, conversational analysis and discourse analysis, are discussed, briefly, here.

Narratives

One of the criticisms of content analysis, and particularly of grounded theory approaches, is that they lead to the fragmentation and decontextualization of data away from the social processes they are meant to represent. However, research that encourages the use of oral or life histories, or uses unstructured interviews, often elicits qualitative data in the form of narratives or stories that lead to more holistic data right from the start. Using narratives is an ideal way of capturing the lived experiences of participants and has been used extensively in settings such as research into medical illness, the study of traumatic events, in education, and studies in the life of organizations. Musson (1998), for example, shows how people's narratives can be used to explain the contradictions, confusions and complexities of working within a modern organization, and how this can illuminate how both individuals and their organization's function.

While different approaches to the analysis of narratives have been put forward, all have a number of common characteristics. First, the text is viewed in the *Gestalt*, that is, within the context and social situation in which it is created. Next comes the formal analysis of the text, including making distinctions between text that constitute narrative passages, and other forms of text. Where researchers generally differ is in their attitude to the status of the text itself. While some take the 'truth' of the narrative at face value, others see narratives as a special way of constructing events, that is, they are 'social constructions located within power structures and social milieux' (Punch, 1998: 223).

Conversational analysis

Conversational analysis is interested in the formal analysis of everyday conversations (Flick, 1998). Primarily, this includes the analysis of natural texts (often the results of transcribed tape recordings) and seeks to specify the formal principles and mechanisms with which participants express themselves in social interactions, or what Hutchby and Wooffitt (1998) term *talk-in-interaction*. Research in conversational analysis was originally limited to the study of everyday conversations such as telephone calls or family conversations, but has been extended to institutional-based conversations such as courtrooms, meetings and various kinds of interviews.

Conversational analysis is less concerned with the formal analysis of language *per se*, than with elements of social interaction such as 'turn taking' or 'opening up closings', interruptions and the distribution of speaking rights, often in relation to various aspects of an institution's functions (Have, 1999). Hence, conversational analysis is very much focused on the issue of context. Meaning or order in conversation can only be understood within the context of local practices and are embedded within concrete contexts. Through turn by turn analysis and the description of conversations, the researcher is able to sense how social order among participants is accomplished (Samra-Fredericks, 1998).

Discourse analysis

The focus of discourse analysis is on how both spoken and written language is used in social contexts. Attention is given to the structure and organization of language with an emphasis on how participants' versions of events are constructed. In contrast to content analysis, discourse analysis rejects the view that language is a transparent medium which merely reflects 'reality'. Analysis becomes focused on recognizing the regularities in language in terms of patterns and repertoires. These repertoires (constructs) do not emanate from the individual as such, but are embedded in culturally and socially constructed situations.

QUALITY IN QUALITATIVE ANALYSIS

In discussing the issue of quality in qualitative research, some commentators resist the temptation to even address such matters as validity and reliability, because, they argue, these concepts were originally developed in a quantitative tradition (Bryman, 1988). Lincoln (1985) also asserts that naturalistic researchers, for example, tend anyway to be more modest and reluctant about making generalizations from their findings. Issues of external validity, then, are not high on their agendas. However, as we shall see, even some of the most enthusiastic adherents of the qualitative approach see the need to address validity and reliability as inescapable, although some do suggest additional quality criteria, some of which they see as of more importance.

Validity

The issue of validity revolves around the question of how far the constructions of the researcher are grounded in the constructions of those being researched (Flick, 1998). Hall and Callery (2001) criticize grounded theory in particular for assuming that the data collected reflect reality, and are independent of, and not influence by, the subjective interpretations of researchers. What is needed, they argue, is for researchers to adopt a *reflexive* stance, through which they critically reflect on their influence on the research process. Self-reflective criticality is strengthened through repetitive checks of the researcher's interpretations (Whittemore et al., 2001). Of course, another approach is to involve those being researched in checking the data for accuracy and in the analysis for the faithfulness of interpretation.

Data can be fabricated, discounted or misinterpreted. One way of avoiding such problems is where research can be validated through replication, but as Dey (1993) cautions, qualitative research is notoriously difficult to replicate. In place of external validation, 'internal' replication may be adopted, whereby other researchers can inspect the procedures through which the research has been conducted. This is much easier, of course, where two researchers collaborate on the same project. Another approach might be to split the data and analyse them in two stages to see if the results are similar.

Establishing principles for validity is all very well, but how do researchers achieve them in practice? Whittemore et al. (2001) present a useful checklist (see Table 13.6) but warn that selection depends upon contextual factors and the purpose of the research.

TABLE 13.6 TECHNIQUES FOR DEMONSTRATING VALIDITY

Type of technique	Technique
Design considerations	Developing a self-conscious research design
	Sampling decisions (i.e. sampling adequacy)
	Employing triangulation
	Giving voice
Data generating	Demonstrating prolonged engagement
	Demonstrating persistent observation
	Providing verbatim transcriptions
	Demonstrating saturation
Analytic	Member checking
	Expert checking
	Testing hypotheses in data analysis
	Exploring rival explanations
	Performing a literature review
	Analysing negative cases
	Memoing
Presentation	Providing an audit trail
	Providing evidence that supports interpretations
	Acknowledging the researcher perspective
	Providing thick descriptions

Source: Adapted from Whittemore et al., *2001*

Activity 13.5

Examine the list in Table 13.6. Which of them would you find useful to implement to aid the validity of your own qualitative research?

Another important feature here is that of external validity, that is, generalizing from the data to other cases or situations. Generalizations can be defined as assertions of enduring value that are context-free (Lincoln and Gubba, 1985: 110). Since sampling in qualitative research tends to be purposive rather than random, and data gathered from a limited number of cases (sometimes one), can we generalize? Lincoln and Gubba (1985) distinguish between two kinds of generalization. The first is nomothetic, based upon a rationalistic, law-like stance, as in the positivist paradigm. The second they term 'naturalistic generalization', which is a more intuitive, ideographic but none the less, empirical approach based upon personal, direct experience. The authors then dismiss the notion of nomothetic generalizations that are truly universal to all times and situations. Local conditions, they contend, make it impossible to generalize. 'If there is a "true" generalization, it is that there can be no generalization' (Lincoln and Guba, 1985: 124).

At best, the results from individual cases allow us to build working hypotheses that can be tested in subsequent cases. As Miles and Huberman (1994) point out, through the use of multiple case studies, attempts are made to match on the basis of underlying theories. As more similar or contrasting cases are used, we can justify, through *replication*, the stability of the findings. Even then, as Dey (1993) asserts, as a basis for generalization, qualitative analysis is more likely to be suggestive than conclusive. At best, rather than generalize, we can see if the findings from Context A can be transferred to Context B.

Reliability

Reliability refers to the stability of findings. A reliable observation, for example, is one that could have been made by any similarly situated observer (Denzin, 1978). For most qualitative approaches, reliability is improved, if not guaranteed, by triangulation, gathering information, for example, from multiple sources or by using multiple data gathering tools. Denzin (1989) offers four kinds of triangulation:

- Data triangulation, where data are gathered using multiple sampling strategies. This can include: *time triangulation*, when data are collected on the same phenomenon over a period of time; *space triangulation*, when data are collected from multiple sites; *person triangulation*, where data are collected at three levels in an organization – for example, individuals, groups and departments.
- Investigator triangulation, using more than one observer in field situations so that observer bias can be reduced (and inter-judge reliability improved). Thus, a training programme would teach observers to keep an 'open mind' and not to become obsessed with their hypothesis (if they start with one). They should not jump towards 'solutions' to a problem as this will tend to make them ignore facts that do not confirm their expectations. In making a study, they are trained to notice *all* aspects of a situation and to deliberately search for unexpected facts, and to seek alternative interpretations. The data will then be checked by other trained colleagues (and even informants) who will, if possible, repeat the observation to see if they get the same results.
- Multiple triangulation, in which a combination of multiple methods, data types, observers and theories are combined in the same investigation. While it is often a practical difficulty to achieve a combination of all of these, it is more common to at least use multiple data levels and methods.
- Methodological triangulation, of which there are two kinds: *within-method,* where the researcher employs varieties of data gathering techniques within the same method, and *between method*, where a variety of different methods are used – for example, quantitative data from a survey with qualitative data from observations.

It should be noted, however, that the significance of reliability is not universally accepted. Glaser (1992), for example, asserts that verification has no place in grounded theory, the task of which is to generate hypotheses, not to test them. This is in sharp contrast to the views of Strauss and Corbin (1994), who suggest that within the data collection and analysis process there is an in-built mandate to strive towards the verification of any resulting hypotheses. For interview data, reliability can be increased through the training of interviewers and through the use of standardized interview schedules. For observations, researchers also need to be trained before they enter the field.

One element of qualitative analysis, conversational analysis, brings with it some different reliability issues. Since conversational analysis is often based on tapes and transcripts of conversations, in terms of reliability, it is fairly obvious that taped conversations will tend to present more reliable evidence than hastily written field notes. But as Peräkylä (1997) warns, video- or audio-recording of events may lose some important aspects of social interaction. These reliability problems include:

- Time. A single recording of events taking place in an organization may be either unenlightening or completely misleading if those events do not represent what typically happens most of the time. Hence, reliability will be improved with a more longitudinal research design, with multiple visits and recordings.
- 'Ambulatory events', that is, the movements of people that simply do not show up on video or audio recordings. One solution is the setting up of multiple cameras to catch these movements.
- Documentary realities. Some conversations (for example, professional people such as doctors or lawyers talking to their clients) may be influenced by the documents (such as forms) they are discussing. Researchers must have access to these documents and include them in the analysis process.

Trustworthiness

Some researchers, particularly those from the naturalistic tradition, argue that trustworthiness is more important than concerns over the validity or reliability that have just been outlined. Skrtic (1985), for example, suggests that this is addressed through a focus on:

- *Transferability* with purposive sampling to illustrate pertinent issues and factors when comparing two contexts for similarity; and thick descriptions to provide evidence for making judgements about similarities between cases.
- *Dependability* through the use of audit trails through the data.
- *Confirmability*, with the audit showing the connections between data and the researcher's interpretations.
- *Credibility*, the use of persistent observations; triangulation (of data, methods, theories and investigations); member checks (where data and interpretations are tested with research participants).

Lincoln and Gubba (1985) argue that credibility can be strengthened through the researcher making a conscious effort to establish confidence in the accuracy of interpretation, and the fit between description and explanation.

To these we can add *authenticity*, which relates analysis and interpretation to the meanings and experiences that are lived and perceived by the subjects of the research. This means the research being aware of the multiple voices contained within the data, and the subtle, sometimes conflicting realities within it. Do the interpretations ring true? Have rival explanations been considered? Davies and Dodd (2002) also suggest that just as important are practices that are honest, open, empathetic, sensitive, respectful and engaging. Perhaps these concepts should also be seen as essential ingredients of research quality.

However, as Johnson and Harris (2002) comment, one problem with qualitative research is that a standard practice for achieving validity, reliability or any other quality indicator has yet to be established. This is because of the variable nature of qualitative research and the relative novelty of many research studies.

Activity 13.6

Evaluate the wide range of software packages for qualitative analysis at the following websites:

http://caqdas.soc.surrey.ac.uk/index.htm
http://www.scolari.co.uk/

SUMMARY

- Qualitative data can have a quality of 'undeniability' because they are rooted in the natural context of field settings.
- The main focus of qualitative research is to understand the ways in which people act and the accounts that people give for these actions.
- In all but the most inductive qualitative approaches, research questions are written, but *when* they are written is one of the features that distinguishes qualitative from quantitative research. In qualitative research, questions are not always written at the start of the study.
- Data are collected using a wide variety of methods, including field research (the most common) but also the use of unobtrusive data, photographs, film, video and other sources.
- The main approaches to qualitative data analysis comprise content analysis and grounded theory. Content analysis involves locating classes or categories within the data. These categories are usually derived from theoretical models. In contrast, grounded theory uses a process of open, axial and selective coding to develop categories and theories inductively from the data.
- Due to the lack of non-probability sampling methods, qualitative analysis is open to accusations of invalidity. However, claims for the validity of results can be strengthened, for example, by eliciting the views of research participants.
- The reliability of qualitative research can be strengthened by using multiple cases, or by supporting assertions using numerous examples, or by verifying the analysis using other researchers. Concepts such as credibility, authenticity, honesty and openness are also important in qualitative research.

(Continued)

SUMMARY OF WEB LINKS

http://caqdas.soc.surrey.ac.uk/index.htm

http://www.scolari.co.uk/

Further reading

Miles, M.B. and Huberman, A.M. (1994) *Qualitative Data Analysis*, 2nd edn. Thousand Oaks, CA: Sage. Still an outstanding source of many and varied qualitative analysis methods.

Flick, U. (1998) *An Introduction to Qualitative Research*. London: Sage. Deals with all the major theories and methods of qualitative research design, including some less well-known approaches such as the use of personal narratives.

Symon, G. and Cassell, C. (1998) (eds) *Qualitative Methods and Analysis in Organisational Research* London: Sage. Presents a refreshing array of qualitative techniques that are dealt with only sparingly by many of the standard texts: Subjects include: life histories, critical incident techniques, qualitative research diaries and pictorial representation.

Locke, K. (2001) *Grounded Theory in Management Research*. London: Sage. Provides a detailed summary of the evolution of grounded theory, and illustrates how it can be applied in a management and organizational context.

Fielding, N. and Lee, R.M. (1998) *Computer Analysis and Qualitative Research*. London: Sage. A valuable introduction to some of the principles of using computers in qualitative research as well as a practical guide to managing data and coding categories.

Suggested answers for Activity 13.2 (selected examples)

There might tend to be more confidence in the validity of results from a comprehensive sample since this covers every case in a given population. Similarly, intensity samples focus on cases that are typical of the population rather than outliers or atypical examples. Deviant case sampling, which looks at extreme cases, may be accused of producing invalid results, but may, in fact, yield illuminating and unexpected data that allow new avenues of exploration. Critical case sampling, with its focus on one case or site, can only provide a strong case for validity if evidence is provided that the case is, indeed, typical of the trait, characteristic or phenomenon under investigation.

14

Writing the Research Report

Chapter objectives

After reading this chapter you will be able to:

- **Write a report that matches your original or evolving research objectives.**
- **Plan and resource the report writing process.**
- **Select from a number of different report formats.**
- **Present your findings in a style, format and structure that is accessible to your intended audience.**

You have planned your research project, adopted an appropriate research methodology, designed valid and reliable data gathering tools and collected and analysed the data. What could be easier than writing up the research report? Actually, it is not as easy as many would imagine. The most carefully planned and skilfully implemented research study will be doomed to failure if you are incapable of presenting the findings in a manner that is engaging, coherent and accessible for your intended audience. As Murray (1994) warns, reports are too often written in a private language that excludes the very people who may have responsibility for actually implementing or assessing the research. One of the keys, therefore, is to keep it simple.

Timing is also important. Most people assume that reports are written at the end of a research project. This is not necessarily the case. Indeed, the more time you can devote to writing sections or chapters of the report during the research process itself, the better. This is because the process of writing is extremely valuable in clarifying your own thoughts, and in finding where gaps and inconsistencies may be emerging in the research. It is better to discover these problems well before the end of the research project so that they can be rectified.

Another concern is that of objectivity. It is likely that you are tackling a research project because you have chosen to (you are interested in the subject), or have been asked to (perhaps it is seen by others as 'your area'). Either way, even though at the start of the project you do not see yourself as an expert, it is probable that you have some interest or connection with the topic. The key here, then, is adopting and maintaining an objective 'distance' from the subject and not getting dragged into some sort of polemical argument. Failure to maintain an objective stance will not only cloud and obscure your writing, it may alienate your audience.

Report writing is (or should be) a creative process. Even using the same sets of data, two researchers will not produce reports that are identical. But report writing is also a skill and, like any skill, it must be learned through practice. It must also be based upon sound principles. Presented in this chapter, then, are some basic approaches to producing a research report that will hopefully complement rather than hinder the research effort that has preceded it. Note that the term 'report' is used here to mean actual reports produced in an organizational context, but many of the principles discussed apply equally to academic dissertations, theses and articles written for the academic literature. These are also discussed with reference to their own specific requirements.

THE REPORT WRITING PROCESS

You will recall that in Chapter 4 and, indeed, throughout this book, the importance of writing clear and unambiguous research objectives has been stressed. It would certainly be a pity if, at the final hour, these objectives were ignored and the report aimed at a completely different set of goals! Of course, it is possible that your objectives may have shifted or even radically changed during the research process itself. This is entirely acceptable, as long as you have clearly articulated what these new objectives are going to be. Even in the most heuristic research approach, the researcher sets off with an intended goal – even though this may become modified through the process of inquiry itself.

Planning the report

Some writers prefer to launch themselves immediately into the writing process, but it is usually prudent to start with at least a draft plan for the report, even if the plan may change during the writing itself. The plan can initially be sketched out on paper or typed straight into a word processed document. The plan might contain the main headings and sub-headings of the report, and references to where notes, files or data sets can be found for when the actual writing process starts. It is nearly always sensible to get this plan evaluated by a reviewer. This person might be your supervisor or tutor if you are undertaking an academic course of study, a peer or co-worker or even the report's organizational sponsor. In seeking this review, make it clear that you want *critical* feedback. Eliciting the views of managers or sponsors is always useful because it enables you to gain some assurance that the report meets with their interests and needs.

In some cases, the planning of the report may be assisted by terms of reference that describe the purposes of the report, its scope, type and readership. Sometimes these terms of reference may be given to you by whoever is commissioning you to carry out the research. Wainwright (1990) suggests that if you have not been given any terms of reference, you should write your own.

Knowing the purpose of the report

Before starting, as Turk and Kirkman (1989) warn, you must begin with a clear idea of what it is you want to achieve. This is not the same as your subject. By focusing on the *aim* of your report, you are considering what it is that the readers want to know, so that it is relevant, interesting and usable for them. Failure to think clearly about the needs, interests and motivations of the target audience is one of the most common reasons why reports fail to fulfil their potential. It often helps to think what it is you expect readers to actually *do* after they have read the report. For example, do you expect them to:

- Request a presentation.
- File the report.
- Pass the report on to another individual or committee.
- Send an e-mail.
- Arrange a meeting.
- Sign a cheque.

Activity 14.1

Examine each of the following words, and select one or more that describe the purpose of your report: describe, explain, instruct, specify, evaluate and recommend, provoke debate but not seem to lead, persuade, concede and apologize, protest, reject.

Knowing your audience

You also need to remember that the report may be read by a variety of people, each of whom has a different interest or motivation for reading it. If it is, say, a technical report, those with technical expertise in this field may be interested in issues of *how* and *why*. Senior managers in an organization, however, may have less time to read all the technical details, but want to get quickly to the issue of *what purpose, what is the cost*, and *where are the resources?* Writing for an academic audience will require a style of writing that includes a strong engagement with the academic literature. So you will need to think of how the report can be written in a way that is accessible to a diverse audience, at least some of whom will not want to read it in its entirety.

Turk and Kirkman (1989) suggest that, before you start, you ask yourself each of the following questions:

- Are all the readers alike?
- What do they already know about the subject?
- What do they need to know?
- What are their attitudes to the subject, to the writer, and to the writer's objectives?
- What are the psychological and physical contexts within which the report will be received?

Booth (1991) also suggests that the writer needs to decide whether the message to be delivered is going to be made explicit or implicit in the report. She argues that it is often better to make the argument implicit, and to lead the reader towards the appropriate conclusion.

Activity 14.2

Taking a report that you intend to write, now add a description of your audience using the bullet points above.

Where to start?

Even if it may seem logical to start writing with an Introduction, this is probably not the best place – indeed, it could be argued that it is easier to write this at the very end (when the whole 'story' of the project is clear). Most researchers find it easiest to begin with the literature review (if the report requires one). There are a number of reasons for this:

- The review will normally have been conducted at an early stage of the research and so can be attempted well before the final phases.
- The process of writing the literature review helps to articulate the objectives, focus and direction of the research.

The literature review, of course, can always be updated and improved at a later stage, but writing a first draft early in the research can provide a solid theoretical and directional underpinning to the entire project. Where you start is obviously up to you. The only point to emphasize is that you should get started on the writing process as soon as possible!

Making and using time

In writing a report, time is one of the most precious, but probably least available, commodities you have at your disposal. It is important, then, to use it wisely and to make as much time available to writing the report as possible. Good project management is the key. At the very start of the research process, you should have allocated a block of time (days, weeks or even months, depending on the scale of the project), for the report writing process. Within this elapsed time schedule, you should also have planned for the writing sessions you need in order to complete the report. If your research and data gathering efforts have overlapped into the report writing phase, then you need to evaluate whether you can complete the report in the planned time, or whether you need to negotiate an extension. What is vital here is that you take some control of decisions, and do not leave requests for extensions until the last minute.

As far as the report writing process is concerned, people tackle this in different ways. According to Saunders et al. (2000), most people can write about 2000 words in a day, but this will depend on their experience, confidence and the complexity of the subject. Some people prefer to devote large blocks of time to writing and to keep going into the night until exhaustion overwhelms them. Others prefer to allocate discrete blocks, spread across a time period. What is important, is that, whatever your preferred style, the time resource you allocate yourself is sufficient to get the job done.

Whatever time you have planned for yourself, you obviously want to make the best use of it. In doing this you might want to:

- Find a place to work where distractions are minimized and where you can think clearly.
- Write at a time of day when you are physically and mentally fresh. Take regular breaks.
- Have access to all the resources you are going to need (a computer for word processing, keeping notes, files, data, and for data analysis, etc.).
- Set yourself challenging but realistic goals for each writing session. This might be a word count – in which case, you could keep a record of your production achievements.

Of course, the report writing process is made more complicated if it is a team effort. The general principles, however, are the same. Plan for the writing of the report and allocate roles and responsibilities. Set deadlines and meet or communicate regularly to see if all team members are on track. Since the timing of the report is now dependent on the speed of the slowest member, it is often prudent to have contingency plans in case the process is held up. For example, can another member of the team or additional staff resources be drafted in to write some more sections or to provide assistance?

Writing the report

After 'completing' the report, always regard this as merely the first draft. Leave it for a few days (if this is possible) before you return to it, so that you will have forgotten the thoughts behind the report and will read what you actually said! You will, inevitably, find not only typing and grammatical mistakes, but also gaps, inconsistencies and errors. It is essential at this stage that you are your own strongest critic. Put yourself into the mind of your audience. Would they understand your writing style? Does the report flow logically? Does it address the audience's needs?

In revising the document, Turk and Kirkman (1989) suggest first reading the draft without stopping, but noting problem passages or words so that you can return to them later. This top-level overview allows you to evaluate the general flow of information and ideas and to see if the structure 'hangs together'. Next, return to the specific problems you identified and amend them. In doing this, pay attention to issues of style.

THE REPORT STYLE AND STRUCTURE

The style and structure of the report will very much depend on what type of report you are producing and for whom. There are, essentially, two kinds of readers: those who commissioned or who are expecting the report, and those who are not expecting the report but who may, none the less, be interested in it. The commissioning group will want to know if this is the report they were waiting for and whether it contains the information they need. The second group will want to know if the report has any relevance to them, and whether it contains any new information. Therefore, for both groups, you need to give the audience information quickly and in an accessible way. It must compete for their limited time and attention. The kinds of criteria readers might apply in deciding whether they read the report or not might include:

- The title – does this sound relevant or interesting to me?
- Do the contents of the report actually match the title?
- How long is the report – what is my investment of time going to be and is it worthwhile?
- How well presented is the report – how confident am I in the abilities of the writer?

The next sections present a number of alternative formats.

Organizational and technical reports

A business report is taken to mean any report written for the purposes of general management or organization, whereas a technical report has, obviously, a more specifically technical focus. Of course, organizational research can often involve the need to understand and act upon technical issues. Some business and technical reports may be written for publication in an academic journal, and so will tend to follow the structure discussed later. Technical reports may be written for organizational purposes and be commissioned or sponsored by an individual or committee within the organization. When undertaking reports of this kind, both you and the sponsor need to be clear about:

- The objectives of the report.
- Access to resources needed to complete it.
- Timescales for delivery.
- The extent to which the report is purely descriptive or analytical. If the latter, are recommendations required?
- The importance, or otherwise, of theoretical underpinning. This, of course, is essential for academic journal articles but may be irrelevant for some kinds of technical report.
- The final intended audience for the report (which may not actually be the initial sponsor) and the style, tone and structure that the report should adopt.

In contrast to academic articles, business and technical reports tend to be much more utilitarian and 'to the point'. White (1997) suggests the following typical structure, but this should not be adhered to rigidly – select sections according to your needs.

Cover   A well-designed cover can help to attract a reader's attention and give a positive impression about the report before it is even read. White (1997) recommends that a cover should include at least four elements: a descriptive title of the report; the names of the report's principle authors, investigators and editors, if applicable; publication number, if the organization requires a record of this; the publication date.

Title page   This is the first page of the report and repeats some of the cover content. For example, it contains a descriptive title of the report, the author's name and the organization's name and address. This page can also include the name of the person who commissioned the report.

Abstract/executive summary   This is designed for busy people who do not usually have the time to read a report in its entirety, and may be between 200 and 500 words long. This summary, then, has to be both comprehensive in its coverage but also very succinct. It should present a short description of the project, plus findings and recommendations. Figures, illustrations and tables are not used.

Table of contents   White (1997) recommends that a table of contents should be used for reports that are over 10 pages long. The table of contents shows all main headings and even sub-headings. Since all headings should fully describe each section, the table of contents not only provides a guide to finding sections, it can actually help to describe what a document is about. Most word processing application programmes will generate a table of contents automatically, but only if you have formatted your report by allocating a style (for example, Heading 1, Heading 2, etc.) to your headings.

List of symbols, abbreviations, definitions   If your report contains complex terms, abbreviations or definitions, then it is helpful to provide an explanation at the beginning. Of course, you will still be required to explain each new term or abbreviation in the main body of your text as it occurs. For example, you will write 'Human Resource Management (HRM)' before alluding to HRM in the remainder of the report.

Introductory material   This might include any of the following:

- The nature of the problem being addressed.
- Why the research was undertaken.
- Any limitations on resources, materials or time in undertaking the research.
- The scope of the research (for example, did the study look at the problem from the perspective of individual employees, departments, sites or the entire organization?)
- An outline of previous work on this topic.

Report of work done   This will probably be the longest section and will, obviously, be determined by your subject, which might be:

- A new product or service. Readers may be interested in its potential uses, the risks involved, and its technical, financial and material requirements. They may also be interested in the life cycle of the product or service, its potential competitors and plans for its development.
- Technical or managerial problems. Readers may be interested in the origins and nature of the problem, whether it is temporary or permanent, options for solving the problem, and which option is selected and why. They may also want to know how and when the recommendations are going to be implemented, and what the outcomes are likely to be.

One of the weaknesses of many reports is that the main findings are buried in the middle or end of the document. Hence, busy managers will have to spend time delving for the nub of the argument. But this is not just an issue of time, it is also one of cognition and understanding. By presenting the important findings or arguments first, subsequent information can then be used to supplement and support them. Readers find it easier to process and assimilate detailed information if they are first given a general framework to work with. This is not to argue that there may not be reports where the argument proceeds like a detective story with the 'solution' arriving at the end, but most readers of business reports will be both irritated and confused by this approach and will want you to get to the point! Herbert (1990) offers a helpful suggestion here: imagine that you have been asked to appear on a serious radio programme to explain your report. Think of how you would have to quickly and succinctly explain *what* you have been investigating, *how*, *why* and with *what results*.

Turk and Kirkman (1989), suggest that reports should be written using a pyramid structure (see Figure 14.1). Since only the first few pages of the report will be read by most readers in an organization, this should contain an accurate summary of the main substance of the report (see Abstract/executive summary, above). The most detailed information, including appendices, will be included at the end of the document.

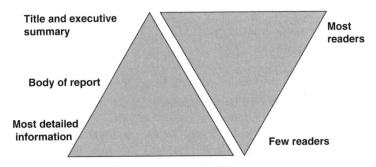

FIGURE 14.1   PYRAMID OF EVIDENCE MODEL FOR REPORT DESIGN
(ADAPTED FROM TURK AND KIRKMAN, 1989)

The main aim of the business report should be to put over the information needed, to those that require it, so that something can be done. It is not an exercise in writing down everything you have learned about the subject, no matter how interesting (to you) this may be. It is worth, however, just qualifying this last statement. It might be worthwhile noting problems encountered in undertaking the research, the false starts made and negative findings recorded, so that other researchers may learn from your experience. Managers who delve this far may also note some of the 'side issues' you were not able to pursue, so that further research might be commissioned. But, overall, try to maintain the focus of the report – keep to the point!

Results/findings   This section should not be a 'dumping ground' for all your research data. Most of the data sets will probably be presented in the appendices. The results section should contain summaries of the data that focus on the main findings of the research. For clarity, it helps if data can be presented in the form of tables or graphs (recall Chapter 12). Note that the Results section should concentrate precisely on this and not discuss the findings. The Discussion section comes next.

Discussion and analysis   This section is where you have an opportunity to draw inferences from the results (what do the data mean?), look at relationships between sets of data and also differences. What was unexpected? What were the causes and what are the likely effects. What do the results mean in terms of options for action? It must be stressed that the Discussion is not an opportunity merely to repeat the results, although reference may need to be made to the findings in drawing out the threads of the analysis. Remember, the Results tell you what has happened, the Discussion/Analysis section aims to understand how and why it happened.

Conclusions   A Conclusion could be merely a number of remarks that 'round off' the report, or it could mean a 'logical outcome' of the report's arguments. The latter is probably preferable in most cases. A conclusion should not be used to repeat findings or facts – it should contain a series of statements that bring together, in a succinct format, what the study has discovered. Berry (1994) warns that Conclusions should not present new evidence, but should relate back to the original purpose and focus of the report.

Recommendations   These should flow logically from the evidence presented by the report, so that there should be no sudden surprises for the reader. This section should also focus completely on these recommendations and not contain other material such as data or discussion that has already been presented. Recommendations are usually presented in a concise format, so the use of a list is entirely appropriate. White (1997) advises that a recommendations section is only relevant if the author has been commissioned to make such recommendations.

Acknowledgements   Turk and Kirkman (1989) recommend limiting acknowledgements to those outside the organization that have provided you with help, and only if this assistance is beyond what one would normally expect from someone in their position. This section should not be used to flatter those who are acknowledged, but to provide the reader with a sense of where some of the information originated.

References   This will be used for citing all the books, journal articles, reports, websites and internal organizational documents used in the study. Only those sources that are actually referenced in the report should be cited, not all those that you read but did not necessarily use. If you want to refer to documents that you are not referencing but which readers might find useful, then place these in a Bibliography section. You might also want to indicate why these sources might be useful.

Appendix for tables, figures and graphs   Some of these tables and figures will probably appear in the main body of the report. Ensure that they are not gratuitous, that is, they should be there for a purpose. Also make sure that they are referred to and described in the body of the text (and not just dumped to stand on their own), and that they appear as close to this description as possible. The citation 'Table' should appear above the table to which it refers, while the citation 'Figure' should appear below the figure (as in this book). This is the convention. More detailed data can be summarized in tables, figures and graphs in the appendix.

Other appendices   These should include any research instruments you have used, such as questionnaires, interview or observation schedules, and any accompanying documentation such as letters sent to survey participants. They might also include copies of e-mails or other communications generated during the process of the research (but remember not to breach confidentiality by revealing the names of research subjects without their permission). Whatever topic is covered in an appendix, it is important that there is a reference to the appendix and its purpose in the main body of the report.

Academic theses and dissertations

An academic thesis or dissertation is very different to an organizational or technical report in that it is usually more comprehensive and expansive. It seeks to marshal *all* the relevant information that relates to the topic or problem, and to support all data and arguments with sources of evidence, so that the way in which a case is built up can be judged (Halpenny, 1976). It also seeks to be original. According to Phillips and Pugh (1994), this could include:

- Carrying out empirical work that has not been done before.
- Using already known material but with a new interpretation.
- Replicating a study that has been done in another country or context.
- Bringing new evidence to bear on an old issue.

How a thesis or dissertation is structured will partly depend on the nature of the research itself, but it is sound advice to sketch out an intended outline at as early a stage as possible. Clearly, this tentative outline may change during the research or writing up process, but it does give the writer a sense of structure and direction (Teitelbaum, 1998). The usual convention for the layout is as follows:

- Title page (which should contain the title, the name of the author and qualifications, a statement of the degree for which the document is being presented, the names of the academic School or Department of the University or college and the date of submission).
- The Abstract (a summary – usually of not more than 300 words – of the content of the thesis).
- Contents page (a listing, giving precise headings for each section and their page numbers).
- Acknowledgements (thanking people and organizations that have assisted in the work).
- The main body of the thesis. This could comprise an Introduction, several chapters dealing with a review of the literature and comprising theoretical issues and arguments (recall Chapter 3), research Methodology, plus Findings, Analysis and Conclusion and/or Recommendations.
- Appendices (if any).
- References (a complete listing of all works cited).

It could be argued that, in some ways, the first and last chapters are the most important as these are what readers tend to remember. The Introduction chapter (often just a few pages in length) will usually be written after the completion of the research and will often contain:

- A broad review, putting the work within a wider context.
- A coherent argument for the significance of the problem being considered.
- An outline of the thesis, showing how the problem was approached.

The final chapter may contain:

- A brief restatement of the problem, now seen from the perspective of what has been learned.
- A clear outline of what has been achieved.
- A discussion of the main recommendations for work in the future.

Between these chapters, of course, we have the all-important literature review. This provides a context for the proposed study and demonstrates why it is important and timely. In order to do this, it sets out to clarify the relationship between the study and previous research on the topic. A very common mistake is that this part of the dissertation reads like a 'laundry list of previous studies' (Rudestam and Newton, 1992: 46). Hence, every paragraph begins, 'Brown found that …', or 'Fletcher argues …'. Recall Figure 3.4 in Chapter 3 and the advice that you should gradually synthesize and focus your ideas, so that all material is linked to the central direction of the study. By the time the reader reaches the Methodology section, he or she should be saying to themselves: 'Yes, these are the questions I too am asking myself and this is what the study should focus on so that knowledge in the field can move forward.'

Academic journal articles

You may undertake research with the specific intention of submitting the outcome for publication to an academic journal, or you may have written a thesis and want to see an edited version of it published. Berry (1994) warns that editors and publishers loath theses. This is because they are written in a cumbersome academic style where length is relatively unrestricted. For a professional reading public, the material will have to be completely reworked, with a succinct and taut prose.

It is also not enough just to decide that you want to publish an article in a journal. The question is: which journal? All journals require contributors to adhere to a specific format. This is usually stated within the journal itself, and normally gives guidance on the structure of articles, writing style, reference system, length and so on. Obviously, this is the first place to look if your report is being written for publication. But you will also find it useful to go beyond this formal outline and in particular to look at:

- The types of articles that have been recently published. What kinds of subjects are of interest to the readers of this journal? Are the research approaches mainly quantitative, qualitative or a mixture of the two, and what epistemological traditions do they follow?
- The formality, or otherwise, of the academic style. In most journals, you should expect a very formal style to be adopted, using the past tense and in the passive voice (for example, 'Fieldwork was undertaken using a structured observation schedule. It was then decided to ….').

- The depth and content of the academic underpinning. Review the reference section of a number of articles. How lengthy is the typical reference section? Is any particular research paradigm favoured?

As Berry (1994) notes, it is usually better to have details of your selected journal's format before writing the article rather than after it. The following Case Study provides an example of what to look out for.

Case Study 14.1   Typical structure for an academic journal article (abridged)

Aims and scope
The International Journal of Human Resource Management is the forum for HRM scholars and professionals world-wide. Concerned with the expanding role of strategic human resource management in a fast-changing global environment, the journal focuses on future trends, drawing on empirical research in the areas of strategic management, international business, organizational behaviour, personnel management and industrial relations.

The journal encourages strategically focused articles on a wide range of issues, including employee participation, human resource flow, reward systems and high commitment work systems. Features include:

- Comparative contributions from both developed and developing countries.
- International data sets.
- Special issues based on conferences and current issues.
- Reviews.

Notes for contributors: Submission of a paper will be taken to imply that it presents original, unpublished work not under consideration for publication elsewhere. Articles should normally be between 7,000 and 8,000 words in length. The Harvard system of referencing should be used. For any other matters of presentation not covered by the above notes, please refer to the usual custom and practice as indicated by the last few issues of the journal.

Source: Adapted and abridged from *The International Journal of Human Resource Management* (2001)

Activity 14.3

Locate at least two academic journals that cover issues within the subject field of your report or thesis. Looking at both the 'Notes for Contributors' and the kinds of articles published, are there any significant differences between the journals in terms of:

- Subject areas.
- Emphasis on approaches to research (qualitative/quantitative) and epistemology.
- Theoretical underpinning in the articles.
- Emphasis on original, empirical work as against descriptions of other people's research.

You will note from Case Study 14.1 that the journal editors have made it as transparent as possible as to what they are looking for. Note also that they want empirical research, not a reworking of past articles or reports. They also provide a list of the kinds of articles they are looking for.

You might want to select a journal that focuses on the subject of your report. On the other hand, you might argue that the journal has failed to publish anything on your subject and that your article would make a vital contribution. This may be so, but do check that the subject is one that is covered in the general rubric of subjects of interest. If you are in doubt about whether a journal might publish your work, you can send an abstract to the journal editor asking if the subject would be worthy of consideration.

In submitting an article, it is advisable to include a short covering letter. This is not an opportunity to recapitulate the rationale, objectives and research methodology and results of the research. The editor will see these clearly from the actual article. The purpose of your letter is simply to offer the article for consideration and to thank the editor for his or her time.

Once you have submitted an article to an academic journal make sure that the editor acknowledges that it has been received. You can then sit back for weeks, and probably months, before you hear whether it is to be published. This is because the article first of all has to be accepted by the editor as worthy of further consideration, after which it will usually be sent to two or perhaps three peer reviewers. The review process is 'blind', that is, your name will not be divulged to the reviewers, who will work completely independently on their evaluations. It frequently happens that one reviewer likes the article and recommends publication and another rejects it. The editor then has to either make a casting decision, or may send the article out for further review. Not surprisingly all this takes time. You are entitled to make the occasional inquiry as to how the review process is going (just in case the busy editor has forgotten about you!), but it is best not to pester editors too much. They have a difficult and often thankless, unpaid task.

The following is a typical outline for an academic article.

Title page   This includes the title itself, that should neatly summarize the main focus of the article. The title page should also include the name of the author and her/his institution, and acknowledgements (especially if the research has received external funding or assistance). The actual title itself should be short, and should specify exactly what the article is about. If the title is rather long, you could consider using the less significant element of it as a 'strap line'. For example:

> *The influence of improved process control systems and resource allocation on widget production through the use of a case study.*

This could read:

> *Case study: widget production improvement – process control systems and resource allocation.*

Abstract   The abstract provides a concise summary of the article (often between 150 and 200 words). The actual length of the abstract will usually be specified by the journal's Note to Contributors. This is a very important section because it may be the only part of the article that some people read. Herbert (1990) suggests that the abstract should contain:

- The main hypothesis.
- A synopsis of the methods used.
- A summary of the major findings.
- A brief mention of subjects and materials.
- The conclusions based on the results.
- Design procedures.

   In addition to the abstract, and perhaps adjacent to it, some journals ask for a list of keywords. In paper-based versions of the journal, these can provide readers with an indication of whether they want to read the article or not. For Web-based abstracting services, typing in one of these keywords will link another researcher to a list of articles containing this keyword, including your article.

Introduction   This explains the purpose of the study, the rationale for undertaking it and some background information. The Introduction also provides an opportunity to outline the main research questions and hypotheses (if any). If the research is based on findings in an organization, it is useful to provide the reader with some additional details on, say, the history of the organization, its size, products or services, mission, etc.

Literature review   After reading the literature review, the reader should understand why the study is being undertaken and how and why it is adding to the store of knowledge. A literature review written for an academic journal will usually be shorter than the kind of very comprehensive review that would be written for an academic thesis or dissertation. It should be self-evident after reading the literature review as to why the study's research questions (and hypotheses, if any) have been selected. Take care, however, not to merely label this section 'Literature review' even though this is what it is. Help and inspire the reader by choosing a title that reflects what the section is really about. If several themes or issues are being addressed, it may be necessary to write a number of literature sections, each with an appropriate heading.

Methodology   This is a key section and will be evaluated meticulously by reviewers and readers, and, of course, by anyone seeking to replicate the findings. The methodology should follow the principles outlined in many chapters in this book, including:

- A description of the research context: what kind of organization or setting, what were the original specifications for the study, what practical or ethical considerations were evident?
- The processes of sample selection: how was the sample selected? When was it selected: at the commencement of the study, or iteratively during it?

- A description of, and justification for, the sample: how many participants were there, what were their characteristics and how representative were they of the population?
- The research procedure, including the kinds of research methodology (experimental, survey, grounded study, etc.), research tools used and evidence for the validity, reliability and credibility of these tools.
- The duration, number and timing of the data gathering sessions: if used, how were interviewers or observers trained, what instructions were given to respondents?
- How were the data analysed?

Results   As the title suggests, this is the section in which you report on your findings. This may be in the form of descriptive text, tables and figures (recall Chapter 12) or through selected quotations. The key word here is 'selected'. Quotations should only be used where the comments themselves are revealing or interesting – they should not be used to carry the main burden of a description or argument. Quotations should also be used sparingly; try to avoid the phenomenon of 'death by quotation'.

Ensure that the results section is precisely this and not a discussion or commentary (which comes in the following section). The easiest way of differentiating between the two sections is that the Results should deal with *what* happened, while the Discussion section should deal with *why* (that is, the analysis). Make sure that you do not mix the two.

Discussion   The Discussion section, using the data (Results), presents answers to the original research questions and/or hypotheses. In doing this, it is particularly important to refer back to the literature review section, so that comparisons and contrasts can be drawn out between what your research found and what the literature suggested you might expect. In some cases you may be confirming the theoretical propositions from the literature, but within new (say, organizational) contexts. In other cases you may be finding relationships between variables that few studies have explored. Remember, all research does not have to be so original or unique that it puts you in line for a Nobel Prize. Nevertheless, unless it has something to add to knowledge, it is unlikely be considered worthy of publication.

References   There are several types of referencing convention, one of the most widely used being the Harvard or author–date system, as used in this book.

Of course, what we have just discussed is quite a conventional format. Journals that take a more inductive, qualitative or ethnographic stance may discourage such a structured approach. The key, as has been suggested, is to look at these journals to see what approach they take.

ETHICAL AND LEGAL CONSIDERATIONS

We have dealt with ethical issues in a number of previous chapters, but it is worth exploring some of them here in the context of writing up the research as well as legal and copyright implications.

The ethics of report writing

Some of the information that your research reveals may be inconvenient, to you, a colleague or a line manager. A study, for example, might reveal shortfalls in efficiency, poor attitudes, errors and just bad organization. As a result, you may be tempted to present the results in a better light than they deserve. However, if the report is at an appropriate level of detail, other readers should be able to compare the data with your findings and recommendations and detect bias or misleading statements.

In terms of the process of producing a report, follow the advice given in previous chapters. If you have promised to respect confidentiality and not to reveal the sources of certain pieces of information, this, obviously, must be adhered to. Ensure that you apply the principles of informed consent both for participation in the study and at the reporting stage (if individuals can be identified).

Legal issues

Legal issues might arise through the process of conducting your research, and also at the report writing stage, for example, where you:

- Reveal your sources of information and use statements made by individuals – are they defamatory, libellous or in breach of sex discrimination laws?
- Present material – has it been published elsewhere and is it copyright? (see next section)
- Make recommendations – do they infringe the law?

Common sense suggests that whenever you are in doubt about whether anything you have written contravenes a legal provision, you should consult a legal expert.

IP and copyright issues

Intellectual property (IP) refers to creations of the mind and includes: inventions, literary and artistic works, names, images, symbols and designs. The four main types of IP are:

- Patents for inventions – new and improved products and processes that are capable of industrial application.
- Trade marks for brand identity – of goods and services, allowing distinctions to be made between different traders.
- Designs for product appearance.
- Copyright for material including literary and artistic material, sound recordings, films, etc.

Copyright laws were first introduced in England in 1710 and now exist in most countries. While the precise nature of national copyright laws varies, the basic premise is that authors need to obtain permission before using another author's document, and must give the author appropriate acknowledgement. Take particular care when tempted to copy material from the Web. While websites are in the 'public domain', this does not mean that they are not protected by copyright laws. It is only safe to copy Web material when the author has abandoned copyright ownership, it is clear that the copyright has expired, or if it is a site owned by the government.

In many countries, what is written by a person while at work, automatically, in most circumstances, becomes the property of their employer. This may well apply to the research report itself.

Activity 14.4

For more details on copyright laws see the following website:
  http://whatiscopyright.org/

In particular take a look at the section of 'Fair Use'.

DEVELOPING A WRITING STYLE AND TONE

The appropriateness of a particular writing style can only be measured in the context of who the report is being written for. Hence, a style that is designed to inspire or enthuse will be very different from one that is meant to criticize or warn. Since the purpose of most reports is functional rather than imaginative, it has been suggested that this style of writing 'should be unobtrusive, an invisible medium, like a window pane through which the information can be clearly seen' (Turk and Kirkman, 1989: 90). Too many writers (particularly those writing scientific or technical documents) use leaden prose, and a stiff, formal style, failing to instil variety into their language.

One of the keys to good style is *readability*, a factor determined by:

* The writer, through the careful selection of material, by signposting, and by using a variety of emphasis.
* The text, in terms of language (structures and vocabulary) and layout (e.g., headings).
* Readers, particularly their motivation and attitudes, and their overall interest in the report.

Booth (1991) suggests that clichés should be avoided, such as 'light at the end of the tunnel' and 'at this moment in time'. Sexist, racist and ageist language must also be avoided, of course, and reference made to particular genders, races or ages only when they are relevant to the subject of the report.

At a practical level, readability is aided by generating a balance between the use of long and short sentences. A report that contains just long, verbose sentences will be difficult to cognitively process and understand; conversely, a report based just on short, staccato sentences will appear disjointed and monotonous. Using sentences that vary in length will aid the reader's attention, concentration and, therefore, understanding. The readability of text can be measured by a variety of indices, one of the most common of which is the Flesch index.

Activity 14.5 Measuring readability

You can measure the readability of the text you are producing using one of a number of alternative measuring indices. Microsoft Word, for example, can be used to give you both a Flesch Reading Ease score and a Flesch–Kincaid Grade Level score. For the Flesch readability score, text is rated on a 100-point scale. The higher the score, the easier the text is to understand. Most documents aim for a score of at least 60–70.

Perform a Flesch readability score on your own report. If this is not already set up in your program, go to the Help facility in Word and type in 'readability'. Follow the instructions to set up the readability statistics tool.

The use of long, technical or unfamiliar words also affects readability. But, it is not the length in itself that is the problem. For example, the word 'organization' has many syllables, but would not cause the average reader any problems. As Turk and Kirkman (1989) warn, it is the combination of unfamiliarity with length that can inhibit readability. Unfamiliarity itself is linked to the frequency with which a word appears. Technical terms, in particular, will only be familiar to an audience that is also knowledgeable and competent in this field. So, in writing technical reports, you need to be particularly careful that either the terms you use are clearly explained, or that they are likely to be well known to your audience. Jargon can be useful because it can be used as a short and convenient way to name new ideas and concepts. Technical reports would be lost without it. But it must also be used with care since, if it is overused, or used in an attempt to give an air of importance, it can obscure the central message of the report.

Turk and Kirkman (1989) also warn against the use of nominalization, that is, the habit of turning verbs into nouns. Take, for example, a perfectly good sentence:

The survey collected data on customer attitudes, showing that ….

Nominalizing the verb in this sentence, 'collected', gives us the following nominalized sentence:

Collection of the data through the survey revealed customer attitudes, which showed that …

Nominalization reduces the effectiveness of the written style because it produces a passive sentence and also forces the writer to insert an additional verb, 'revealed'. While it is tempting to use passive forms of writing because they add a sense of detachment and perhaps spurious objectivity to the report, they also make it longer, more complex and lacking in dynamism.

The tone of a report relates to the general mood of the finished text. It is important, for example, not to betray personal feelings such as anger, frustration, jealously, resentment or anxiety in the report, even if you are feeling these emotions. The overall tone of a report should reflect the nature of its message.

THE REVIEW PROCESS

It is difficult to overstate the importance of a review process. The research task is usually a long and arduous one, sometimes involving unexpected and unwelcome surprises. You have struggled through it and probably along the way become not only interested but quite committed to its subject and even its findings. You are also probably quite tired and even a little bored at reading or re-reading what you have written. You are, therefore, the very last person who should be evaluating and reviewing your work! You are now in desperate need of an 'outsider's' detached view of what you have created. Selecting an appropriate reviewer may be difficult, so plan this well in advance. In 'commissioning' the review, ask that the reviewer be as constructively critical as possible, since it is far better to identify real problems now rather than after the project has been delivered. Ask the reviewer to consider, in the light of the intended audience, the:

- Overall argument: is it understandable, consistent and congruent with the stated aims of the project?
- Structure of the report – is it logical and easy to follow?
- Language and tone – is it suitable and consistent?
- Presentation of the report – is the look and 'feel' appropriate?
- Grammar and punctuation – are they accurate?

If the report is intended for a very senior audience, then you will need to go through a number of iterations, ideally using a number of experienced and expert reviewers. If the report is a dissertation or thesis, intended for assessment as part of an academic programme, then obtaining a review from someone familiar with the subject matter would be useful.

PRESENTATIONS

Sometimes you might be asked to present both a written report and give an aural presentation, or even just a presentation alone. Academic kinds of presentation can take the form of a 'viva' where you are questioned by a group of experts, which usually includes your project supervisor and at least one external academic (usually in the role of the external examiner). The format for such a meeting can vary widely. In some parts of continental Europe, for example, the viva is an open event, at which members of the public may not only attend, but also ask questions.

In a business environment, the presentation may be to a project team or a management or executive board. The style and depth of the presentation will be largely determined by whether the recipients of the presentation have previously read the report. If they have read the report or are at least familiar with it, then you should concentrate on the background, highlight key points, and summarize implications and recommendations (if any). In giving aural presentations it is particularly important to be able to anticipate questions (especially difficult ones). It helps if you are able to be critically reflective about your own work and have the skill of identifying the weaknesses and contradictions in your report. If you fail to do this, recipients of the aural presentation will do this for you – probably to your discomfort.

If recipients have not read the report, your role is to summarize its aims, methodology and findings as clearly as possible and to point listeners to key sections if they wish to refer to them in more detail at a later time. It is important not to get too bogged down in detail or to confuse or alienate the audience.

SUMMARY

- Understand the needs and interests of your intended audience and write for them.
- Plan the report writing process, allowing yourself sufficient time to write the report and resources to aid its completion.
- Different structures are required for case study reports, organizational and technical reports and academic dissertations and journal articles.
- A common structure for an organizational report is one that presents the substantive arguments and findings at the beginning, using the rest of the report to support them.
- Dissertations and theses usually contain an abstract, an Introduction, several theoretical chapters, plus chapters on research Methodology, Findings, Analysis and Conclusion and/or Recommendations.
- The precise structure of journal articles is determined by the journal in question, but such articles will usually contain, amongst other sections, a strong, theoretical underpinning.
- Some of the main ethical considerations to think about when writing up research include maintaining confidentiality and taking care not to breach copyright laws. Be particularly careful when copying material from the Web.
- Style and presentation are important for the impact of a research report and are improved through practice and redrafting. Expert reviewers are of value in this process.

Summary of web links

http://whatiscopyright.org/

Further reading

Turk, C. and Kirkman, J. (1989) *Effective Writing: Improving Scientific, Technical and Business Communication*, 2nd edn. London: E.&F.N. Spon. A very readable book that offers a wealth of practical advice on writing reports.

Rudestam, K.E. and Newton, R.R. (1992) *Surviving your Dissertation: A Comprehensive Guide to Content and Process*. Newbury Park, CA: Sage. Provides practical guidance on selecting topics, and what the literature review, methods and results chapters should contain.

Research and Change in the Real World

15 Action research and change

Chapter objectives

After reading this chapter you will be able to:

- **Distinguish between action research and other research methodologies.**
- **Distinguish between the variety of approaches within action research.**
- **Plan a project, keeping in mind some of the potential limitations of action research.**
- **Describe the processes involved in conducting an action research project, and methods for gathering data.**

Part E of this book is devoted to action research because this methodology symbolizes much of what modern research is about – analysing the world but also trying to change it. Whereas some research paradigms may be content to add to the store of knowledge, action research asks the question: 'What can I do about it?' In addressing real world problems, the action researcher becomes directly involved in the research process as a *change agent*, devoted not only to studying organizations and processes but also to improving them. Contrast this with other research paradigms where the researcher is seen as a detached scientist, intent on avoiding any action that might bias or tarnish the results. Action research, in contrast, is committed and intentional but also informed and systematic. Lincoln (2001) sees strong connections, for example, between action research and constructivism, both of which claim the impossibility of value-free knowledge. But action researchers do not simply throw themselves into the research process. As we will see, there are planning, implementation and ethical issues that need addressing.

The term 'action research' was first coined by Lewin in 1946, by which he meant a process through which theory building and research on practical problems should be combined. Given the context of post-war reconstruction in which the theory was developed, it is not surprising that Lewin viewed action research as a way of improving social behaviour and encouraging social change. But his approach to such change was similar to the contemporary, traditional, scientific paradigm in that it recognized the value of experimentation and the importance of creating knowledge. But, while traditional science begins with substantial knowledge about hypothetical relationships, action research begins with very few facts. Lewin also argued that it was important to conduct social experiments in natural, social settings, not in the artificial world of controlled laboratory environments. Action research is also gestaltist in origin, that is, it sees issues as only being understood not through the study of a single variable, but within a holistic, complex social system.

Unfortunately, Lewin never wrote a systematic statement of his views before his death in 1947. Hence, as Dickens and Watkins (1999) note, there is still no definitive approach to action research and no unified theory. However, according to Bowling (1997, cited in Badger, 2000), Lewin's concept of action research as a means of social engineering has now been replaced by one that emphasizes raising awareness, empowerment and collaboration. There are still, however, a number of disparate definitions and characterizations of action research. McKay and Marshall (2001) even claim that the practice of action research is somewhat enigmatic, with few guidelines for action researchers to follow. This chapter, however, hopes, within the constraints just identified, to offer some guidelines to practice.

WHAT IS ACTION RESEARCH?

The term action research is a generic one and has been used to describe a bewildering range of activities and methods. In brief, however, action research is an approach that 'focuses on simultaneous action and research in a participative manner' (Coghlan and Brannick, 2001: 7). Within this approach there are varied methodologies, each with their own priorities and modes of inquiry (although there are as many overlaps and similarities between the approaches as there are distinctions). Some, for example, focus on how communities can enact change, particularly challenging issues such as injustice and social exclusion. Others are based in a more organizational context and may include how professional practitioners can improve their own professional practice. All approaches, however, have at least three common features:

- Research subjects are themselves researchers or involved in a democratic partnership with a researcher.
- Research is seen as an agent of change.
- Data are generated from the direct experiences of research participants.

A mode of action research that takes this latter point particularly seriously is *participatory action research* (PAR). McTaggart (1997) warns that participation is much more than mere involvement. Authentic participation means immersing people in the focus of the enquiry and the research method, and involving them in data collection and analysis. One of the primary aims of PAR is to transform situations or structures in an egalitarian manner. Hence, it has been used to deal with issues such as inner-city and rural poverty, education, mental health, disability and domestic violence. In the 1990s, however, PAR has also been taken up as a legitimate research approach by powerful agencies such as government departments, universities and multinational companies. In 1999, for example, the World Bank commissioned a 'Consultation with the Poor' involving over 20,000 people in 23 countries. Gaventa and Cornwall argue that the key element in PAR is a process of reflection, social learning and the development of 'critical consciousness' (2001: 76). This is particularly so among oppressed groups of people, where non-experts play a central role (Park, 2001).

In contrast, another type of action research is what Coghlan (2001) terms '*insider action research*', in which managers are engaged in action research projects in their own organizations. Often, these projects are undertaken as part of an academic programme of study such as an executive MBA. The kinds of issues addressed often include systems improvement, organizational learning and the management of change. One of the advantages of adopting insider action research is that managers have an intimate knowledge of the organization being studied – they know its culture, its jargon and its personal networks. They can also participate freely in discussions or merely observe what is going on without people necessarily being aware that they are being researched. On the other hand, it may be difficult at times to maintain a sense of detachment and it may sometimes prove difficult for an insider to cross departmental, hierarchical or network boundaries.

An alternative approach is *external action research*, where the researcher may be independent of the professional context, but work within it and alongside professional practitioners (for example, business leaders, managers, trainers or health professionals) to achieve change. Hence, action research is a process of collaboration for bringing about change. The exact nature of this collaboration, however, may be problematic.

Activity 15.1

Examine each of the following statements, only two of which are typical of action research statements. Which are they?

1 What is happening here?
2 How can I improve the quality of my professional practice?
3 How can this research method be improved?
4 What implications does my research have for all practitioners in my profession?

Suggested answers are provided at the end of the chapter.

Another approach to action research is *action science,* which attempts to integrate practical problem solving with theory building and change. Friedman (2001) acknowledges that it is difficult to locate a single, comprehensive definition of action science, but suggests that it involves a form of social practice which integrates both the production and use of knowledge in order to promote learning with and among individuals and systems. The objective of action science is to help practitioners to 'discover the tacit choices they have made about their perceptions of reality, about their goals and about their strategies for achieving them (Friedman, 2001: 160). To achieve this, communities of practice are created in which both practitioners and researchers make explicit their interpretations, which can then be made subject to rigorous testing for their validity.

Gummesson (2000) divides action science into *societal action science* and *management action science*. The former is concerned with the kinds of macro social, political and economic issues that arise, say, when a company is threatened with closure. This could involve, for example, a participatory study by groups of workers who are directly threatened by the closure. Such an approach stems from a belief that research should not lie in the hands of 'professional experts', who will have their own agendas and subjective biases.

Management action science is focused on a company as a business. Here, the action researcher has the difficult task of tackling issues and producing results that are of value to both science and to business. Thus, from a theoretical perspective, the action researcher will seek to contribute to knowledge, understanding and theoretical perspectives. But this must also be knowledge that can be applied and 'validated in action' (Gummesson, 2000: 119). This means that the life of the action scientist is often prone to role conflict and ambiguity. Another aspect of management action science is that it is interactive, that is, it requires close collaboration between the researcher and the company client. Again, this may pose problems for the researcher who may be pressurized to change original research designs in the interests of producing short-term actionable results.

Some important differences between participant action research and action science are highlighted by Whyte (1991). Action science focuses more heavily on interpersonal relationships, but also requires the intervention team to keep control of both the intervention and the research process (often as detached observers). In contrast, participatory action research, for example, involves greater sharing of control between practitioners and researchers.

Finally, *cooperative inquiry* is related to action research in that both focus on research *with* people rather than research *on* people. Where cooperative inquiry differs is in the way collaboration between researchers and participants takes place. Heron and Reason describe how co-subjects become 'immersed in and engaged with their action and experience' (2001: 180). They develop a degree of co-openness to what is happening through deep experiential engagement, often generated through music, drawing, drama and dance.

We can see, then, that action research involves quite a varied range of approaches to research both in terms of the relationship between researcher and participants and the focus of the research itself. Table 15.1 provides a summary of the kinds of action research projects that have been undertaken in different sectors.

TABLE 15.1   SECTORS WHERE ACTION RESEARCH PROJECTS HAVE BEEN
USED

Sector	Type of project
Education	School curriculum
	Evaluation
	Classroom processes
	Parent participation
Health	Infant health programmes
	Drug abuse programmes
	Health promotion projects
	Community health projects
Social work	Youth programmes
	Parenting programmes
Organizational development	Planning
	Change processes
	Training programmes
	Human resource development
Urban and economic development	Urban planning projects
	Community planning projects
	Housing needs surveys
	Youth housing needs

Source: Adapted from Stringer, 1999.

THE ACTION RESEARCH PROCESS

McNiff et al. (1996) caution that it is wise at the outset to be very realistic about what action research can achieve. You may also have to recognize that it is easier to change your own perspectives and professional practice than that of others. The success of an action research project will depend, in large measure, on your success with working with other people, so you need to identify the range of people who will be involved. These will certainly include *participants*, who may include colleagues or fellow employees. It is essential to pay very close attention to gaining access and to maintaining relationships. This is helped by keeping participants informed about the progress of the research and by thanking them for their assistance. But other possible collaborative sources might include:

- *Critical colleagues*, those who work with you and who may be willing to discuss your research, critically but supportively. It is advisable to negotiate the ground rules for engagement at the start of the project.
- *Adviser/mentor/tutor*, whose role is to challenge your thinking so that the direction of the project can be refocused or ideas reshaped.
- *Action research colleagues*, who may be fellow students on a taught programme or colleagues in a professional development programme. These people are key for providing support and sharing information and resources.

377

- *The validating group* of colleagues, managers or fellow professionals who may be used to comment critically on the outcomes of the project (see Validating action research p. 387).

Failure to engage the cooperation of people who can give you advice and support may actually endanger your project (see Case Study 15.2).

As Stringer (1999) shows, the aim of action research is not to present finalized 'answers' to problems, but to reveal the different truths and realities (constructions) held legitimately by different groups and individuals. People with identical information will interpret it in different ways, depending on their previous experiences, worldview and culture. The task of action researchers, therefore, it to:

> *Develop a context in which individuals and groups with divergent perceptions and interpretations can formulate a construction of their situation that makes sense to them all – a joint construction.* (Stringer, 1999: 45)

The action research process itself, as originally conceived by Lewin, is a cyclical one, working through a series of steps including planning, action and observing and evaluating the effects of that action. Note that these stages overlap, meaning that some activities are running in parallel to each other. For example, a team could plan a project, and begin to execute some change, but then modify these plans on the basis of lessons learnt through action. Each of these steps is continually monitored to make adjustments as needed (see Figure 15.1). McTaggart (1997) suggests an alternative approach. Rather than see this as an entire project, a good way to begin is to collect some initial data in an area of general interest (a reconnaissance), then to reflect before making a plan for action. Hence, execution (albeit on a small scale) proceeds planning.

While this section has looked at action research as a neatly planned and orderly process, Dickens and Watkins warn that this is not always the case and that 'it can go forward, backward, and all directions at once' (1999: 135). We will explore each of the core action research stages in more detail next.

Planning: getting the focus right

Choosing a focus for the action research project may, at first sight, seem a relatively simple task, yet it is one that often causes researchers the most difficulty. This is because there are often so many issues that could be addressed, the problem is prioritizing between them. One of the keys to identifying a suitable research topic is having a sense of commitment to improvement (McNiff et al., 1996). If undertaking research within your own professional practice, you could, for example, ask yourself questions such as:

- How can I reduce my stress levels at work?
- How can we improve the quality of the consultancy and advice we give in the organization?

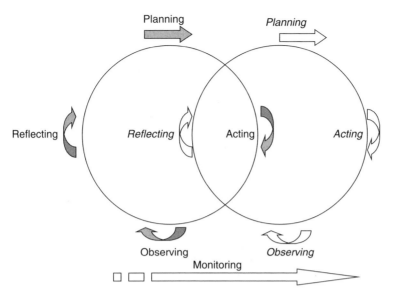

FIGURE 15.1   THE ACTION RESEARCH MODEL

- How can we achieve better working relationships within the company's project teams?

But there is an important difference between focusing on an issue that you consider vital or interesting and one that can actually be practically addressed. You must, then, also consider the matter of feasibility – do I have the time, access to participants and resources to actually tackle this issue and to bring about change? If the answer to the above question is 'Yes' then you will probably want to start with at least a tentative working hypothesis: 'If I do this, then it is likely that X might happen'. Unlike experimental research, this is not an attempt to identify causal relationships between variables. It is trying to identify the kinds of actions that can lead to positive change.

This means meeting with stakeholders to obtain a consensus on the actions that are planned. As Stringer (1999) makes clear, it is essential that the voices of all are heard, so that appropriate goals can be set. For planning purposes, the focus becomes one of establishing:

- *Why* activities are required.
- *What* actions need to be taken.
- *How* tasks are to be accomplished.
- *Who* is to be responsible for each activity.
- *Where* the tasks are going to be performed.
- *When* the activities are going to commence and when they are to be completed.

Mumford (2001) advises that a formal 'action' document should be drawn up with precise specifications of processes, objectives and outputs, and that this should be signed by both management and the researcher and given to all interested parties. Avison et al. (2001) refer to such a document as 'action warrants' that define the authority under which action can be taken, specifying the balance of authority between researchers and internal organizational participants. Sometimes projects may not begin with an action warrant because they are relatively informal or the precise nature and scope of the problem have not been defined, or it is initially not seen as serious. Once the problem and research objectives become clearer, then an organization may decide it needs the sort of formal control structures that an action warrant can specify.

In aiming to get the focus of the research project right, it is vital to make our own, personal values explicit, so that we can explore the relationship between these values and our own behaviour. Although we all have value systems, we may be forced by organizational constraints to act in ways that contradict them. For example, a manager might believe strongly in democratic forms of work organization, but act in quite authoritarian ways towards employees. Action research:

> is a way of working that helps us to identify the things we believe in and then work systematically and collaboratively one step at a time, to making them come true. (McNiff et al., 1996)

Activity 15.2

In planning your own action research project, (a) make a list of the likely participants (other than yourself); (b) identify those who might be prepared to give you critical advice and support; (c) select a suitable action research subject; (d) formulate a provisional hypothesis for the project.

If you are coming into an action research project from the outside, you will need to make contact with key stakeholders and interest groups as quickly as possible. These groups might include not only those people most directly concerned with the issue, but also managers and sponsors. As we saw in Chapter 10, it may also be necessary to contact, and get to know, unofficial opinion leaders or gatekeepers.

Acting: gathering evidence

Having identified the focus of your research, the next step is deciding what sort of actions to initiate and then what data to gather. It is usually best to focus on the kinds of performance indicators that show whether you, or others who are the focus of your research, are being effective in initiating change or not. Hence, if you were looking at improving communications between yourself and a group of clients, then you could try to locate critical incidents of when communication was progressing well, and when it was subject to problems. Data collection should be as comprehensive as possible, because important insights may only emerge once the data are being analysed. This means that you may have to use a wide range of data gathering tools, such as interviews (individual and focus groups), participant or non-participant observation, informal meetings and document analysis. For every piece of data, ensure that you record the date, time, place and the people who were present. Transcripts of conversations and records of meetings should be authenticated by getting them signed by a relevant participant.

The main problem is knowing how much data to gather without the process becoming unwieldy and unmanageable. As usual, the key is aiming to achieve a representative selection from the possible range of data. So, if you are trying to investigate the working relationships of a team of 20 people, one approach would be to chose four of them, if you were sure that they were typical of the group as a whole. Stringer (1999) also advises you should ensure that the diversity of groups in a social setting are represented. For example, in conducting an action research project amongst the parents of school children, it would be important to ensure that different social classes and ethnic groups were represented.

Stringer also suggests four alternative frameworks for assisting the data gathering process, namely:

- *Interpretative questions.* Participants might be encouraged to work through these in order to extend their understanding of the problem. These questions might include: what are the key elements of the problem? How is the problem affecting us? Who is being affected?
- *Organizational review.* Participants should focus on analysing various features of their organization, including: the general mission or purpose of the organization; its goals and objectives; the structure of the organization, including roles and responsibilities and the efficiency or otherwise with which they are conducted; the factors that inhibit the enactment of these responsibilities.
- *Problem analysis.* This is similar to concept mapping, only here participants are asked to identify the problem itself, the antecedents that led up to it and the major consequences that have ensued.
- *Concept mapping.* This is used by stakeholders to understand how different key elements in the problem relate to each other. The facilitator begins by drawing a word that sums up the central problem. Participants then add new labels to the chart that represent other elements associated with the problem. They then decide how the issues are linked. An example of a concept map is illustrated in Figure 15.2.

Observing: analysing the impact

Since action research is about taking action and often involves experimentation, action researchers have to take note of the impact of their actions. This might include providing authentic descriptions of what has been achieved. These may be either factual (for example, transcripts of conversations), subjective (such as,

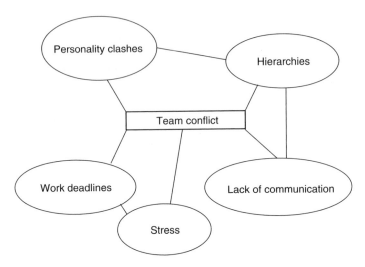

FIGURE 15.2 THE DATA GATHERING PROCESS: CONCEPT MAPPING OF TEAM
CONFLICT WITHIN A WORKPLACE

diaries and personal reflections) or fictionalized accounts that preserve the anonymity of participants but are used to highlight issues explicitly.

On the other hand, the impact analysis might take the form of meetings of stakeholders to examine what has been achieved. This is not a case of looking at the techniques and procedures that guide action research, but exploring the 'sense of unity that holds people to a collective vision of their world and inspires them to work together for the common good' (Stringer, 1999: 121). There should be opportunities for participants to discuss their contributions and to describe what they will do and the way in which they will go about it. The key to action is participation, a shared intent, positive working relationships and inclusivity. Of course, disagreements and antagonisms might arise. The role of the action researcher is to maintain a neutral stance and to act as a mediator to heal conflict.

Reflecting: evaluating the impact of the project

As we have seen, the aim of action research is the attainment of change. So how will you evaluate that change has actually taken place? The best approach, before you even start the project, is to identify what criteria constitute evidence of change. Then, select a piece of evidence from the data that you think demonstrates this change and have the evidence judged (validated) by others. The individual action researcher is not in a position to say whether their actions have had an impact – it is for participants in the project to judge for themselves. But action research is not just about fostering change in organizations, it is about generating learning amongst the action research participants. This too needs to be a focus of reflection – what was learned, what is its value, can it be applied elsewhere?

Having cycled through the planning, acting, observing and reflecting stages (often a number of times), what should the action researcher have to show for it? Coghlan (2001) suggests that the outputs of action research should include evidence of:

- How researchers engaged in the steps of action research, how they recorded their data and how they were a true reflection of what was studied.
- How they challenged and tested their own assumptions and interpretations of what was happening on a continual basis.
- How they accessed different views of what was happening showing both confirming and contradictory interpretations.
- How these interpretations and analysis were grounded in academic theory and how this theory both confirmed and challenged the analysis.

In contrast, Stringer (1999) argues that good action research projects have no well-defined ending. Instead, new realities emerge that extend the process of inquiry. What people should do is celebrate these achievements. Mumford (2001), however, talks explicitly about 'getting out' of the action research setting through the action researcher successfully handing over the knowledge needed by the group he or she has been working with, so that they can continue to solve their own problems. Hence, successful action research projects are not just about bringing about change in organizations, communities or networks, but about changing and empowering people.

THE ROLE OF RESEARCHERS AND PARTICIPANTS

In contrast to many other research methodologies, in action research the role of the researcher is seen as more of a facilitator than an 'expert'. Stringer (1999) contrasts action research with surveys, which he says are often limited in scope and 'frequently riddled with the agendas, interests, and perspectives of the people who commissioned or constructed them' (Stringer, 1999: 26). In action research, the researcher is a catalyst for achieving change by stimulating people to review their practices and to accept the need for change. But the researcher is not there to offer blueprints but to enable people to develop their own analysis of the issues facing them and the potential solutions. This might mean getting people to consider a range of possible solutions and their consequences. Once a plan has been decided, the role of the action researcher is to help in its implementation through analysing any weaknesses in the plan and by helping to locate resources (including human resources and the development of the necessary skills for the plan's success).

Given the facilitative role of the action researcher, the relationships and working processes between researcher and participants are of central importance. According to Stringer (1999), action research seeks to develop and maintain non-exploitative social and personal relationships and to enhance the social and emotional lives of those who participate. It is organized in democratic, therapeutic and equitable ways that should engender a community spirit. Table 15.2 summarizes some of the key elements that contribute to this.

TABLE 15.2 ELEMENTS THAT CONTRIBUTE TO COMMUNITY RELATIONSHIPS
IN ACTION RESEARCH

Working principle	Principle as implemented in action research community
Relationships	Promote feelings of equality for all involved
	Maintain harmony
	Resolve conflicts openly
	Encourage cooperative relationships
Communication	Listen attentively to people
	Be truthful and sincere
	Act in socially and culturally appropriate ways
	Regularly advise others as to what is happening
Participation	Enable significant levels of involvement
	Enable people to perform significant tasks
	Provide support for people as they learn to act for themselves
	Deal personally with people rather than with their representatives or agents
Inclusion	Maximize the involvement of all relevant individuals
	Ensure cooperation of other groups, agencies and organizations
	Ensure that all relevant groups benefit from activities

Source: Adapted from Stringer, 1999

Activity 15.3

Take a look at the wealth of action research sources at:
  http://www.goshen.edu/soan/soan96p.htm
Evaluate some of these sources and note any that may be of value in the
future.

METHODS OF DATA GATHERING

After planning the action research project, the next question is how to gather the data. As in most research methods, a variety of techniques are available, many of them already discussed in some detail in this book. The key, however, it to ensure that data gathering is systematic and provides a permanent record of what has taken place. As usual, it is important to use a variety of methods if possible to allow for triangulation.

Diaries

Whatever data gathering tool is used, it is probably advisable to keep a diary throughout the action research project as it can, as a minimum, provide a factual description of events, dates and people. But diaries are useful for a whole number of other purposes, including providing:

- An *aide-mémoire* of short notes for later reflection.
- A detailed portrait of events to provide a 'thick description' for later reports.
- A reflective account through which the researcher makes tentative interpretations of events, or through which the researcher records personal feelings and anxieties in order to try to understand them.
- An analytical tool that could contain a framing of the original research focus and a provisional analysis of the data as they are gathered.

If the action research project is a collaborative one, then it is also possible to write collaborative diaries. These can be written independently, and so provide a way of triangulating and checking for different recall or interpretations of events. Alternatively, they could be written interactively. The Internet offers some flexible facilities here. For example, one researcher could send an e-mail offering opinions or reflections on a topic to a co-researcher who would reply; the original researcher would reply to this, and so on. Hence, an interactive document is produced around a specific theme. Once the theme is exhausted, one of the researchers could send an e-mail on another subject. Alternatively, using a computer-based discussion forum, a group of action researchers or project participants could debate and comment on subjects through a continuous flow of threaded discussions.

Observations, interviews and questionnaires

Entire chapters of this book have been devoted to these data gathering methods and it is not the intention merely to repeat what has already been said. However, one way in which action research uses these methods differently, is that they are used in *collaboration* with others. Take the example of a group of consultants who frequently have to make presentations to company chief executives. They could set up an action research project in which they observe and video each other's practice presentations and give feedback.

It is usually unwise to use a questionnaire in action research unless there are really good reasons for doing so. This is because they do not help to generate the forms of collaborative problem solving that action research requires. But the use of questionnaires is valid for discovering information that could not be ascertained in any other way, or for evaluating the effect of an action research intervention – again, if data cannot be gathered using other methods.

Photography, audio and video recordings

These media can be used either to stimulate discussion or recall events during the research process, or as a means of capturing evidence in data gathering. In the case of the research process, participants may sometimes need visual evidence to remind them of a situation or just to stimulate ideas. Photographs or video can be used to present evidence of changes that perhaps the action research project has achieved. In the case of video, this is particularly true if we are talking about changes in human behaviour.

Audio is valuable because it can be used as a kind of talking diary that captures an entire conversation (McNiff et al., 1996). Of course, this will often mean that the tape will have to be transcribed before it can be analysed. You may find it useful either to play the tape to your critical friends, or to show them the transcript of the conversation.

Memory work

Memory work is used to uncover and analyse earlier understandings of social behaviour in personal and professional situations through the framework of current understanding. First used by feminist researchers, participants write stories about events or situations they have experienced in their lives. These narratives, which are written in the third person to create a sense of detachment, are then discussed and analysed by the group. Each member of the group then rewrites their original text in the light of the comments they have received. In the final phase, the original and rewritten texts of all group members are compared by the group. According to Schratz (1996), what is important is that the memory work process allows the group to explore issues and to learn.

An illustration of how action research data collection methods can be used in practice is given in Case Study 15.1.

Case Study 15.1 Improving children's health through action research

The aim of the action research project was to improve the provision of child health surveillance in a community context (doctor's surgeries rather than hospitals) and to develop a written framework for child health surveillance. The study was conducted over a 12 month period in 28 surgeries within one health district. Participants comprised between two and 11 primary care staff from each surgery, including at least one doctor and health visitor.

As is typical of action research projects, data were collected using a variety of methods, namely: direct observation of baby clinics by the research team, questionnaires to parents, semistructured interviews with team members and analysis of child care health surveillance reviews recorded in personal child health records. The 28 practices were randomly assigned to two groups comprising 14 practices in each, with one of the groups used for the action research study, the other being the control.

In the action research group, action researchers facilitated team meetings in each practice at 4-monthly intervals. At these meetings, the data collected from the observations, questionnaires and interviews were discussed. This allowed the teams to analyse how child health care surveillance could be improved and what kind of changes should be made.

(Continued)

The results did not reveal a statistically significant difference between the two groups of practices in terms of parent satisfaction or return rate of child health surveillance reviews. But the teams involved in the action research project did decide to make changes in aspects of their professional practice. Communication and the use of child health records improved, and health visitors reported a greater feeling of empowerment. A framework for child health surveillance was developed that was acceptable to the practice teams.

Source: Adapted from Hampshire, 2000

Activity 15.4

Given the research aim in Case Study 15.1, to what extent do you think that action research was the appropriate research methodology?

Suggested answers are provided at the end of the chapter.

VALIDATING ACTION RESEARCH

Given that action research can involve the quite personal observations and analysis of the researcher, using small samples or individual case studies, the issue of validation is certainly no less important for this than for other research methodologies. According to McNiff et al. (1996), the purpose of validation in action research is to:

- Test out key arguments with a critical audience to identify where there is a lack of clarity or focus.
- Sharpen claims to new knowledge and ensure that the data match these claims.
- Develop new ideas.

The starting place for establishing claims for the validity of action research is with the researcher. McNiff (1988) suggests that the researcher needs to demonstrate publicly that he or she has followed a system of disciplined inquiry. This includes checking that any judgements made about the data are reasonably fair and accurate.

Validation can be quite an informal process, but may also involve the use of formal groups, especially selected to scrutinize the outcomes of an action research project. These could include critical colleagues, advisers or mentors, or fellow action research colleagues working on the project. If formal groups are used, it is important to ensure that participants both understand and can empathize with the context of the research. Ideally, the group should also contain members from outside the context who can provide a more detached and independent perspective.

Waterman (1998) argues that the process of validation in action research is strengthened by the 'to-ing and fro-ing' between the elements in the action research spiral (planning, acting, observing and reflection). Typically, action researchers are not satisfied with one turn of the action research spiral but will repeat the process several times, allowing for the refinement of ideas and practices.

Of course, as we saw in Chapter 14, not all of those involved in action research would agree that validity is a necessary or feasible objective. Lincoln and Guba (1985), you may recall, argue that instead of validity, the aim, certainly of qualitative research, should be to establish the credibility of the research through forging confidence in the accuracy of its interpretations. As Grønhaug and Olson (1999) note, if the validity of research is founded on a notion of scientific knowledge, based upon rigorous testing of falsification, then action research may prove lacking. However, claims for the generalizability of findings may be made on the basis of systematic comparison of such findings with the results from other settings, and by conducting more research to examine the robustness of the generalizations. In a sense, this is not too dissimilar to Flick's (1998) notion of case study replication (see Chapter 6).

ETHICS

The issue of ethics has been raised in nearly every chapter of this book, and this last chapter is no exception. Action research is deeply embedded in an existing social organization, and failure to respect the general procedures of that organization will jeopardize the process of improvement. Badger (2000) suggests that, at least superficially, action research seems to pose few ethical dilemmas because it is based on a philosophy of collaboration for the mutual benefit of researchers and participants. Lathlean (1996, cited in Badger, 2000) contrasts action research with the 'smash and grab' approach of both positivist and interpretative traditions, who complete their study and leave their subjects to 'clear up the mess'. Taking note of ethical principles for action research, however, still involves the usual array of requirements for negotiated access, confidentiality and allowing participants the right to withdraw.

Negotiating access

Access needs to be negotiated at various levels: within organizations or communities, with individuals and with parents, guardians or supervisors.

Organizations and communities

You will probably first need to negotiate access to organizations or communities or to management in your own organization. After establishing contact, you will need to define your aims and objectives and get their agreement, in writing, to your research project. Be honest about what you are about to do, and if your objectives change, notify the sponsors immediately. Also note the warning of

Coghlan and Brannick (2001) that doing action research in your own organization is a political act which might even be construed by some as subversive.

Participants

Make it clear that they are not 'subjects' but participants and co-researchers. You are studying yourself in relation to them or their relationship to others. Either way, they are central to your research. However, while most commentators on action research tend to emphasize the democratic and inclusive nature of the action research process, Avison et al. (2001) argue that either practitioners or researchers have the upper hand in most aspects of control and authority. Their relationship, then, is not balanced in a democratic sense, so opening up the potential for the abuse of power, influence and authority.

Parents, guardians or supervisors

Particularly if you are dealing with parents or guardians you need to inform them in writing of your intentions and to elicit their agreement, also in writing. You need to ensure that your research does not infringe any equal opportunities or human rights legislation.

Activity 15.5

Take a look at the UN Convention of the Rights of the Child at:
   http://www.unicef.org/crc/crc.htm
Look particularly at issues of non-discrimination (Article 2), best interests of the child (Article 3), freedom of expression (Article 13), disabled children (Article 23), education (Articles 28 and 29).

Maintaining an ethical stance

Promise of confidentiality   You need to make it clear that you will not reveal any information that is confidential or sensitive in nature, unless prior permission is obtained. If organizations and individuals are content to allow you to use the names of participants then you can do this, but otherwise use numbers or initials for identification. You also need to protect the confidentiality of your data, by getting other participants to check both the data and your interpretation of them for accuracy and balance. In some work situations, however, merely describe someone's role in an organization might immediately identify an individual. You need to negotiate or warn these individuals before publishing any report.

The right to withdraw   Research participants must know that they can withdraw from the research at any time, and this right to withdraw must be respected. Lathlean (1996, cited in Badger, 2000), however, notes that action research might involve the use of observation of group activity from which individuals could not withdraw, especially when the activity is related to collective working practices.

Communication Keep participants informed about the objectives of the project and how it is progressing. One idea is to produce project reports, but limit the distribution of these only to the relevant interested parties. Communication should be used as a means of eliciting and encouraging suggestions and participation.

Maintaining good faith Never take anything for granted and try to anticipate areas where possible misunderstandings could arise. Check with people to see if their interpretations are the same as yours. Indeed, Mumford (2001) suggests that participants should be actively involved in writing up any final report or recommendations. Participants should also be consulted as to how descriptions of the action research project are to be published (Coghlan and Brannick, 2001).

By following these criteria it should be possible to ensure that the outcomes are objective and truthful in the sense that the understanding of meaning is directed towards the achievement of a possible consensus amongst actors (Winter, 1996). However, as Tickle (2001) points out, action researchers often face a practical dilemma between keeping all participants informed of what is happening and maintaining confidentiality.

Activity 15.6

Taking note of the ethical issues outlined above, return to your plan for your action research project and include a set of ethical principles that you will need to address. In doing this, consider any documentation in the organization that deals with these issues and make yourself aware of any processes (such as gaining permission for conducting the research from senior managers or committees). Make a note of any ethical problems you potentially face in your research diary, and maintain a reflective record of how you deal with them.

LIMITATIONS OF ACTION RESEARCH

While we have identified the effectiveness of the action research approach in particular settings, like any research paradigm, it has its potential drawbacks and limitations. Hampshire (2000) reports on action research projects in the field of primary health care, where significant amounts of time and effort have to be expended on maintaining collaborative networks. Since action research studies, typically, take longer to complete than other approaches, staff turnover and people leaving the project can be disruptive. Also, while new knowledge generated through studies may lead to practical results, these may not be widely reported in the academic literature – hence, they do not reach the public domain, and their application to other situations may be limited. Another problem is that of generalizability. Many action research projects are fairly unique or idiosyncratic in nature. Badger also warns that due to its very contextual focus, action research may only be capable of allowing 'tentative generalization' (2000: 202). On the whole, action researchers seem fairly divided as to whether generalization of the results of an action research project is either feasible or, indeed, worthwhile.

An honest evaluation of an actual action research project is presented by Waterson (2000) in the next, and last, Case Study.

Case Study 15.2 The real world – when an action research project goes wrong

In the mid–1990s in the UK, the role of social services departments was changed from being an assessor and provider of social care, to an assessor only, with care being purchased from public and private sector sources, depending on which was most appropriate. This new policy generated new forms of work responsibility and management priorities. Waterson (2000) reports on three phases of an action research project within one social service region that explored issues of organizational progress in making these changes, problems that required solving and strategic questions that had emerged.

Despite the commitment of the researcher and the care with which the research was planned and undertaken, major problems ensued. During the latter phases of the project, the preliminary findings were forcefully challenged by the main management client. Interestingly, he objected to the qualitative nature of the research reports and appeared to want a more positivistic, deductive perspective, including the use of statistics. New statements had to be inserted into the report at the insistence of senior managers. The final circulation of the report was restricted to a small number of senior managers, not to all the many staff involved in providing information, as had been agreed at the outset. Partly as a result of these difficulties, the impact of the project was minimal.

Why did this disappointing outcome occur? Waterson is instructive in pointing to some of the causes. She argues that one problem was the multiple agendas of those involved in the project. The task of the researcher is to create knowledge that is reliable and trustworthy. The ground-level social workers, however, were primarily preoccupied with the immediate needs of their clients. Senior managers faced the challenges of implementing a radical government policy. These multiple agendas eventually led to conflicts that the action research reports emerging from the project simply could not hide. As Waterson succinctly comments, there is an underlying assumption in action research that researchers are powerful change agents when, in fact, it is senior managers who have the power to block change. She therefore recommends that action researchers:

- Use an independent mentor to provide support and advice.
- Bring in co-workers (researchers).
- Engage more proactively in contact with senior managers.
- Establish a steering group with the involvement of an external researcher.
- Make explicit at the outset the sort of action research model that is being used.
- Discuss strategies for making sure that the validity of all participants' contributions is recognized and that ways of handling conflict are planned.
- Emphasize that research findings on their own cannot achieve change.

Activity 15.7

Evaluate the recommendations at the end of Case Study 15.2. Do you agree with them? Are they all practical? Are there any other recommendations that you would make to strengthen the potential success of an action research project?

SUMMARY

- Action research is used to address real world problems, with the researcher becoming actively involved in the research process as a change agent.
- Often, action researchers are professional practitioners who use action research methodology as a means of researching into and changing their own professional practice.
- Action research involves a cyclical process of planning, acting, observing and reflecting.
- Methods of data collection include: diaries and logs, documents, observations, questionnaires, interviews, memory work (writing stories about events) and the analysis of photographs, audio and video recordings.
- The data gathered through action research can be validated through eliciting the views of critical colleagues, advisers or mentors or fellow action researchers.
- Action research must avoid the 'smash and grab' mentality. The usual ethical principles must be adhered to, including negotiating access, promises of confidentiality, guaranteeing the right of participants to withdraw and checking to see if participants agree with the interpretations emerging from the research.
- One of the drawbacks of action research is that it often takes considerable resources, including time, to complete. Also many action research projects tend to be fairly unique and difficult to generalize. However, claims for generalizability may be strengthened by the replication of findings across a number of contexts.

SUMMARY OF WEB LINKS

http://www.goshen.edu/soan/soan96p.htm
http://www.unicef.org/crc/crc.htm

Further reading

Coghlan, D. and Brannick, T. (2001) *Doing Action Research in Your Own Organization.* London: Sage. An accessible book that deals both with the principles and processes of action research, and the challenges of conducting an internal action research project.

Reason, P. and Bradbury, H. (eds) (2001) *Handbook of Action Research: Participative Inquiry and Practice.* London: Sage. Aptly called a handbook since this very comprehensive volume contains chapters on the many approaches to action research as well as a wide range of case studies

Stringer, E.T. (1999) *Action Research,* 2nd edn. Thousand Oaks, CA: Sage. A comprehensive and practical guide for those intending to conduct an action research project.

Whyte, W.F. (ed.) (1991) *Participatory Action Research.* Newbury Park, CA: Sage. Describes some of the principles of participatory action research, which are then illustrated through a series of case studies.

Suggested answers for Activity 15.1

Action research asks 'What is happening here?' and is a process that seeks to improve the professional practice of the action researcher and those colleagues who take part in the project. Since the focus is often highly localized and contextual, it does not usually make strong claims for generalizability and, hence, would rarely claim to be able to change practices across a profession.

Suggested answers for Activity 15.4

Since the focus of the project is on improvement and change within a professional context, action research would appear to be an ideal methodology. This methodology encourages the active engagement of a range of participants who, through the action research process, come to value their contribution and to 'own' the changes that are made.

Glossary of Terms

Accretion measure	A type of unobtrusive measure that arises from the deposit of material (e.g. graffiti or litter) that can be analysed as having a significance.
Action research	Research that involves close collaboration between researchers and practitioners, and which usually aims to achieve measurable, practical benefits for the company, organization or community.
Analysis of variance (ANOVA)	A statistical test used to determine whether there are differences between two or amongst three or more groups on one or more variables. ANOVA is determined using the F-test.
Analytic survey	A survey design that uses a quasi-experimental approach that attempts to measure the impact of independent variables on dependent variables, while controlling for extraneous variables.
Anonymity	An assurance that data will not be traceable to participants in a research project.
A posteriori	The outcome of, and dependent on, observation or direct experience.
A priori	A term indicating an idea derived from theory rather than practice.
Areas of acceptance or rejection	For a one-tailed hypothesis test, the area of rejection is either the upper or lower tail of the distribution. For a two-tailed test both tails are used.
Association	The tendency of two events to occur together. When applied to variables it is more usual to refer to this as a correlation.
Attrition	The reduction in the number of people involved in a study. If more participants withdraw from one group than another, this can threaten the internal validity of a study.
Audit trail	The presentation of material gathered within a naturalistic enquiry that allows other researchers to trace the original researcher's analysis and conclusions.

Behaviour sampling	An observational sampling method in which subjects are observed and occurrences of particular types of behaviour are recorded.
Bias	In general, any influence that distorts the results of a study. In statistics, a case of systematic error in a statistical result.
Case	The smallest unit of analysis; an element of a sample or population.
Case study	A research design focusing on one person or sample. Case studies provide limited information on a single issue, person or organization. There are dangers in generalizing from such limited samples, but results may be indicative of trends.
Categorical data	Data that include both nominal and ordinal data.
Cell	Area containing values in a table of data.
Census	The measurement of a complete population rather than a sample – particularly useful when researching organizations.
Central tendency	A measure of the typicality or centrality of a set of scores, the main measures of which are the mean, median and mode.
chi-square distribution	Statistical test used with nominal data to determine if patterns or characteristics are common across populations.
chi-square test	How well observed data fit an expected or theoretical distribution.
Closed question	A question where the possible answers are predetermined.
Cluster sampling	A sampling strategy involving successive sampling of units or clusters, progressing from larger units to smaller ones.
Coding	The process of transforming raw data into a standardized format for data analysis. In qualitative research this means attaching numerical values to categories; in qualitative research it means identifying recurrent words, concepts or themes.
Coding frame	A template of key coding instructions for each variable in a study (e.g. Agree = 1).
Concept mapping	Producing a diagram showing the relationship between concepts in order to understand them.
Concurrent validity	The extent to which test scores represent an individual's current ability. For example, are the results of a recent aptitude test similar to the individual's current work performance?
Confidence interval	This identifies a range of values that includes the true population value of a particular characteristic at a specified probability level (usually 95 per cent).

Confounding variable	A variable, other than the variable(s) under investigation, which may distort the results of experimental research, and so has to be controlled for.
Construct	The particular way in which an individual expresses meaning about a concept.
Construct validity	The extent to which an instrument measures a theoretical concept (construct) under investigation.
Content analysis	The examination of qualitative data by either qualitative or quantitative methods by systematically identifying special characteristics (classes or categories).
Content validity	An estimate of the extent to which a research tool takes items from the subject domain being addressed, including not only cognitive topics but also behaviours.
Contingency table	A display of frequencies for two or more variables.
Control group	As part of an experimental design, a group *not* given the intervention so that the effects of the intervention on the experimental group can be compared with it.
Controlled variable	A variable, the effect of which has to be eliminated, in researching the relationship between dependent and independent variables.
Convenience sampling	A non-probability sampling strategy that uses the most conveniently accessible people to participate in the study.
Conversational analysis	The formal analysis of everyday conversations, often based upon transcribed tape recordings.
Core category	The central category that is used in grounded theory to integrate all the categories identified.
Correlation	The extent of an association between and among inter-dependent variables such that when one variable changes, so does the other. Variables that are independent are not correlated.
Correlation coefficient (*r*)	A measure of the linear relationship between two numerical values made on the same set of variables. It ranges from −1 (a perfectly negative relationship) to +1 (a perfectly positive relationship), with 0 meaning no relationship. Linear relationships can be measured by Pearson's product moment correlation; changes in one variable causing changes in another in a fixed direction can be measured by Kendall's coefficient of rank correlation or Spearman's rank correlation coefficient.
Covert participant	Someone who participates in the activities of a research study without revealing his or her identity as a researcher.

Credibility	Seen by some supporters of qualitative approaches as more important than validity or reliability. Established through building confidence in the accuracy of data gathering and interpretation.
Criterion-related validity	Assessed through comparing the scores on an instrument with one or more external criteria such as a well-established existing test.
Critical value (of a distribution)	The absolute value that a test statistic must exceed if the null hypothesis is to be rejected.
Cross sectional	A study in which data are collected at one time only, usually for a large number of cases.
Data	Findings and results which, if meaningful, become information.
Data saturation	The point at which data collection can cease, because data have become repetitive with the emergence of no new themes or ideas.
Deductive approach	Experimental approach that uses a priori questions or hypotheses that the research will test.
Degrees of freedom	The number of components in results that are free to vary. Measured by the number of categories minus 1.
Dependent t-test (also referred to as a paired t-test or a one-sample t-test)	Compares the difference or changes in ratio or interval variables that is observed for two paired or matched groups. It can also be used for before and after measures on the same group.
Dependent variable	A variable that forms the focus of research, and depends on another (the independent or explanatory variable).
Descriptive statistics	Statistical methods used to describe data collected from a specific sample (e.g. mean, mode, median, range, standard deviation).
Design	An approach to the collection of data that combines a validity of results with an economy of effort. Includes decisions on the case site, sample, data collection and analysis.
Deviation	The difference between the value of a variable and the mean of its distribution.
Dichotomous variable	Nominal variables that have only two outcomes such as Yes/No, True/False, etc.
Discourse analysis	The study of how both spoken and written language is used in social contexts.
Distribution	Values (e.g. age in years, scores on an aptitude test, length of service in an organization) of a variable or characteristic (e.g. knowledge, behaviour, age, income or attitude) and the frequency of occurrence.

Emic view	A term used by ethnographers to refer to an insider's view of his or her own world (see etic).
Empirical data	The results of experiments or observations used to check the validity of assertions.
Empiricism	The idea that valid knowledge can only be derived from what is observable, measurable or experienced.
Episodic records	Archival records that are insufficiently complete to allow for the identification of trends.
Epistemology	A branch of philosophy that considers the criteria for determining what constitutes and what does not constitute valid knowledge.
Ethics	The study of standards of conduct and values, and in research, how these impact on both the researcher and research subjects.
Ethnography	A qualitative approach that seeks out the perspectives about the culture of individuals, groups or systems occurring in settings or 'fields'. Originally associated with anthropology and sociology.
Ethnomethodology	A research tradition that argues that people continually redefine themselves through their interactions with others.
Etic view	A term used by ethnographers to describe an outsider's view of a specific cultural group (see emic).
Evaluation	The systematic collection of data about the characteristics of a programme, product, policy or service. Often performed to identify opportunities for change and improvement.
Expected frequencies	Frequencies that are observed in a contingency table if the null hypothesis is true.
Expected value	The mean of a sample distribution of a test statistic.
Experimental group	In experimental research, the group of subjects who receive the experimental treatment, in contrast to the control group who do not.
Experimental research	A research methodology based upon cause-and-effect relationships between independent and dependent variables by means of the manipulation of independent variables, control and randomization.
Ex post facto	Research that is completed after changes have already occurred in the independent variables and without random assignment of the objects in the study.
External validity	The extent to which research results can be generalized to the population as a whole.
Extraneous variable	A variable that needs to be controlled for because it has the potential to adversely affect the results of a study.

Face validity	The extent to which a measuring instrument appears to be measuring what it claims to measure.
Field notes	Notes written when conducting interviews or observations in the field. They may include the researcher's personal comments or interpretations.
Fieldwork	The gathering of data at a research site.
Filter question	A question designed to exclude some respondents or direct them to later questions in a questionnaire.
Fisher's exact test	Used to test the null hypothesis that nominal characteristics are not associated. Usually used when the sample size is too small for the chi-square test.
Focal sampling	An observational sampling method in which a sampling unit (person, group, etc.) is observed for a specific time period and all measures of behaviour are recorded.
Focus group	A group interview, usually framed around one issue.
Frame	A repository of items from which a sample can be chosen (e.g. an organization's internal telephone directory or an electoral register).
Frequency	The number of items in a class or category.
Frequency count	Calculation of frequencies to determine how many items fit into a category (e.g. number of sales per product, members of a team, men and women in the workforce).
F-value	A statistic produced by performing an analysis of variance, indicating whether differences in means occurred by chance.
Gatekeepers	Individuals who have the power or influence to grant or refuse access to a field or research setting.
Generalizability	The extent to which the results of a study based upon evidence drawn from a sample can be applied to a population as a whole. Often referred to as external validity.
Goodness-of-fit	How well a given set of data fit a distribution. It may be measured by the chi-square statistic.
Grounded theory	An inductive approach to the analysis of qualitative data involving open, axial and selective coding.
Grouped data	Data that have been collected into groups or classes for ease of reading or for assisting calculations.
Hermeneutics	An approach based on the interpretation of literary texts and human behaviour.
Hypothesis	A statement that should be capable of measurement about the relation between two or more variables. Testing hypotheses, and especially the null hypothesis, is part of inferential statistics.

Hypothetico-deductive method	Procedures through which a hypothesis is deduced from a theory and expressed in terms of a relationship between two or more variables. Measurements are then made from which the hypothesis is either accepted or rejected.
Ideographic	An approach that emphasizes that explanation of human behaviour is only possible through gaining access to participants' subjective interpretations or culture.
Independent variable	Used to explain or predict a result or outcome on the dependent variable.
Induction	The development of theory or inferences from observed or empirical reality. It is associated with naturalism and the 'grounded theory' approach to theory formation. It is the opposite of deduction.
Inductive approach	The establishment of facts on which theories or concepts are later built, moving from specifics to generalizations.
Inference	An assertion made on the basis of something else observed.
Inferential statistics	Used to draw inferences from a sample being studied to a larger population that the sample is drawn from.
Information	Data expressed in a way that has meaning.
Informed consent	The obtaining of voluntary participation in a research project based on a full understanding of the likely benefits and risks.
Instrument	A tool such as a questionnaire, survey or observation schedule used to gather data as part of a research project.
Internal validity	The extent to which changes in the dependent variable can be attributed to the independent variable, rather than to an extraneous variable.
Inter-observer reliability	The extent to which two or more observers agree on what they have seen.
Interval scale	A quantifiable, continuous scale that has an arbitrary zero point (for example, the Fahrenheit and Celsius temperature scales). Unlike ratio scales (where a score of 120 represents a figure twice as large as a score of 60), an IQ score of 120 (interval data) is not twice as large as one of 60.
Leading question	A question that suggests a possible answer, and hence promotes bias.
Likert scale	A scale in which items represent different sub-concepts of the measured object and responses are presented to indicate different degrees of agreement or disagreement with the item.
Literature review	The selection of documents (published and unpublished) on a topic, that contain information, ideas and evidence,

	and the evaluation of these documents in relation to a particular piece of research.
Longitudinal study	A research study that examines phenomena over a relatively long period of time.
Manipulation	Intentionally changing the value of an independent variable.
Mann Whitney U-test	See Wilcoxon rank-sum test.
Maturation	A threat to internal validity caused by changes in the value of the dependent variable that occurs without any intervention by the researcher.
Mean	The arithmetic average of observations. A measure of central tendency for interval or ratio data.
Measures of central tendency	Used in descriptive statistics, comprising measures of the mean, median and mode.
Measures of dispersion	Descriptive statistics that describe the spread of numerical data. They include measures of the range, standard deviation and percentiles.
Median	A measure of central tendency where 50 per cent of observations are above it and 50 per cent below.
Meta-analysis	Quantitative techniques for synthesizing the results of a large number of studies of a particular issue or topic.
Method	The systematic approach towards the collection of data so that information can be obtained.
Methodology	The analysis of, and the broad philosophical and theoretical justification for, a particular method used in research, for example, action research.
Mode	A measure of central tendency comprising the value of the observation that occurs most frequently.
Mortality	A threat to the validity of the research caused by subjects prematurely withdrawing from the study.
Narratives	The use of oral or life histories to capture personal lived experiences.
Naturalistic paradigm	A paradigm that assumes that there are multiple interpretations of reality and that the goal of researchers is to work with people to understand how they construct their own reality within a social context.
Nominal scale	Describes characteristics that have no numerical value (e.g. the name of organizations, products, departments, etc). Sometimes referred to as a categorical scale.
Nomothetic	Approaches that seek to construct a deductively tested set of general theories that explain and predict human behaviour. It is the opposite of ideographic.

Non-parametric tests	Tests that do not make any assumption that the population is normally distributed (sometimes called distribution-free tests). These include all tests involving the ranking of data, including Kendall's rank correlation and Spearman's rho.
Non-probability sampling	Techniques used to draw a sample in such a way that the findings will require judgement and interpretation before being applied to a population. Often necessary in practice.
Normal distribution	Based on the assumption that the distribution of a population will be a smooth, bell-shaped curve that is symmetric around the mean and where the mean, median and mode are equal. Symbolized by the Greek letter mu (μ).
Null hypothesis (H_0)	A statement of the relationship between two variables which argues that no difference exists in the means, scores or other numerical values obtained for the two groups. These differences are statistically significant when the null hypothesis is rejected – suggesting that a difference does, in fact, exist.
Observed frequencies	Frequency scores actually obtained through research – in contrast to expected frequencies (see above).
One-sample *t*-test	Also known as a dependent *t*-test or paired *t*-test. Used for comparing a variable across two groups or within one group over time.
One-tailed test	The area of a normal distribution curve showing the region of rejection for the null hypothesis where the direction predicted by the hypothesis is known.
One-way ANOVA	Used to test for differences for studies with one dependent variable with ratio or interval data. This test uses the *F*-statistic.
Ontology	The study of the essence of phenomena and the nature of their existence.
Open question	A question without fixed categories of answers.
Operational definition	A concise statement that assigns meaning to a construct or variable by specifying the activities necessary to measure it.
Ordinal scale	An ordering or ranking of values with no implication that the differences between the values are equal. Examples include: Strongly agree, Agree, Disagree and Strongly disagree; Frequently, Often, Sometimes, Never.
Paired sample	Two samples in which each member is paired with a member in the other sample (e.g. comparing the output of two groups of assembly-line workers). The paired *t*-test is used to measure whether any differences on the random variable (e.g. output) are significant.

Paradigm	A perspective or worldview based upon sets of values and philosophical assumptions, from which distinctive conceptualizations and explanations of phenomena are proposed.
Parameter	The population value of a distribution such as the mean.
Parametric test	Tests that assume that the data for a population are normally distributed. Examples include t-tests and the F-test. To be used for interval and ratio numerical data, but not ordinal data.
Participant observation	Qualitative research, when a researcher both collects data and becomes involved in the site of the study.
Participatory action research	A research tradition in which people themselves act as participants to investigate their own reality.
Pearson product moment	A statistical formula for calculating the correlation coefficient between two variables. Assumes that both variables are interval and that the relationship between them is linear.
Percentile	A number that indicates the percentage of a distribution that is above or below that number. A statement that a person scored on the 75th percentile indicates that 75 per cent of the others scored the same or below this.
Phenomenology	The search for how participants experience and give meaning to an event, concept or phenomenon.
Pilot survey	A small-scale survey carried out before a large-scale one to evaluate processes and research tools such as questionnaires.
Plausibility	An assessment of whether any truth claim is likely to be true, given the present state of knowledge. Associated with postmodern critiques.
Population	The totality of people, organizations, objects or occurrences from which a sample is drawn.
Positivism	A philosophical assumption that the purpose of theory is application and that the truth can be distinguished from untruth, and that the truth can be determined by either deduction or by empirical support.
Postal survey	A survey in which survey instruments such as questionnaires are distributed by post.
Postmodernism	A set of theories that argue that objective truth is unobtainable. All we have is 'truth claims' that are partial, partisan and incomplete.
Post-positivism	Sometimes referred to as anti-positivism, a research tradition that rejects the belief that human behaviour can be investigated through the use of the methods of scientific inquiry.

Post-test	A test that occurs after a treatment has been administered in an experimental study.
Predictive validity	The extent to which scores on an instrument can predict a subject's future behaviour in relation to the test's content (e.g. do scores on an engineering aptitude test predict the ability to perform engineering tasks?)
Pre-test	A test that occurs before a treatment has been administered in an experimental study.
Probability sampling	Techniques used to ensure that a sample is representative of the population, so that findings can be generalized to that population.
Probe	An interviewing technique in which the interviewer seeks clarification and elaboration of a respondent's answers.
Proposition	A formal statement that relates two or more concepts.
Purposive sampling	A non-probability sampling strategy in which participants are selected on the basis that they are considered to be typical of a wider population.
p-value	The probability of obtaining the results of a statistical test by chance. It is calculated after the statistical test. If less than the alpha value (α) which is set before the test, then the null hypothesis is rejected.
Qualitative methods	Techniques by which qualitative data are collected and analysed.
Quantitative methods	The systematic and mathematical techniques used to collect and analyse quantitative data.
Quasi-experimental design	Approach using elements of experimental design such as the use of a control group, but without the ability to randomly select the sample.
Quota sampling	A non-probability sampling strategy in which various strata are identified by the researcher who ensures that these strata are proportionately represented within the sample to improve its representativeness.
Random sampling	The method of drawing a proportion of a population such that all *possible* samples have the same probability of being selected.
Range	The difference between the largest observation and the smallest in a sample of a set of variables.
Rank	The position of a member of a set in an order.
Ratio scales	A measurement in which equal differences between points correspond to equal differences on the scale. Used for characteristics where there is an absolute zero point that does have some meaning, that is, an absence

of the construct being measured (in contrast to interval scales where the zero is arbitrary) – for example, zero length on a ruler.

Reactivity	The potential for the behaviour of research subjects to change due to the presence of the researcher.
Realism	A research philosophy that presumes that a knowable, objective reality exists.
Reflexivity	The monitoring by a researcher of her or his impact on the research situation being investigated. A stance associated with postmodernism and anti-realism.
Reliability	The degree to which an instrument will produce similar results at a different period.
Representative sample	A sample in which individuals are included in proportion to the number of those in the population who are like them.
Research design	A strategic plan for a research project, setting out the broad structures and features of the research.
Research methodology	Approaches to systematic inquiry developed within a particular paradigm with associated epistemological assumptions (e.g. experimental research, survey research, grounded theory, action research).
Research question	A specific formulation of the issues that a research project will address, often describing general relationships between and among variables that are to be tested.
Sample	A set of objects, occurrences or individuals selected from a parent population for a research study.
Sampling bias	Distortion occurring when a sample is not representative of the population from which it has been drawn.
Sampling error	The fluctuations in the value of a statistic from different samples drawn from the same population.
Sampling frame	A complete list of the people or entities in the entire population to be addressed by a research study, from which a random sample will be drawn.
Secondary analysis	A reworking of data that have already been analysed to present interpretations, conclusions or knowledge additional to, or different from, those originally presented.
Significance level	The probability of rejecting a true null hypothesis. This should be chosen before a test is performed and is called the alpha value (α). Alpha values are usually kept small (0.05, 0.01 or 0.001), because it is important not to reject the null hypothesis when it is true (a Type I error), that is, there is no difference between the means of the groups being measured.
Skewed distribution	An asymmetrical distribution, positively skewed meaning the larger frequencies being concentrated towards the

lower end of the variable, and negatively skewed, towards the higher end.

Snowball sampling
A non-probability sampling strategy through which the first group of participants is used to nominate the next cohort of participants.

Spearman's rank-order correlation (Spearman's rho)
Used to describe the relationship between two ordinal characteristics or one ordinal and one ratio/interval characteristic. Represented by the symbol r_s.

Standard deviation
A measure of the spread of data about the mean (average), symbolized by the Greek letter sigma (σ), or the square root of the variance.

Statistical inference
A procedure using the laws of probability to generalize the findings from a sample to an entire population from which the sample was drawn.

Statistical significance
See Significance level.

Stratified sampling
Drawing a sample from a specified strataum – for example, from a company's rural, out-of-town and town centre stores.

Subjects
A term most frequently used in positivist research to describe those who participate in a research study.

Survey
An investigation into one or more variables in a population that may involve the collection of both qualitative and quantitative data.

Symbolic interactionism
A school of sociology in which people are seen as developing a sense of identity through their interactions and communication with others.

Theoretical sampling
The selection of participants within a naturalistic inquiry, based on emerging findings during the progress of the study to ensure that key variables are adequately represented.

Theoretical sensitivity
Often used in grounded theory, involves maintaining an awareness of the subtleties of meaning in data.

Thick description
A detailed account of life 'inside' a field of study. Associated with humanistic ethnography but rejected by postmodern ethnography as just selective or partial descriptions.

Time sampling
An observational method in which data are collected at periodic intervals.

Time series
A set of measures on a single variable collected over time.

Traces
An unobtrusive measure in which physical evidence is collected to provide evidence about social behaviour.

Triangulation
The use of a variety of methods or data sources to examine a specific phenomenon either simultaneously or sequentially in order to improve the reliability of data.

t- test	A test used on the means of small samples to measure whether the samples have both been drawn from the same parent population.
Two-tailed test	The two areas of a normal distribution curve showing the regions of rejection for the null hypothesis where the direction predicted by the hypothesis is not known (hence the need for two tails).
Type I error	An error that occurs when the null hypothesis is rejected when it is true and a researcher concludes that a statistically significant relationship exists when it does not.
Type II error	An error that occurs when the null hypothesis is accepted when it is false and a researcher concludes that no significant relationship exists when it does.
Unit of analysis	The set of objects (individuals, organizations or events) on which the research is focused.
Unobtrusive measures	A non-reactive method of data collection using sources such as archives, documents or the Web.
Validity	The degree to which data in a research study are accurate and credible.
Variable	A characteristic that is measurable, such as income, attitude, colour etc.
Variance	The differences measured in repeated trials of a procedure. The standard deviation squared – a measure of dispersion.
Verification	Drawing the implications from a set of empirical conclusions to theory.
Vignette	A data collection technique involving the posing of a hypothetical or real scenario to a respondent for their comments.
Wilcoxon rank–sum test	A non-parametric test for comparing ordinal data from two dependent samples or interval/ratio data that is not normally distributed.
Wilcoxon test	A non-parametric test for a difference between two samples where the samples are non-normally distributed and the measurement scale on the dependent variable is ordinal.

References

Alford, R.R. (1998) *The Craft of Inquiry: Theory, Methods, Evidence.* New York: Oxford University Press.

American Psychological Association (1992) *American Psychological Association Ethical Principles of Psychologists and Code of Conduct.* Retrieved 23 November 2001 from http://www.apa.org/ethics/code.html#materials.

Arksey, H. and Knight, P. (1999) *Interviewing for Social Scientists.* London: Sage.

Atkinson, P. and Coffey, A. (1997) 'Analysing documentary realities', in D. Silverman (ed.), *Qualitative Research: Theory, Methods and Practice.* London: Sage.

Avison, D., Baskerville, R. and Myers, M. (2001) 'Controlling action research projects', *Information Technology and People*, 14(1): 28–45.

Badger, T.G. (2000) 'Action research, change and methodological rigour', *Journal of Nursing Management*, 8: 201–207.

Bailey, C.A. (1996) *A Guide to Field Research.* Thousand Oaks, CA: Pine Forge Press.

Bales, R.F. (1950) *Interaction Process Analysis: A Method for the Study of Small Groups.* London: University of Chicago Press.

Ballantine, J., Levy, M., Martin, A., Munro, I. and Powell, P. (2000) 'An ethical perspective on information systems evaluation', *International Journal of Agile Management Systems*, 2/3: 233–41.

Beed, T.W. and Stimson, R.J. (1985) (eds) *Survey Interviewing: Theory and Techniques.* North Sydney: George Allen & Unwin.

Begley, C.M. (1996) 'Using triangulation in nursing research', *Journal of Advanced Nursing*, 24: 122–8.

Berg, B.L. (1995) *Qualitative Research Methods for the Social Sciences*, 2nd edn. Needham Heights, MA: Allyn & Bacon.

Berry, R. (1994) *The Research Project: How To Write It*, 3rd edn. London: Routledge.

Black, T.R. (1993) *Evaluating Social Science Research.* London: Sage.

Black, T.R. (1999) *Doing Quantitative Research.* London: Sage.

Boote, J. and Mathews, A. (1999) '"Saying is one thing: doing is another": the role of observation in marketing research', *Qualitative Market Research: An International Journal*, 2(1): 15–21.

Booth, P.F. (1991) *Report Writing*, 2nd edn. Huntingdon: Elm Publications.

Bramley, P. and Kitson, B. (1994) 'Evaluating training against business criteria', *Journal of European Industrial Training*, 18 (1): 10–14.

Brewer, J.D. (2000) *Ethnography.* Buckingham, Philadelphia: Open University Press.

Bryman, A. (1988) *Quantity and Quality in Social Research.* London: Routledge.

Burgess, R.G. (1984) *In the Field: An Introduction to Field Research.* London: Routledge.

Campbell, C.P. (1997) 'Training course/program evaluation: principles and practice', *Journal of European Industrial Training*, 22(8): 323–44.

Campbell, D.T. and Stanley, J.C. (1963) *Experimental and Quasi-experimental Designs for Research*. Chicago, IL: Rand McNally.

Cannell, C.F. (1985) 'Overview: response bias and interviewer variability in surveys', in T.W. Beed and R.J. Stimson (eds), *Survey Interviewing: Theory and Techniques*. North Sydney: George Allen & Unwin.

Carrigan, M. and Kirkup, M. (2001) 'The ethical responsibility of marketers in retail observational research: protecting stakeholders through the ethical "research covenant"', *International Review of Retail, Distribution and Consumer Research*, 11(4): 415–35.

Carroll, S. (1994) 'Questionnaire design affects response rate', *Marketing News*, 28(12): 25–7.

Charmaz, K. (1995) 'Grounded theory', in J.A. Smith, R. Harré and L.V. Langenhove (eds), *Rethinking Methods in Psychology*. London: Sage.

Chia, R. (2002) 'The Production of Management Knowledge: Philosophical Underpinnings of Research Design', in D. Partington (ed.), *Essential Skills for Management Research*. London: Sage.

Clarke, A. (1999) *Evaluation Research: An Introduction to Principles, Methods and Practice*. London: Sage.

Coghlan, D. (2001) 'Insider Action Research Projects: Implications for Practising Managers' *Management Learning*, 32(1): 49–60.

Coghlan, D. and Brannick, T. (2001) *Doing Action Research in Your Own Organization*. London: Sage.

Cohen, L. and Manion, L. (1997) *Research Methods in Education*, 4th edn. London: Routledge.

Copas, A.J. and Farewell, V.T. (1998) 'Dealing with non-ignorable non-response by using an "enthusiasm-to-respond" variable', *Journal of the Royal Statistical Society*, 161(3): 385–96.

Cressey, P. (1932) *The Taxi-Dance Hall*. Chicago, IL: University of Chicago Press.

Creswell, J.W. (1994) *Research Design: Qualitative and Quantitative Approaches*. Thousand Oaks, CA: Sage.

Crotty, M. (1998) *The Foundation of Social Research: Meaning and Perspectives in the Research Process*. London: Sage.

Czaja, R. and Blair, J. (1996) *Designing Surveys: A Guide to Decisions and Procedures*. Thousand Oaks, CA: Sage.

Davenport, T.H. and Prusak, L. (2000) *Working Knowledge: How Organizations Manage What They Know*. Boston, MA: Harvard Business School Press.

Davies, D. and Dodd, J. (2002) 'Qualitative research and the question of rigor', *Qualitative Health Research*, 12(2): 279–89.

Davies, S. (2001) 'New Techniqes and Technologies of Surveillance in the Workplace', Computer Security Research Centre, The London School of Economics. Retrieved 17 November from www.msf-itpa.org.uk/juneconf3.shtml.

De Laine, M. (2000) *Fieldwork, Participation and Practice*. London: Sage.

Delanty, G. (1997) *Social Science: Beyond Constructivism and Realism*. Buckingham: Open University Press.

Denzin, N.K. (1978) *The Research Act*. New York: McGraw-Hill.

Denzin, N.K. (1989) *Sociological Methods*. New York: McGraw-Hill.

De Vaus, D.A. (1986) *Surveys in Social Research*. London: George Allen & Unwin.

De Vaus, D.A. (2002) *Surveys in Social Research*, 5th edn. London: George Allen & Unwin.

Dey, I. (1993) *Qualitative Data Analysis*. London: Routledge.

Dey, I. (1999) *Grounding Grounded Theory: Guidelines for Qualitative Inquiry.* London: Academic Press.

Dewey, J. (1933) *How We Think.* London: D.C. Heath & Co.

Diamantopoulos, A. and Schlegelmilch, B.B. (1997) *Taking the Fear out of Data Analysis.* London: Harcourt Brace.

Dickens, L. and Watkins, K. (1999) 'Action Research: Rethinking Lewin', *Management Learning,* 30(2): 127–40.

Diener, E. and Crandall, R. (1978) *Ethics in Social and Behavioural Research.* Chicago, IL: University of Chicago Press.

Dillman, D.A. (2000) *Mail and Internet Surveys: The Tailored Design Method,* 2nd edn. Chichester: John Wiley.

Dochartaigh, N. (ed.) (2002) *The Internet Research Handbook: A Practical Guide for Students and Researchers in the Social Sciences.* London: Sage.

Douglas, J.D. (1976) *Investigative Social Research: Individual and Team Field Research.* Beverly Hills, CA: Sage.

Easterby-Smith, M. (1994) *Evaluations, Management Development, Training and Education.* Aldershot: Gower.

Easterby-Smith, M., Thorpe, R. and Lowe, A. (1991) *Management Research: An Introduction.* London: Sage.

Elger, A. and Smith, C. (1998) 'Exit, voice and "mandate": management strategies and labour practices of Japanese firms in Britain', *British Journal of Industrial Relations,* 36(2): 185–207.

Ellen, R.F (ed.) (1984) *Ethnographic Research: A Guide to General Conduct.* London: Academic Press.

Featherstone, M. (2000) 'Archiving cultures', *British Journal of Sociology,* 51(1): 161–84.

Ferguson, S.D. (2000) *Researching the Public Opinion Environment: Theories and Methods.* Thousand Oaks, CA: Sage.

Fetterman, D.M. (1989) *Ethnography Step by Step.* Newbury Park, CA: Sage.

Fielding, J. and Gilbert, N. (2000) *Understanding Social Statistics.* London: Sage.

Fielding, N. and Lee, R.M. (1998) *Computer Analysis and Qualitative Research.* London: Sage.

Fink, A. (1995a) *How to Sample in Surveys.* Thousand Oaks, CA: Sage.

Fink, A. (1995b) *The Survey Handbook.* Thousand Oaks, CA: Sage.

Fink (1995c) *How to Analyze Survey Data.* Thousand Oaks, CA: Sage.

Flanders, N.A. (1970) *Analyzing Teaching Behaviour.* London: Addison–Wesley.

Flick, U. (1998) *An Introduction to Qualitative Research.* London: Sage.

Foddy, W. (1993) *Constructing Questions for Interviews and Questionnares: Theories and Practice in Social Research.* Cambridge: Cambridge University Press.

Friedman, V.J. (2001) 'Action Science: creating communities of inquiry in communities of practice', in P. Reason and H. Bradbury (eds), *Handbook of Action Research: Participative Inquiry and Practice.* London: Sage.

Gans, H.J. (1999) 'Participant observation in the era of "ethnography", *Journal of Contemporary Ethnography,* 28(5): 540–8.

Gaventa, J. and Cornwall, A. (2001) 'Power and Knowledge', in P. Reason and H. Bradbury (eds), *Handbook of Action Research: Participative Inquiry and Practice.* London: Sage.

Gill, J. and Johnson, P. (1997) *Research Methods for Managers,* 2nd edn. London: Paul Chapman.

Gillham, B. (2000) *Developing a Questionnaire.* London: Continuum.

Glaser, B.G. (1992) *Basics of Grounded Theory Analysis.* Mill Valley, CA: Sociology Press.

Glaser, B.G. and Strauss, A. (1967) *The Discovery of Grounded Theory: Strategies for Qualitative Research.* Chicago, IL: Aldine.

Gomm, R., Hammersley, M. and Foster, P. (2000) 'Case Study and Generalisation', in R. Gomm, M. Hammersley and P. Foster (eds), *Case Study Method: Key Issues, Key Texts.* London: Sage.

Gray, D., Griffin, C. and Nasta, T. (2000) *Training to Teach in Further and Adult Education.* Cheltenham: Stanley Thornes.

Grønhaug, K. and Olson, O. (1999) 'Action research and knowledge creation: merits and challenges', *Qualitative Market Research: An International Journal,* 2(1): 6–14.

Guba, E.G. (1985) 'The content of emergent paradigm research', in Y.S. Lincoln (ed.), *Organizational Theory and Inquiry.* Newbury Park, CA: Sage.

Gummesson, E. (2000) *Qualitative Methods in Management Research.* Thousand Oaks, CA: Sage.

Habermas, J. (1972) *Knowledge and Human Interests.* London: Heinemann.

Hakim, C. (1993) 'Research analysis of administrative records', in M. Hammersley (ed.), *Social Research: Philosophy, Politics and Practice.* London: Sage.

Hakim, C. (2000) *Research Design: Successful Designs for Social and Economic Research,* 2nd edn. London: Routledge.

Hall, T. (2000) 'At home with the young homeless', *International Journal of Social Research Methodology,* 3(2): 121–33.

Hall, W.A. and Callery, P. (2001) 'Enhancing the rigor of grounded theory: incorporating reflexivity and relationality', *Qualitative Health Research,* 11(2): 257–72.

Halpenny, F.G. (1976) 'The thesis and the book', in E. Harman and I. Montagnes (eds), *The Thesis and the Book.* Toronto: University of Toronto Press.

Hammersley, M. (1992) *What's Wrong with Ethnography?* London: Routledge.

Hampshire, A.J. (2000) 'What is action research and can it promote change in primary care?', *Journal of Evaluation in Clinical Practice,* 6(4): 337–43.

Hancock, D.R. and Flowers, C.P. (2001) 'Comparing social desirability responding on World Wide Web and paper-administered surveys', *Educational Technology Research and Development,* 49(1): 5–13.

Hart, C. (1998) *Doing a Literature Review.* London: Sage.

Hart, C. (2001) *Doing a Literature Search.* London: Sage.

Hartley, J. (2001) 'Employee surveys: strategic aid or hand-grenade for organisational and cultural change?', *The International Journal of Public Sector Management,* 14(3): 184–204.

Have, P.T. (1999) *Doing Conversational Analysis: A Practical Guide.* London: Sage.

Hedrick, T.E., Bickman, L. and Rog, D.J. (1993) *Applied Research Design: A Practical Guide.* Newbury Park, CA: Sage.

Heron, J. and Reason, P. (2001) 'The practice of co-operative inquiry: research "with" rather than "on" people', in P. Reason and H. Bradbury (eds), *Handbook of Action Research: Participative Inquiry and Practice.* London: Sage.

Herrera, C.D. (1999) 'Two arguments for "covert methods" in social research', *British Journal of Sociology,* 50(2): 331–43.

Herbert, M. (1990) *Planning a Research Project: A Guide for Practitioners and Trainees in the Helping Professions.* London: Cassell Educational.

Hosker, I. (2002) *Social Statistics: Data Analysis in Social Science Explained.* Taunton: Studymates.

House, E.R. (1980) *Evaluating with Validity.* Beverly Hills, CA: Sage.

Hughes, J. and Sharrock, W. (1997) *The Philosophy of Social Research.* London: Addison Wesley Longman.

Hutchby, I. and Wooffitt, R. (1998) *Conversational Analysis: Principles, Practices and Applications.* Cambridge: Polity Press.

Jankowicz, A.D. (1991) *Business Research Projects for Students.* London: Chapman & Hall.

Jarvis, P. (1995) *Adult and Continuing Education: Theory and Practice.* London: Routledge.

Jobber, D. and O'Reilly, D. (1996) 'Industrial mail surveys: techniques for inducing response', *Marketing and Intelligence*, 14(1): 29–34.

Johnson, P. and Harris, D. (2002) 'Qualitative and quantitative issues in research design', in D. Partington (ed.), *Essential Skills for Management Research.* London: Sage.

Keats, D.M. (2000) *Interviewing: A Practical Guide for Students and Professionals.* Buckingham: Open University Press.

Kelly, G.A. (1955) *The Psychology of Personal Constructs.* New York: Norton.

Kenyon, E. and Hawker, S. (1999) '"Once would be enough": some reflections on the issue of safety for lone researchers', *International Journal of Social Research Methodology*, 2(4): 313–27.

Keppel, G., Saufley, W.H. and Tokunaga, H. (1992) *Introduction to Design and Analysis*, 2nd edn. New York: W.H. Freeman and Company.

Kerlinger, F.N. (1986) *Foundations of Behavioural Research*, 3rd edn. Orlando, FL: Holt, Rinehart and Winston.

Kettner, M. (1993) 'Scientific knowledge, discourse ethics and consensus formation in the public domain', in E. Winkler and J. Coombs (eds) *Applied Ethics.* Oxford: Blackwell.

Kidder, L.H. (1981) 'Qualitative research and quasi-experimental frameworks', in M.B. Brewer and B.E. Collins (eds), *Scientific Inquiry and the Social Sciences.* San Fransisco, CA: Jossey-Bass.

Kirkpatrick, D.L. (1959) 'Techniques for evaluating training programmes', *Journal of the American Society of Training Directors*, 13(3–9): 21–6.

Kirkup, M. and Carrigan, M. (2000) 'Video surveillance research in retailing; ethical issues', *International Joural of Retail and Distribution Management*, 28(11): 470–80.

Korac-Kakabadse, N., Kakabadse, A. and Kouzmin, A. (2002) 'Ethical considerations in management research: a "truth" seeker's guide', in D. Partington (ed.), *Essential Skills for Management Research.* London: Sage.

Kuhn, T.S. (1970) *The Structure of Scientific Revolutions*, 2nd edn. Chicago, IL: University of Chicago Press.

Lee, R.M. (2000) *Unobtrusive Measures in Social Research.* Buckingham: Open University Press.

Lewin, K. (1946) 'Action research and minority problems', *Journal of Social Issues*, 2(4): 34–6.

Lieberson, S. (2000) 'Small N's and big conclusions: an examination of the reasoning in comparative studies based on a small number of cases', in R. Gomm, M. Hammersley, and P. Foster (eds), *Case Study Method: Key Issues, Key Texts.* London: Sage.

Lincoln, Y.S. (1985) 'The substance of the emergent paradigms: implications for researchers', in Y.S. Lincoln (ed.), *Organizational Theory and Inquiry.* Newbury Park, CA: Sage.

Lincoln, Y.S. (2001) 'Engaging sympathies: relationships between action research and social constructivism', in P. Reason and H. Bradbury (eds), *Handbook of Action Research: Participative Inquiry and Practice.* London: Sage.

Lincoln, Y.S. and Guba, E.G. (1985) *Naturalistic Inquiry.* Newbury Park, CA: Sage.

Lincoln, Y.S. and Guba, E.G. (2000) 'The only generalisation is: there is no generalisation', in R. Gomm, M. Hammersley and P. Foster (eds), *Case Study Method: Key Issues, Key Texts.* London: Sage.

Locke, K. (2001) *Grounded Theory in Management Research.* London: Sage.

Lofland, J. and Lofland, L.H. (1984) *Analyzing Social Situations,* 2nd edn. Belmont, CA: Wadsworth.

Mailbase (2002) *Copyright of email messages.* Retrieved 28 June 2002 from http://www.mailbase.ac.uk/docs/copyright.html.

Mangione, T.W. (1995) *Mail Surveys: Improving the Quality.* Thousand Oaks, CA: Sage.

Market Research Society *Code of Conduct.* Retrieved 3 May 2002 from http://www.mrs.org.uk/.

Mayring, P. (1983) Qualitative Inhaltsanclyse. Grundlagen and Techniken, 7th edn Weinheim: Deutscher Studien Verlag.

McBurney, D.H. (1998) *Research Methods,* 4th edn. Pacific Grove, CA: Brookes/Cole.

McKay, J. and Marshall, P. (2001) 'The dual imperatives of action research', *Information Technology and People,* 14(1): 46–59.

McNiff, J. (1988) *Action Research: Principles and Practice.* London: Routledge.

McNiff, J., Lomax, P. and Whitehead, J. (1996) *You and Your Action Research Project.* London: Routledge.

McTaggart, R. (1997) 'Guiding principles for partipatory action research', in R. McTaggart (ed.), *Participatory Action Research.* Albany, NY: State University of New York Press.

Merriam, S.B., Johnson-Bailey, J., Lee, M., Ntseane, G. and Muhamad, M. (2001) 'Power and positionality: negotiating insider/outsider status within and across cultures', *International Journal of Lifelong Education,* 20(5): 405–16.

Meyer, P. (2000) 'Could net polling hasten demise of phone surveys?', *USA Today,* 31 October.

Miles, M.B. and Huberman, A.M. (1994) *Qualitative Data Analysis,* 2nd edn. Thousand Oaks, CA: Sage.

Morris, L.L., Fitz-Gibbon, C.T. and Freeman, M.E. (1987) *How to Communicate Evaluation Findings.* Newbury Park, CA: Sage.

Motulsky, H. (1995) *Intuitive Biostatistics.* Oxford University Press. Retrieved 4 January, 2001 from http://www.graphpad.com/www/book/Choose.htm.

Moustakas, C. (1990) *Heuristic Research: Design, Methodology, and Applications.* Newbury Park, CA: Sage.

Mumford, E. (2001) 'Advice for an action researcher', *Information Technology and People,* 14(1): 12–27.

Murray, D.M. (1994) 'Write research to be read', in M. Langenbach, C. Vaugn, and L. Aagaard (eds), *An Introduction to Educational Research.* Needham Heights, MA: Allyn and Bacon.

Musson, G. (1998) 'Life histories', in G. Symon and C. Cassell (eds), *Qualitative Methods and Analysis in Organisational Research.* London: Sage.

Oakley, A. (1999) 'Paradigm wars: some thoughts on a personal and public trajectory', *International Journal of Social Research Methodology,* 2(3): 247–54.

Oppenheim, A.N. (1992) *Questionnaire Design, Interviewing and Attitude Measurement.* London: Pinter.

Park, P. (2001) 'Knowledge and participatory research', in P. Reason and H. Bradbury (eds), *Handbook of Action Research: Participative Inquiry and Practice.* London: Sage.

Partington, D. (2002) 'Grounded theory', in D. Partington (ed.), *Essential Skills for Management Research.* London: Sage.

Patton, M.Q. (1984) 'Data collection: options, strategies and cautions', in L. Rutman (ed.), *Evaluation Research Methods: A Basic Guide,* 2nd edn. Newbury Park, CA: Sage.

Patton, M.Q. (1990) *Qualitative Evaluation and Research Methods*, 2nd edn. Newbury Park, CA: Sage.

Peräkylä, A. (1997) 'Reliability and validity in research based on tapes and transcripts', in D. Silverman (ed.), *Qualitative Research: Theory, Methods and Practice*. London: Sage.

Perry, C. (1998) 'Processes of a case study methodology for postgraduate research marketing', *European Journal of Marketing*, 32(9/10): 785–802.

Phillips, E.M. and Pugh, D.S. (1994) *How to get a PhD: A Handbook for Students and Their Supervisors*, 2nd edn. Buckingham: Open University Press.

Pink, S. (2001) *Doing Visual Ethnography*. London: Sage.

Popper, K.R. (1968) *The Logic of Scientific Discovery*, 2nd edn. London: Hutchinson.

Punch, K.F. (1998) *Introduction to Social Research: Quantitative and Qualitative Approaches*. London: Sage.

Punch, S. (2002) 'Interviewing strategies with young people: the "Secret Box", stimulus material and task-based activities', *Children and Society*, 16: 45–56.

QAA (Quality Assurance Agency for Higher Education) (2000) *Code of Practice for the Assurance of Academic Quality and Standards in Higher Education, Section 7: Programme Approval, Monitoring and Review*. Gloucester: QAAHE.

Raimond, P. (1993) *Management Project: Design, Research and Presentation*. London: Chapman & Hall.

Reason, P. and Bradbury, H. (2001) (eds) *Handbook of Action Research: Participative Inquiry and Practice*. London: Sage.

Reay, D.G. (1994) *Evaluating Training*. London: Kogan Page.

Reinharz, S. (1992) *Feminist Methods in Social Research*. New York: Oxford University Press.

Robson, C. (1993) *Real World Research*. Oxford: Blackwell.

Rowe, C. (1995) 'Incorporating competence into the long-term evaluation of training development', *Industrial and Commercial Training*, 27(2): 3–9.

Rudestam, K.E. and Newton, R.R. (1992) *Surviving your Dissertation: A Comprehensive Guide to Content and Process*. Newbury Park, CA. Sage.

Samra-Fredericks, D. (1998) 'Conversational analysis', in G. Symon and C. Cassell (eds), *Qualitative Methods and Analysis in Organisational Research*. London: Sage.

Sapsford, R. (1999) *Survey Research*. London: Sage.

Saunders, M., Lewis, P. and Thornhill, A. (2000) *Research Methods for Business Students*, 2nd edn. London: Prentice-Hall.

Scheurich, J.J. (1997) *Research Methods in the Postmodern*. London: Falmer.

Schofield, J.W. (2000) 'Increasing the generalisability of qualitative research', in R. Gomm, M. Hammersley and P. Foster (eds), *Case Study Method: Key Issues, Key Texts*. London: Sage.

Schratz, M. (1996) 'Collaborative, self-critical and reciprocal inquiry through memory work', in O. Zuber-Skerritt (ed.), *New Directions in Action Research*. London: Falmer Press.

Scriven, M. (1967) 'The methodology of evaluation', in R.W. Tyler, R.M. Gagne and M. Scriven (eds), *Perspectives of Curriculum Evaluation*. Chicago, IL: Rand McNally.

Scriven, M. (1973) 'Goal free evaluation', in E.R. House (ed.), *School Evaluation*. Berkeley, CA: McCutchan.

Sekaran, U. (1992) *Research Methods for Business*, 2nd edn. New York: John Wiley.

Sixsmith, J. and Murray, C.D. (2001) 'Ethical issues in the documentary data analysis of internet posts and archives', *Qualitative Health Research*, 11(3): 423–32.

Skrtic, T.M. (1985) 'Doing naturalistic research into educational organizations', in Y.S. Lincoln (ed.), *Organizational Theory and Inquiry*. Newbury Park, CA: Sage.

Slack, F. and Rowley, J. (2001) 'Observation: perspectives on research methodologies for leisure managers', *Management Research News*, 24(1/2): 35–42.

Sleeman, P. (2002) 'Archives and statistics', in N. Dochartaigh (ed.), *The Internet Research Handbook: A Practical Guide for Students and Researchers in the Social Sciences.* London: Sage.

Stake, R.E. (2000) 'The case study method in social inquiry', in R. Gomm, M. Hammersley and P. Foster, (eds), *Case Study Method: Key Issues, Key Texts.* London: Sage.

Strauss, A.L. (1987) *Qualitative Analysis for Social Scientist.* New York: Cambridge University Press.

Strauss, A.L. and Corbin, J. (1994) 'Grounded theory methodology: an overview', in N.K. Denzin and Y.S. Lincoln (eds), *Handbook of Qualitative Research.* London: Sage.

Strauss, A.L. and Corbin, J. (1998) *Basics of Qualitative Research*, 2nd edn. Thousand Oaks, CA: Sage.

Stringer, E.T. (1999) *Action Research*, 2nd edn. Thousand Oaks, CA: Sage.

Symon, G. and Cassell, C. (eds) (1998) *Qualitative Methods and Analysis in Organisational Research.* London: Sage.

Teitelbaum, H. (1998) *How to Write a Thesis*, 4th edn. New York: Macmillan General Reference.

Tesch, R. (1991) 'Software for qualitative researchers: analysis needs and program capabilities' in N. Fielding and R.M. Lee (eds), *Using Computers in Qualitative Research.* London: Sage.

Tesch, R. (1994) 'The contribution of a qualitataive method: phenomenological research', in M. Langenbach, C. Vaugn and L. Aagaard (eds), *An Introduction to Educational Research.* Needham Heights, MA: Allyn and Bacon.

Tickle, L. (2001) 'Opening windows, closing doors: ethical dilemmas in educational action research', *Journal of Philosophy of Education*, 35(3): 345–59.

Travers, M. (2001) *Qualitative Research Through Case Studies.* London: Sage.

Turk, C. and Kirkman, J. (1989) *Effective Writing: Improving Scientific, Technical and Business Communication*, 2nd edn. London: E.&F.N. Spon.

Vazquez-Montilla, E., Reyes-Blanes, M.E., Hyun, E. and Brovelli, E. (2000) 'Practices for culturally responsive interviews and research with Hispanic families', *Multicultural Perspective*, 2(3): 3–7.

Vinten, G. (1994) 'Participant observation: a model for organizational investigation?', *Journal of Managerial Psychology*, 9(2): 30–8.

Wainwright, G. (1990) *Report Writing*, 2nd edn. Shrewsbury: Management Update.

Warr, P., Bird, M. and Rackman, N. (1970) *Evaluation of Management Training.* Aldershot: Gower.

Waterman, H. (1998) 'Embracing ambiguities and valuing ourselves: issues of validity in action research', *Journal of Advanced Nursing*, 28(1): 101–5.

Waterson, J. (2000) 'Balancing research and action: reflections on an action research project in a social services department', *Social Policy and Administration*, 34(4): 494–508.

Webb, E.J., Campbell, D.T., Schwartz, R.D. and Sechrest, L. (1966) *Unobtrusive Measures: Nonreactive Research in the Social Sciences.* Chicago, IL: Rand McNally.

Weiss, C.H. (1984) 'Increasing the likelihood of influencing decisions', in L. Rutman (ed.), *Evaluation Research Methods: A Basic Guide*, 2nd edn. Newbury Park, CA: Sage.

Wengraf, T. (2001) *Qualitative Research Interviewing: Biographic Narrative and Semi-Structured Methods.* London: Sage.

White, J.H. (1997) *Creating Effective Technical Documents.* New York: ASME Press.

Whittemore, R., Chase, S.K. and Mandle, C.L. (2001) 'Validity in qualitative research', *Qualitative Health Research*, 11(4): 522–37.

Whyte, W.F. (1991) (ed.) *Participatory Action Research*. Newbury Park, CA: Sage.

Whyte, W.F. (1991) 'Compring PAR and Action Science', in W.F. Whyte (ed.), *Participatory Action Research*. Newbury Park, CA: Sage.

Wield, D. (2002) 'Planning and organising a research project', in S. Potter (ed.), *Doing Postgraduate Research*. London: Sage.

Williams, D. (1996) 'Research proposals', in T. Greenfield, (ed.), *Research Methods: Guidance for Postgraduates*. London: Arnold.

Williams, M. and May, T. (1996) *Introduction to the Philosophy of Social Research*. London: Routledge.

Wilson, K. and Roe, B. (1998) 'Interviewing older people by telephone following initial contact by postal survey', *Journal of Advanced Nursing*, 27: 575–81.

Winkler, A.C. and McCuen, J.R. (1985) *Writing the Research Paper: A Handbook*, 2nd edn. New York: Harcourt Brace Jovanovich.

Winkler, E. and Coombs, J. (eds) *Applied Ethics*. Oxford: Blackwell.

Winter, R. (1996) 'Some principles and procedures for the conduct of action research', in O. Zuber-Skerritt (ed.), *New Directions in Action Research*. London: Falmer Press.

Wolcott, H.F. (1994) *Transforming Qualitative Data: Description, Analysis and Interpretation*. Thousand Oaks, CA: Sage.

Yin, R.K. (1993) *Applications of Case Study Research*. Thousand Oaks, CA: Sage.

Yin, R.K. (1994) *Case Study Research: Design and Methods*, 2nd edn. Thousand Oaks, CA: Sage.

Index

417